PRINCIPLES OF ARBITRATION LAW

Stephen J. Ware

Professor of Law
University of Kansas

Ariana R. Levinson

Professor of Law
Brandeis School of Law
University of Louisville

CONCISE HORNBOOK SERIES™

WEST
ACADEMIC
PUBLISHING

© 2017 LEG, Inc. d/b/a West Academic
444 Cedar Street, Suite 700
St. Paul, MN 55101
1-877-888-1330

Printed in the United States of America

ISBN: 978-1-68328-568-7

For

Adam and Spencer Ware

&

Kathy and Stanley Levinson

Preface ·

Arbitration law has a long history. Even "modern" arbitration statutes like the Federal Arbitration Act are now nearly a century old. And the last few decades have witnessed the growth of a large body of legal doctrine—from statutes, judicial decisions, and other sources—focused on arbitration. This book is written with the goal of providing a clear and reliable summary of that body of law, so this book should be useful to lawyers and scholars researching arbitration law and to students learning about arbitration.

We thank the people who contributed helpful suggestions for this book: Ted St. Antoine, Hiro Aragaki, Rick Bales, Chris Drahozal, Michael Z. Green, John Head, David Horton, Jay McCauley, and Peter (Bo) Rutledge. In addition, we thank the student research assistants who helped with various portions of this book, Travis Fiechter, Corey Music, Jennifer Reynolds, and Chapman Williams. Finally, we are grateful for the support we have received from the University of Kansas and the University of Louisville.

As we expect to write future editions of this book, we welcome comments and suggestions.

STEPHEN J. WARE
Professor of Law
University of Kansas
ware@ku.edu
(785) 864-9209

ARIANA R. LEVINSON
Professor of Law
University of Louisville
Brandeis School of Law
a.levinson@louisville.edu
(502) 852-0794

December 2, 2016

Note to Teachers

This Hornbook is designed to be used as the primary or secondary text in a law school course. In the United States, casebooks, rather than Hornbooks or other treatises, are the primary texts in most law school courses, and casebooks work well at the center of law school courses that emphasize Socratic dialog and "thinking like a lawyer." By contrast, many teachers of dispute-resolution, including arbitration, design their courses to develop a wider array of practice skills, generally through the use of role-playing exercises. We believe this Hornbook is especially well-suited to be the primary text for such courses. Because this book is clear and concise, students reading it can quickly gain a solid understanding of arbitration's central concepts and legal doctrines. This efficient use of time enables the teacher to devote many class sessions to role-playing exercises, and discussion of them. Excellent role-playing exercises are available from several sources, including:

- Willamette University Center for Dispute Resolution http://www.willamette.edu/modules/simbank/login.cgi

- Harvard Program on Negotiation http://www.pon. harvard.edu/store/

- University of Missouri Center for the Study of Dispute Resolution http://law.missouri.edu/drle/teaching/ simulations-and-exercises-various-simulations-and-materials/

- Employment Law Arbitration Exercises, developed by Gary Spitko, Santa Clara University School of Law, gspitko@gmail.com

- Securities Dispute Resolution Triathlon, St. John's University School of Law Hugh L. Carey Center for Dispute Resolution & FINRA, http://www.stjohns.edu/ law/hugh-l-carey-center-dispute-resolution/securities-dispute-resolution-triathlon

- American Bar Association Law Student Competitions http://abaforlawstudents.com/events/law-student-competitions/practical-skills-competitions/competition -videos/

- American Bar Association's Dispute Resolution Resource Database http://www.americanbar.org/ directories/dispute-resolution.html

Of course, individual instructors can also create their own role-playing exercises.

Also helpful in teaching practice skills is viewing others engage in arbitration hearings and processes. As with role-playing exercises, excellent videos are available from several sources, including:

- The Pennsylvania State University School of Labor and Employment Relations Labor Arbitration Case Study: The Suspension of Nurse Kevin http://lser.la.psu.edu/documents/Abitration_flier-1.pdf/view

- YouTube, Labor Management Arbitration Excerpts, Part I & II, https://www.youtube.com/watch?v=Zka LoZOKf4I

- American Bar Association, Advanced Arbitration Insight: 20/20, http://shop.americanbar.org/eBus/Store/ProductDetails.aspx?productId=214114

- American Bar Association Law Student Competitions http://abaforlawstudents.com/events/law-student-competitions/practical-skills-competitions/competition-videos/

- The Center for American and International Law, Arbitral Advocacy, Mock Arbitration Proceedings and Commentary, http://www.cailaw.org/Institute-for-Transnational-Arbitration/onlineeducation/video-library/arbitral-advocacy.html

In addition to serving as the primary text for arbitration courses that emphasize role-playing exercises, this Hornbook can also serve as the primary text for arbitration seminars. In a seminar course, students generally read scholarly articles and write their own substantial papers. Before venturing into a field of scholarship, students generally need a solid foundation in the field's central concepts and legal doctrines. This book provides that foundation with only a limited amount of reading, thus enabling students to devote substantial time to the seminar's more-advanced work of reading scholarly articles and writing original papers.

Acknowledgments

The following authors and publishers gave permission to reprint excerpts from copyright material.

American Arbitration Association, Commercial Arbitration Rules, R–13(b), 17, 18 (2013). Reprinted with permission.

Gary B. Born, International Commercial Arbitration (2009), reprinted with permission of author.

Margaret L. Moses, The Principles and Practice of International Commercial Arbitration (2008), with permission of Cambridge University Press.

Summary of Contents

Table of Contents

PRINCIPLES OF ARBITRATION LAW

Chapter 1

WHAT IS ARBITRATION

Table of Sections

§ 1   Arbitration Defined

Arbitration is private (non-government) adjudication.[1] Arbitrators, selected by the disputing parties (directly or indirectly),[2] are the adjudicators in arbitration. In contrast, judges and jurors are the adjudicators in *litigation*, which is adjudication in a government forum, a court.

In addition to being "private" in the non-governmental sense, arbitration is also usually "private" in the confidential sense.[3] But it does not have to be. Arbitration could occur on a busy city sidewalk in full view of the public and it would still be *private* adjudication. In short, the essence of arbitration is that it is a private-sector

---

[1]   " 'Adjudication' refers to the process by which final, authoritative decisions are rendered by a neutral third party who enters the controversy without previous knowledge of the dispute." Alan Scott Rau, Edward F. Sherman & Scott R. Peppet, Processes of Dispute Resolution: The Role of Lawyers 21 (4th ed. 2006). "The traditional model of arbitration is precisely that of the 'private tribunal'—private individuals, chosen voluntarily by the parties to a dispute in preference to the 'official' courts, and given power to hear and 'judge' their 'case.' " Id. at 599. See also Gary B. Born, International Commercial Arbitration 1743 (2009) (describing "the adjudicative character of international arbitration, in which the arbitrators are obligated to decide the parties' dispute impartially and objectively, based upon the law and evidence the parties present."); Lon Fuller, The Forms and Limits of Adjudication, 92 Harv.L.Rev. 353, 364 (1978) ("the distinguishing characteristic of adjudication lies in the fact that it confers on the affected [disputing] party a peculiar form of participation in decision, that of presenting proofs and reasoned arguments for a decision in his favor."); Ian R. Macneil, Richard E. Speidel & Thomas J. Stipanowich, Federal Arbitration Law § 2.6.1, at 2:37 n.1 (1994) ("Arbitration is a form of adjudication because the parties participate in the decisional process by presenting evidence and reasoned arguments to an arbitrator whose final decision should be responsive to the dispute as presented.")

[2]   See § 36(a).

[3]   See § 37(b).

alternative to government courts. It is to the court system what private schools are to public schools, or what private housing is to public housing.

§ 2   Contractual Arbitration and Non-Contractual Arbitration; Constitutional Right to Jury Trial

Arbitration can be divided into two types, contractual and non-contractual.[4] The duty to arbitrate a dispute can be created by contract or by other law. If the duty to arbitrate is created by contract, then enforcement of that duty is unlikely to violate the constitutional right to a jury trial. Courts typically hold that, by forming a contract to arbitrate, a party waives its right to a trial by jury.[5] In contrast, the parties to non-contractual arbitration have

---

[4]   See § 78(a).

[5]   See, e.g., Harrington v. Atl. Sounding Co., 602 F.3d 113, 126 (2d Cir.2010) ("courts may not rely on the uniqueness of an agreement to arbitrate, which necessarily waives jury trial, as a basis for a state-law holding that enforcement would be unconscionable. It is well-settled that waivers of jury trial are fully enforceable under the FAA.") (internal quotations omitted); Caley v. Gulfstream Aerospace Corp., 428 F.3d 1359, 1371 (11th Cir.2005) (the "agreement to arbitrate and waiver of jury trial rights are governed by contract principles and are not subject to the heightened knowing and voluntary standard argued by plaintiffs"); American Heritage Life Ins. Co. v. Orr, 294 F.3d 702, 711 (5th Cir.2002) (" '[t]he Seventh Amendment does not confer the right to a trial, but only the right to have a jury hear the case once it is determined that the litigation should proceed before a court. If the claims are properly before an arbitral forum pursuant to an arbitration agreement, the jury trial right vanishes.' ") (quoting Cremin v. Merrill Lynch, Pierce, Fenner & Smith, Inc., 957 F.Supp. 1460, 1471 (N.D.Ill.1997)); Sydnor v. Conseco Fin.Servicing Corp., 252 F.3d 302, 307 (4th Cir. 2001) ("the right to a jury trial attaches in the context of judicial proceedings after it is determined that litigation should proceed before a court."); Geldermann, Inc. v. Commodity Futures Trading Comm'n, 836 F.2d 310, 323–24 (7th Cir.1987) ("In a non-Article III forum the Seventh Amendment simply does not apply. Because we hold that Geldermann is not entitled to an Article III forum, the Seventh Amendment is not implicated.") (citations omitted); https://www.westlaw.com/ Document/I96e66eedfabc11d983e7e9deff98dc6f/View/FullText.html?transitionType= Default&contextData=(sc.Default)&VR=3.0&RS=da3.0&fragmentIdentifier=co_pp_ sp_661_904 Hays Grp., Inc. v. Biege, 193 P.3d 1028, 1030 (Or.App.2008) (parties waived jury right by agreeing to arbitrate); Adler v. Fred Lind Manor, 153 Wash. 2d 331, 360–61, 103 P.3d 773, 789 (2004)("by knowingly and voluntarily agreeing to arbitration, a party implicitly waives his right to a jury trial by agreeing to an alternate forum, arbitration"); In re Ball, 665 N.Y.S.2d 444, 447 (N.Y.App.Div.1997); Mugnano-Bornstein v. Crowell, 677 N.E.2d 242, 247 (Mass.App.Ct.1997); Long v. DeGeer, 753 P.2d 1327, 1329 (Okla.1988).

The Seventh Amendment, preserving the right to jury trial, is one of the few provisions of the Bill of Rights that constrains only federal, not state, government. See Curtis v. Loether, 415 U.S. 189, 192 n.6 (1974). The Seventh Amendment applies in federal, not state, court. Gasperini v. Ctr. for Humanities, Inc., 518 U.S. 415, 418 (1996); GTFM, LLC v. TKN Sales, Inc., 257 F.3d 235, 245 (2d Cir.2001). While many state constitutions contain a provision that similarly protects the right to trial by jury, see Martin H. Redish, Legislative Response to Medical Malpractice Insurance Crisis: Constitutional Implications, 55 Tex.L.Rev. 759, 797 (1977), the Federal Arbitration Act prevails in a conflict between it and a state constitutional provision. See U.S. Const. art. VI, § 2 (the Supremacy Clause). Thus, an arbitration agreement's effectiveness as a waiver of the right to jury trial is determined solely by federal, rather

rarely waived the right to a jury trial. Therefore, non-contractual arbitration generally must be non-binding to avoid violating this right.[6]

Non-contractual, yet binding, arbitration is discussed as part of labor arbitration in sections 56 and 61, and as explicitly non-contractual at the end of this book, under the heading "Processes Similar to Arbitration."[7] Otherwise, the term "arbitration" is used throughout this book to mean "contractual arbitration."

§ 3   Arbitration Law Summarized

(a) Post-Dispute and Pre-Dispute Agreements to Arbitrate

A dispute goes to arbitration only when the parties have contracted to send it there.[8] Sometimes parties with an existing dispute contract to send that dispute to arbitration. Such *post-dispute* arbitration agreements (or "submission agreements") are relatively rare and non-controversial.[9] More common, and more controversial, are *pre-dispute* arbitration agreements. These are contracts containing a clause providing that, if a dispute arises, the parties will resolve that dispute in arbitration rather than in court. These arbitration clauses typically are written broadly to cover any dispute the parties' transaction might produce, but also can be written more narrowly to cover just some potential disputes.[10] Arbitration clauses

---

than state, law unless the arbitration agreement is one of the few not governed by the FAA. See § 4(d).

[6]   See § 78.

[7]   See id.

[8]   See, e.g., Howsam v. Dean Witter Reynolds, Inc., 537 U.S. 79, 83 (2002) ("'arbitration is a matter of contract and a party cannot be required to submit to arbitration any dispute which he has not agreed so to submit.'" (quoting United Steelworkers v. Warrior & Gulf Naval Co., 363 US 574, 582 (1960)); Int'l Broth. of Elec. Workers, Local 21 v. Ill. Bell Telephone Co., 491 F.3d 685, 687 (7th Cir.2007) (same); First Options of Chicago, Inc. v. Kaplan, 514 U.S. 938, 943 (1995)("arbitration is simply a matter of contract between the parties"); Granite Rock Co. v. Int'l Bhd. of Teamsters, 561 U.S. 287, 297 (2010) ("a court may order arbitration of a particular dispute only where the court is satisfied that the parties agreed to arbitrate *that dispute*.") (emphasis in original).

[9]   See Christopher R. Drahozal & Samantha Zyontz, Private Regulation of Consumer Arbitration, 79 Tenn.L.Rev. 289, 346 (2012) (noting 96.3% of cases arose out of pre-dispute agreements, while only 3.7% arose out of post-dispute agreements to arbitrate); Lewis L. Maltby, Out of the Frying Pan, into the Fire: The Feasibility of Post-Dispute Employment Arbitration Agreements, 30 Wm.Mitchell L.Rev. 313, 319 (2003) (analyzing the American Arbitration Association data on the infrequency of post-dispute arbitration clauses in employment cases).

Post-dispute arbitration agreements resemble settlement agreements, which are discussed in Stephen J. Ware, Principles of Alternative Dispute Resolution Ch. 3 (3d ed. 2016).

[10]   See §§ 30–31.

appear in a wide variety of contracts including those relating to employment, credit, goods, services, and real estate.

(b) Enforcement of Arbitration Agreements

In the case of most contracts containing pre-dispute arbitration clauses, like most contracts generally, the parties never have any dispute. If the parties do have a dispute, however, the arbitration clause likely will be enforceable, so a party who would rather litigate than arbitrate will nevertheless have to perform its agreement to arbitrate. If, for example, Seller sues Buyer despite an arbitration agreement between them, Buyer can get a court to stay or dismiss Seller's lawsuit.[11] As a result of the court's order, Seller's only forum to pursue its claim is arbitration.[12] Another possibility is that Seller asserts a claim against Buyer in arbitration but Buyer simply refuses to participate in arbitration. Seller can get a court order compelling Buyer to participate.[13] In this manner, the court enforces Buyer's agreement to arbitrate.

(c) The Arbitration Process

Not only does the parties' contract determine *whether* a dispute goes to arbitration, the contract also determines *what occurs* during arbitration.[14] Like any *adjudication*,[15] arbitration involves the presentation of evidence and argument to the adjudicator. The presentation of evidence and argument in *litigation* is governed by rules of procedure and evidence enacted by government. In contrast, the rules of procedure and evidence in arbitration are, with few exceptions, whatever the contract says they are.[16] Arbitration agreements commonly provide for less discovery and motion practice than is typical of litigation and commonly provide for fewer rules of evidence than are typical in litigation.[17] But the parties are free to draft their agreement almost any way they like. Arbitration privatizes procedural law by largely allowing parties to create their own customized rules of procedure and evidence. In short, arbitration is a creature of contract.

---

[11]   See § 4(c).

[12]   With respect to this dispute, arbitration has replaced litigation as the default process of dispute resolution. Disputing parties who have previously agreed to arbitrate can contract into some other process of dispute resolution, but if they do not do so then each party has the right to have the dispute resolved in arbitration. See Stephen J. Ware, Principles of Alternative Dispute Resolution § 1.7(b) (3d ed.2016).

[13]   See § 4(c).

[14]   See §§ 35–38.

[15]   See supra note 1.

[16]   See §§ 35–37.

[17]   Id.

(d) Enforcement of Arbitrator's Decision or "Award"

Arbitration agreements typically provide that the arbitrator's decision (or "award") will be final and binding. Once an arbitrator renders an award, either party may obtain court enforcement of that award. Judicial enforcement may not be needed because losing parties often comply with arbitration awards. Nevertheless, the winning party can get a court order *confirming* the arbitration award; confirmation converts the award into a judgment of the court.[18] A confirmed arbitration award in favor of the plaintiff (or "claimant") is enforced in the same manner as other court judgments: through orders to turn over property, judgment liens, writs of execution, garnishment, etc. Arbitration awards also are enforced through the preclusion of court actions. An arbitration award in favor of the defendant (or "respondent") precludes the plaintiff from litigating the claim that was already resolved in arbitration.[19]

Judicial enforcement of arbitration awards is an example of courts enforcing contracts. Refusing to comply with the arbitrator's award breaches the arbitration agreement, which is, in part, a promise to comply with the arbitrator's award.

---

[18]   See § 39.

[19]   Id.

Chapter 2

SOURCES OF CONTEMPORARY AMERICAN ARBITRATION LAW

Table of Sections

---

§ 4   Federal Law

(a) Sources of Federal Arbitration Law

The Federal Arbitration Act ("FAA")[1] is by far the most important source of arbitration law in the United States. There are other sources of federal arbitration law but they govern only specific types of arbitration, such as labor arbitration[2] and international arbitration.[3] State arbitration law is much less important than the FAA because the FAA has a broad reach and preempts conflicting state law.[4]

(b) Pro-Contract

The FAA, enacted in 1925, is resolutely pro-contract. FAA § 2 says that arbitration agreements "shall be valid, irrevocable, and enforceable, save upon such grounds as exist at law or in equity for the revocation of any contract."[5] This language reflects an intent to

---

[1]   9 U.S.C. §§ 1–16, 201–08, 301–07.

[2]   See § 48–61.

[3]   See §§ 62–76.

[4]   See §§ 6–18.

[5]   The full text of § 2 is as follows:

A written provision in any maritime transaction or a contract evidencing a transaction involving commerce to settle by arbitration a controversy thereafter arising out of such contract or transaction, or the refusal to

place arbitration agreements "upon the same footing as other contracts" and to reverse judicial hostility to the enforcement of arbitration agreements.[6] The FAA's enactment was "motivated, first and foremost, by a congressional desire to enforce agreements into which parties had entered."[7]

(c) Court Orders to Arbitrate; Specific Performance of Arbitration Agreements

The FAA requires courts to use an especially powerful remedy in enforcing arbitration agreements. While money damages are the ordinary remedy for breach of contract,[8] specific performance is the FAA's remedy for breach of an arbitration agreement. An example will illuminate this point.

Suppose Seller sues Buyer despite an arbitration agreement between them. If Seller's suit occurred prior to the enactment of the FAA,[9] the court would allow Seller's litigation to proceed.[10] The court would deny Buyer's motion to stay or dismiss Seller's case. In other words, pre-FAA courts would not specifically enforce "executory"

---

perform the whole or any part thereof, or an agreement in writing to submit to arbitration an existing controversy arising out of such a contract, transaction, or refusal, shall be valid, irrevocable, and enforceable, save upon such grounds as exist at law or in equity for the revocation of any contract.

9 U.S.C. § 2.

[6]   H.R.Rep.No. 68–96, at 2 (1924). "Despite its lengthy history and popular acceptance, the common law courts did not welcome arbitration. The earliest judicial hostility reflected a concern for defense of judges' turf (and perhaps of the fees that came with the turf.)" Laura J. Cooper, Dennis R. Nolan & Richard A. Bales, ADR in the Workplace 3 (2d Ed. 2005). See e.g., Tobey v. County of Bristol, et al., 23 Fed. Cas. 1313 (1845) (Story, J.) (arbitrators "are not ordinarily well enough acquainted with the principles of law or equity, to administer either effectually, in complicated cases; and hence it has often been said, that the judgment of arbitrators is but rusticum judicium").

[7]   Volt Info. Sciences, Inc. v. Board of Trustees, 489 U.S. 468, 478 (1989); Dean Witter Reynolds v. Byrd, 470 U.S. 213, 220 (1985); Javitch v. First Union Sec., Inc., 315 F.3d 619, 625 (6th Cir.2003) ("the FAA is at bottom a policy guaranteeing the enforcement of private contractual arrangements") (internal quotations and citations omitted). See also Buckeye Check Cashing, Inc. v. Cardegna, 546 U.S. 440, 443 (2006) ("To overcome judicial resistance to arbitration, Congress enacted the Federal Arbitration Act (FAA), 9 U.S.C. §§ 1–16. Section 2 embodies the national policy favoring arbitration and places arbitration agreements on equal footing with all other contracts.")

[8]   See Joseph M. Perillo, Calamari & Perillo on Contracts § 14.1 (6th ed.2009).

[9]   Suits brought in the courts of two states, New York and New Jersey, are exceptions to this generalization. These two states enacted statutes providing specific enforcement for arbitration agreements a few years before the FAA's 1925 enactment. See Ian R. Macneil, American Arbitration Law: Reformation, Nationalization, Internationalization 34–47 (1992).

[10]   See Ian R. Macneil, Richard E. Speidel & Thomas J. Stipanowich, Federal Arbitration Law, § 4.3.2.2 (1994) (explaining that in the period 1800–1920, agreements to arbitrate future disputes were not enforced with remedy of specific performance); Wesley A. Sturges, Commercial Arbitration and Awards § 87 (1930).

arbitration agreements—that is, agreements to arbitrate that have not yet been performed.

Buyer could still seek money damages for Seller's breach of the arbitration agreement, but how would the amount of those damages be calculated? To put the non-breaching party in the position it would have been in had the contract been performed,[11] the court would have to predict the results of both arbitration and litigation, then award as damages the difference (in terms of value to the non-breaching party) between the two. The speculativeness of such an approach is daunting and courts did not use this method of remedying breaches of executory arbitration agreements. A court might instead award nominal damages of one dollar or so,[12] but Buyer would receive no meaningful remedy for Seller's breach. In short, Seller could breach its arbitration agreement without legal consequence.

Alternatively, suppose that Seller asserted a claim against Buyer in arbitration but Buyer simply refused to participate in arbitration. Prior to the FAA, Seller could not get a court order compelling Buyer to participate in arbitration.[13] If Seller wanted to pursue its claim against Buyer, Seller would have to do so in litigation. Seller would have no meaningful remedy for Buyer's breach of the arbitration agreement. Buyer could breach its arbitration agreement with impunity.

The FAA changed the result in both of these Seller/Buyer scenarios. Under the FAA, the remedy for breach of an arbitration agreement is specific performance, that is, an order to arbitrate.

Consider, first, Seller's suit against Buyer. A plaintiff who sues, despite an arbitration agreement with the defendant, is in breach of that agreement. By staying the lawsuit, a court effectively orders the plaintiff to perform the agreement to arbitrate. This stay[14] follows from FAA § 3, which says:

---

[11]   This is the way to calculate the "expectation damages" normally awarded for breach of contract. See Restatement (Second) of Contracts §§ 344 & 347 (1981).

[12]   See Munson v. Straits of Dover S. S. Co., 102 F. 926 (2d Cir.1900) (holding that plaintiff, who sought damages in the form of lawyer's fees and costs incurred in defending a lawsuit for breach of agreement to arbitrate, was entitled to nominal damages only.)

[13]   Two states, New York and New Jersey, enacted statutes providing specific enforcement for arbitration agreements a few years before the FAA's 1925 enactment. See Macneil, supra note 9.

[14]   Some courts only stay the lawsuit while others dismiss it, a significant difference because dismissals are immediately appealable but, under FAA § 16(b)(1), stays are not. Compare, e.g., Hewitt v. St. Louis Rams P'ship, 409 S.W.3d 572, 574 (Mo.Ct.App.2013) ("Rather than dismissal, the proper course of action for the trial court, upon finding an agreement to arbitrate, is to stay the action pending arbitration."); Taylor v. Leslie's Poolmart, Inc., No. 12–2205–STA-tmp, 2013 WL 1314416, at *2 (W.D.Tenn.Mar.28, 2013) ("Therefore, the parties are directed to

> If any suit or proceeding be brought in any of the courts of the United States upon any issue referable to arbitration under an agreement in writing for such arbitration, the court in which such suit is pending, upon being satisfied that the issue involved in such suit or proceeding is referable to arbitration under such an agreement, shall on application of one of the parties stay the trial of the action until such arbitration has been had in accordance with the terms of the agreement, providing the applicant for the stay is not in default in proceeding with such arbitration.[15]

Now consider the second scenario, Buyer's refusal to arbitrate Seller's claim against it. A defendant who refuses to participate in arbitration will be ordered by a court to do so. This order follows from FAA § 4, which says, in part:

> A party aggrieved by the alleged failure, neglect, or refusal of another to arbitrate under a written agreement for arbitration may petition any United States district court * * * for an order directing that such arbitration proceed in the manner provided for in such agreement * * * . The court shall hear the parties, and upon being satisfied that the making of the agreement for arbitration or the failure to comply therewith is not in issue, the court shall make an

---

proceed to arbitration. Furthermore, having satisfied itself that the parties entered into a written agreement to arbitrate the issues in this suit, the Court will stay the proceedings."); Lloyd v. Hovensa, LLC., 369 F.3d 263, 269 (3d Cir.2004) ("the plain language of § 3 affords a district court no discretion to dismiss a case where one of the parties applies for a stay pending arbitration."); Adair Bus Sales, Inc. v. Blue Bird Corp., 25 F.3d 953, 955 (10th Cir.1994) ("where a defendant moved for a stay pending arbitration under 9 U.S.C. § 3, the District court erred in instead entering a dismissal and the proper course would have been to enter the stay"), with Soucy v. Capital Mgmt. Servs., L.P., No. 14 C 5935, 2015 WL 404632, at *6 (N.D. Ill. Jan. 29, 2015) ("The Seventh Circuit . . . has repeatedly affirmed district courts' decisions dismissing suits where all of the claims must be arbitrated according to the agreement."); Knall Bev., Inc. v. Teamsters Local Union No. 293 Pension Plan, 744 F.3d 419, 421 (6th Cir. 2014) ("[T]he district court correctly ruled that the Act requires that this claim be arbitrated, and properly dismissed the case without prejudice."); Ozormoor v. T-Mobile USA, Inc., 2009 WL 4408187, *3 (6th Cir.2009) (rejecting argument "that 9 U.S.C. § 3 requires district courts to stay suits pending arbitration rather than dismiss them."); Alford v. Dean Witter Reynolds, Inc., 975 F.2d 1161, 1164 (5th Cir.1992) ("[t]he weight of authority clearly supports dismissal of the case when all of the issues raised in the district court must be submitted to arbitration"); Green v. Ameritech Corp., 200 F.3d 967, 973 (6th Cir.2000) (same); Sparling v. Hoffman Const. Co., Inc., 864 F.2d 635, 638 (9th Cir.1988); Choice Hotels Intern., Inc. v. BSR Tropicana Resort, Inc., 252 F.3d 707, 709–10 (4th Cir.2001) ("Notwithstanding the terms of § 3, however, dismissal is a proper remedy when all of the issues presented in a lawsuit are arbitrable."); Bercovitch v. Baldwin School, Inc., 133 F.3d 141, 156 & n.21 (1st Cir.1998) (remanding to dismiss or stay).

[15]   9 U.S.C. § 3.

order directing the parties to proceed to arbitration in accordance with the terms of the agreement * * * .[16]

To summarize, FAA §§ 3 and 4 require courts to enforce arbitration agreements with orders of specific performance. Rather than ordering the payment of money, courts order parties in breach of arbitration agreements to perform their agreements, that is, to arbitrate. Failure to obey such an order can be contempt of court.[17]

(d) Broad Applicability

The FAA applies to a written arbitration agreement[18] "in any maritime transaction or a contract evidencing a transaction involving commerce."[19] FAA § 1 defines "commerce" to mean interstate or international commerce.[20] The Supreme Court interprets this

---

[16]   9 U.S.C. § 4.

[17]   See Wal-Mart Stores, Inc. v. PT Multipolar Corp., 202 F.3d 280, 1999 WL 1079625, *2 (9th Cir.1999) (affirming contempt order against party who violated injunction against litigating in Indonesian courts, rather than performing its agreement to arbitrate); General Teamsters Union Local No. 439 v. Sunrise Sanitation Services, Inc., 2006 WL 2091947 (E.D.Cal.2006)(denying contempt motion in context of labor arbitration, rather than FAA); Ernest v. Lockheed Martin Corp., 2009 WL 1698505, at *4 (D.Colo.2009)("Plaintiff's counsel has been abusive, unprofessional and refused to arbitrate in clear defiance of my July 29, 2008 Order. However, it appears that immediately prior to and after Defendant filed the instant [contempt] motion, Plaintiff's counsel started complying, and his conduct has significantly improved. Based on the more recent record, I find that an order of contempt is not appropriate at this time.")

[18]   An oral arbitration agreement may be unenforceable. The FAA requires courts to enforce only "written" arbitration agreements, as do most state arbitration statutes. See Unif. Arbitration Act §§ 1, 2, 7 U.L.A. 102, 240 (2005). But another federal statute, the Electronic Signatures in Global and National Commerce Act, has been interpreted as amending the FAA to require enforcement of electronic, as well as written, agreements. See Campbell v. General Dynamics Gov't Systems cor., 407 F.3d 546, 556 (1st Cir.2005). And the Revised Uniform Arbitration Act uses the word "record" instead of "writing" and defines "record" to mean "information that is inscribed on a tangible medium or that is stored in an electronic or other medium and is retrievable in perceivable form." Unif. Arbitration Act (2000) §§ 1, 6(a) & cmt. 1, 7 U.L.A. 10, 22–23 (2005). "The requirement of a writing of the FAA is distinct from any statute of frauds that might otherwise apply to the transaction." Christopher R. Drahozal, Commercial Arbitration: Cases and Problems 93 (2d ed.2006).

Arbitration clauses in documents other than contracts may not be enforceable. For example, the only cases to address whether arbitration clauses in trusts are enforceable have concluded that they are not. In re Calomiris, 894 A.2d 408 (D.C. 2006); Schoneberger v. Oelze, 96 P.3d 1078 (Ariz.Ct.App.2004). See generally David Horton, The Federal Arbitration Act and Testamentary Instruments, 90 N.C.L.Rev. 1027 (2012).

[19]   9 U.S.C. § 2.

[20]   "Commerce" is defined as:

    commerce among the several States or with foreign nations, or in any Territory of the United States or in the District of Columbia, or between any such Territory and another, or between any such Territory and any State or foreign nation, or between the District of Columbia and any State or Territory or foreign nation, but nothing herein contained shall apply to contracts of

language broadly to reach all transactions affecting interstate or international commerce.[21] So interpreted, FAA § 1's definition of commerce is extremely broad, bringing the vast majority of arbitration agreements within the coverage of the FAA.[22]

There is, however, an exception to the extremely broad reach of the FAA. FAA § 1 says "nothing herein contained shall apply to contracts of employment of seamen, railroad employees, or any other class of workers engaged in foreign or interstate commerce."[23] Arbitration agreements falling within this "employment exclusion" are not governed by the FAA.[24] In addition, arbitration clauses in collective bargaining agreements fall outside the FAA for a different reason. Collective bargaining agreements are not "contracts of employment" because they are contracts between the employer and union, rather than the employer and employee; they set the terms of employment that will govern (separate, often unwritten,) contracts between the employer and employees.[25] A separate federal statute,

---

employment of seamen, railroad employees, or any other class of workers engaged in foreign or interstate commerce.

9 U.S.C. § 1.

[21]   Citizens Bank v. Alafabco, Inc., 539 U.S. 52, 56–57 (2003)("We have interpreted the term 'involving commerce' in the FAA as the functional equivalent of the more familiar term 'affecting commerce'—words of art that ordinarily signal the broadest permissible exercise of Congress' Commerce Clause power. * * *[The FAA] provides for the enforcement of arbitration agreements within the full reach of the Commerce Clause.") (internal quotes and citations omitted). See also Allied-Bruce Terminix Co. Inc., v. Dobson, 513 U.S. 265, 281–82 (1995).

[22]   For exceptions, see Garrison v. Palmas Del Mar Homeowners Ass'n, Inc., 538 F.Supp.2d 468, 475 (D. P.R.2008) ("these deeds are inherently intrastate and do not constitute 'transactions involving commerce' within the meaning of the FAA"); Arkansas Diagnostic Center, P.A. v. Tahiri, 257 S.W.3d 884, 891–92 (Ark.2007) (employment agreement); Brown v. Hyatt Corp., 128 F.Supp.2d 697, 699–700 (D.Haw.2000); Baronoff v. Kean Development Co., Inc., 818 N.Y.S.2d 421, 424–25 (N.Y.Sup.Ct.2006); Ex parte Webb, 855 So.2d 1031 (Ala.2003); City of Cut Bank v. Tom Patrick Construction, Inc., 963 P.2d 1283 (Mont.1998).

[23]   9 U.S.C. § 1.

[24]   Most employment arbitration agreements do not fall within this exclusion. In other words, most employment arbitration agreements are governed by the FAA. See § 46.

[25]   See J.I. Case Co. v. N.L.R.B., 321 U.S. 332 (1944).

Collective bargaining between employer and the representatives of a unit, usually a union, results in an accord as to terms which will govern hiring and work and pay in that unit. The result is not, however, a contract of employment except in rare cases; no one has a job by reason of it and no obligation to any individual ordinarily comes into existence from it alone. The negotiations between union and management result in what often has been called a trade agreement, rather than in a contract of employment. Without pushing the analogy too far, the agreement may be likened to the tariffs established by a carrier, to standard provisions prescribed by supervising authorities for insurance policies, or to utility schedules of rates and rules for service, which do not of themselves establish any relationships but which do govern the terms of the shipper or insurer or customer relationship whenever and with whomever it may be established.

the Labor Management Relations Act ("LMRA"), governs collective bargaining agreements and their arbitration clauses.[26] The important area of labor arbitration is governed primarily by the LMRA, rather than the FAA.[27]

§ 5   State Law

(a) Arbitration Law

Prior to the 1925 enactment of the FAA, only two states required courts to enforce pre-dispute arbitration agreements with the remedy of specific performance, that is, orders to arbitrate.[28] The 1925 law in all other states provided no meaningful remedy against a party in breach of its promise to arbitrate. Since 1925, nearly every state has changed its law to require courts to order performance of arbitration agreements. Now, only Alabama still refuses such enforcement of pre-dispute arbitration agreements.[29]

Many states have adopted the Uniform Arbitration Act ("UAA"), drafted in 1955, or the Revised Uniform Arbitration Act ("RUAA"), drafted in 2000.[30] The UAA and RUAA are both similar to the FAA. There are few, if any, inconsistencies between either uniform act and the FAA. But the UAA, and especially the RUAA, are longer than the FAA, covering some topics not addressed by the FAA.[31]

This book discusses state arbitration law only where that law differs from federal law. Where state and federal arbitration law are the same, nothing turns on the question of which applies.

Id. at 334–35.

[26]   See § 52.

[27]   See § 50.

[28]   Macneil, supra note 9, at 34–47.

[29]   Id. at 57 ("only three states—Alabama, Mississippi, and West Virginia—have yet to adopt modern arbitration statutes", that is, statutes making pre-dispute arbitration agreements specifically enforceable). See Ala. Code § 8–1–41(3) (1975)("The following obligations cannot be specifically enforced: * * * An agreement to submit a controversy to arbitration"). Mississippi and West Virginia state law now seems to provide for such enforcement. See Covenant Health & Rehab. of Picayune v. Estate of Moulds ex rel. Braddock, 14 So.3d 695, 698 (Miss.2009)(" 'this Court will respect the right of an individual or an entity to agree in advance of a dispute to arbitration' " (quoting IP Timberlands Oper. Co., v. Denmiss Corp., 726 So.2d 96, 104 (Miss.1998)); Board of Educ. v. W. Harely Miller, Inc., 236 S.E.2d 439, 447–48 (W.Va.1977) ("all arbitration provisions in all contracts which indicate that the parties intended to arbitrate their differences rather than litigate them are presumptively binding, and specifically enforceable.").

[30]   The UAA, drafted by the National Conference of Commissioners on Uniform State Laws, is currently enacted in 27 states. See Unif. Arbitration Act (1956), 7 U.L.A. 99 (2009). The RUAA, also drafted by the National Conference of Commissioners on Uniform State Laws, has been enacted by 12 states, plus the District of Columbia. See Unif. Arbitration Act (2000), 7 U.L.A. 1 (2009).

[31]   Macneil, Speidel & Stipanowich, supra note 10, § 5.4.2 (regarding the UAA).

(b) Non-Arbitration Law

The FAA, UAA, and RUAA are not a complete statement of all the law governing arbitration.[32] These statutes presuppose, and often incorporate, existing law in areas such as contract and agency.[33] In other words, lots of non-arbitration law applies to arbitration. Most of this non-arbitration law is state common law. The common law of contracts is especially important to arbitration. Much of arbitration law is basically an application of general contract law to a particular sort of contract, the arbitration agreement.[34] For that reason, much of the language of this book—and even some of its organization—is borrowed from contract law.

---

[32]   Id. § 10.6.2.1 (Supp.1999).

[33]   Id. ("contract law alone is an insufficient foundation for the FAA. The FAA also presupposes the existence of a whole corpus of general law: property, torts, agency, corporations, criminal, and regulation, to mention a few of countless possible examples.")

[34]   See, e.g., §§ 22–26, 29–32.

Chapter 3

FAA PREEMPTION
OF STATE LAW

Table of Sections

1. THE EVOLUTION OF CASE LAW ON FAA PREEMPTION
Table of Sections

§ 6   Federal Arbitration Law as (Non-Preemptive) Procedural Law

The relationship between federal and state law is one of the most important and complex topics in arbitration law. The starting point is the Supremacy Clause of the United States Constitution, which says that—so long as a federal law is within the scope of federal power—that federal law is supreme over conflicting state law.[1] Consider, for example, a case in which Defendant is liable to Plaintiff under state tort and contract law. If Defendant can show that enforcement of that state law would conflict with a federal statute, such as the Employee Retirement Income Security Act ("ERISA"), then Defendant wins the case.[2] What would have been the result under state law is reversed by federal law. What has just been said about the preemptive effect of ERISA can also be said about all federal *substantive* law. Federal substantive law preempts inconsistent state law, and this is true whether the case is heard in federal or state court.[3] In contrast, federal *procedural* law does not necessarily preempt state law.[4] For instance, the Federal Rules of Civil Procedure do not preempt inconsistent state law because the Federal Rules of Civil Procedure only apply in federal court and the "inconsistent" state law, the state rules of civil procedure, only apply in state court. There is no conflict because each governs in its own forum.

The same was true of federal and state arbitration law prior to the FAA's 1925 enactment. Federal arbitration law governed only in

---

[1]   U.S. Const. art. VI, cl. 2 ("This Constitution, and the Laws of the United States which shall be made in Pursuance thereof; and all Treaties made, or which shall be made, under the Authority of the United States, shall be the supreme Law of the Land; and the Judges in every State shall be bound thereby, any Thing in the Constitution or Laws of any State to the Contrary notwithstanding.")

[2]   See, e.g., Aetna Health Inc. v. Davila, 542 U.S. 200, 210–14 (2004) ("respondents' state causes of action fall within the scope of ERISA * * * and are therefore completely pre-empted by ERISA") (internal quotations omitted); Pilot Life Insurance Co. v. Dedeaux, 481 U.S. 41, 45–47 (1987).

[3]   Howlett v. Rose, 496 U.S. 356, 367 (1990) ("Federal law is enforceable in state courts * * * because the Constitution and laws passed pursuant to it are as much laws in the States as laws passed by the state legislature. The Supremacy Clause makes those laws 'the supreme Law of the Land,' and charges state courts with a coordinate responsibility to enforce that law according to their regular modes of procedure.")

[4]   "No one disputes the general and unassailable proposition * * * that States may establish the rules of procedure governing litigation in their own courts." Felder v. Casey, 487 U.S. 131, 138 (1988). However, "Federal law takes state courts as it finds them only insofar as those courts employ rules that do not impose unnecessary burdens upon rights of recovery authorized by federal laws." Id. at 150 (internal quotations omitted).

federal court and state arbitration law governed only in state court.[5] Scholars disagree about whether the FAA was designed to preserve or change this state of affairs. While many believe that the FAA was originally understood to be merely a *procedural* law governing only in federal courts, some evidence suggests that those who enacted the FAA understood its key provision, § 2, to be *substantive* federal law governing in both federal and state courts.[6] Whatever the original understanding at the time of the FAA's enactment, all agree that many decades passed before courts began to hold that the FAA applies in state court and thus preempts inconsistent state law.

§ 7   Federal Arbitration Law as (Preemptive) Substantive Law

Until the late 1950's, no case held that the FAA applies in state court or preempts inconsistent state law.[7] In 1959, the Second Circuit held that the FAA § 2 was "federal substantive law * * * equally applicable in state or federal court."[8] It was not until 1984 that the Supreme Court applied the FAA to a state court case, *Southland Corp. v. Keating,*[9] and held that FAA § 2 preempts inconsistent state law. *Southland* stated that "The Federal Arbitration Act rests on the

---

[5]   Ian R. Macneil, American Arbitration Law 21–24 (1992); Ian R. Macneil, Richard E. Speidel & Thomas J. Stipanowich, Federal Arbitration Law § 10.1 (1994 & Supp.1999).

[6]   Compare, e.g., Macneil, supra note 5, 92–121 (only federal courts), with Christopher R. Drahozal, In Defense of Southland: Reexamining the Legislative History of the Federal Arbitration Act, 78 Notre Dame L.Rev. 101, 123 (2002)("The language of [FAA] section 2 broadly makes 'valid, irrevocable, and enforceable' both pre-dispute and post-dispute arbitration agreements. Nothing in the language of the section limits its application to cases in the federal courts"; "By contrast, the remaining sections of the FAA by their terms apply only in federal court"). This topic continues to inspire passionate criticism of the Supreme Court. See Brown ex rel. Brown v. Genesis Healthcare Corp., 724 S.E.2d 250, 278 (2011) ("With tendentious reasoning, the United States Supreme Court has stretched the application of the FAA from being a procedural statutory scheme effective only in the federal courts, to being a substantive law that preempts state law in both the federal and state courts."), vacated by, Marmet Health Care Center, Inc. v. Brown, 132 S.Ct. 1201 (2012).

[7]   Macneil, supra note 5, at 122–38.

[8]   Robert Lawrence Co., Inc. v. Devonshire Fabrics, Inc., 271 F.2d 402 (2d Cir.1959).

> To be sure much of the Act is purely procedural in character and is intended to be applicable only in the federal courts. But Section 2 declaring that arbitration agreements affecting commerce or maritime affairs are 'valid, irrevocable, and enforceable' goes beyond this point and must mean that arbitration agreements of this character, previously held by state law to be invalid, revocable or unenforceable are now made 'valid, irrevocable, and enforceable.' This is a declaration of national law equally applicable in state or federal courts.

Id. at 407.

[9]   465 U.S. 1, 11 (1984).

authority of Congress to enact substantive rules under the Commerce Clause."[10]

This *Southland* holding[11] was reaffirmed in a 1995 Supreme Court case, *Allied-Bruce Terminix Cos. v. Dobson*.[12] So it is now well-established doctrine that FAA § 2 applies in state court. However, state-court applicability is not clear as to other provisions of the FAA, some of which expressly indicate that they apply only in federal court. The Supreme Court still has not decided whether § 2 is the only provision of the FAA that applies in state court.[13]

§ 8   The FAA Creates No Federal Jurisdiction

While the Supreme Court has established that FAA § 2 is substantive law,[14] it is unusual federal substantive law because it creates no federal jurisdiction.[15] Ordinarily, a party asserting its federal rights is entitled to have a federal court hear its claims. But that is not true of parties asserting FAA rights. Those parties must use state court unless they can point to some other source of federal jurisdiction.[16] As the Supreme Court explained in *Vaden v. Discover Bank*,[17]

> As for jurisdiction over controversies touching arbitration, however, the [FAA] is something of an anomaly in the realm of federal legislation: It bestows no federal jurisdiction but rather requires for access to a federal forum an independent jurisdictional basis over the parties' dispute. Given the

---

[10]   Id.

[11]   Southland is discussed in § 7.

[12]   513 U.S. 265, 281 (1995).

[13]   The cases discussed throughout §§ 4–9 clearly hold that FAA § 2 applies in state court. Whether FAA §§ 3 and 4 apply in state court is discussed in § 11. The possible application of FAA § 10 in state court is discussed in § 44(d).

[14]   See § 7.

[15]   Southland, 465 U.S. 1, 16 n.9 (1984).

> While the Federal Arbitration Act creates federal substantive law requiring the parties to honor arbitration agreements, it does not create any independent federal-question jurisdiction under 28 U.S.C. § 1331 (1976) or otherwise. This seems implicit in the provisions in § 3 for a stay by a "court in which such suit is pending" and in § 4 that enforcement may be ordered by "any United States district court which, save for such agreement, would have jurisdiction under Title 28, in a civil action or in admiralty of the subject matter of a suit arising out of the controversy between the parties." Ibid.

Id. (citations omitted). In contrast, the international sections of the FAA, 9 U.S.C. §§ 201–208 and 301–307, do create federal jurisdiction. See Vaden v. Discover Bank, 556 U.S. 49, 58 (2009) ("Chapter 2 of the FAA, not implicated here, does expressly grant federal courts jurisdiction to hear actions seeking to enforce an agreement or award falling under the Convention on the Recognition and Enforcement of Foreign Arbitral Awards.")

[16]   See Macneil, Speidel & Stipanowich, supra note 5, § 9.2.1.

[17]   556 U.S. 49, 58 (2009).

substantive supremacy of the FAA, but the Act's nonjurisdictional cast, state courts have a prominent role to play as enforcers of agreements to arbitrate.[18]

When do federal courts have jurisdiction to play their own roles as "enforcers of agreements to arbitrate"? The *Vaden* case began with a (state-law) breach-of-contract claim brought in state court, followed by state-law counterclaims, also asserted in state court. The counterclaims, however, were preempted by federal banking law so the plaintiff (defending against the counterclaims) argued that this federal question gave a federal court jurisdiction to compel arbitration of the case.[19] The Supreme Court rejected this argument because of the "longstanding well-pleaded complaint rule," which is that "a suit arises under federal law only when the plaintiff's statement of his own cause of action shows that it is based upon federal law. Federal jurisdiction cannot be predicated on an actual or anticipated defense. * * * Nor can federal jurisdiction rest upon an actual or anticipated counterclaim."[20] In sum, "a party seeking to compel arbitration may gain a federal court's assistance only if, 'save for' the [arbitration] agreement, the entire, actual 'controversy between the parties,' as they have framed it, could be litigated in federal court."[21] In cases lacking federal jurisdiction, such as *Vaden*, the party seeking to compel arbitration can seek such an order from a state court.

2.   PREEMPTION OF STATE LAW IMPEDING CONTRACT ENFORCEMENT
Table of Sections

Sec.

---

[18]   Id. at 1271–72 (internal quotations omitted).

[19]   Id. at 1268–69. See 28 U.S.C. § 1331 (giving federal courts jurisdiction over "all civil actions arising under the Constitution, laws, or treaties of the United States.").

[20]   Id. at 1272 (internal quotations omitted). "Under the well-pleaded complaint rule, a completely preempted counterclaim remains a counterclaim and thus does not provide a key capable of opening a federal court's door." Id. at 1276.

[21]   Id. at 1275 (quoting 9 U.S.C. § 4). "[F]ederal jurisdiction cannot be invoked on the basis of a defense or counterclaim. Parties may not circumvent those rules by asking a federal court to order arbitration of the portion of a controversy that implicates federal law when the court would not have federal-question jurisdiction over the controversy as a whole. It does not suffice to show that a federal question lurks somewhere inside the parties' controversy, or that a defense or counterclaim would arise under federal law." Id. at 1278.

---

§ 9   Generally

The FAA is resolutely pro-contract. FAA § 2 says that arbitration agreements "shall be valid, irrevocable, and enforceable, save upon such grounds as exist at law or in equity for the revocation of any contract."[22] This language reflects an intent to place arbitration agreements "upon the same footing as other contracts" and to reverse judicial hostility to arbitration agreements.[23] The FAA's enactment was "motivated, first and foremost, by a congressional desire to enforce agreements into which parties had entered."[24] Accordingly, the Supreme Court has repeatedly emphasized that it seeks "to ensure the enforceability, according to their terms, of private agreements to arbitrate."[25]

The resolutely pro-contract stance of FAA § 2 frequently conflicts with state law. In the event of such a conflict, the state law is unenforceable because it is preempted by the FAA.[26]

The following sections discuss the most important area of FAA preemption, the enforceability of executory arbitration agreements, that is, agreements to arbitrate that have not yet been performed.[27]

---

[22]   9 U.S.C. § 2.

[23]   H.R.Rep. No. 68–96, at 2 (1924). For an argument that the Supreme Court "invest[s] undue importance in [this] critical passage from a House Report," see Hiro N. Aragaki, Equal Opportunity for Arbitration, 58 U.C.L.A. L.Rev. 1189, 1235–39 (2011).

[24]   Volt Info. Sciences, Inc. v. Board of Trustees, 489 U.S. 468, 478 (1989). See also Buckeye Check Cashing, Inc. v. Cardegna, 546 U.S. 440, 443 (2006) ("To overcome judicial resistance to arbitration, Congress enacted the Federal Arbitration Act (FAA), 9 U.S.C. §§ 1–16. Section 2 embodies the national policy favoring arbitration and places arbitration agreements on equal footing with all other contracts.")

[25]   Mastrobuono v. Shearson Lehman Hutton, Inc., 514 U.S. 52, 57 (1995)(quoting Volt Info. Sciences, Inc. v. Board of Trustees, 489 U.S. 468, 476 (1989)). See also AT & T Mobility LLC v. Concepcion, 563 U.S. 333, 343 (2011) ("The principal purpose of the FAA is to ensure that private arbitration agreements are enforced according to their terms.") (internal quotations omitted).

[26]   U.S. Const. art. VI, cl. 2 ("This Constitution, and the Laws of the United States which shall be made in Pursuance thereof; and all Treaties made, or which shall be made, under the Authority of the United States, shall be the supreme Law of the Land; and the Judges in every State shall be bound thereby, any Thing in the Constitution or Laws of any State to the Contrary notwithstanding.")

[27]   See §§ 10–14.

Other issues relating to FAA preemption of state law are discussed throughout this book as they arise amid various topics.

§ 10   State Law Prohibiting Courts from Enforcing Arbitration Agreements

The clearest case for FAA preemption is state law making arbitration agreements unenforceable. For example, Alabama courts have declared that pre-dispute arbitration agreements are "void."[28] The Supreme Court held in *Allied-Bruce Terminix Cos., Inc. v. Dobson*,[29] that the FAA preempts this Alabama law.[30]

§ 11   State Law Prohibiting Courts from Enforcing Arbitration Agreements with the Remedy of Specific Performance

While the previous paragraph discussed Alabama case law declaring that pre-dispute arbitration agreements are void, Alabama also has a statute that goes not quite as far in the anti-arbitration direction. This statute prohibits courts from enforcing arbitration agreements with the remedy of specific performance, that is, orders to arbitrate.[31] While the Supreme Court held in *Allied-Bruce Terminix Cos., Inc. v. Dobson*, that the FAA preempts this statute,[32] Justice Thomas's dissent pointed out that this statute does not, by its terms, make arbitration agreements unenforceable but merely limits the remedies courts can use in enforcing arbitration agreements.[33] For example, the Alabama statute permits courts to award money damages for breach of an arbitration agreement. Therefore, Justice Thomas concluded, the Alabama statute does not conflict with the FAA's requirement that arbitration agreements be "valid, irrevocable and enforceable."[34]

On behalf of the *Allied-Bruce* majority, one can note that the ineffectiveness of money damages as a remedy for breach of executory

---

[28]   See, e.g., Wells v. Mobile County Bd. of Realtors, 387 So.2d 140, 144 (Ala.1980). See generally Stephen J. Ware, *The Alabama Story: Arbitration shows law's connection to politics, culture*, DISP. RESOL. MAG. 24 (Summer 2001).

[29]   513 U.S. 265 (1995).

[30]   Id. at 281. See also State ex rel. Wells v. Matish, 600 S.E.2d 583, 591 n.7 (W.Va.2004) ("The Federal Arbitration Act pre-empts state law * * * [so] state courts cannot apply state statutes that invalidate arbitration agreements." (citation omitted)).

[31]   Ala.Code § 8–1–41(3) (1975) ("The following obligations cannot be specifically enforced: * * * An agreement to submit a controversy to arbitration").

[32]   513 U.S. 265, 281 (1995).

[33]   See 513 U.S. at 293 (Thomas, J. dissenting) ("A contract surely can be 'valid, irrevocable, and enforceable' even though it can be enforced only through actions for damages."); id. at 294 ("the [Alabama] statute does not itself make executory arbitration agreements invalid, revocable, or unenforceable").

[34]   9 U.S.C. § 2.

arbitration agreements is the main problem the FAA was enacted to solve.[35] Central to the FAA is its requirement that courts enforce arbitration agreements with the remedy of specific performance. Accordingly, the FAA directly conflicts with, and therefore preempts, a state law precluding specific performance as a remedy for breach of an arbitration agreement.

Here, however, the text of the FAA cuts against preemption. The portions of the FAA requiring courts to enforce arbitration agreements with the remedy of specific performance are FAA §§ 3 and 4.[36] The text of these provisions indicates that they apply only in federal, not state, court. FAA § 3 covers "any suit or proceeding * * * brought in any of the courts of the United States."[37] FAA § 4 is even clearer, applying to "any United States district court."[38]

The Supreme Court has not directly resolved the question of whether, despite this apparently limiting language, FAA §§ 3 and 4 nevertheless apply in state court. In 1984, the Supreme Court first applied § 2 of the FAA to a state court case, *Southland Corp. v. Keating*.[39] In 1983, the year preceding *Southland*, the Court said that "state courts, as much as federal courts, are obliged to grant stays of litigation under § 3 of the Act."[40] But *Southland* backtracked: "we do not hold that §§ 3 and 4 of the Arbitration Act apply to proceedings in state courts."[41] And in 1989, the Supreme Court stated: "we have never held that §§ 3 and 4, which by their terms appear to apply only to proceedings in federal court, are nonetheless applicable in state court."[42] The 1995 *Allied-Bruce* case reaffirmed *Southland* but did not discuss whether FAA §§ 3 and 4 apply in state court. However, the effect of *Southland* and *Allied-Bruce* is to require state courts to enforce arbitration agreements with the remedy of specific performance, that is, orders to arbitrate. In effect, *Southland* and *Allied-Bruce* have made the core of FAA §§ 3 and 4 (specific performance) applicable in state court even while maintaining that

---

[35]   See § 4(c).

[36]   See id.

[37]   9 U.S.C. § 3.

[38]   9 U.S.C. § 4.

[39]   465 U.S. 1, 11 (1984).

[40]   Moses H. Cone Mem'l Hosp. v. Mercury Constr.Corp., 460 U.S. 1, 26 n.34 (1983).

[41]   See Southland, 465 U.S. 1, 16 n.10 (1984).

[42]   Volt Info.Sciences, Inc. v. Bd. of Trustees of the Leland Stanford Junior Univ., 489 U.S. 468, 477 n.6 (1989). Accord Vaden v. Discover Bank, 556 U.S. 49, 70 (2009) ("This Court has not decided whether §§ 3 and 4 apply to proceedings in state courts, and we do not do so here.") (citing Volt).

it is still an open question whether those provisions technically apply in state court.[43]

§ 12   State Law Making Arbitration Agreements Unenforceable with Respect to Certain Claims

The FAA preempts state law making arbitration agreements unenforceable with respect to certain claims. An example of such a law appeared in *Southland Corp. v. Keating*,[44] which involved an arbitration clause in a franchise agreement for a convenience store. Franchisees sued Southland alleging a variety of claims including torts, breach of contract, and breach of the disclosure requirements of a California statute, the California Franchise Investment Law ("CFIL").[45] The trial court granted Southland's motion to compel arbitration of all claims except those based on the CFIL.[46] The trial court ruled that the dispute should be split, with one claim litigated and other claims arbitrated.[47] The Supreme Court of California agreed, enforcing the arbitration agreement with respect to all claims except for one.[48] In other words, it held that the franchisees' tort and contract claims were *arbitrable* but their CFIL claims were not.[49]

The California courts' rationale for treating CFIL claims differently from tort or contract claims is the language of the CFIL, which says that "any stipulation purporting to waive compliance with

---

[43]   See Southland, 465 U.S. at 24 (O'Connor, J., dissenting) ("the Court reads [FAA] § 2 to require state courts to enforce § 2 rights using procedures that mimic those specified for federal courts by FAA §§ 3 and 4."); Macneil, Speidel & Stipanowich, supra note 5, § 10.8.2.4, at 10:91–10:92 (Supp.1999) ("although the Court holds that FAA §§ 3 and 4 do not govern state courts, it is equally clear that FAA § 2, which does govern them, carries with it duties indistinguishable from those imposed on federal courts by FAA §§ 3 and 4.").

While the Court has made the core of FAA §§ 3 and 4 applicable in state court, some of its details have been held not to apply in state court. Rosenthal v. Great Western Fin.Sec.Corp., 926 P.2d 1061 (Cal.1996)(FAA § 4's jury trial right for issues about the making of the arbitration agreement not applicable in state court); St. Fleur v. WPI Cable Systems/Mutron, 879 N.E.2d 27, 33 (Mass.2008) (same; state court should apply state statute otherwise similar to FAA § 4 rather than FAA § 4).

[44]   465 U.S. 1 (1984).

[45]   Id. at 4. See Cal.Corp.Code Ann. §§ 31000 et seq. (West 1977).

[46]   465 U.S. at 4.

[47]   This raises questions about whether one action should be stayed while the other proceeds and about possible conflicting rulings in the two actions. See KPMG LLP v. Cocchi, 132 S.Ct. 23 (2011) ("when a complaint contains both arbitrable and nonarbitrable claims, the [FAA] requires courts to 'compel arbitration of pendent arbitrable claims when one of the parties files a motion to compel, even where the result would be the possibly inefficient maintenance of separate proceedings in different forums.' ") (quoting Dean Witter Reynolds Inc. v. Byrd, 470 U.S. 213 (1985)).

[48]   465 U.S. at 5.

[49]   This is an issue of statutory arbitrability, not contractual arbitrability. Statutory arbitrability law is discussed further in §§ 27–28. Contractual arbitrability is discussed in §§ 29–31.

any provision of this law is void."[50] The California Supreme Court interpreted this language to void an agreement to arbitrate CFIL claims.[51] Whether the California court was correct in treating an arbitration clause as a waiver of statutory compliance is an interesting question,[52] but the United States Supreme Court did not address it in *Southland*. The Court deferred to the California Supreme Court as the highest interpreter of California statutes. The Court therefore considered only whether the California statute, as interpreted by California's highest court, was preempted by federal law.

Southland held that the California statute, as interpreted by California's highest court, was preempted by FAA § 2 which says that arbitration agreements "shall be valid, irrevocable, and enforceable, save upon such grounds as exist at law or in equity for the revocation of any contract."[53] The Supreme Court in *Southland* explained that the CFIL conflicts with, and is therefore preempted by, FAA § 2.

> We agree, of course, that a party may assert general contract defenses such as fraud to avoid enforcement of an arbitration agreement. We conclude, however, that the defense to arbitration found in the California Franchise Investment Law is not a ground that exists at law or in equity "for the revocation of any contract" but merely a ground that exists for the revocation of arbitration provisions in contracts subject to the California Franchise Investment Law.[54]

Justice Stevens' dissent in *Southland* argued that "a state policy of providing special protection for franchisees * * * can be recognized without impairing the basic purposes of the federal statute."[55] The majority rebutted Stevens' analysis.

> If we accepted this analysis, states could wholly eviscerate Congressional intent to place arbitration agreements "upon the same footing as other contracts," simply by passing statutes such as the Franchise Investment Law. We have rejected this analysis because it is in conflict with the Arbitration Act and would permit states to override the

---

[50] Cal.Corp.Code § 31512 (West 1977).

[51] 465 U.S. at 10.

[52] Compare § 44 (courts sometimes confirm and enforce arbitration awards that do not apply the law), with Shearson American Express, Inc. v. McMahon, 482 U.S. 220, 229 (1987) ("[b]y agreeing to arbitrate a statutory claim, a party does not forgo the substantive rights afforded by the statute.")

[53] 9 U.S.C. § 2.

[54] Southland, 465 U.S. at 16 n.11.

[55] Southland, 465 U.S. at 21 (Stevens, J., dissenting).

declared   policy   requiring   enforcement   of   arbitration
agreements.[56]

Courts may decline to enforce arbitration agreements only on "such
grounds as exist at law or in equity for the revocation of any
contract."[57] In other words, the FAA requires parties who deny the
enforceability of an arbitration agreement to find their arguments in
contract law, not in some other body of law.[58]

Many states have law analogous to the California law held
preempted in *Southland*. That is, many states' laws prohibit
enforcement of pre-dispute arbitration agreements with respect to
certain categories of claims, such as tort claims, personal injury
claims, or medical malpractice claims.[59] These laws are preempted
by the FAA because they create a ground for denying enforcement to
arbitration agreements that is not a ground "for the revocation of any
contract."[60] For example, the Supreme Court's 2012 decision in

---

[56]   Southland, 465 U.S. at 16 n.11 (quoting H.R.Rep.No. 68–96, supra note 23).

[57]   9 U.S.C. § 2.

[58]   AT & T Mobility LLC v. Concepcion, 563 U.S. 333, 343 (2011) (FAA § 2
"permits agreements to arbitrate to be invalidated by generally applicable contract
defenses, such as fraud, duress, or unconscionability, but not by defenses that apply
only to arbitration or that derive their meaning from the fact that an agreement to
arbitrate is at issue.") (internal quotations and citations omitted). The *AT & T* case is
discussed in § 34.

[59]   See, e.g., Ark. Code Ann. 16–108–230(b)(1) (personal injury); Ga. Code Ann. 9–
9–2(c)(10) (personal injury); Iowa Code Ann. 679A.1(2)(c) (tort); Kan. Stat. Ann. 5–
401(c)(3) (tort); Mont. Code Ann. 27–5–114(2)(a) (personal injury); Neb. Rev. Stat. 25–
2602.01(e), (f) (workers compensation, personal injury tort, Fair Employment
Practices Act); N.C. Gen. Stat. 90–21.60(a) ("all claims for damages for personal injury
or wrongful death based on alleged negligence in the provision of health care"); S. C.
Code Ann. 15–48–10(b)(3) (medical malpractice).

[60]   9 U.S.C. § 2. See, e.g., Perry v. Thomas, 482 U.S. 483, 490–91 (1987) (FAA
preempts state law denying enforcement of agreements to arbitrate California Labor
Code claims); Ting v. AT & T, 319 F.3d 1126, 1147 (9th Cir.2003)(FAA preempts
California's Consumer Legal Remedies Act); Shepard v. Edward Mackay Enterprises,
Inc., 56 Cal.Rptr.3d 326 (Ct.App.2007)(FAA preempts California statute denying
enforcement of agreements to arbitrate bodily injury or wrongful death claims arising
out of real estate transactions); Triad Health Management of Georgia, III, LLC v.
Johnson, 679 S.E.2d 785, 789–90 (Ga.App.2009)(FAA preempts Georgia statute
denying enforcement of agreements to arbitrate medical malpractice claims); Macneil,
Speidel & Stipanowich, supra note 5, § 16.6.1 (Supp.1999) (such "state public policy
defense law is the clearest possible example of state arbitration law, which is
superseded by the FAA." Id. at 16:155).

Nevertheless, California courts hold that the FAA does not preempt state law
prohibiting enforcement of pre-dispute arbitration agreements with respect to claims
for injunctive relief under certain state statutes. Cruz v. Pacificare Health Sys., Inc.,
66 P.3d 1157 (Cal.2003); Broughton v. Cigna Healthplans, 988 P.2d 67 (Cal.1999). The
Ninth Circuit limited these California holdings. Kilgore v. KeyBank, Nat. Ass'n, 718
F.3d 1052 (9th Cir.2013) (en banc) (FAA preempts Broughton-Cruz rule except in
narrow circumstances in which the injunctive relief sought mostly benefits the general
public rather than the individual party pursuing the claim). See also Christopher R.
Drahozal, Federal Arbitration Act Preemption, 79 Ind. L.J. 393, 416 (2004)

Marmet Health Care Center, Inc. v. Brown, held that the FAA preempted a rule of West Virginia case law that prohibited enforcement of pre-dispute arbitration agreements with respect to personal injury negligence claims against nursing homes.[61]

§ 13   State Law Making Arbitration Agreements in Certain Types of Transactions Unenforceable

Many states prohibit enforcement of arbitration agreements in certain types of transactions, such as consumer contracts, adhesion contracts, insurance contracts, or employment contracts.[62] These transaction-focused anti-arbitration laws differ from the claim-focused anti-arbitration laws discussed in the previous section. For example, a breach of contract claim might arise out of a consumer transaction and a tort claim might arise out of a transaction between businesses. An anti-arbitration law focused on consumer transactions would apply to the first example but not the second, while an anti-arbitration law focused on tort claims would apply to the second example but not the first. However, like claim-focused anti-arbitration laws, state laws prohibiting enforcement of arbitration agreements in certain types of transactions are (with the possible exceptions of those relating to insurance[63] and employment[64]) preempted by the FAA because they create a ground for denying enforcement of certain arbitration agreements that is not a ground "for the revocation of any contract."[65]

("*Broughton* and its progeny exhibit the exact same hostility to arbitration that the U.S. Supreme Court has found objectionable in its FAA preemption cases to date.")

    [61]   132 S.Ct. 1201, 1203–04 (2012)

    [62]   See, e.g., Ark.Code Ann. 16–108–201(b)(2) (2004) (insurance contracts); Ga.Code Ann. 9–9–2(c)(3), (6) (West 2003) (insurance contracts, consumer contracts); Iowa Code Ann. 679A.1(2)(a), (b) (adhesion contracts, employment contracts); Kan.Stat.Ann. 5–401(c)(1) (2001) (insurance contracts); Baxter v. John Weitzel, Inc., 871 P.2d 855 (Kan.Ct.App.1994) (employment contracts); Ky.Rev.Stat.Ann. 336.700(2) (West 2006) (employment contracts); id. 417.050(2) (West 2006) (insurance contracts); Md. Code Ann., Cts. & Jud. Proc. 3–206.1 (consumer insurance contracts) (West 2002); Mo.Ann.Stat. 435.350 (West 1992) (adhesion contracts, insurance contracts); Mont.Code Ann. 27–5–114(2)(b), (c) (2009) (insurance contracts, property contracts); N.Y.Gen.Bus.Law 399–c(2)(b) (McKinney 1996) (consumer contracts); Ohio Rev.Code Ann. 2711.01(B)(1) (West 2009) (real estate contracts); R.I.Gen.Laws 10–3–2 (2006) (employment contracts, insurance contracts); S.C.Code Ann. 15–48–10(b)(2) (2005) (employment contracts); S.D.Codified Laws 21–25A–3 (2004) (insurance contracts).

    [63]   See § 18.

    [64]   See §§ 46–47.

    [65]   9 U.S.C. § 2. See also Preston v. Ferrer, 552 U.S. 346, 356 (2008) (FAA preempts state statute denying enforcement to arbitration agreements in talent agency contracts); Sutcliffe v. Mercy Clinics, Inc., 856 N.W.2d 382 (Iowa Ct.App.2014) (FAA preempts Iowa statute denying enforcement to employment arbitration agreements); Am. Fin. Serv. Assn. v. Burke, 169 F.Supp.2d 62, 68 (D.Conn.2001) (FAA preempts state statute denying enforcement to arbitration clauses in high-cost home loan agreements); Durkin v. CIGNA Property & Cas. Corp., 942 F.Supp. 481, 485 n.2 (D.Kan.1996) ("The Kansas Uniform Arbitration Act specifically excludes employment

Some state statutes do not go as far as forbidding enforcement of *all* arbitration agreements in a particular type of transaction, but nevertheless make *some* arbitration clauses in just that type of transaction unenforceable. For example, a California statute says that "a provision in a franchise agreement restricting venue to a forum outside this state is void with respect to any claim arising under or relating to a franchise agreement involving a franchise business operating within this state."[66] The Ninth Circuit held that this statute was preempted by the FAA because it applies only to forum selection clauses and only to franchise agreements; it therefore does not apply to "any contract," as required by FAA § 2.[67]

§ 14 State Law Raising the Standard of Assent for Contract Formation

Formation of a contract requires a manifestation of assent by each party.[68] Assent is typically manifested by signing a document or saying certain words, but can be accomplished in other ways as well. Mutual manifestation of assent is required to form an arbitration agreement, just as it is required to form any contract.[69]

Contract law has long grappled with assent issues in the context of form contracts presented to consumers on a take-it-or-leave-it basis. For example, a comment to the Restatement (Second) of Contracts says that:

> A party who makes regular use of a standardized form of agreement does not ordinarily expect his customers to understand or even to read the standard terms * * * .

---

contracts. Kan.Stat.Ann. § 5–401(c)(2) (Supp.1995). State law is preempted, however, to the extent that it conflicts with the FAA").

[66]   Cal.Bus. & Prof.Code § 20040.5.

[67]   Bradley v. Harris Research, Inc., 275 F.3d 884, 888–890 (9th Cir.2001). Accord KKW Enterprises, Inc. v. Gloria Jean's Gourmet Coffees Franchising Corp., 184 F.3d 42 (1st Cir.1999); Flint Warm Air Supply Co., Inc. v. York Intern.Corp., 115 F.Supp.2d 820, 827 (E.D.Mich.2000) (FAA preempts Michigan statute denying enforcement to agreements to arbitrate franchise disputes "outside this state.") See also OPE Intern. LP v. Chet Morrison Contractors, Inc., 258 F.3d 443 (5th Cir.2001) (FAA preempts Louisiana statute invalidating contract provisions requiring arbitration of any disputes outside of state.) But see Keystone, Inc. v. Triad Sys.Corp., 971 P.2d 1240, 1245–46 (Mont.1998) (Montana statute voiding out-of-state forum-selection clauses is consistent with the FAA because the Montana statutes apply to both arbitration clauses and other forum-selection clauses.)

In adopting the Revised Uniform Arbitration Act, New Mexico added a provision making a "disabling civil dispute clause"—a provision that provides for a less convenient forum, reduced access to discovery, a limited right to appeal, the inability to join class actions, or the like—voidable by consumers, borrowers, tenants and employees in arbitration. N.M.Stat.Ann. §§ 44–7A–1(b)(4), 44–7A–5 (Supp.2003).

[68]   See generally E. Allan Farnsworth, Contracts ch.3 (4th ed.2004); Joseph M. Perillo, Calamari & Perillo on Contracts § 2.1 (6th ed.2009).

[69]   See § 22.

Customers do not in fact ordinarily understand or even read the standard terms. They trust to the good faith of the party using the form and to the tacit representation that like terms are being accepted regularly by others similarly situated. But they understand that they are assenting to the terms not read or not understood, subject to such limitations as the law may impose.[70]

One such legal limitation holds that the consumer does not assent to a form contract term if the "other party has reason to believe that the [consumer] would not have accepted the agreement if he had known that the agreement contained the particular term."[71] This doctrine protects consumers from a form contract term which is "bizarre or oppressive," "eviscerates the non-standard terms explicitly agreed to," or "eliminates the dominant purpose of the transaction."[72]

States may apply to arbitration agreements this generally-applicable contract law regarding assent without risking FAA preemption.[73] Because this sort of law applies to all contracts, states may apply it to arbitration agreements while remaining faithful to the FAA's goal of placing arbitration agreements "upon the same footing as other contracts."[74] Indeed, states would be unfaithful to this goal if they applied a lower standard of assent to arbitration agreements than to other contracts. Conversely, states may not apply a higher standard of assent to arbitration agreements than to other contracts.

For example, the FAA preempts the following Montana statute: "Notice that a contract is subject to arbitration * * * shall be typed in underlined capital letters on the first page of the contract; and unless such notice is displayed thereon, the contract may not be subject to arbitration."[75] *Doctor's Associates, Inc. v. Casarotto*,[76] involved a franchise agreement that did not comply with this statute because the arbitration clause was on page nine and in ordinary type.[77] The Supreme Court held that the Montana statute is preempted by the

---

[70]   Restatement (Second) of Contracts § 211 cmt. b (1981).

[71]   Id. § 211 cmt. f.

[72]   Id.

[73]   The Restatement's reasonable expectations doctrine was applied to an arbitration agreement in Broemmer v. Abortion Servs. of Phoenix, LTD., 840 P.2d 1013, 1017 (Ariz.1992) ("The Restatement focuses our attention on whether it was beyond plaintiff's reasonable expectations to expect to arbitrate her medical malpractice claims").

[74]   H.R.Rep. No. 68–96, at 2 (1924). See § 9.

[75]   Mont.Code Ann. § 27–5–114(4) (1995). This language was deleted from the statute in 1997.

[76]   517 U.S. 681 (1996).

[77]   Id. at 684–85.

FAA because the Montana statute "conditions the enforceability of
arbitration agreements on compliance with a special notice
requirement not applicable to contracts generally."[78] The FAA
"precludes States from singling out arbitration provisions for suspect
status, requiring instead that such provisions be placed 'upon the
same footing as other contracts.' "[79] Other state laws preempted on
the reasoning of *Casarotto* are numerous.[80]

Despite *Casarotto*, the Montana Supreme Court continues to
hold arbitration agreements to a higher standard of assent than it
holds contracts generally.[81] The Montana Supreme Court's rationale
is that arbitration agreements waive a constitutional right (the right
to jury trial) and Montana courts require all contracts (not just
arbitration agreements) that waive constitutional rights, to the
higher standard of assent, "knowing and voluntary" assent.[82] On the
other hand, this Montana law may be preempted by FAA § 2, which
says that to be a permissible ground for the revocation of an

---

[78]   Id. at 687.

[79]   Id.

[80]   With the possible exceptions of state statutes relating to insurance, see § 18,
and employment, see §§ 46–47, other statutes preempted on the reasoning of *Casarotto*
include: Cal.Bus. & Prof.Code § 7191(a) (arbitration clauses in certain residential
contracts shall contain prescribed notice in at least ten-point roman boldface type or if
in red print in at least eight-point boldface type); Colo.Rev.Stat.Ann. § 13–64–403(d)(4)
(arbitration clauses in agreements for medical services shall contain prescribed notice
in at least ten-point boldface type); Ga.Code Ann. 9–9–2(c)(8), (9) (arbitration clause
must be initialed); N.Y.Pub. Health Law §§ 4406–a(2), (3) (arbitration provisions of
health maintenance organization contracts must be in at least twelve-point boldface
type immediately above spaces for the signature); R.I.Gen.Laws § 10–3–2 (arbitration
clauses in insurance contracts must be immediately before the testimonium clause or
the signature of the parties); S.C.Code Ann. § 15–48–10(a) (arbitration clause must be
underlined and capitalized, or rubber-stamped prominently, and on first page); Munoz
v. Green Tree Financial Corp., 542 S.E.2d 360, 364 (S.C.2001) (holding the statute's
requirements are preempted by the FAA); S.D.Codified Laws § 21–25B–3 (arbitration
clauses relating to medical services must be in twelve-point boldface type immediately
above the space for signature); Tenn.Code Ann. § 29–5–302(a) (arbitration clause in
certain contracts must be signed or initialed by the parties); Vt.Stat.Ann.tit. 12,
§ 5652(b) (arbitration clause must be signed by parties and displayed prominently).
See also In re Nexion Health at Humble, Inc., 173 S.W.3d 67 (Tex.2005)(FAA preempts
Texas statute requiring the signature of a party's counsel on arbitration agreements
in personal injury cases).

[81]   Kelker v. Geneva-Roth Ventures, Inc., 303 P.3d 777, 786 (Mont.2013)
("Outside the arbitration context, our generally applicable principles of contract law
presume that '[a]bsent incapacity to contract, ignorance of the contents of a written
contract is not a ground for relief from liability' under its provisions. . . . Because an
arbitration provision waives fundamental rights, however, we have applied a more
stringent standard when faced with a consumer's claim that she has not read or
understood the arbitration clause in a contract."); Kortum-Managhan v. Herbergers
NBGL, 204 P.3d 693, 699 (Mont.2009); Kloss v. Edward D. Jones & Co., 54 P.3d 1
(Mont.2002).

[82]   "Montana law generally applicable to the waiver of constitutional rights,
requires that the waiver will not be lightly presumed; that it must be proved to have
been made voluntarily, knowingly and intelligently—typically by the party seeking
the waiver; and that it will be narrowly construed." Kloss, 54 P.3d. at 16.

arbitration agreement, it must be a ground for the revocation of "any contract." Not "any contract that waives constitutional rights," but "any contract." This issue is not limited to Montana; it arises whenever a state (by case law, statute or constitution) raises the standard of assent for arbitration agreements and some, but not all, other contracts.[83]

3.   CHOICE-OF-LAW CLAUSES
Table of Sections

§ 15   Introduction

Because of the United States Constitution's Supremacy Clause, when there is a conflict between federal and state law, the federal law prevails.[84] In this regard, federal arbitration law is no different from any other federal law[85] and the FAA preempts many state laws.[86] However, otherwise-preempted state arbitration law may nevertheless govern particular parties if those parties have, by contract, chosen to be governed by that state law. With respect to at least some topics, parties have the power to form an enforceable arbitration agreement providing that any dispute they have will be governed by state arbitration law, instead of by the FAA.[87] The parties' power to do this is found in the Supreme Court's opinion in *Volt Information Sciences, Inc. v. Board of Trustees of the Leland Stanford Junior University*.[88]

---

[83]   Stephen J. Ware, Contractual Arbitration, Mandatory Arbitration and State Constitutional Jury-Trial Rights, 38 U.S.F.L.Rev. 39, 44–48 (2003).

[84]   U.S. Const. art. VI, cl. 2 ("This Constitution, and the Laws of the United States which shall be made in Pursuance thereof; and all Treaties made, or which shall be made, under the Authority of the United States, shall be the supreme Law of the Land; and the Judges in every State shall be bound thereby, any Thing in the Constitution or Laws of any State to the Contrary notwithstanding.")

[85]   See §§ 6–7.

[86]   See §§ 9–14.

[87]   See, e.g., Alan Scott Rau, Federal Common Law and Arbitral Power, 8 Nev. L.J. 169, 203 n.108 (2007) ("parties may choose to subject themselves to state rather than federal rules of arbitration—as long as their intention to do so is particularly explicit.")

[88]   489 U.S. 468 (1989).

§ 16   The *Volt* Case

Volt involved an arbitration clause in a construction contract. The California trial court stayed arbitration pending resolution of related litigation,[89] as a California statute permitted.[90] In contrast, the FAA probably does not permit such a stay.[91] The California Court of Appeal held that California arbitration law, rather than the FAA, applied because the construction contract included a choice-of-law clause stating that the contract would be "governed by the law of the place where the project is located."[92] The project at issue was located in California.[93] The California Court of Appeal held that the parties "have agreed, as we interpret their choice of law provision, that the laws of California, of which [the stay provision] is certainly a part, are to govern their contract."[94] It also held "that enforcement of the arbitration agreement in accordance with the chosen California rules of procedure does not create a conflict with the [FAA], since the purpose of the [FAA] was to ensure that private agreements to arbitrate are enforceable contracts."[95] The United States Supreme Court agreed and affirmed.[96]

While the Supreme Court's opinions in *Volt* included a dissent, the Court was unanimous in ruling that parties can make an enforceable agreement that California arbitration law, rather than the FAA, determines whether to stay arbitration pending resolution of related litigation. The majority in *Volt* affirmed the holding that the parties in *Volt* had made such an agreement. While the dissenting justices did not believe the parties in *Volt* had made such an agreement, the dissenters did agree that the parties had the power to make such an agreement. The dissent said that parties "are free if they wish to write an agreement to arbitrate outside the coverage of the FAA. Such an agreement would permit a state rule, otherwise preempted by the FAA, to govern their arbitration."[97] So the Court unanimously held that, at least with respect to some topics, parties have the power to form an enforceable arbitration agreement

---

[89]   Board of Trustees of the Leland Stanford Junior Univ. v. Volt Info.Sciences, Inc., 240 Cal.Rptr. 558, 559 (Ct.App.1987), aff'd, 489 U.S. 468 (1989).

[90]   Cal.Civ.Proc.Code § 1281.2(c)(4). This provision is quoted in § 33, n.59.

[91]   See § 33.

[92]   Volt, 240 Cal.Rptr. at 559.

[93]   Id.

[94]   Id.

[95]   Id.

[96]   Volt Info. Sciences, Inc., v. Board of Trustees of the Leland Stanford Junior Univ., 489 U.S. 468, 479 (1989).

[97]   Id. at 485 (Brennan, J., dissenting).

providing that their dispute will be governed by state arbitration law, instead of by the FAA.

What divided the majority and dissent in *Volt* was whether the parties in that case had exercised their power to make an enforceable agreement providing for California arbitration law, rather than the FAA. The *Volt* Court's majority did not review, but accepted as a matter of state law, the California Court of Appeal's interpretation of the choice-of-law clause "to mean that the parties had incorporated the California rules of arbitration into their arbitration agreement."[98] In contrast, the dissent stated "I can accept neither the state court's unusual interpretation of the parties' contract, nor this Court's unwillingness to review it."[99] The dissent correctly pointed out that "the normal purpose of such choice-of-law clauses is to determine that the law of one State rather than that of another State will be applicable; they simply do not speak to any interaction between state and federal law."[100] The choice-of-law clause in *Volt* is best interpreted as the parties' choice of California law over other state law, rather than California law over federal law. The California Court of Appeal misinterpreted the contract.

So the narrow question dividing the Supreme Court in *Volt* was whether to correct the California court's misinterpretation of the contract. The majority chose not to, while dissent would have done so. Ordinarily, the Supreme Court reviews *de novo* state court rulings on federal law but defers to state courts on matters of state law.[101] Contract interpretation is usually a matter of state law, but arbitration agreements are also the subject of federal law. The FAA provides that arbitration agreements "shall be valid, irrevocable, and enforceable, save upon such grounds as exist at law or in equity for the revocation of any contract."[102]

States could easily nullify this federal command if the Supreme Court did not police state courts' creative interpretation of arbitration agreements. Suppose that Alabama courts interpreted every arbitration agreement before them as embodying the parties' choice to be governed by Alabama arbitration law, rather than the FAA. Alabama law holds that pre-dispute arbitration agreements are void.[103] So if Alabama courts interpreted all arbitration agreements

---

[98]   Id. at 474.

[99]   Id. at 481 (Brennan, J., dissenting).

[100]   Id. at 488 (Brennan, J., dissenting) (citing authority).

[101]   Erwin Chemerinsky, Federal Jurisdiction § 10.1 (4th ed.2003) ("The Court may decide only questions of federal law. The Court has no authority to decide matters of state law in reviewing the decisions of state courts.")

[102]   9 U.S.C. § 2.

[103]   See § 10.

before them as embodying the parties' choice to be governed by Alabama law, then the FAA's primary command—that arbitration agreements be enforced—would not apply in Alabama courts. By ruling on contract interpretation, ordinarily a matter of state law, Alabama courts would effectively nullify a federal statute.

In contrast, no similar nullification of the FAA's primary command was effected by the California court's ruling, affirmed in *Volt*. Alabama arbitration law is diametrically opposed to the FAA, while California arbitration law is fairly similar to the FAA. California arbitration law is generally supportive of arbitration and enforcement of arbitration agreements.[104] *Volt* expressly noted that California arbitration law is "manifestly designed to encourage resort to the arbitral process."[105] So the Supreme Court might well review contract interpretation by Alabama courts in the example just given, even though the Court's majority refused to review contract interpretation by the California court in *Volt*.[106]

§ 17 Case Law Since *Volt*

Since *Volt*, the Supreme Court has twice considered whether parties contracted out of FAA preemption of state law by including a general choice-of-law clause in their arbitration agreement. In both cases, *Mastrobuono v. Shearson Lehman Hutton, Inc.*,[107] and *Preston v. Ferrer*,[108] the Court held that the parties did not contract out of FAA preemption.

Mastrobuono involved a contract between investors and their securities broker. The contract contained both an arbitration clause and a clause stating that the contract "shall be governed by the laws of the State of New York."[109] New York law at the time prohibited arbitrators from awarding punitive damages.[110] When the arbitrator

---

[104] Cal.Civ.Proc.Code §§ 1281–1281.9 (West 1982).

[105] Volt, 489 U.S. at 476.

[106] See Woodmen of World Life Ins. Soc. v. White, 35 F.Supp.2d 1349, 1354 (M.D.Ala.1999) ("Volt and Mastrobuono are distinguishable from the case at hand because the Alabama rule which the Defendants now seek to apply would render the arbitration agreement within the contract to which the parties agreed unenforceable, while the agreements in Volt and Mastrobuono dealt only with procedural issues and, even where the state law was enforced, the state law actually fostered arbitration."); Webb v. R. Rowland & Co., 800 F.2d 803, 804–07 (8th Cir.1986) (refusing to interpret Missouri choice-of-law clause as choice of Missouri arbitration law over the FAA because Missouri law would have prohibited enforcement of the arbitration clause). See also § 25(b)(discussing Supreme Court decisions constraining state courts' discretion regarding what is usually a state-law issue, unconscionability).

[107] 514 U.S. 52 (1995).

[108] 552 U.S. 346, 356 (2008)(FAA preempts state statutory provision denying enforcement to arbitration agreements in talent agency contracts).

[109] 514 U.S. at 52, 58–59.

[110] Id. at 55.

awarded punitive damages to the investor, the broker (citing *Volt*) asked the court to vacate that portion of the arbitrator's award on the ground that New York law governed.[111] The Supreme Court rejected the broker's argument and confirmed the award of punitive damages.[112]

Unlike *Volt*, which began in state court, the *Mastrobuono* case began in federal court. So in *Mastrobuono* the Supreme Court could interpret the contract as it wished, without considering whether to defer (as it did in *Volt*) to a state court's interpretation of the contract.[113] The *Mastrobuono* Court rightly interpreted the contract as not requiring application of New York's law prohibiting arbitrators from awarding punitive damages. Among other things, the Court suggested that the choice-of-law clause was simply a choice of New York law over the law of other states, rather than a choice to avoid FAA preemption of New York law. The Court did this by pointing out that the broker wrongly interpreted the contract's choice of "the laws of the State of New York" to "include[ ] the caveat, 'detached from otherwise-applicable federal law.' "[114]

The 2008 *Preston* case involved a contract with an arbitration clause and a clause providing that the "agreement shall be governed by the laws of the state of California."[115] Preston sought to arbitrate his claim for payment for services he rendered to Ferrer.[116] Preston's demand for arbitration was countered by Ferrer's petition to the California Labor Commissioner charging that the contract was unenforceable under the California Talent Agencies Act (CTAA),[117] which vests the Labor Commissioner with exclusive original jurisdiction to determine whether a particular agreement is subject to a California statute that requires parties to exhaust administrative remedies before resorting to arbitration.[118] In other words, Preston wanted the case decided in arbitration and Ferrer wanted at least some preliminary portion of the case decided by the Labor Commissioner.

Had there been no choice-of-law clause, the case would have been sent to arbitration simply because that is what the agreement

---

[111]   Id. at 54–55.

[112]   Id. at 64.

[113]   Whether to so defer is the issue that split the majority and dissent in *Volt*. See § 16.

[114]   Mastrobuono, 514 U.S. at 55.

[115]   552 U.S. at 361.

[116]   Id. at 350.

[117]   Cal.Lab.Code Ann. § 1700 et seq. (West 2003 and Supp.2008).

[118]   Preston, 552 U.S. at 356 (citing Cal.Lab.Code Ann. § 1700.44(a)).

provided and the agreement is enforceable under the FAA.[119] The CTAA purports to make portions of that arbitration agreement unenforceable, but the FAA preempts conflicting state law.[120] One question in *Preston* was whether the parties contracted out of this preemption by including in their contract a California choice-of-law clause. In answering "no," the *Preston* Court distinguished *Volt* and was "guided by [its] more recent decision" in *Mastrobuono*.[121] The *Preston* Court concluded that the California choice-of law clause should be read to incorporate "prescriptions governing the substantive rights and obligations of the parties, but not the State's 'special rules limiting the authority of arbitrators.' "[122]

In sum, *Mastrobuono* and *Preston* reinforce *Volt's* main holding—that parties can contract out of at least some aspects of FAA preemption—but indicate that it typically takes more than a general choice-of-law clause to do so. Similarly, most lower-court cases treat a general choice-of-law clause as a choice among states, rather than a choice of the chosen state over the FAA.[123] For parties to contract

---

[119] See § 12. See also AT & T Mobility LLC v. Concepcion, 563 U.S. 333, 342 (2011) (citing *Preston* for the proposition that "When state law prohibits outright the arbitration of a particular type of claim, the analysis is straightforward: The conflicting rule is displaced by the FAA.")

[120] Preston, 552 U.S. at 356 ("Procedural prescriptions of the TAA thus conflict with the FAA's dispute resolution regime in two basic respects: First, the TAA, in § 1700.44(a), grants the Labor Commissioner exclusive jurisdiction to decide an issue that the parties agreed to arbitrate, see Buckeye, * * * ; second, the TAA, in § 1700.45, imposes prerequisites to enforcement of an arbitration agreement that are not applicable to contracts generally, see Doctor's Associates, Inc., * * * .")

[121] Id. at 361.

[122] Id. at 363 (quoting Mastrobuono, 514 U.S. at 63–64). See Supreme Court Addresses Volt's Choice-of-Law Trap: Is the End of the Problem in Sight?, 64 J. Disp. Resol. 22 (May–July 2009) (noting that what is significant about Preston "but largely overlooked" is that it "departs from the approach in Volt, which left the interpretation of choice-of-law cases to the state courts.")

[123] See Oberwager v. McKechnie Ltd., 2009 WL 3358469, *2 (3d Cir.) ("[A] generic choice of law provision is insufficient to evidence the clear intent necessary to opt out of the FAA's d efault regime"); BNSF R. Co. v. Alstom Transp., Inc., 777 F.3d 785, 790 (5th Cir. 2015) ("arbitration under non-FAA [state] rules [only] if a contract expressly references state arbitration law"); Sovak v. Chugai Pharm. Co., 280 F.3d 1266, 1270 (9th Cir.2002) (choice-of-law clause did not choose Illinois arbitration law over the FAA); Dominium AustinPartners, LLC v. Emerson, 248 F.3d 720, 729 n.9 (8th Cir.2001) (citing UHC Mgmt. Co., Inc. v. Computer Scis. Corp., 148 F.3d 992, 997 (8th Cir.1998)) ("The construction of an agreement to arbitrate is governed by the FAA unless the agreement expressly provides that state law should govern."); Porter Hayden Co. v. Century Indem.Co., 136 F.3d 380, 382 (4th Cir.1998)("The Supreme Court has, however, squarely rejected the argument that a federal court should read a contract's general choice-of-law provision as invoking state law of arbitrability and displacing federal arbitration law."); Ferro Corp. v. Garrison Indus., Inc., 142 F.3d 926, 937 (6th Cir.1998)("the choice-of-law clause is not an 'unequivocal inclusion' of the Ohio rule which arguably holds [the opposite of the FAA rule]"; PaineWebber Inc. v. Elahi, 87 F.3d 589, 594 (1st Cir.1996)("Following the principles and analysis set forth in Mastrobuono, we * * * find that the choice-of-law clause in this case is not an expression of intent to adopt New York caselaw [on question of the arbitration timing]"); National Union Fire Insurance Co. of Pittsburgh, Pa. v. Belco Petroleum

out of FAA preemption, they need more specific language stating not only which state's law they choose to govern the merits of any dispute, but also that they want this state's arbitration law.[124]

4. INSURANCE ARBITRATION

Table of Sections

Sec.

§ 18   McCarran-Ferguson and the FAA

---

§ 18   McCarran-Ferguson and the FAA

FAA preemption of state law has an added complication in the insurance context because of the McCarran-Ferguson Act,[125] which states:

(a) State regulation

The business of insurance, and every person engaged therein, shall be subject to the laws of the several States which relate to the regulation or taxation of such business.

(b) Federal regulation

No Act of Congress shall be construed to invalidate, impair, or supersede any law enacted by any State for the purposes of regulating the business of insurance, * * * unless such Act specifically relates to the business of insurance. * * * [126]

Some state laws that would otherwise be preempted by federal law are protected from that preemption by McCarran-Ferguson. For example, McCarran-Ferguson precludes application of the FAA to certain insurance cases, leaving those cases to state arbitration law.

Corp., 88 F.3d 129, 135 (2d Cir.1996) ("[T]he choice-of-law clause is not an unequivocal inclusion of a New York rule that requires the preclusive effect of a prior arbitration to be decided by the court."); Jung v. Ass'n of Am. Med. Colleges, 300 F.Supp.2d 119, 153 (D.D.C.2004) ("Numerous courts of appeals have concluded that Mastrobuono requires that the intent of the contracting parties to apply state arbitration rules or law to arbitration proceedings must be explicitly stated in the contract and that under Mastrobuono, a general choice of law provision does not evidence such intent.")

The exceptions include Ekstrom v. Value Health, Inc., 68 F.3d 1391, 1393 (D.C.Cir.1995); Restaurant Consulting Servs., Inc. v. Mountzuris, 253 F.Supp.2d 45, 51 (D.Mass.2003)("Because the agreement calls for the use of Massachusetts law in determining the rights and obligation of the parties, the Massachusetts Uniform Arbitration Act, rather than the Federal Arbitration Act, applies.").

[124] Foulger-Pratt Residential Contracting, LLC v. Madrigal Condominiums, LLC, 779 F. Supp. 2d 100, 110 (D.D.C. 2011) (while "a generic choice of law clause is insufficient to displace the FAA, * * * In this case * * * the parties included a specific clause stating that '[t]his [a]greement to arbitrate shall be specifically enforceable pursuant to and interpreted under the laws of the District of Columbia.' [and thus] specifically and unambiguously evidences their clear choice of D.C. law rather than the FAA to govern their agreement to arbitrate.")

[125] 15 U.S.C. §§ 1011–1015.

[126] 15 U.S.C. § 1012(a)–(b).

The challenge then, is to identify which state laws are protected from FAA preemption by McCarran-Ferguson.

The Supreme Court holds that, to be protected from preemption by McCarran-Ferguson, a state "law must not just have an impact on the insurance industry, but be specifically directed toward that industry."[127] For this reason, McCarran-Ferguson does not protect from FAA preemption state laws regulating arbitration generally, even when those laws are applied to insurance arbitration.[128] In contrast, McCarran-Ferguson does protect from FAA preemption a Kansas statute providing that arbitration clauses in insurance policies are unenforceable, while arbitration clauses in other contracts are enforceable.[129] McCarran-Ferguson also protects from FAA preemption certain state law regarding insurance company liquidations and receiverships.[130] In the international arbitration context, courts are divided on the extent to which McCarran-Ferguson protects state law from preemption by the most important arbitration treaty, the New York Convention.[131]

---

[127] Pilot Life Insurance Co. v. Dedeaux, 481 U.S. 41, 50 (1987).

[128] See Miller v. Nat'l Fidel.Life Ins.Co., 588 F.2d 185, 187 (5th Cir.1979)(where state insurance code contains no provisions relating to arbitration, applying the FAA to an insurance arbitration clause does not—to use McCarran-Ferguson's language— "invalidate, impair, or supersede any state law regulating the business of insurance."); Hart v. Orion Ins. Co., 453 F.2d 1358, 1360 (10th Cir.1971); Hamilton Life Ins.Co. v. Republic Nat'l Life Ins.Co., 408 F.2d 606, 611 (2d Cir.1969)("arbitration statutes * * * are not statutes regulating the business of insurance, but statutes regulating the method of handling contract disputes generally."); Ainsworth v. Allstate Ins.Co., 634 F.Supp. 52 (W.D.Mo.1985).

[129] Mutual Reinsurance Bureau v. Great Plains Mutual Ins.Co., Inc., 969 F.2d 931 (10th Cir.1992); Friday v. Trinity Universal of Kansas, 939 P.2d 869 (Kan.1997). For other cases finding that McCarran-Ferguson protects a state law from FAA preemption, see American Bankers Ins. Co. of Florida v. Inman, 436 F.3d 490 (5th Cir.2006); McKnight v. Chicago Title Ins. Co., Inc., 358 F.3d 854, 859 (11th Cir.2004); Standard Sec.Life Ins.Co. v. West, 267 F.3d 821, 823 (8th Cir.2001); Nat'l Home Ins. Co. v. King, 291 F.Supp.2d 518, 530 (E.D.Ky.2003); Imbler v. PacifiCare of Cal., Inc., 126 Cal.Rptr.2d 715, 723 (Ct.App.2002); Allen v. Pacheco, 71 P.3d 375, 384 (Colo.2003); United Ins. Co. of America v. Office of Ins. Regulation, 985 So.2d 665 (Fla.App.2008); Love v. Money Tree, Inc. 614 S.E.2d 47, 50 (Ga.2005); In re Kepka, 178 S.W.3d 279, 292–93 (Tex.Ct.App.2005); Kruger Clinic Orthopaedics, LLC v. Regence BlueShield, 138 P.3d 936, 940–41 (Wash.2006); State, Dept. of Transp. v. James River Ins. Co., 292 P.3d 118 (Wash.2013). But see Little v. Allstate Ins. Co., 705 A.2d 538, 541 (Vt.1997).

With respect to federal crop insurance, courts find that the FAA preempts state arbitration law. State of Kansas ex rel. Todd v. United States, 995 F.2d 1505, 1511 (10th Cir.1993); In re 2000 Sugar Beet Crop Ins. Litigation, 228 F.Supp.2d 992 (D.Minn.2002); IGF Ins. Co. v. Hat Creek P'ship, 76 S.W.3d 859 (Ark.2002).

[130] See Corcoran v. Universal Reinsurance Corp., 713 F.Supp. 77 (S.D.N.Y.1989); Ideal Mut. Ins. Co. v. Phoenix Greek Gen'l Ins.Co., 1987 WL 28636 (S.D.N.Y.1987); Washburn v. Corcoran, 643 F.Supp. 554 (S.D.N.Y.1986).

[131] Compare, e.g., Safety Nat.Cas.Corp. v. Certain Underwriters At Lloyd's, London, 587 F.3d 714, 731 (5th Cir.2009) ("implemented treaty provisions, self-executing or not, are not reverse-preempted by state law pursuant to the McCarran-Ferguson Act"); Goshawk Dedicated v. Portsmouth Settlement Co. I, 466 F.Supp.2d 1293, 1306 (N.D.Ga.2006) ("the [New York] Convention prevails over the McCarran-

Ferguson Act"), with Stephens v. American International Insurance Co., 66 F.3d 41 (2d Cir.1995)(anti-arbitration provision in the Kentucky Insurers Rehabilitation and Liquidation Law protected by McCarran-Ferguson from preemption by the Federal Arbitration Act provision implementing New York Convention).

Chapter 4

FORMATION OF ENFORCEABLE ARBITRATION AGREEMENTS

Table of Sections

      (4)   Family Law: Child Custody

   (b)   Arbitrability with Strings Attached: The "Effectively Vindicate" Doctrine

The FAA is not a complete statement of all the law governing arbitration.[1] The FAA presupposes, and often incorporates, state law in areas such as contract and agency. In other words, lots of general state law applies to arbitration. The area of general state law with the most frequent application to arbitration is contract law. The following sections survey the law regarding formation of enforceable contracts as that law applies to arbitration agreements.[2] Before doing so, however, it discusses a special twist of contract law that applies when the contract has an arbitration clause. That twist is the separability doctrine.[3]

1.   SEPARABILITY
Table of Sections

§ 19   The *Prima Paint* Case

The separability doctrine is complex so it can best be understood by starting with the facts of the Supreme Court case that adopted the doctrine, *Prima Paint Corp. v. Flood & Conklin Manufacturing Co.*[4] F & C sold Prima Paint a list of F & C's customers and promised not to sell paint to those customers for six years.[5] F & C also promised to act as a consultant to Prima Paint during these six years.[6] This

---

[1]   See § 5(b).

[2]   See §§ 22–26.

[3]   This special twist of contract law also applies when the contract has a forum-selection clause naming a particular court, rather than arbitration, as the chosen forum. Christopher R. Drahozal, Buckeye Check Cashing and the Separability Doctrine, 1 YB Arb. & Med. 55, 83–89 (2009). Also somewhat analogous are cases involving choice-of-law clauses and jury-waiver clauses. Id.

[4]   388 U.S. 395 (1967).

[5]   Id. at 397.

[6]   Id.

consulting agreement included an arbitration clause.[7] Prima Paint did not make the payments provided for in the consulting agreement.[8] Prima Paint contended that F & C had fraudulently represented that it was solvent and able to perform its contract, but was in fact insolvent and intended to file for bankruptcy shortly after executing its consulting agreement with Prima Paint.[9]

F & C served on Prima Paint a "notice of intention to arbitrate."[10] Prima Paint then sued in federal court for rescission of the consulting agreement because of the alleged misrepresentation and for an order enjoining F & C from proceeding with arbitration.[11] F & C cross-moved to stay the suit pending arbitration.[12] The trial court granted F & C's motion and the Second Circuit dismissed Prima Paint's appeal.[13] The Supreme Court affirmed.

Although the Court ruled against Prima Paint, the Court did not address Prima Paint's argument that F & C fraudulently induced Prima Paint to sign the consulting agreement. In fact, the Court held that no court should address this argument because it raised an issue for the arbitrator to resolve.

The Court said that its result is compelled by FAA § 4, which provides that if

> [a] party [claims to be] aggrieved by the alleged failure * * * of another to arbitrate * * * [t]he court shall hear the parties, and upon being satisfied that the making of the agreement for arbitration or the failure to comply therewith is not in issue, the court shall make an order directing the parties to proceed to arbitration * * * . If the making of the arbitration agreement or the failure, neglect, or refusal to perform the same be in issue, the court shall proceed summarily to the trial thereof.[14]

More simply, § 4 says that the court shall not order the parties to arbitration if "the making *of the arbitration agreement*" is in issue.[15] If the making of the arbitration agreement *is* in issue then the court must proceed to trial on that issue. If the trial determines that the parties made an arbitration agreement then the court must order the

---

7   Id. at 398.

8   Id.

9   Id.

10   Id.

11   Id. at 398–99.

12   Id. at 399.

13   Id.

14   9 U.S.C. § 4.

15   Id. (emphasis added).

parties to arbitration. Conversely, if the trial determines that the parties did not make an arbitration agreement then the court must not order the parties to arbitration. In short, FAA § 4 rests on the basic premise that the parties should be ordered to arbitration if, but only if, they have contracted to be there.

Prima Paint held that there would be no trial on the question of whether the parties made an arbitration agreement because Prima Paint alleged fraud in the inducement *of the consulting contract*, not in the inducement *of the arbitration agreement*.[16] The term "arbitration agreement," as used in FAA § 4, refers specifically to the arbitration clause itself, not more broadly to the consulting contract of which the arbitration clause was a part. If Prima Paint had argued that there was fraud "directed to the arbitration clause itself,"[17] then the making of the arbitration agreement would have been at issue and Prima Paint would have been entitled to a trial on that issue.[18] But the Supreme Court held that FAA § 4 "does not permit the federal court to consider claims of fraud in the inducement of the contract generally."[19]

This holding is known as the separability doctrine because it treats the arbitration clause as if it is a separate contract from the contract containing the arbitration clause, that is, the "container contract." The *Prima Paint* Court held that:

> arbitration clauses as a matter of federal law are "separable" from the contracts in which they are embedded, and that where no claim is made that fraud was directed to the arbitration clause itself, a broad arbitration clause will be held to encompass arbitration of the claim that the contract itself was induced by fraud.[20]

While the separability doctrine has its critics, its practical benefits can be appreciated by considering what would happen without it. Without the separability doctrine, if Prima Paint was to allege fraudulent inducement of the consulting agreement then a court would "proceed summarily to the trial thereof."[21] A court would decide whether F & C made a fraudulent misrepresentation. If the court found that F & C had not made a fraudulent misrepresentation, then the court would refer F & C's claim (for payment) to arbitration.

---

16   Prima Paint, 388 U.S. at 404–06.

17   388 U.S. at 402.

18   See, e.g., Moseley v. Electronic & Missile Facilities, Inc., 374 U.S. 167 (1963) (cited in Prima Paint); Engalla v. Permanente Medical Group, Inc., 938 P.2d 903 (Cal.1997).

19   Prima Paint, 388 U.S. at 404.

20   Id.

21   9 U.S.C. § 4.

But Prima Paint's defense for its non-payment *is* F & C's misrepresentation, so the court would have already decided the issue of the case it was sending to arbitration.

In the absence of the separability doctrine, courts deciding whether to send disputes to arbitration often would, as in this example, become entangled with the merits of the dispute. If the court sent a dispute to arbitration after effectively ruling on the merits, the arbitrator would have two choices. The arbitrator could reconsider the merits *de novo*, which would require the parties to adjudicate the merits twice and create the possibility of inconsistent results.[22] Or the arbitrator could rubber-stamp the court's view of the merits, which would make the arbitration agreement effectively unenforceable because the parties would get a court's, rather than an arbitrator's, decision on the merits.

§ 20   The *Buckeye* Case and Separability in State Courts

The Supreme Court case adopting the separability doctrine, *Prima Paint Corp. v. Flood & Conklin Manufacturing Co.*,[23] was decided in 1967. Despite this ruling from the highest court in the land, during the following four decades many courts did not apply the separability doctrine.[24] To some extent, this was due to doubt about whether *state* courts had to apply the separability doctrine or were free to depart from it.[25] The belief that states were free to depart from

---

[22]   See Ian R. Macneil, Richard E. Speidel & Thomas J. Stipanowich, Federal Arbitration Law § 15.3.5.1 (1994 & Supp.1999) (discussing Rush v. Oppenheimer & Co., 681 F.Supp.1045 (S.D.N.Y. 1988), in which a broker allegedly told Rush, a customer, that "there was no need to read [the documents], that they were just a formality and that they were just like the documents at Drexel."

The court treated this allegation as an attack on the arbitration clause in particular, but upheld the clause on its merits. In doing so it made several findings of facts pertaining to Rush's not being misled. Is the arbitrator bound by those findings of fact when Rush attacks the entire agreement for misrepresentation before the arbitrator?

There is much to be said for giving no preclusive effect to the court's determinations when the substantive dispute goes on to arbitration. In other words, the arbitrator should decide de novo whether the defect in the underlying contract exists.

Macneil et al., § 15.3.5.1.

[23]   388 U.S. 395 (1967).

[24]   There were "a wide range of cases where *Prima Paint* issues were in fact present, but where the courts * * * refused to apply them or simply ignored their presence." Macneil, Speidel & Stipanowich, supra note 22, § 15.3.2, at 15:28.

[25]   See, e.g., Atcas v. Credit Clearing Corp. of Am., 197 N.W.2d 448 (Minn.1972) (recognizing Prima Paint but declining to the adopt the separability doctrine); Marks v. Bean, 57 S.W.3d 303 (Ky.App.2001) (same); City of Blaine v. John Coleman Hayes & Associates, Inc., 818 S.W.2d 33, 37–38 (Tenn.App.1991) (same). None of these cases continues to be good law. The Wyoming Supreme Court thought "the 'separability doctrine' espoused by *Prima Paint* ha[d] been modified by subsequent United States

the separability doctrine followed from the fact that *Prima Paint*'s reasoning rested on FAA §§ 3 and 4, which by their terms appear to apply only to proceedings in federal court.[26]

The Supreme Court resolved that question in the 2006 case of *Buckeye Check Cashing, Inc. v. Cardegna*,[27] holding that the separability doctrine applies in state court and preempts any inconsistent state law.[28] *Buckeye* said that, "[a]lthough § 4, in particular, had much to do with *Prima Paint*'s understanding of the rule of severability, this rule ultimately arises out of § 2, the FAA's substantive command that arbitration agreements be treated like all other contracts."[29] As FAA § 2 does apply in state court, *Buckeye* held "that, regardless of whether the challenge is brought in federal or state court, a challenge to the validity of the contract as a whole, and not specifically to the arbitration clause, must go to the arbitrator."[30] In short, *Buckeye* holds that state courts must apply the separability doctrine or "*Prima Paint*'s rule of severability" as *Buckeye* called it.[31]

While *Buckeye* held that the separability doctrine "ultimately arises out of [FAA] § 2", *Buckeye* did not explain this as thoroughly as a much earlier Second Circuit opinion, *Robert H. Lawrence Co. v. Devonshire Fabrics, Inc.*:[32]

> That the Arbitration Act envisages a distinction between the entire contract between the parties on the one hand and the arbitration clause of the contract on the other is plain on the face of the statute. Section 2 does not purport to affect the contract as a whole. On the contrary, it makes "valid, irrevocable, and enforceable" only a "written provision in any maritime transaction or a contract evidencing a transaction involving commerce to settle by arbitration a controversy thereafter arising out of such contract or transaction."
>
> * * *
>
> The agreement described in Section 2 is the arbitration "provision" or clause of the principal contract. If this

---

Supreme Court rulings." Fox v. Tanner, 101 P.3d 939, 943 (Wyo.2004) (citing First Options of Chicago, Inc. v. Kaplan, 514 U.S. 938 (1995), Doctor's Associates, Inc. v. Casarotto, 517 U.S. 681 (1996), Howsam v. Dean Witter Reynolds, Inc., 537 U.S. 79 (2002)).

26   See § 11.

27   546 U.S. 440 (2006).

28   Id. at 445–47.

29   Id. at 445.

30   Id. at 449.

31   Id. at 447.

32   271 F.2d 402 (2d Cir.1959).

arbitration clause was induced by fraud, there can be no arbitration; and if the party charging this fraud shows there is substance to his charge, there must be a judicial trial of that question before a stay [of litigation] can issue * * * . It is not enough [that] there is substance to the charge that the contract to deliver merchandise of a certain quality was induced by fraud.[33]

The Supreme Court used similar reasoning in a post-*Buckeye* case, *Rent-A-Center, West, Inc. v. Jackson*,[34] which said:

[FAA] § 2 states that a "written provision" "to settle by arbitration a controversy" is "valid, irrevocable, and enforceable" *without mention* of the validity of the contract in which it is contained. Thus, a party's challenge to another provision of the contract, or to the contract as a whole, does not prevent a court from enforcing a specific agreement to arbitrate.[35]

In sum, the Supreme Court has reaffirmed the separability doctrine adopted in *Prima Paint* but has shifted the doctrine's foundation from FAA § 4 to FAA § 2.[36] As § 2 applies in state court, the separability doctrine applies in state, as well as federal, court and thus preempts inconsistent state law.[37]

§ 21 Applications of Separability

(a) Contract Formation vs. Defenses to Enforcement of Contract

While fraud was the basis of the challenge to the arbitration agreement in *Prima Paint*, illegality was the basis in *Buckeye*. The contract containing the arbitration clause in *Buckeye* was a payday loan's "Deferred Deposit and Disclosure Agreement," pursuant to which Buckeye provided Cardegna with cash in exchange for a personal check in the amount of the cash plus a finance charge.[38]

---

[33] Id. at 409–11.

[34] 561 U.S. 63 (2010).

[35] Id. at 2778.

[36] Id. at 1209.

[37] This preemption applies both to the question of whether an arbitrator or court will resolve an issue and to the question of whether an arbitrator or administrative agency will resolve an issue. Preston v. Ferrer, 552 U.S. 346, 349–50 (2008) ("Does the FAA override not only state statutes that refer certain state-law controversies initially to a judicial forum, but also state statutes that refer certain disputes initially to an administrative agency? We hold today that, when parties agree to arbitrate all questions arising under a contract, state laws lodging primary jurisdiction in another forum, whether judicial or administrative, are superseded by the FAA.") This case is discussed supra § 17.

[38] Buckeye, 546 U.S. at 442.

Cardegna sued, "alleging that Buckeye charged usurious interest rates and that the Agreement violated various Florida lending and consumer-protection laws, rendering it criminal on its face."[39] The Florida Supreme Court in *Buckeye* distinguished *Prima Paint* on the ground that

> in *Prima Paint*, the claim of fraud in the inducement, if true, would have rendered the underlying contract merely voidable. In [*Buckeye*], however, the underlying contract at issue would be rendered void from the outset if it were determined that the contract indeed violated Florida's usury laws. Therefore, if the underlying contract is held entirely void as a matter of law, all of its provisions, including the arbitration clause, would be nullified as well.[40]

The Florida Supreme Court was not alone in making this distinction; several other courts had also applied the separability doctrine to voidable-contract arguments but not to void-contract arguments.[41] After the United States Supreme Court's decision in *Buckeye*, however, it is clear that the separability doctrine applies to void-contract arguments as well as to voidable-contract arguments.

Open questions remain, however. In *Buckeye* the Supreme Court said:

> The issue of the contract's validity is different from the issue of whether any agreement between the alleged obligor and obligee was ever concluded. Our opinion today addresses only the former, and does not speak to the issue decided in the cases cited by respondents (and by the Florida Supreme Court), which hold that it is for courts to decide whether the alleged obligor ever signed the contract, *Chastain v. Robinson-Humphrey Co.*, 957 F.2d 851 (C.A.11 1992), whether the signor lacked authority to commit the alleged principal, *Sandvik AB v. Advent Int'l Corp.*, 220 F.3d 99 (C.A.3 2000); *Sphere Drake Ins. Ltd. v. All American Ins. Co.*, 256 F.3d 587 (C.A.7 2001), and whether the signor lacked the mental capacity to assent, *Spahr v. Secco*, 330 F.3d 1266 (C.A.10 2003).[42]

---

[39]   Id.

[40]   Cardegna v. Buckeye Check Cashing, Inc., 894 So.2d 860, 863 (Fla.2005).

[41]   Jolley v. Welch, 904 F.2d 988 (5th Cir.1990); Three Valleys Mun.Water Dist. v. E.F.Hutton & Co., 925 F.2d 1136, 1140–41 (9th Cir.1991); Rainbow Investments, Inc. v. Super 8 Motels, Inc., 973 F.Supp. 1387, 1390–91 (M.D.Ala.1997); Allstar Homes, Inc. v. Waters, 711 So.2d 924, 927 (Ala.1997).

[42]   546 U.S. at 444 n.1.

Thus *Buckeye* does not preclude courts from hearing arguments about whether any arbitration agreement between the alleged obligor and obligee was ever concluded, that is, formed. Similarly, an earlier Supreme Court case, *First Options of Chicago, Inc. v. Kaplan*,[43] also suggests that the separability doctrine does not apply to arguments that a particular party never formed an arbitration agreement.

In *First Options*, Kaplan contended that he never formed an arbitration agreement with First Options, although he conceded that his wholly-owned company, MKI, had done so.[44] The arbitrators decided that they had the power to rule on whether Kaplan had formed an arbitration agreement with First Options and ruled that he had.[45] Kaplan sought to have the arbitration award vacated,[46] and the Supreme Court ruled for Kaplan, affirming the Third Circuit's holding that Kaplan did not form an arbitration agreement with First Options.[47] In so doing, the Court ruled that the Third Circuit correctly reviewed the arbitrators' contrary decision "independently" (de novo), rather than under the deferential standard of review FAA § 10 requires courts to use when reviewing an arbitrator's decisions on matters properly before the arbitrator.[48] Thus, *First Options* supports the proposition that courts, not arbitrators, decide whether a party has formed an arbitration agreement.

Moreover, a 2002 Supreme Court case, *Howsam v. Dean Witter Reynolds, Inc.*,[49] cites *First Options* for the proposition that "a gateway dispute about whether the parties are bound by a given arbitration clause raises a 'question of arbitrability' for a court [rather than an arbitrator] to decide."[50] Finally, in a 2010 labor arbitration case, *Granite Rock Co. v. Int'l Bhd. of Teamsters*, the Supreme Court cited *First Options* and *Buckeye* for the proposition that it is "well settled that where the dispute at issue concerns contract formation, the dispute is generally for courts to decide."[51]

---

43 514 U.S. 938, 944 (1995).

44 Id. at 941.

45 Id.

46 Id.

47 Id. at 947 ("We conclude that, because the Kaplans did not clearly agree to submit the question of arbitrability to arbitration, the Court of Appeals was correct in finding that the arbitrability of the Kaplan/First Options dispute was subject to independent review by the courts.")

48 Id. at 943. See §§ 42–44 (discussing FAA § 10).

49 537 U.S. 79 (2002).

50 Id. at 84.

51 Granite Rock Co. v. Int'l Bhd. of Teamsters, 561 U.S. 287, 297 (2010). *Granite Rock* involved the question "when (not whether) the [collective bargaining agreement] that contains the parties' arbitration clause was ratified and thereby formed." Id. at 2856.

FORMATION OF ENFORCEABLE
ARBITRATION AGREEMENTS

Thus it now seems clear that the separability doctrine does not apply to the question whether a particular party formed an arbitration agreement,[52] but only to questions about defenses to the enforcement of that agreement.[53] Following this distinction would send to courts questions about mutual assent,[54] consideration,[55] and agency (authority to assent on behalf of others),[56] while sending to arbitrators questions about misrepresentation (fraud in the

---

[52] Id. at 2857–58 ("courts should order arbitration of a dispute only where the court is satisfied that neither the formation of the parties' arbitration agreement nor (absent a valid provision specifically committing such disputes to an arbitrator) its enforceability or applicability to the dispute is in issue.") However, a party who has formed an arbitration agreement may have enforce-ably delegated to the arbitrator issues about the scope of the agreement, including issues about the parties with whom it has agreed to arbitrate. Contec Corp. v. Remote Solution, Co., 398 F.3d 205, 208 (2d Cir.2005) (requiring signatory to arbitration agreement to arbitrate issue of whether it was obligated to arbitrate with non-signatory to agreement). Compare Microchip Tech. Inc. v. U.S. Philips Corp., 367 F.3d 1350, 1358 (Fed. Cir. 2004) (non-signatory to arbitration agreement not obligated to arbitrate whether it was obligated to arbitrate with signatory to agreement: "the district court must determine whether Microchip was a successor party to the 1983 agreement before any issue may be referred to arbitration under that agreement. It was not error for the district court to deny Philips' motion to compel arbitration pending resolution of that question").

[53] Clayton v. Davidson Contractors, LLC, 2015 WL 1880973, at *7 (Tenn.Ct.App.2015)("When read together, Prima Paint, Buckeye, Rent-A-Center, and Granite Rock stand for the proposition that the court resolves two types of issues relating to an agreement to arbitrate: (1) a challenge to the validity of the specific arbitration clause sought to be enforced; and (2) a challenge to the formation of a contract, which may include an agreement to arbitrate.")

[54] See § 22; Will-Drill Resources, Inc. v. Samson Resources Co., 352 F.3d 211, 215 (5th Cir.2003); Opals on Ice Lingerie v. Body Lines Inc., 320 F.3d 362 (2d Cir. 2003); Chastain v. Robinson-Humphrey Co., 957 F.2d 851 (11th Cir.1992); Jolley v. Welch, 904 F.2d 988, 993–94 (5th Cir.1990); Vallejo v. Garda CL Southwest, Inc., 948 F.Supp.2d 720, 2013 WL 2417898 (S.D.Tex.2013). See also In re Neutral Posture, Inc., 135 S.W.3d 725 (Tex.App.2003)(whether parties' agreement to arbitrate expired by its terms is a question of the very existence of agreement to arbitrate and, thus, an issue of substantive arbitrability reserved for judicial determination, rather than a question to be determined by an arbitrator).

[55] See § 23.

[56] Sandvik AB v. Advent Int'l Corp., 220 F.3d 99, 107 (3d Cir.2000) ("the District Court was correct in determining that it must decide whether Huep's signature bound Advent before it could order arbitration."); Sphere Drake Ins. Ltd. v. All American Ins. Co., 256 F.3d 587, 591 (7th Cir.2001) (court decides whether agent had authority to bind the principal to arbitration agreement unless parties agreed to send that question to arbitration); Midwest Mem'l Grp., LLC v. Singer, No. 301861, 2012 WL 470203, at *5 (Mich. Ct. App. Feb. 14, 2012) (trial court had the power to decide * * * Smart signed [arbitration agreements]in an individual capacity and did not have the power to bind plaintiffs to the agreements."); Global Travel Mktg., Inc. v. Shea, 908 So.2d 392 (Fla.2005) (parent had authority to bind minor to arbitration clause); Hojnowski v. Vans Skate Park, 901 A.2d 381 (N.J.2006) (same); Cross v. Carnes, 724 N.E.2d 828 (Ohio App. 1998) (court holds that parent had authority to bind minor to arbitration clause, and sends to arbitrators the question of whether parent had authority to bind minor to the rest of the container contract).

inducement),[57] mistake,[58] duress,[59] undue influence,[60] incapacity,[61] unconscionability,[62] impracticability, frustration of purpose,[63] the

[57]   Prima Paint, 388 U.S. 395 (1967).

[58]   Masco Corp. v. Zurich American Ins.Co., 382 F.3d 624, 629–30 (6th Cir.2004); Unionmutual Stock Life Ins.Co. of Am. v. Beneficial Life Ins.Co., 774 F.2d 524, 528–29 (1st Cir.1985). But see Shoels v. Klebold, 375 F.3d 1054, 1066 (10th Cir.2004) (without discussing *Prima Paint* or the separability doctrine, court hears—rather than sending to arbitrator—argument that arbitration agreement was voidable due to mistake).

[59]   SBRMCOA, LLC v. Bayside Resort, Inc., 707 F.3d 267, 274 (3d Cir.2013) (under *Buckeye*, "the Condominium Association's coercion claim is arbitrable because it is a challenge to the validity (rather than the formation) of the" contract containing the arbitration clause); Service Corp. Intern. v. Lopez, 162 S.W.3d 801, 810 (Tex.App.2005) ("duress * * * issue relates to the contract as a whole and not solely the arbitration provision. It is therefore an issue to be decided in arbitration"); In re FirstMerit Bank, N.A., 52 S.W.3d 749, 756 (Tex.2001) ("The defenses of unconscionability, duress, fraudulent inducement, and revocation * * * must specifically relate to the Arbitration Addendum itself, not the contract as a whole, if they are to defeat arbitration. Defenses that pertain to the entire installment contract can be arbitrated.") But see Flannery v. Tri-State Div., 402 F.Supp.2d 819, 825 (E.D.Mich.2005) ("plaintiff's claim of duress challenges the existence of the contract itself, and therefore relates to all the clauses and provisions in it, including the arbitration clause. The argument that the arbitration clause is invalid and unenforceable, therefore, is not barred by the rule in *Prima Paint*.")

[60]   Merrill Lynch, Pierce, Fenner & Smith, Inc. v. Haydu, 637 F.2d 391 (5th Cir.1981) (duress and undue influence); Lake Erie Towing v. Walter, 2007 WL 2907496, at*7–8 (N.D.Ohio 2007) ("The Defendants' Undue Influence Claim Challenges the Contract Generally and Therefore Belongs in Front of the Arbitrator, not the Court.").

[61]   Courts have split on the question of mental incapacity. Compare, e.g., Spahr v. Secco, 330 F.3d 1266, 1273 (10th Cir.2003) (court decides defense of mental incapacity); In re Morgan Stanley & Co., Inc., 293 S.W.3d 182, 190 (Tex.2009)("Prima Paint reserves to the court issues like the one here, that the signor lacked the mental capacity to assent. Accordingly, the trial court did not abuse its discretion in declining to yield the question to the arbitrator."), with Primerica Life Ins.Co. v. Brown, 304 F.3d 469, 472–73 (5th Cir.2002) (arbitrator decides defense of mental incapacity). See, e.g., Stephen K. Huber, The Arbitration Jurisprudence of the Fifth Circuit: Round IV, 39 Tex. Tech L. Rev. 463, 476 (2007) (disapproving Primerica as not "sensible" for ignoring the distinction between contract defenses and contract formation); Alan Scott Rau, Everything You Really Need to Know About "Separability" in Seventeen Simple Propositions, 14 Am. Rev. Int'l Arb. 1, 15–16 (2003) (criticizing Primerica as a "bizarre and inexplicable" misreading of the separability doctrine).

A related question is a minor's lack of capacity to contract. See H & S Homes, L.L.C. v. McDonald 823 So.2d 627 (Ala.2001) (limited discovery allowed on minority issue at time of motion to compel arbitration in the trial court); Douglass v. Pflueger Hawaii, Inc., 135 P.3d 129 (Haw.2006).

[62]   Substantive unconscionability of contract terms other than the arbitration clause is an issue for the arbitrator, Bob Schultz Motors, Inc. v. Kawasaki Motors Corp., U.S.A., 334 F.3d 721 (8th Cir.2003), while substantive unconscionability of the arbitration clause is generally an issue for the court. Banc One Acceptance Corp. v. Hill, 367 F.3d 426 (5th Cir.2004). For a discussion of procedural unconscionability, see infra note 147.

[63]   Unionmutual Stock Life Ins. Co. of Am. v. Beneficial Life Ins. Co., 774 F.2d 524, 528–29 (1st Cir. 1985) ("[T]he arbitration clause is separable from the contract and is not rescinded by * * * [defendant]'s attempt to rescind the entire contract based on * * * frustration of purpose."); Commonwealth Edison Co. v. Gulf Oil Corp., 541 F.2d 1263, 1271 (7th Cir. 1976).

statute of frauds, the statute of limitations,[64] and illegality.[65] To reiterate, these latter issues are sent to the arbitrator if they are challenges to the container contract as a whole. In contrast, if they are challenges "directed to the arbitration clause itself,"[66] then they are presumptively heard by courts.

(b) Delegation Clauses

The previous section explained that the separability doctrine sends to arbitrators arguments based on defenses to contract enforcement if they are challenges to the whole contract containing the arbitration clause, but not if they are directed to the arbitration clause itself. However, even challenges directed to the arbitration clause itself are heard by arbitrators if the parties have agreed to have them heard by arbitrators. This was the case in *Rent-A-Center, West, Inc. v. Jackson*,[67] in which the Supreme Court enforced a contract clause that said:

> [t]he Arbitrator, and not any federal, state, or local court or agency, shall have exclusive authority to resolve any dispute relating to the interpretation, applicability, enforceability or formation of this Agreement including, but not limited to any claim that all or any part of this Agreement is void or voidable.[68]

In *Rent-A-Center*, Jackson argued that the arbitration agreement was unconscionable so he should be free to litigate, rather than arbitrate, his claims against Rent-A-Center.[69] The Supreme Court rejected Jackson's argument on the ground that the just-quoted "delegation" clause constituted his agreement to arbitrate the question of whether other portions of his arbitration agreement were

---

[64]   Allianz Glob. Risk U.S. Ins. Co. v. Gen. Elec. Co., 470 F. App'x 652, 654 (9th Cir. 2012) (citing Rent-a-Center for the proposition that "The parties' remaining contentions regarding the statute of limitations, which go to the enforceability of the contract as a whole, are for the arbitrator to decide"). See also Howsam v. Dean Witter Reynolds, Inc., 537 U.S. 79 (2002); O'Keefe Architects, Inc. v. CED Construction Partners, Ltd., 2006 WL 2971783 (Fla. Oct.19, 2006).

[65]   Buckeye, 546 U.S. 440 (2006). Nitro-Lift Technologies, L.L.C. v. Howard, 133 S.Ct. 500, 503 (2012) (whether employee's non-competition agreement is void as against public policy to be determined by arbitrator rather than court; "attacks on the validity of the contract, as distinct from attacks on the validity of the arbitration clause itself, are to be resolved by the arbitrator in the first instance, not by a federal or state court.")

[66]   Prima Paint, 388 U.S. at 402. Accord Buckeye, 546 U.S. at 449 ("a challenge to the validity of the contract as a whole, and not specifically to the arbitration clause, must go to the arbitrator.")

[67]   561 U.S. 63 (2010).

[68]   Id. at 2775.

[69]   Id.

unconscionable.[70] By contrast, had Jackson argued that the delegation clause itself was unconscionable then that argument would, the Supreme Court suggested, be heard by a court, rather than sent to arbitration.[71] In other words, the Court seems to treat the delegation clause as separable from the broader arbitration clause in much the same way the separability doctrine treats an arbitration clause as separable from the still-broader container contract.[72] And just as delegation clauses should not prevent courts

---

[70]   Id. at 2777–79.

[71]   "[U]nless Jackson challenged the delegation provision specifically, we must treat it as valid under § 2, and must enforce it under §§ 3 and 4, leaving any challenge to the validity of the Agreement as a whole for the arbitrator." Id. at 2779. Few reported cases since *Rent-A-Center* address arguments that the delegation clause is unconscionable or otherwise unenforceable. Most of these enforce the delegation clause. See Tiri v. Lucky Chances, Inc., A136675, 2014 WL 1961845 (Cal. Ct. App. May 15, 2014) (rejecting argument that delegation clause was unconscionable, "[t]hus, it will be for the arbitrator to consider the conscionability of the agreement as a whole"); id. at *9 ("the inescapable import of Rent-A-Center is that clear delegation clauses in employment arbitration agreements are substantively unconscionable only if they impose unfair or one-sided burdens that are different from the clauses' inherent features and consequence" and "the trial court lacked the authority to rule on the enforceability of the agreement because the parties' delegation of this authority to the arbitrator was clear"); Halliday v. Beneficial Fin. I, Inc., 2:12–CV–708, 2013 WL 693022 (S.D. Ohio Feb. 26, 2013) ("Because the Court concludes that the delegation provision is not unconscionable, the threshold issue of whether the remainder of the arbitration clause is unconscionable is a matter for arbitration * * * . As required by Rent-A-Center v. Jackson, the Court defers to arbitration the issues, raised by plaintiffs, of whether the arbitration rider itself is unconscionable and whether it should be given effect. Here, the Court enforces only the delegation clause."); Dean v. Draughons Jr. Coll., Inc., 917 F. Supp. 2d 751, 763 (M.D. Tenn. 2013) (enforcing delegation clause and sending to arbitration the issue whether the arbitration agreement was enforceable: "[T]o the extent the plaintiffs seek to challenge the enforceability of the Arbitration Clause (or any terms contained therein), they will need to address those objections to the arbitrator pursuant to the Delegation Clause"); Chung v. Nemer, 2012 WL 5289414 (N.D. Cal. Oct. 25, 2012) (enforcing the delegation clause and granting defendant's motion to compel arbitration).

[72]   Jack M. Graves & Yelena Davydan, Competence-Competence and Separability-American Style in International Arbitration and International Commercial Law: Synergy, Convergence and Evolution 165 (2011). See also David Horton, The Federal Arbitration Act and Testamentary Instruments, 90 N.C.L.Rev. 1027, 1058 n.181 (2012). ("[T]he Court conceptualized the delegation clause as an independent arbitration clause ('an agreement to arbitrate threshold issues concerning the arbitration agreement') within a broader contract to arbitrate (the Mutual Agreement to Arbitrate Claims).")

   For cases applying *Rent-A-Center*, see, e.g., Momot v. Mastro, 652 F.3d 982, 988 (9th Cir.2011) (finding that language in arbitration agreement providing that parties agree to arbitrate any dispute that " 'arises out of or relates to . . . the validity or application of any of the provisions of this Section 4' . . . constitutes 'an agreement to arbitrate threshold issues concerning the arbitration agreement' " under *Rent-A-Center*); Hawkins v. Region's, 944 F. Supp. 2d 528, 530 (N.D. Miss. 2013) ("While the holding in *Jackson* leaves a number of unanswered questions, it appears to place a heavy burden on plaintiffs to make challenges which are tailored specifically to arbitration *delegation* clauses within contracts, rather than to the contract as a whole or even to arbitration clauses within those contracts. * * * The court recognizes that the Supreme Court's decision in Jackson might be regarded by some as creating a legal

from hearing contract-defenses to the delegation clause itself, delegation clauses should not prevent courts from hearing arguments that the alleged contract containing the delegation clause was, in fact, not formed.[73]

(c) Conditions to Arbitration

The previous paragraphs explained that, in the absence of an enforceable *Rent-a-Center*-type delegation clause, courts may hear contract defenses "directed to the arbitration clause itself." In contrast, one might also use a phrase like "defenses to arbitration" to refer to arguments that arbitration should not occur because a contractual time limit to start arbitration has expired or contractual preconditions to start arbitration have not been satisfied. Such arguments, the Supreme Court held in *Howsam v. Dean Witter Reynolds, Inc.*, should be heard by the arbitrator even if they are directed to the arbitration clause itself.[74] *Howsam* said "procedural questions which grow out of the dispute and bear on its final disposition are presumptively not for the judge, but for an arbitrator, to decide."[75] As examples, the Court endorsed authorities stating that the "arbitrator should decide whether the first two steps of a grievance procedure were completed, where these steps are prerequisites to arbitration," and "whether prerequisites such as time limits, notice, laches, estoppel, and other conditions precedent to an obligation to arbitrate have been met, are for the arbitrators to decide."[76] Other courts have added to this list the place (venue) of arbitration.[77]

"black hole" which inevitably sucks in disputes and sends them to arbitration (at least in cases involving a delegation clause).")

[73]   Dixon v. Daymar Colleges Grp., LLC, No. 2012–SC–000687–DG, 2015 WL 1544450, at *5 (Ky. Apr. 2, 2015), reh'g denied (Sept. 23, 2015) ("Rent-A-Center has a limited application: when the 'validity of a written agreement to arbitrate' is in question, i.e., when a party challenges whether an arbitration agreement is legally binding. When a party challenges whether the arbitration agreement—and, by extension, the delegation provision—was in fact agreed to, Rent-A-Center's analytical approach does not apply.")

[74]   537 U.S. 79, 84–85 (2002).

[75]   Id.

[76]   Id.

[77]   LodgeWorks, L.P. v. C.F. Jordan Const., LLC, 506 F. App'x 747, 750 (10th Cir.2012); Fin. Servs. v. W. Va. Univ. Hosps., Inc., 660 F.3d 643, 655 (2d Cir.2011) ("venue is a procedural issue that [the] arbitrators should address in the first instance.").

2.   FORMATION
Table of Sections

Leaving aside the separability doctrine,[78] the state law of contract formation applies to arbitration agreements. The general requirements to form a contract are: (1) mutual manifestations of assent, and (2) consideration.[79] These contract-formation requirements apply to arbitration agreements.

§ 22   Mutual Manifestations of Assent

(a) Contract Law's Objective Approach

Formation of a contract requires a manifestation of assent by each party. Assent is typically manifested by signing a document or saying certain words, but can be accomplished in other ways as well. The process by which parties manifest assent is often called "offer and acceptance."[80]

The FAA presupposes and incorporates state law regarding assent to form a contract.[81] In other words, mutual manifestation of

---

[78]   See §§ 19–21.

[79]   E. Allan Farnsworth, Contracts ch.2–3 (4th ed.2004).

[80]   See generally Joseph M. Perillo, Calamari & Perillo on Contracts ch.2 (6th ed.2009).

[81]   See, e.g., First Options of Chicago, Inc. v. Kaplan, 514 U.S. 938, 944 (1995) ("[w]hen deciding whether the parties agreed to arbitrate a certain matter * * * courts generally * * * should apply ordinary state-law principles that govern the formation of contracts."); Doctor's Associates Inc. v. Casarotto, 517 U.S. 681, 685 (1996) ("state law, whether of legislative or judicial origin, is applicable if that law arose to govern issues concerning the validity, revocability, and enforceability of contracts generally."); Delmore v. Ricoh Americas Corp., 667 F.Supp.2d 1129, 1138–39 (N.D.Cal.2009) ("the FAA requires courts to look to relevant state law when deciding whether the parties agreed to arbitrate a particular matter. * * * California law requires courts to determine the existence of mutual assent to a contract based upon objective and outward manifestations of the parties.")

assent is required to form an arbitration agreement, just as it is required to form any contract.[82] Most state arbitration statutes also generally presuppose and incorporate the general contract law regarding assent.[83]

In contrast, some states' laws apply a higher standard of assent to arbitration agreements than to other contracts. Consider for example, the Montana statute at issue in the Supreme Court case, *Doctor's Associates, Inc. v. Casarotto*:[84] "Notice that a contract is subject to arbitration * * * shall be typed in underlined capital letters on the first page of the contract; and unless such notice is displayed thereon, the contract may not be subject to arbitration."[85] The Supreme Court held that the FAA preempts this Montana statute because the Montana statute "conditions the enforceability of arbitration agreements on compliance with a special notice requirement not applicable to contracts generally."[86] As the *Casarotto* opinion stated, the FAA "precludes States from singling out arbitration provisions for suspect status, requiring instead that such provisions be placed 'upon the same footing as other contracts.' "[87]

The Supreme Court's approach (in *Casarotto* and other cases) applies general contract law's standards of assent to arbitration agreements.[88] In particular, general contract law usually holds that parties manifest assent to standard forms they sign regardless of whether they read or understand the terms on the forms.[89] A party

---

[82]   See, e.g., General Impact Glass & Windows Corp. v. Rollac Shutter of Texas, Inc., 8 So.3d 1165, 1167 (Fla.Dist.Ct.App.2009) ("The documents exchanged between the parties during the course of their dealings are devoid of any expression of an intent to resolve future disputes in arbitration. The terms and conditions, which Rollac urges this Court to consider as a part of the contract, were never signed by General Impact, and were never expressly incorporated into or attached to any of the documents that formed the contract between the parties. The provision relating to alternative dispute resolution on Rollac's website and in the Rollac catalog was part of a separate collateral document. Because that separate document was not incorporated into the writings exchanged between the parties, General Impact is not bound by it.").

[83]   See Unif. Arbitration Act § 1 (1956), 7 U.L.A. 102 (2005); Unif. Arbitration Act (2000) § 6(a), 7 U.L.A. 22 (2005).

[84]   517 U.S. 681 (1996).

[85]   Mont.Code Ann. § 27–5–114(4) (1995). This language was deleted from the statute in 1997.

[86]   Doctor's Assoc., Inc. v. Casarotto, 517 U.S. 681, 687 (1996).

[87]   Id.

[88]   See, e.g., First Options of Chicago, Inc. v. Kaplan, 514 U.S. 938, 944 (1995)("[w]hen deciding whether the parties agreed to arbitrate a certain matter * * * courts generally * * * should apply ordinary state-law principles that govern the formation of contracts.")

[89]   See § 14 (discussing Restatement (Second) of Contracts § 211 (1981)). See, e.g., Schnabel v. Trilegiant Corp., 697 F.3d 110, 123 (2d Cir. 2012)("A person can assent to terms even if he or she does not actually read them, but the offer must nonetheless make clear to a reasonable consumer both that terms are being presented and that

signing a standard form is, however, relieved of a particular term on that form if the party who drafted the form "has reason to believe" that the non-drafting party would not have signed if he had known "that the writing contained [the] particular term."[90] In other words, the non-drafting party is relieved of a particular term if the drafting party should have known that that term would have been a deal-breaker had the non-drafting party noticed it. Under this test, to avoid an arbitration clause the non-drafting party must persuade the court that the drafting party should have known that if the non-drafting party had noticed the arbitration clause, the non-drafting party would have refused to sign the form. This objective test is unlikely to result in the non-enforcement of many arbitration clauses because few non-drafting parties can make a convincing case that they would not have assented to the form contract containing an arbitration clause had they known of the clause.

However, general contract law also includes the unconscionability defense (discussed below) that can turn on subjective assent and a fair number of arbitration clauses have been held unconscionable.[91]

(b) Common Assent Issues

(1) Assent Through an Agent

A few recurring issues generate much of the litigation on assent to arbitration. One is whether a party (the principal) who did not assent to an arbitration agreement is nevertheless bound by it because someone else (the agent) assented to it on behalf of the

---

they can be adopted through the conduct that the offeror alleges constituted assent."); Sydnor v. Conseco Financial Servicing Corp., 252 F.3d 302 (4th Cir.2001) ("[an] elementary principle of contract law is that a party signing a written contract has duty to inform himself of its contents before executing it, and in the absence of fraud or overreaching, he will not be allowed to impeach the effect of the instrument by showing that he was ignorant of its contents or failed to read it."); Delmore v. Ricoh Americas Corp., 667 F.Supp.2d 1129, 1138–39 (N.D.Cal.2009) ("Delmore's signature on the confidentiality agreement and initial on the arbitration clause is objective evidence of his assent to its terms. The unambiguous language of the agreement put Delmore on notice that, by initialing this paragraph and signing the agreement, he agreed to arbitrate any claims he had.") (citations omitted); Booker v. Robert Half Int'l., Inc., 315 F.Supp.2d 94 (D.D.C.2004) (employee's manifestation of assent to arbitration agreement enforceable under "objective law" of contracts, notwithstanding an employee's failure to read or understand it or employer's failure to explain it); Aguillard v. Auction Mgmt. Corp., 908 So.2d 1, 22 (La.2005) ("It is well settled that a party who signs a written instrument is presumed to know its contents and cannot avoid its obligations by contending that he did not read it, that he did not understand it, or that the other party failed to explain it to him.").

90   Restatement (Second) of Contracts § 211(3) (1981).

91   See § 25 (procedural unconscionability encompasses not only the employment of sharp bargaining practices and the use of fine print and convoluted language, but a lack of understanding and an inequality of bargaining power).

principal. Basic agency law allows one party to act through another,[92] for example, to form a contract.[93] In fact, for some parties the only way to form a contract is through an agent. For example, a corporation can form a contract only through the actions of its agents,[94] who often, but not always, are employees of the corporation.[95] Some cases involve the issue whether a corporation or other organization is bound by an arbitration agreement because of assent manifested on its behalf by its agent.[96]

Agency issues can arise in other contexts as well.[97] For example, does a lawyer have authority to bind his client to an arbitration agreement?[98] Some agency cases involve family members. Courts have determined whether a parent had authority to bind her child to

---

[92]   See Restatement (Third) of Agency 1.01 (2006).

Agency is the fiduciary relationship that arises when one person (a "principal") manifests assent to another person (an "agent") that the agent shall act on the principal's behalf and subject to the principal's control, and the agent manifests assent or otherwise consents so to act.

Id.

[93]   "Perhaps the really distinguishing characteristic of the agent is that he represents his principal contractually, which means that, given proper authorization, the agent makes contracts or conducts negotiations of a business nature on behalf of his principal and by which his principal is bound." William A. Gregory, The Law of Agency and Partnership 113 (3d ed.2001).

[94]   "That a corporation can act only through agents is too elementary a proposition to require the citation of authority." William Meade Fletcher, 2 Fletcher Cyclopedia of the Law of Private Corporations § 434 (2005). Corporations are not the only parties that must act through their agents to form contracts. That is also true of other business organizations and other non-human parties such as governments.

[95]   "The servant, qua servant, has no power to bind his master in contract. It is apparent, however, that one can be and often will be employed in a capacity where he is alternatively or simultaneously a servant and an agent. So an express company's truck driver may be a servant in driving the truck and an agent when receiving a package and signing a bill of lading binding his company to deliver it." William A. Gregory, The Law of Agency and Partnership 114 (3d ed.2001).

[96]   Merrill Lynch Inv. Managers v. Optibase, Ltd., 337 F.3d 125, 130 (2d Cir.2003)("mutual benefits derived from affiliation * * * insufficient to bind a non-signatory on agency principles to an arbitration agreement signed by an affiliate"); Thomson-CSF, S.A. v. Am. Arbitration Ass'n, 64 F.3d 773, 777 (2d Cir.1995) (agency principles do not bind parent corporation to arbitration agreement signed by subsidiary before parent bought subsidiary); Three Valleys Mun. Water Dist. v. E.F. Hutton & Co., Inc., 925 F.2d 1136 (9th Cir.1991) ("On remand, the district court must first determine whether the signatory had authority to bind the other plaintiffs to the agreements containing the arbitration clauses.").

[97]   Scone Investments, L.P. v. American Third Market Corp., 992 F.Supp. 378, 381 (S.D.N.Y.,1998) (broker signed arbitration agreement on customer's behalf); In re Labatt Food Service, L.P., 279 S.W.3d 640 (Tex.2009) (employee's arbitration agreement requires employee's wrongful death beneficiaries to arbitrate their wrongful death claims against employer even though they did not sign the agreement).

[98]   Compare Brooks v. BDO Seidman, LLP, 883 N.Y.S.2d 450 (N.Y.Sup.Ct.2009) (authority), with Louis Michel, Inc. v. Whitecourt Constr. Co., 189 N.E. 767 (N.Y.Ct.App.1934) (no authority).

an arbitration agreement,[99] and whether an adult child had authority to bind her elderly parent to an arbitration agreement.[100]

(2) Assent by Performance

In some cases, the document containing the arbitration clause was never signed by all of the parties and the issue is whether the non-signing parties manifested assent to the arbitration clause by performing the contract.[101] If the arbitration clause appears on a "stuffer" mailed with a monthly bank statement or credit card bill, for example, the question is whether the customer's continued use of the bank account or credit card constitutes assent to the arbitration clause.[102] A similar issue arises when an insurance policy contains an arbitration clause and the policyholder performs by paying for the insurance, rather than canceling it.[103] The performance-as-assent

---

[99]   Global Travel Mktg., Inc. v. Shea, 908 So.2d 392 (Fla.2005)(parent had authority to bind minor to arbitration clause); Hojnowski v. Vans Skate Park, 901 A.2d 381 (N.J.2006)(same).

[100]   Covenant Health Rehab. of Picayune, L.P. v. Brown, 949 So.2d 732 (Miss.2007) (adult daughter of the patient, acting as a healthcare surrogate, had the authority to contractually bind her mother in healthcare matters), overruled on other grounds, Covenant Health & Rehabilitation of Picayune, LP v. Estate of Moulds ex rel., 14 So.3d 695 (Miss.2009).

[101]   Compare, e.g., Herrington v. Union Planters Bank, N.A., 113 F.Supp.2d 1026, 1028–32 (S.D.Miss.2000) (finding assent by bank customer who received a letter and revised "Deposit Account Agreement and Disclosure", "plaintiffs could have simply declined to accept the arbitration provision by terminating their account before the effective date of the amendment"), with Ex parte Cain, 838 So.2d 1020 (Ala.2002) (manufacturer's unilateral inclusion of arbitration provision in homeowner's manual allegedly placed in mobile home was insufficient as a matter of law to show that purchaser assented to all the contents therein).

[102]   Compare, e.g., Ineman v. Kohl's Corp., 2015 WL 1399052, at *4 (W.D. Wis. Mar. 26, 2015) (under the laws of Delaware, Ohio or Wisconsin "a credit card agreement becomes enforceable once a cardholder uses the card"); Krutchik v. Chase Bank USA, N.A., 531 F.Supp.2d 1359, 1364–65 (S.D.Fla.2008) (assent); Hutcherson v. Sears Roebuck & Co., 793 N.E.2d 886 (Ill.Ct.App.2003) (assent); MBNA America Bank, N.A. v. Bibb, 2009 WL 1750220 (N.J.Super.App.Div.,2009)("the cardholder's decision to use the card provides the requisite assent to the terms of the offer extended by the card's issuance, such that a contract is formed."), with Badie v. Bank of Am., 79 Cal.Rptr.2d 273 (Cal.Ct.App.1998)(no assent); Union Planters Bank, Nat'l Ass'n v. Rogers, 912 So.2d 116 (Miss.2005)(no assent); Kortum-Managhan v. Herbergers NBGL, 204 P.3d 693, 699 (Mont.2009)(no assent).

[103]   Am. Bankers Ins. Co. of Florida v. Tellis, No. 1131244, 2015 WL 3935260, at *5 (Ala. June 26, 2015)("although the policyholders did not execute stand-alone arbitration agreements or necessarily even read or receive the insurance policies containing the arbitration provisions, they have nevertheless manifested their assent to those policies and, necessarily, the arbitration provisions in them, by accepting and acting upon the policies, inasmuch as they all affirmatively renewed their policies and paid their premiums, thus ratifying the policies").

issue also arises when goods,[104] services,[105] or payments[106] are delivered with documents that purport to be a contract containing terms including an arbitration clause. Finally, the issue of assent by performance occurs when an employer presents an employee with an employee handbook containing an arbitration clause and the question is whether the employee's continued performance of the job constitutes assent to the arbitration clause.[107]

(3)   Is the Document a Contract?

Another assent issue commonly arises with employee handbooks. A handbook signed by the employee may contain both an arbitration clause and language arguably stating that the handbook is not a legally-binding contract.[108]

---

[104]   Compare, e.g., Hill v. Gateway 2000, Inc., 105 F.3d 1147 (7th Cir.1997) (assent); Levy v. Gateway 2000, Inc., 1997 WL 823611 (N.Y.Sup.Ct.1997) (assent); Kahan Jewelry Corp. v. Venus Casting, Inc., 847 N.Y.S.2d 366, 372 (N.Y.Sup.Ct.2007) ("As UCC § 2–201(2) would make other terms of the Delivery Receipt binding, if not objected to within ten days of receipt, the FAA requires the arbitration clause in the Delivery Ticket also to be enforced if it was not objected to within such ten day period."), with Klocek v. Gateway, Inc., 104 F.Supp.2d 1332 (D.Kan.2000) (no assent), dismissed for lack of subject matter jurisdiction, 2000 WL 1372886 (D.Kan.Sept.6, 2000); Reedy v. Cincinnati Bengals, Inc., 758 N.E.2d 678 (Ohio Ct.App.2001) (no assent); DeFontes v. Dell, Inc., 984 A.2d 1061 (R.I.2009)(no assent).

[105]   Savetsky v. Pre-Paid Legal Servs., Inc., 2015 WL 1519066, at *3 (N.D. Cal. Apr. 3, 2015) (the contract language does not "make clear to a reasonable consumer both that terms are being presented and that they can be adopted through the conduct that the offeror alleges constitutes assent.")

[106]   Cook's Pest Control, Inc. v. Rebar, 852 So.2d 730, 737 (Ala.2002) (service-provider assented to terms—eliminating arbitration clause—customer enclosed with payment).

[107]   Compare, e.g., Hardin v. First Cash Fin. Services, Inc., 465 F.3d 470 (10th Cir.2006) (assent); Berkley v. Dillard's Inc., 450 F.3d 775, 777 (8th Cir.2006) (assent); May v. Higbee Co., 372 F.3d 757 (5th Cir.2004)(assent), Hightower v. GMRI, Inc., 272 F.3d 239 (4th Cir.2001)(assent); Rangel v. Hallmark Cards, Inc., 2010 WL 781722 (D.Kan.2010)(assent), with Campbell v. Gen. Dynamics Gov't Sys. Corp., 407 F.3d 546, 559 (1st Cir. 2005) ("General Dynamics has produced no evidence that any historical use of personnel handbooks in the workplace would have suggested that the reissued handbook carried contractual significance"); Lee v. Red Lobster Inns of Am., 92 Fed.Appx. 158 (6th Cir.2004) (no assent).

[108]   Compare, e.g., Patterson v. Tenet Healthcare, Inc., 113 F.3d 832, 834–35 (8th Cir.1997) (although handbook did not create a binding contract, "the arbitration clause is separate from the other provisions of the handbook and * * * constitutes an enforceable contract."), with Etienne v. Hang Tough, Inc., 2009 WL 1140040, at *3 (S.D.Fla.2009) (arbitration clause not binding); Ex Parte Beasley, 712 So.2d 338 (Ala.1998) (same); Hubner v. Cutthroat Commc'n, Inc., 80 P.3d 1256 (Mont.2003) (same). Somewhat analogous issues are raised by documents stating that the arbitration clause may not be enforceable. See, e.g., Winter v. Window Fashions Professionals, Inc., 83 Cal.Rptr.3d 89, 91 (Ct.App.2008) ("The franchise agreement requires binding arbitration. The arbitration will occur at Dallas County, Texas with the costs being borne by the losing party. This provision may not be enforceable under California law.")

(4)   Incorporation by Reference

Incorporation by reference is another assent issue that arises in some arbitration cases because the parties signed a document that does not contain an arbitration clause and the issue is whether that document effectively incorporates by reference a different document that does contain an arbitration clause. The Supreme Court's 2012 decision in *CompuCredit Corp. v. Greenwood*, enforced an arbitration agreement incorporated by reference in a consumer's application for a credit card.[109] As the dissent pointed out, "The contract signed by cardholders did not itself require arbitration. Rather, it incorporated by reference an 'enclosed insert' providing that all disputes would be resolved by arbitration."[110]

Other courts require more to incorporate an arbitration agreement. For example, the West Virginia Supreme Court held that U-Haul's rental contract did not incorporate an addendum's arbitration agreement because the rental agreement's mention of the addendum was "brief" and "general" and "U-Haul's practice was to provide customers a copy of the Addendum only after the Rental Agreement had been executed."[111]

(5)   Websites

New assent issues have arisen along with the growth of the Internet; an increasing number of cases address arbitration clauses found on websites. Courts generally enforce websites' "clickwrap" agreements, that is, agreements requiring a site's user to "consent to any terms or conditions by clicking on a dialog box on the screen in order to proceed with a transaction."[112] For example, the Tenth Circuit enforced AT & T's arbitration agreement because "U-verse customers are given notice of the U-verse terms and must

---

[109]   CompuCredit Corp. v. Greenwood, 132 S.Ct. 665, 668 (2012). See also Jureczki v. Banc One Texas, N.A., 252 F.Supp.2d 368 (S.D.Tex.2003)(Texas law required bank account depositors to arbitrate a dispute since they executed a signature card which contained a provision acknowledging receipt of and agreement to be bound by bank's account rules and regulations, which included arbitration provision, despite depositors' claim they never received terms and conditions); Robert J. Denley Co., Inc. v. Neal Smith Const.Co., Inc., 2007 WL 1153121, at *2–4 (Tenn.Ct.App.2007) (mutual assent when a signed contract referenced a separate arbitration document).

[110]   CompuCredit Corp. v. Greenwood, 132 S.Ct. 665, 677 (2012) (Sotomajor, J. dissenting).

[111]   State ex rel. U-Haul Co. of W. Virginia v. Zakaib, 752 S.E.2d 586, 598 (2013), cert. denied sub nom. W. Virginia ex rel. U-Haul Co. of W. Virginia v. Zakaib, 135 S.Ct. 59 (2014). See also Etienne v. Hang Tough, Inc., 2009 WL 1140040 (S.D.Fla.2009) (no assent to arbitrate because acknowledgment form did not incorporate by reference the arbitration provision of the Handbook).

[112]   Hancock v. Am. Tel. & Tel. Co., 701 F.3d 1248, 1255 (10th Cir. 2012).

affirmatively manifest assent to the terms by clicking 'I Acknowledge' and 'I Agree' buttons."[113]

However, the Second Circuit held that "a consumer's clicking on a download button does not communicate assent to contractual terms if the offer did not make clear to the consumer that clicking on the download button would signify assent to those terms."[114] Similarly, the Ninth Circuit held "that where a website makes its terms of use available via a conspicuous hyperlink on every page of the website but otherwise provides no notice to users nor prompts them to take any affirmative action to demonstrate assent, even close proximity of the hyperlink to relevant buttons users must click on—without more—is insufficient."[115]

(6) Exchange of Documents

Back in the old paper-based economy, merchants still engage in the "battle of the forms" in which one form (either the buyer's purchase order or the seller's acknowledgment) contains an arbitration clause, while the other does not. These cases, decided under Uniform Commercial Code § 2–207, sometimes find assent to arbitration and sometimes do not.[116]

§ 23   Consideration

Consideration is required to form a contract.[117] Perhaps the most obvious consideration for a promise to arbitrate is a reciprocal

---

[113]   Id. at 1257.

[114]   Specht v. Netscape Commc'ns Corporation, 306 F.3d 17, 29–30 (2d Cir.2002); id. at 20 ("a reasonably prudent Internet user in circumstances such as these would not have known or learned of the existence of the license terms before responding to defendants' invitation to download the free software, * * * defendants therefore did not provide reasonable notice of the license terms. In consequence, plaintiffs' bare act of downloading the software did not unambiguously manifest assent to the arbitration provision contained in the license terms.")

[115]   Nguyen v. Barnes & Noble Inc., 763 F.3d 1171, 1178–79 (9th Cir. 2014). See also Schnabel v. Trilegiant Corp., 697 F.3d 110, 127 (2d Cir. 2012) (no assent to arbitration because website "effectively obscured the details of the terms and conditions and the passive manner in which they could be accepted");

[116]   Aceros Prefabricados, S.A. v. TradeArbed, Inc., 282 F.3d 92, 100 (2d Cir.2002) ("arbitration agreements do not, as a matter of law, constitute material alterations to a contract; rather, the question of their inclusion in a contract under section 2–207(2)(b) is answered by examining, on a case-by-case basis, their materiality under a preponderance of the evidence standard as we would examine any other agreement."); ICC Chem. Corp. v. Vitol, Inc., 425 F. App'x 57, 59 (2d Cir. 2011) (arbitration agreement became part of contract under UCC 2–702(2)(b) because not a "material alteration")); PCS Nitrogen Fertilizer, L.P. v. Christy Refractories, L.L.C., 225 F.3d 974 (8th Cir.2000); Dorton v. Collins & Aikman Corp. 453 F.2d 1161 (6th Cir.1972); Dumont Telephone Co. v. Power & Telephone Supply Co., 962 F.Supp.2d 1064, 1079–80 (N.D.Iowa 2013)(arbitration clause became part of contract).

[117]   See generally Perillo, supra note 80, ch.4.

promise to arbitrate.[118] Most arbitration agreements obligate both parties to pursue their claims in arbitration. Each party's promise to do so serves as consideration for the other's promise to do so.[119]

In contrast, some arbitration agreements obligate one party to pursue its claims in arbitration, while allowing the other party to pursue its claims in litigation.[120] Such agreements are said by some courts to "lack mutuality," and some of these courts refuse to enforce the promise to arbitrate on the ground that there is no reciprocal promise to arbitrate.[121] However, other courts hold that the consideration for a promise to arbitrate can be anything that would constitute consideration for any sort of contract, that is, any promise or performance.[122]

---

[118] See Macneil, Speidel & Stipanowich, supra note 22, § 17.4.3 (Supp.1999). See also Lombardi v. DirecTV, Inc., 549 Fed.Appx. 617, 619 (9th Cir. 2013) (holding that reciprocal promises between satellite television service provider and customers to arbitrate all claims with the exception of theft of service provided sufficient consideration for arbitration agreement under Arizona and Illinois law); Lara v. Onsite Health, Inc., 896 F.Supp.2d 831, 838 (N.D. Cal. 2012) (finding employer and employee's reciprocal promises to arbitrate any and all employment disputes provided adequate consideration for arbitration agreement); Hancock v. American Tel. & Tel. Co., 804 F.Supp.2d 1196 (W.D. Okla. 2011) (holding that reciprocal promises to arbitrate between customer and Internet service provider were sufficient consideration for arbitration agreement under Florida law); In re Odyssey Healthcare, Inc., 310 S.W.3d 419, 424 (Tex. 2010) (finding "[m]utual promises to submit all employment disputes to arbitration is sufficient consideration for such agreements").

[119] In re 24R, Inc., 324 S.W.3d 564, 566 (Tex. 2010) ("Mutual agreement to arbitrate claims provides sufficient consideration to support an arbitration agreement.")

[120] Such agreements may be unconscionable. See § 25.

[121] See, e.g., Noohi v. Toll Bros., Inc., 708 F.3d 599, 607 (4th Cir. 2013) ("Maryland's highest court specifically rejected the notion that consideration for an underlying contract can serve as consideration for an arbitration provision within that contract."); Hull v. Norcom, Inc., 750 F.2d 1547, 1550 (11th Cir.1985) ("the consideration exchanged for one party's promise to arbitrate must be the other party's promise to arbitrate at least some specified class of claims"); Gonzalez v. W. Suburban Imps., Inc., 411 F.Supp.2d 970, 972–73 (N.D.Ill.2006); Vassilkovska v. Woodfield Nissan, Inc., 830 N.E.2d 619 (Ill.App.Ct.2005); The Money Place, LLC v. Barnes, 78 S.W.3d 714 (Ark.2002); Stirlen v. Supercuts, Inc., 60 Cal.Rptr.2d 138, 150 (Ct.App.1997).

Whether this result is required by the separability doctrine, see §§ 19–21, is the subject of debate. Compare, e.g., Stevens/Leinweber/Sullens, Inc. v. Holm Development and Management, Inc., 795 P.2d 1308, 1313 (Ariz.App.1990) ("Because under the separability doctrine the arbitration provision is an independent and separate agreement, Holm Development cannot 'borrow' consideration from the principal contract to support the arbitration provision. As a result, we conclude that the arbitration provision, which clearly lacks mutuality, is void for lack of consideration."), with Wilson Electrical Contractors, Inc. v. Minnotte Contracting Corp., 878 F.2d 167, 169 (6th Cir.1989).

[122] See, e.g., Fazio v. Lehman Bros., Inc., 340 F.3d 386, 397 (6th Cir.2003)("mutuality is not a requirement of a valid arbitration clause if the underlying contract is supported by consideration"); Harris v. Green Tree Fin. Corp., 183 F.3d 173, 179–80 (3d Cir.1999); Doctor's Associates, Inc. v. Distajo, 66 F.3d 438 (2d Cir.1995); Wilson Elec.Contractors. v. Minnotte Contractors Corp., 878 F.2d 167

The other set of cases raising doubts about consideration are those involving promises to arbitrate employment disputes where the employment is terminable at-will.[123] Suppose an employer asks an at-will employee (or job applicant) to sign a document providing that he or she will arbitrate any claims the employee may have against the employer. If the employee signs and later seeks to litigate such claims, the employee may argue that his or her promise to arbitrate was unsupported by consideration. The employer may point to its promise to pay salary and benefits as consideration.[124] But some courts hold that this promise is illusory (not a promise at all) because the employer could fire the employee at any time, even a moment after the arbitration agreement was signed.[125] If employment has actually continued for a period of time after the employee's promise to arbitrate, however, some courts hold this continued employment constitutes consideration for the employee's promise.[126] In addition, if the employer has promised to arbitrate its claims against the employee then that promise should serve as consideration for the at-

---

(6th Cir.1989); Molton, Allen & Williams, LLC v. Continental Cas. Ins. Co., 2010 WL 780353, *5–6 (N.D.Ill.2010) ("when a separate arbitration agreement is not at issue * * * arbitration provisions are enforceable where the larger contract at issue is supported by consideration."); Green Tree Agency, Inc. v. White, 719 So.2d 1179 (Ala.1998); Willis Flooring, Inc. v. Howard S. Lease Constr.Co. & Assoc., 656 P.2d 1184 (Alaska 1983). Macneil, Speidel & Stipanowich, supra note 22, § 17.4.2 (Supp.1999). See Restatement (Second) of Contracts § 71 (1981).

[123]   For a brief discussion of employment-at-will, see § 59(a).

[124]   Koveleskie v. SBC Capital Markets, Inc., 167 F.3d 361, 368 (7th Cir.1999) ("plaintiff's contract with SBC was supported by adequate consideration. First, [plaintiff] signed the [arbitration agreement] in exchange for SBC's promise to employ her.")

[125]   Compare Gibson v. Neighborhood Health Clinics, Inc., 121 F.3d 1126 (7th Cir.1997)("when an employer has made no specific promise, the mere fact of continued employment does not constitute consideration for the employee's promise"); Cheek v. United Healthcare of the Mid-Atlantic, Inc., 835 A.2d 656 (Md.2003)(arbitration agreement in which employer reserved the right to alter, amend, modify, or revoke the arbitration agreement at any time and without notice, was unenforceable for lack of consideration, even though employer had not exercised that option against employee; employer's promise to arbitrate was illusory, and the employment could not serve as consideration for the arbitration agreement); Sniezek v. Kansas City Chiefs Football Club, 402 S.W.3d 580, 585 (Mo. Ct. App. 2013) (continued employment not consideration for at-will employee's promise to arbitrate her claims); Thompson v. Bar-S Foods Co., 174 P.3d 567, 577 (Okla.2007)(no consideration because document signed by employee allowed employer to modify arbitration clause at any time without notice), with Hadnot v. Bay, Ltd., 344 F.3d 474 (5th Cir.2003)(offer of at-will employment by employer was consideration for agreement to arbitrate any disputes arising out of employment); Adkins v. Labor Ready, Inc., 303 F.3d 496 (4th Cir.2002) (arbitration agreement contained in temporary employment agency's application was supported by consideration, consisting of mutual agreement to be bound by the arbitration process notwithstanding at-will employee status).

[126]   Pomposi v. GameStop, Inc., 2010 WL 147196, at *6 (D.Conn.2010)("where an individual's employment is at will, continued employment is sufficient consideration to render an arbitration agreement binding."); Rupert v. Macy's, Inc., 2010 WL 2232305, at *8 (N.D.Ohio 2010); Raasch v. NCR Corp., 254 F.Supp.2d 847, 864 (S.D.Ohio 2003).

will employee's promise to arbitrate.[127] And even if the employer has not promised to arbitrate its claims, some courts have held that the employer's promise to abide by the arbitrator's decisions on the employee's claims serves as consideration for the at-will employee's promise to arbitrate.[128]

3.   CONTRACT LAW DEFENSES TO ENFORCEMENT
Table of Sections

§ 24   Defenses Subject to the Separability Doctrine

FAA § 2 says that arbitration agreements "shall be valid, irrevocable, and enforceable, save upon such grounds as exist at law or in equity for the revocation of any contract."[129] Accordingly, the defenses to enforcement of arbitration agreements are the same as the defenses to other contracts. They include misrepresentation, duress, undue influence, mistake, impracticability, frustration of purpose, the statute of limitations, the statute of frauds, and illegality. However, these defenses are subject to the separability doctrine.[130] The separability doctrine holds that arbitrators, not courts, hear challenges to the enforceability of arbitration agreements unless those challenges are "directed to the arbitration

---

[127]   In re 24R, Inc., 324 S.W.3d 564, 566–67 (Tex. 2010) ("Mutual agreement to arbitrate claims provides sufficient consideration to support an arbitration agreement. At-will employment does not preclude employers and employees from forming subsequent contracts, so long as neither party relies on continued employment as consideration for the contract.")

[128]   Circuit City Stores, Inc. v. Najd, 294 F.3d 1104, 1108 (9th Cir.2002)(employer's promise to be bound by the arbitration process served as adequate consideration for agreement requiring binding arbitration of employees' claims, though employer was not required to submit any of its claims against employees to arbitration); Michalski v. Circuit City Stores, Inc., 177 F.3d 634, 637 (7th Cir.1999); Johnson v. Circuit City Stores, 148 F.3d 373, 378 (4th Cir.1998); Slaughter v. Stewart Enterprises, Inc., 2007 WL 2255221, at *11 (N.D.Cal.2007); JTH Tax, Inc. v. Lee, 2007 WL 1795751, *5 (E.D.Va.2007) (employer's agreement to be bound to arbitrator's decision was adequate consideration).

[129]   9 U.S.C. § 2.

[130]   See §§ 19–21.

clause itself" rather than to the whole contract containing that clause.[131] Under the separability doctrine, arbitrators rather than courts will address the aforementioned defenses in most cases because those defenses are rarely "directed to the arbitration clause itself."[132] A party alleging that its arbitration agreement is unenforceable due to one of the grounds listed above will likely be sent to arbitration to make that argument. As arbitrators' decisions are rarely published,[133] few reported decisions apply these contract-law defenses to arbitration agreements.

The contract-law defense that is most often directed to the arbitration clause itself and thus most likely to be heard by a court is unconscionability.[134]

§ 25   Unconscionability

(a) Generally

Unconscionability is often thought of as coming in two forms: procedural and substantive. Procedural unconscionability relates to the process of contract formation. It encompasses "not only the employment of sharp bargaining practices and the use of fine print and convoluted language, but a lack of understanding and an inequality of bargaining power."[135] In contrast, substantive unconscionability refers simply to terms that are "unreasonably favorable" to one side.[136] "Most cases of unconscionability involve a combination of procedural and substantive unconscionability, and it is generally agreed that if more of one is present, then less of the other is required to defeat enforcement."[137]

The separability doctrine holds that arbitrators rather than courts hear defenses to the enforceability of arbitration agreements unless those defenses are "directed to the arbitration clause itself" rather than to the whole contract containing that clause.[138] Unconscionability is often a defense directed to the arbitration clause itself.[139] Therefore, unconscionability arguments are often heard by

---

[131]   See Prima Paint Corp. v. Flood & Conklin Mfg. Co., 388 U.S. 395, 402 (1967).

[132]   See § 21. See also Macneil, Speidel & Stipanowich, supra note 22, § 19.2.1.

[133]   See § 37(f).

[134]   See, e.g., Banc One Acceptance Corp. v. Hill, 367 F.3d 426 (5th Cir.2004).

[135]   Farnsworth, supra note 79, § 4.28, at 301.

[136]   Id.

[137]   Id. at 302.

[138]   See Prima Paint Corp. v. Flood & Conklin Mfg. Co., 388 U.S. 395, 402 (1967). See §§ 19–.21.

[139]   Allegations of procedural unconscionability require the court to consider, in the course of analyzing the validity of the arbitration provision, the circumstances surrounding the making of the entire agreement. So such allegations, if not combined with allegations that the arbitration clause is substantively unconscionable, may be

courts, as opposed to arbitrators.[140] This generates many reported decisions from which one can get an impression of the sorts of arbitration clauses that are, and are not, likely to be held unconscionable.

The Supreme Court seems to take a narrow view of the unconscionability doctrine.[141] Consider, for example, *Gilmer v. Interstate/Johnson Lane Corp.*,[142] which enforced a securities industry employee's agreement to arbitrate any dispute arising out of his employment.[143] The entire securities industry, at the time, required all employees in certain job categories to agree to arbitration as a condition of employment.[144] Justice Stevens' dissent in *Gilmer* raised "concern about the inequality of bargaining power between an entire industry on the one hand, and an individual * * * employee on the other."[145] The Supreme Court's majority responded that

> [m]ere inequality of bargaining power * * * is not a sufficient reason to hold that arbitration agreements are never enforceable in the employment context * * *. Of course, courts should remain attuned to well-supported claims that the agreement to arbitrate resulted from the sort of fraud or overwhelming economic power that would provide grounds for the revocation of any contract. There is no indication in this case, however, that Gilmer, an

---

subject to the separability doctrine. Jenkins v. First American Cash Advance of Georgia, LLC, 400 F.3d 868, 877 (11th Cir.2005) ("the FAA does not permit a federal court to consider claims alleging the contract as a whole was adhesive.") See also Nagrampa v. MailCoups, Inc., 469 F.3d 1257, 1264 (9th Cir.2006) (en banc) (court addresses procedural unconscionability issue because the California law "requires the court to consider, in the course of analyzing the validity of the arbitration provision, the circumstances surrounding the making of the entire agreement.")

[140] However, even challenges directed to the arbitration clause itself are heard by arbitrators if the parties have agreed to have them heard by arbitrators. See § 21 (discussing Rent-A-Center, West, Inc. v. Jackson, 561 U.S. 63 (2010)). For discussions of courts sending unconscionability decisions, especially procedural unconscionability decisions, to arbitrators, see Karen Halverson Cross, Letting the Arbitrator Decide Unconscionability Challenges, 26 Ohio St.J. on Disp.Resol. 1, 44–49 (2011); Aaron-Andrew P. Bruhl, The Unconscionability Game: Strategic Judging and the Evolution of Federal Arbitration Law, 83 N.Y.U.L.Rev. 1420 (2008).

[141] G. Richard Shell, Contracts in the Modern Supreme Court, 81 Cal.L.Rev. 431, 492 (1993). None of the Court's decisions since 1993 alter this conclusion. See, e.g., AT & T Mobility LLC v. Concepcion, 563 U.S. 333, 343 (2011); Rent-A-Center, West, Inc. v. Jackson, 561 U.S. 63 (2010).

[142] 500 U.S. 20 (1991).

[143] While *Gilmer* did not use the word "unconscionability", it discussed related concepts, like "inequality of bargaining power" and "overwhelming economic power." Id. at 33. Regarding the interplay of state and federal law with respect to unconscionability, see § 25(b).

[144] See Stephen J. Ware, Employment Arbitration and Voluntary Consent, 25 Hofstra L.Rev. 83, 114–15 & nn.151–52 (1996).

[145] Gilmer, 500 U.S. at 43 (Stevens, J., dissenting).

experienced businessman, was coerced or defrauded into agreeing to the arbitration clause in his registration application. As with the claimed procedural inadequacies discussed above, this claim of unequal bargaining power is best left for resolution in specific cases.[146]

Gilmer, then, indicates that parties raising unconscionability challenges to arbitration clauses face an uphill battle. Nevertheless, unconscionability challenges to arbitration clauses sometimes succeed.

These successes usually occur in the context of take-it-or-leave-it form contracts and are especially likely to occur if the arbitration clause lacks clarity or conspicuousness.[147] Courts have held unconscionable arbitration clauses that:

- allow the party drafting the clause to pursue its claims in litigation, while requiring the non-drafting party to pursue its claims in arbitration,[148]

---

[146]   Gilmer, 500 U.S. at 33.

[147]   Many courts treat adhesion contracts, or at least those between parties of "unequal bargaining power," as presumptively procedurally unconscionable. See, e.g., Quilloin v. Tenet HealthSystem Phila., Inc., 673 F.3d 221, 235 (3d Cir. 2012) ("[U]nder Pennsylvania law, a contract is generally considered to be procedurally unconscionable if it is a contract of adhesion"); Kilgore v. KeyBank, N.A., 718 F.3d 1052, 1063 (9th Cir. 2013) (quoting Ting v. AT & T, 319 F.3d 1126, 1148 (9th Cir. 2003)) (noting under California law, contracts of adhesion are procedurally unconscionable); Quality Bank v. Cavett, 788 N.W.2d 629, 632 (N.D. 2010) ("Courts presume adhesion contracts are procedurally unconscionable.") Thus with procedural unconscionability so easily shown, the arguments about adhesive arbitration agreements tend to focus on substantive unconscionability.

However, giving the adhering party 30 days to opt out of the arbitration clause while leaving the rest of the contract in force has been held to remove the element of procedural unconscionability. Circuit City Stores, Inc. v. Ahmed, 283 F.3d 1198, 1199 (9th Cir.2002); Owings v. T-Mobile USA, Inc., 978 F. Supp. 2d 1215, 1224 (M.D. Fla. 2013)("that the consumer may opt-out of arbitration within thirty days of signing the agreement obviates any argument of procedural unconscionability."); Freedman v. Comcast Corp., 988 A.2d 68, 86 (Md.App.2010) (arbitration provision was not procedurally unconscionable as a contract of adhesion because of a clear and conspicuous opt-out provision). See also Johnson v. Career Sys. Dev., 2010 WL 292667, at *4 (W.D.Ky.2010) (arbitration clause not procedurally unconscionable "if there are other alternative options available to the party having less bargaining power," such as finding a new job).

[148]   Compare, e.g., Pokorny v. Quixtar, Inc., 601 F.3d 987, 1001 (9th Cir.2010) ("Requiring one party to arbitrate its claims but not the other is a paradigmatic form of substantive unconscionability under California law."); Iberia Credit Bureau, Inc. v. Cingular Wireless LLC, 379 F.3d 159, 168–69 (5th Cir.2004) (unconscionable); Armendariz v. Foundation Health Psychcare Services, Inc., 99 Cal.Rptr.2d 745 (Cal.2000) (unconscionable); Iwen v. U.S. West Direct, 977 P.2d 989 (Mont.1999) (unconscionable); Arnold v. United Companies Lending Corp., 511 S.E.2d 854 (W.Va.1998) (unconscionable); Taylor v. Butler, 142 S.W.3d 277 (Tenn.2004) (unconscionable); Caplin Enterprises, Inc. v. Arrington, 2011–CT–01332–SCT, 2014 WL 1875364 (Miss. May 8, 2014) (unconscionable), with Oblix, Inc. v. Winiecki, 374 F.3d 488, 491 (7th Cir.2004) (not unconscionable); Bess v. Check Express, 294 F.3d

- require the non-drafting party to pay a significant portion of fees charged by the arbitrator or arbitration organization,[149]

- require the non-drafting party to pay its own attorney's fees even when bringing a claim under which successful plaintiffs are entitled to have such fees paid by the defendant,[150]

- prohibit class actions,[151]

- severely limit discovery,[152]

- severely limit remedies, such as punitive damages,[153]

1298 (11th Cir.2002) ("while the agreement requires only Colburn to arbitrate his disputes, without mentioning PayDay's rights or obligations in this regard, this lack of mutuality does not, in and of itself, render the arbitration agreement unconscionable); Harris v. Green Tree Fin. Corp., 183 F.3d 173 (3d Cir.1999); Green Tree Fin. Corp. of Alabama v. Wampler, 749 So.2d 409, 416 (Ala.1999) (fact that borrower must arbitrate while lender may litigate, standing alone, does not warrant a finding of unconscionability). See also Penn v. Ryan's Family Steak Houses, Inc., 269 F.3d 753 (7th Cir.2001) (holding unenforceable contracts among employer, employee and arbitration provider that resulted in employee, but not employer, promising to arbitrate).

See also § 23.

149 Compare, e.g., Ting v. AT&T, 319 F.3d 1126, 1151 (9th Cir.2003) (fees excessive and unconscionable); Ingle v. Circuit City Stores, Inc. 328 F.3d 1165 (9th Cir.2003) (same); Armendariz v. Foundation Health Psychcare Services, Inc., 99 Cal.Rptr.2d 745 (Cal.2000) (same); Brower v. Gateway 2000 Inc., 676 N.Y.S.2d 569, 574 (App.Div.1998) (same); D.R. Horton, Inc. v. Green, 96 P.3d 1159 (Nev.2004) (same), with Carbajal v. H & R Block Tax Services, Inc., 372 F.3d 903, 906 (7th Cir. 2004) (arbitration clause in a loan agreement is not rendered unconscionable by its provision requiring parties to bear their own costs of arbitration); Shadeh v. Circuit City Stores, Inc., 334 F.Supp.2d 938 (W.D.Ky.2004) (Under Kentucky law, agreement to arbitrate employment disputes was not rendered unenforceable by cost-splitting provision, under which employee's exposure for costs was limited to greater of $500 or three percent of annual income); Norwest Fin. Mississippi, Inc. v. McDonald, 905 So.2d 1187, 1196 (Miss.2005); Leeman v. Cook's Pest Control, Inc., 2004 WL 2757414 (Ala.2004); Lovey v. Regence BlueShield of Idaho, 72 P.3d 877 (Idaho 2003); State ex rel. Wells v. Matish, 600 S.E.2d 583 (W.Va.2004).

See also § 36(c).

150 Adler v. Fred Lind Manor, 103 P.3d 773 (Wash.2004); Sec. Serv. Fed. Credit Union v. Sanders, 264 S.W.3d 292, 298–301 (Tex.Ct.App. 2008) (arbitration agreements' attorney-fee provisions unenforceable because in conflict with Texas Deceptive Trade Practices-Consumer Protection Act, but severable from arbitration agreement, and arbitration agreement otherwise enforceable).

151 See § 34.

152 Compare, e.g., Armendariz v. Foundation Health Psychcare Services, Inc., 99 Cal.Rptr.2d 745 (Cal.2000), with Roman v. Superior Court, 92 Cal.Rptr.3d 153, 164–65 (Cal.Ct.App.2009) (clause allowing arbitrator to deny depositions not unconscionable).

See also § 36(d).

153 Booker v. Robert Half Int'l, 413 F.3d 77 (D.C.Cir.2005); Ingle v. Circuit City Stores, Inc. 328 F.3d 1165 (9th Cir.2003); Armendariz v. Foundation Health Psychcare Services, Inc., 99 Cal.Rptr.2d 745 (Cal.2000); Young Seok Suh v. Superior Court, 105

- shorten limitations periods,[154]

- require the arbitration to be confidential,[155]

- require the arbitrators to be members of occupations similar to that of the drafting party,[156]

- give the drafting party greater control than the non-drafting party in the selection of the arbitrator,[157]

- give the drafting party the power to unilaterally modify the arbitration clause,[158] and

---

Cal.Rptr.3d 585, 595–96 (Ct.App.2010) (American Health Lawyers Association arbitration rules); State ex rel. Dunlap v. Berger, 567 S.E.2d 265 (W.Va.2002).

See also § 38.

[154] Compare Ingle v. Circuit City Stores, Inc. 328 F.3d 1165 (9th Cir.2003); Parilla v. IAP Worldwide Services, VI, Inc., 368 F.3d 269 (3d Cir.2004) (agreement unconscionable because it required that "Employee must present Employee's claim in written form to the Company within thirty (30) calendar days of the event which forms the basis of the claim, unless a different time for presentation of the claim is provided for by the [AAA Rules]."); Adler v. Fred Lind Manor, 103 P.3d 773 (Wash.2004), with In re Cotton Yarn Antitrust Litigation, 505 F.3d 274, 288 (4th Cir.2007) ("statutory limitations periods can be contractually shortened, so long as the contractual period is not unreasonably short").

[155] Pokorny v. Quixtar, Inc., 601 F.3d 987, 1001 (9th Cir.2010) ("Another indicator of substantive unconscionability is the confidentiality requirement"); Ting v. AT&T, 319 F.3d 1126, 1151–52 (9th Cir. 2003); Plaskett v. Bechtel Int'l, 243 F.Supp.2d 334, 340–45 (D.V.I.2003); Eagle v. Fred Martin Motor Co., 809 N.E.2d 1161, 1180–83 (Ohio Ct.App.2004); McKee v. AT&T Corp., 191 P.3d 845, 858 (Wash.2008) ("A confidentiality clause in a contract of adhesion is a one-sided provision designed to disadvantage claimants and may even help conceal consumer fraud. Confidentiality unreasonably favors repeat players such as AT & T."). On the other hand, see Parilla v. IAP Worldwide Services, VI, Inc., 368 F.3d 269 (3d Cir.2004) (not unconscionable); Bettencourt v. Brookdale Senior Living Communities, Inc., 2010 WL 274331, at *7–8 (D.Or.2010); Hutcherson v. Sears Roebuck & Co., 793 N.E.2d 886, 897 (Ill.App.Ct.2003); Vasquez-Lopez v. Beneficial Or., Inc., 575, 152 P.3d 940, 953 (Or.Ct.App.2007) ("nonconfidential information, while not officially reported, is widely available to plaintiffs' lawyers through informal networks and organizations. Thus, any advantage conferred on repeat players and their counsel is marginal and, we conclude, it is roughly offset by the advantage that privacy about their financial affairs confers on plaintiffs.")

[156] See § 36(a)(3).

[157] See id.

[158] Compare, e.g., Al-Safin v. Circuit City Stores, Inc., 394 F.3d 1254, 1259 (9th Cir.2005); Circuit City Stores, Inc. v. Mantor, 335 F.3d 1101,1107 (9th Cir.2003); Ingle v. Circuit City Stores, Inc. 328 F.3d 1165, 1179 (9th Cir.2003), with Iberia Credit Bureau, Inc. v. Cingular Wireless LLC, 379 F.3d 159 (5th Cir.2004) (change-in-terms provision did not render the clause unconscionable);Pomposi v. Gamestop, Inc., 2010 WL 147196, at *12–13 (D.Conn.2010); Martin v. Citibank, Inc., 567 F.Supp.2d 36, 45 (D.D.C.2008) (requirement that employer provides thirty days notice of prospective modifications to arbitration agreement "affords employees sufficient protection against inequitable assertions of power"); SouthTrust Corp. v. James, 880 So.2d 1117 (Ala.2003).

- place the location of arbitration far from the non-drafting party.[159]

(b) The FAA's Constraint on the Scope of the Unconscionability Doctrine

The FAA constrains the extent to which courts may hold arbitration clauses unconscionable. To see this, consider *Doctor's Associates, Inc. v. Casarotto*,[160] in which the United States Supreme Court enforced an arbitration clause in a take-it-or-leave-it franchise agreement. The Court did this despite the following protest by Montana Supreme Court Justice Trieweiler, who authored that court's opinion in *Casarotto*:

> In Montana, we are reasonably civilized and have a sophisticated system of justice * * * .
>
> * * *
>
> What I would like the people in the federal judiciary, especially at the appellate level, to understand is that due to their misinterpretation of congressional intent when it enacted the Federal Arbitration Act, and due to their naive assumption that arbitration provisions and choice of law provisions are knowingly bargained for, [Montana's] procedural safeguards and substantive laws are easily avoided by any party with enough leverage to stick a choice of law and an arbitration provision in its pre-printed contract and require the party with inferior bargaining power to sign it.
>
> The procedures we have established, and the laws we have enacted, are either inapplicable or unenforceable in the process we refer to as arbitration.
>
> * * *
>
> To me, the idea of a contract or agreement suggests mutuality. There is no mutuality in a franchise agreement, a securities brokerage agreement, or in any other of the agreements which typically impose arbitration as the means for resolving disputes. National franchisors, like the defendant in this case, and brokerage firms, who have been the defendants in many other arbitration cases, present

---

[159] Domingo v. Ameriquest Mortg. Co., 70 Fed.Appx. 919 (9th Cir.2003); Bolter v. Superior Court, 104 Cal.Rptr.2d 888, 894 (Ct.App.2001); Patterson v. ITT Consumer Fin. Corp., 18 Cal.Rptr. 2d 563 (Ct.App.1993); Swain v. Auto Services, Inc., 128 S.W.3d 103, 108 (Mo.Ct.App.2003).

[160] 517 U.S. 681 (1996).

form contracts to franchisees and consumers in which choice of law provisions and arbitration provisions are not negotiable, and the consequences of which are not explained. The provision is either accepted, or the business or investment opportunity is denied. Yet these provisions * * * do, in effect, subvert our system of justice as we have come to know it. If any foreign government tried to do the same, we would surely consider it a serious act of aggression.

Furthermore, if the Federal Arbitration Act is to be interpreted as broadly as some of the decisions from our federal courts would suggest, then it presents a serious issue regarding separation of powers. What these interpretations do, in effect, is permit a few major corporations to draft contracts regarding their relationship with others that immunizes them from accountability under the laws of the states where they do business, and by the courts in those states. With a legislative act, the Congress, according to some federal decisions, has written state and federal courts out of business as far as these corporations are concerned. They are not subject to California's labor laws or franchise laws, they are not subject to our contract laws or tort laws. They are, in effect, above the law.

These insidious erosions of state authority and the judicial process threaten to undermine the rule of law as we know it.[161]

Suppose that these views are widespread among Montana judges and suppose that Montana courts hold unconscionable every take-it-or-leave-it arbitration agreement before them. By so ruling, Montana courts could effectively nullify the FAA with respect to a huge class of contracts. Countering that threat, the Supreme Court said that FAA § 2 "precludes States from singling out arbitration provisions for suspect status, requiring instead that such provisions be placed 'upon the same footing as other contracts.' "[162] As Montana courts enforce many take-it-or-leave-it contracts without arbitration clauses,[163] Montana courts would be singling out arbitration

---

[161]   Casarotto v. Lombardi, 886 P.2d 931, 939–40 (Mont.1994).

[162]   Doctor's Associates, 517 U.S. at 682.

[163]   See, e.g., Lee v. USAA Cas. Ins. Co., 22 P.3d 631, 636–37 (Mont.2001); Brabeck v. Employers Mut.Cas.Co., 16 P.3d 355, 357 (Mont.2000); Counterpoint, Inc. v. Essex Insurance Co., 967 P.2d 393 (Mont.1998); Stutzman v. Safeco Ins.Co., 945 P.2d 32 (Mont.1997).

provisions for suspect status if they refused to enforce any take-it-or-leave-it contracts with arbitration clauses.

Notice, however, that Montana courts would be doing this through contract law's unconscionability doctrine, ordinarily an area of state, rather than federal, law. Ordinarily, the United States Supreme Court defers to state courts on matters of state law.[164] For example, the United States Supreme Court accepts that Montana contract law is whatever the Montana Supreme Court says it is. But the United States Supreme Court has shown that it will police state courts' expansive use of the unconscionability doctrine against arbitration agreements to prevent that doctrine from effectively nullifying the FAA with respect to take-it-or-leave-it contracts. In the 1980's and 1990's, the Court warned that state courts may not "rely on the uniqueness of an agreement to arbitrate as a basis for a state-law holding that enforcement would be unconscionable, for this would enable the court to effect what * * * the state legislature cannot."[165] Then in the 2011 case of *AT & T Mobility LLC v. Concepcion*, the Court followed through on this warning and held that a California case law rule on the unconscionability of arbitration agreements prohibiting class actions was preempted by the FAA.[166]

The *AT & T* opinion said "The overarching purpose of the FAA, evident in the text of §§ 2, 3, and 4, is to ensure the enforcement of arbitration agreements according to their terms so as to facilitate streamlined proceedings."[167] The Court's reasoning built on this premise that an important purpose of the FAA was to enforce agreements in which parties choose the more streamlined process (arbitration) over the more elaborate process (litigation). The Court suggested that the FAA would preempt (hypothetical) state law deeming unconscionable arbitration agreements lacking "judicially monitored discovery,"[168] "adherence to the Federal Rules of Evidence,"[169] or "arbitration-by-jury"[170] because requiring arbitration to include these aspects of litigation would effectively

---

[164] Erwin Chemerinsky, Federal Jurisdiction § 10.3.2 (4th ed.2003).

[165] Doctor's Associates, 517 U.S. at 687–88 n.3; Perry v. Thomas, 482 U.S. 483, 493 n.9 (1987). Has the Montana Supreme Court successfully evaded these rulings? See § 14 nn.81–82 (discussing Kloss v. Edward D. Jones & Co., 54 P.3d 1 (Mont.2002)). See also Scott J. Burnham, The War Against Arbitration in Montana, 66 Mont. L. Rev. 139, 200 (2005) ("the Montana Supreme Court [in *Kloss*] has now accomplished what the legislature was unable to do * * * It is possible that the higher court will right this wrong, or even that a reconstituted Montana Supreme Court will see things differently. Until that time, however, arbitration is dead in Montana.")

[166] 563 U.S. 333 (2011). The AT & T case is discussed in greater detail in § 34.

[167] 563 U.S. 333 (2011).

[168] Id. at 1748.

[169] Id.

[170] Id. at 1751, n.7.

convert the more streamlined process into the more elaborate process, so it would no longer be "arbitration," as that process was envisioned by those who enacted the FAA.[171] Similarly, the Court held that state law "[r]equiring the availability of classwide arbitration interferes with fundamental attributes of arbitration and thus creates a scheme inconsistent with the FAA."[172] In 2015, the Court supplemented *AT & T* with *DirecTV v. Imburgia*, which policed state court interpretation of arbitration agreements where the state court at least arguably engaged in an unusual interpretation to try to preserve the very state law held preempted by *AT & T*.[173]

(c) Arbitration Organizations' Policing Against Unconscionability

Courts are not the only entities policing the fairness of arbitration. Some of the leading arbitration organizations have enacted policies on the subject.[174] For example, the American Arbitration Association has a "Due Process Protocol" for employment disputes.[175] The AAA has refused to administer arbitration under agreements that do not comply with the protocol.[176] After one such refusal, a court allowed the employee to litigate claims, rejecting the employer's argument that the court should instead appoint an arbitrator outside the AAA.[177]

§ 26   Waiver of the Right to Arbitrate

Contract rights can be waived.[178] Accordingly, one defense to enforcement of an arbitration agreement is that the party seeking to

---

[171]   In fact, arbitration is generally less elaborate than litigation; arbitration agreements commonly provide for less discovery and motion practice than is typical of litigation and commonly provide for fewer rules of evidence than are typical of litigation. But the parties are free to draft their agreement almost any way they like. See §§ 35–37. The *AT & T* Court said that "[p]arties could agree to arbitrate pursuant to the Federal Rules of Civil Procedure, or pursuant to a discovery process rivaling that in litigation. Arbitration is a matter of contract, and the FAA requires courts to honor parties' expectations. * * * But what the parties in the aforementioned examples would have agreed to is not arbitration as envisioned by the FAA, lacks its benefits, and therefore may not be required by state law." 563 U.S. 333 (2011).

[172]   Id. at 1748.

[173]   136 S.Ct. 463 (2015).

[174]   See, e.g., Amer. Arb. Ass'n, Consumer Due Process Protocol, https://adr.org/aaa/ShowPDF?doc=ADRSTG_005014 (last visited Mar.11, 2017); JAMS Policy on Consumer Arbitrations Pursuant to Pre-Dispute Clauses Minimum Standards of Procedural Fairness (2009), https://www.jamsadr.com/consumer-minimum-standards/ (last visited Mar.11, 2017).

[175]   Amer. Arb. Ass'n, Employment Due Process Protocol, https://www.adr.org/sites/default/files/document_repository/Employment%20Due%20Process%20Protocol_0.pdf (last visited Apr.16, 2017).

[176]   Martinez v. Master Protection Corp., 12 Cal.Rptr.3d 663 (Ct.App.2004).

[177]   Id. at 674–75.

[178]   Farnsworth, supra note 79, § 8.19.

enforce the agreement has waived its right to do so. For example, suppose that Buyer and Seller have an arbitration clause in their contract for the sale of goods. If Seller sues Buyer then Seller is in breach of its promise to arbitrate and Buyer has the right to compel arbitration of Seller's claim.[179] Suppose, however, that Buyer does not promptly ask the court to compel arbitration. Instead, Buyer participates in litigation before asking the court to compel arbitration. The court may refuse to compel arbitration on the ground that Buyer waived its right to compel arbitration by participating in litigation. Most courts hold that the court (rather than arbitrator) should decide whether a party has waived its right to compel arbitration,[180] but a few cases are to the contrary.[181]

When courts decide whether waiver of the right to compel arbitration has occurred, they often look to "whether the opposing party would be prejudiced by a subsequent order requiring it to submit to arbitration."[182] This is a fact-specific inquiry that generally

---

[179]   See § 4(c).

[180]   JPD, Inc. v. Chronimed Holdings, Inc., 539 F.3d 388, 394 (6th Cir.2008) ("Howsam [v. Dean Witter Reynolds, Inc., 537 U.S. 79 (2002)] did not disturb the traditional rule that the courts presumptively resolve waiver-through-inconsistent-conduct claims."); Ehleiter v. Grapetree Shores, Inc., 482 F.3d 207, 217–18 (3d Cir.2007) ("[T]he Supreme Court did not intend its pronouncements * * * to upset the 'traditional rule' that courts, not arbitrators, should decide the question of whether a party has waived its right to arbitrate by actively litigating the case in court."); Marie v. Allied Home Mortg. Corp., 402 F.3d 1 (1st Cir.2005) (the issue of waiver by conduct is for the court, and not for the arbitrator, at least in situations where the alleged waiver occurred due to conduct before the court); Tristar Fin.Ins.Agency, Inc. v. Equicredit Corp. of Am., 97 Fed. Appx. 462, 464, 2004 WL 838633 (5th Cir.2004)(same); Blanco v. Sterling Jewelers Inc., 2010 WL 466760, at *4 (D.Colo.2010); Scott v. First Union Securities, Inc., 761 N.Y.S.2d 770 (N.Y.Sup.2003) (same),

[181]   Nat'l Am.Ins.Co. v. Transamerica Occidental Life Ins.Co., 328 F.3d 462, 466 (8th Cir.2003); Bellevue Drug Co. v. Advance PCS, 333 F. Supp. 2d 318, 324 (E.D. Pa. 2004) (overturned on other grounds) (relying on Howsam v. Dean Witter Reynolds, Inc., 537 U.S. 79 (2002), for the proposition that "the issue of whether the defendant, by litigating in this Court the present case, has waived the right to demand arbitration should properly be presented in the first instance to the arbitrator"). Howsam said "the presumption is that the arbitrator should decide 'allegation[s] of waiver, delay, or a like defense to arbitrability.'" Id. at 84 (quoting Moses H. Cone Memorial Hosp. v. Mercury Constr. Corp., 460 U.S. 1, 24–25 (1983)).

[182]   Mutual Assurance, Inc. v. Wilson, 716 So.2d 1160, 1163 (Ala.1998)(quoting Companion Life Ins. Co. v. Whitesell Manufacturing, Inc., 670 So.2d 897, 899 (Ala.1995)). See also Patten Grading & Paving, Inc. v. Skanska USA Building, Inc., 380 F.3d 200, 206 (4th Cir.2004) ("participation in litigation activity alone will not suffice, as the dispositive question 'is whether the party objecting to arbitration has suffered actual prejudice.'") (citing MicroStrategy, Inc. v. Lauricia, 268 F.3d 244, 249 (4th Cir.2001)); Perry Homes v. Cull, 258 S.W.3d 580, 594 (Tex.2008) ("of the twelve regional circuit courts, ten require a showing of prejudice and the other two treat it as a factor to consider"); Steele v. Lundgren, 935 P.2d 671 (Wash.1997). But see St. Mary's Med. Ctr. of Evansville, Inc. v. Disco Aluminum Prods. Co., 969 F.2d 585, 590–91 (7th Cir.1992)("prejudice is but one relevant circumstance to consider in determining whether a party has waived its right to arbitrate"); Raymond James Fin. Services, Inc. v. Saldukas, 896 So.2d 707 (Fla.2005).

turns on the costs the opposing party has incurred in litigating,[183] and whether the party now seeking arbitration has benefitted from features of litigation, such as extensive discovery, that may not be available to it in arbitration.[184]

Courts have held that parties waived the right to compel arbitration by filing litigation pleadings,[185] engaging in litigation discovery,[186] or removing to federal court.[187] In contrast, other courts have declined to find a waiver by parties who engaged in similar litigation conduct.[188] Courts are more likely to find waiver by

---

[183]   Compare, e.g., Gen.Star Nat'l Ins.Co. v. Administratia Asigurarilor de Stat, 289 F.3d 434, 438 (6th Cir.2002) ("for 17 months, Astra remained idle while General Star incurred the costs associated with this action"), with Rose v. Volvo Const. Equipment North America, Inc., 2007 WL 846123, at *7 (N.D.Ohio 2007) ("Unlike the party in *Gen. Star Nat'l Ins. Co.* who failed to assert its right to arbitrate until after a default judgment had been entered against it, in the instant case, EHHE requested that this court * * * compel arbitration less than five months after" complaint).

[184]   Alan Scott Rau, Edward F. Sherman & Scott R. Peppet, Processes of Dispute Resolution: The Role of Lawyers 728 (4th ed.2006).

[185]   Robinson v. Food Service of Belton, Inc., 415 F.Supp.2d 1221 (D.Kan.2005)(defendant did not seek to compel arbitration until after filing amended answer listing arbitration as affirmative defense and counterclaims against parties it later sought to compel to arbitrate); Lapidus v. Arlen Beach Condominium Ass'n Inc., 394 So.2d 1102 (Fla.Dist.Ct.App.1981); Ex Parte Prendergast, 678 So.2d 778 (Ala.1996).

[186]   Rankin v. Allstate Ins. Co., 336 F.3d 8 (1st Cir.2003)(Defendant insurance company waived its right to arbitrate by waiting until discovery had closed and the long-scheduled trial date had almost arrived before invoking the arbitration clause); In re Citigroup, Inc., 376 F.3d 23 (1st Cir.2004)(15 depositions); Com-Tech Assoc. v. Computer Assoc. Int'l, Inc., 938 F.2d 1574 (2d Cir.1991); Ex Parte Smith, 706 So.2d 704, 705 (Ala.1997); Green Tree Servicing, LLC v. McLeod, 15 So.3d 682, 694 (Fla.Dist.Ct.App.2009) ("a party's participation in discovery related to the merits of pending litigation is activity that is generally inconsistent with arbitration. Such activity-considered under the totality of the circumstances-will generally be sufficient to support a finding of a waiver of a party's right to arbitration."); MS Credit Center, Inc. v. Horton, 926 So.2d 167, 180 (Miss.2006).

[187]   Ex Parte Hood, 712 So.2d 341, 345 (Ala.1998).

[188]   See, e.g., Hill v. Ricoh Americas Corp., 603 F.3d 766 (10th Cir.2010)(employer did not waive its right to arbitration by failing to demand arbitration until four months after its answer);

Patten Grading & Paving, Inc. v. Skanska USA Building, Inc., 380 F.3d 200, 206 (4th Cir.2004)("party's filing of minimal responsive pleadings, such as an answer or compulsory counter-claim, are not necessarily inconsistent with an intent to pursue arbitration"); Sharif v. Wellness Int'l Network, Ltd., 376 F.3d 720 (7th Cir.2004)(parties did not waive right to arbitrate under distributorship agreements, even though they waited 18 months after action was filed to seek to compel arbitration and filed four motions to dismiss before filing motion to compel arbitration); Tristar Fin.Ins.Agency, Inc. v. Equicredit Corp. of Am., 97 Fed.Appx. 462, 464, 2004 WL 838633 (5th Cir.2004)(filing motions, conducting discovery); Coca-Cola Bottling Co. of New York, Inc. v. Soft Drink and Brewery Workers Union Local 812, Int'l Brotherhood of Teamsters, 242 F.3d 52 (2d Cir.2001)(Union did not waive its right to arbitrate employer's suit by answering complaint, claiming a violation of temporary restraining order, entering into a protective order and stipulation for discovery, and obtaining substantial discovery); Walker v. J.C. Bradford & Co., 938 F.2d 575 (5th Cir.1991); Stifel, Nicolaus & Co., Inc. v. Freeman, 924 F.2d 157 (8th Cir.1991).

plaintiffs who initiate litigation before seeking arbitration than by defendants who respond in litigation before seeking arbitration.[189] If a court does find that a party has waived the right to compel arbitration then the dispute will be resolved in litigation rather than arbitration.[190] A court may even decline to enforce a contract clause providing that participation in litigation "shall not be deemed a waiver of a party's right to demand arbitration or to continue arbitration."[191]

4. NON-CONTRACT LAW DEFENSES TO ENFORCEMENT: FEDERAL STATUTORY CLAIMS AND PUBLIC POLICY
Table of Sections

The previous sections primarily discuss contract law.[192] Those sections survey the law regarding the formation of enforceable contracts as that law applies to a particular type of contract, the arbitration agreement. In contrast, the next two sections note the rare occasions when non-contract law provides a defense to the enforcement of an arbitration agreement.

---

[189] See, e.g., Grumhaus v. Comerica Securities, Inc., 223 F.3d 648 (7th Cir.2000)(shareholders litigated their claims for several months and waited several months after dismissal of their complaint and more than one year after filing initial action to demand arbitration formally, and rights and remedies underlying the different claims were the same); Aguilar v. Lerner, 12 Cal.Rptr.3d 287 (Cal.2004)(client who filed a lawsuit against attorney alleging professional malpractice, thereby waived his rights to arbitrate under the mandatory fee arbitration act, even though lawsuit also sought resolution of attorney fee dispute).

[190] Of course, the parties can form a post-dispute agreement to use some other process, but if they do not then litigation is the default process. See Stephen J. Ware, Principles of Alternative Dispute Resolution § 1.5(b) (3d ed.2016).

[191] Republic Ins. Co. v. PAICO Receivables, LLC, 383 F.3d 341, 348 (5th Cir.2004). See also S & R Co. of Kingston v. Latona Trucking, Inc., 159 F.3d 80 (2d Cir.1998).

[192] See §§ 19–26.

§ 27   Toward Universal Arbitrability

Consider domestic United States arbitration (as opposed to international arbitration) prior to the 1980's. Nearly all domestic arbitration occurred in two contexts: (1) labor disputes and (2) disputes among businesses.[193] With arbitration limited to these contexts, the sorts of issues resolved in arbitration were also generally limited. Arbitration was usually limited to contract issues. Disputes in the labor context focus on alleged breaches of collective bargaining agreements,[194] and disputes among businesses also tend to revolve around contract interpretation and performance. Prior to the 1980's, arbitration seemed largely confined to contract claims and little attention was given to the arbitration of non-contract claims. Then the Supreme Court revolutionized arbitration law.

The Court's 1980's revolution centered on "statutory arbitrability." An *arbitrable* claim is one with respect to which a pre-dispute arbitration agreement will be enforced.[195] Consider, for example, a contract between Buyer and Seller obligating each party to arbitrate any "controversy or claim arising out of or relating to this contract, or the breach thereof." If a dispute arises and one party seeks to litigate, while the other seeks to arbitrate, a court will have to decide whether to hear the case or to order arbitration. Assuming there is no generally applicable contract defense,[196] a court will order arbitration if, for example, Seller alleges that Buyer failed to pay, or Buyer alleges that Seller breached a warranty. By sending contract and warranty claims to arbitration over the objection of a party, a court holds that such claims are arbitrable.

But what if Buyer alleges that Seller violated the antitrust laws? Until the 1980's, courts held that antitrust claims were not arbitrable.[197] That is, if either party sought to litigate rather than arbitrate the antitrust claim, a court would have heard the antitrust claim on the merits, rather than order arbitration of it. In our

---

[193]   See Mitsubishi Motors Corp. v. Soler Chrysler-Plymouth, Inc., 473 U.S. 614, 650 (1985) (Stevens, J., dissenting) (referring to "the undisputed historical fact that arbitration has functioned almost entirely in either the area of labor disputes or in 'ordinary disputes between merchants as to questions of fact' ").

[194]   See § 48.

[195]   This discussion of "statutory arbitrability" should be contrasted with § 30's discussion of "contractual arbitrability." The latter is the case-by-case question of whether the particular contract should be interpreted to send to arbitration a particular claim. Contractual arbitrability is a question of contract interpretation, while statutory arbitrability is a question of statutory interpretation.

[196]   See §§ 19–26.

[197]   See, e.g., American Safety Equip.Corp. v. J.P.Maguire & Co., 391 F.2d 821, 828 (2d Cir.1968) (declaring antitrust claims "inappropriate for arbitration"). But see Mitsubishi Motors Corp., 473 U.S. 614, 640 (1985)(holding an agreement to arbitrate a claim arising under the Sherman Antitrust Act enforceable).

example, the court may have concluded that Buyer and Seller agreed to arbitrate Buyer's antitrust claim because it, like the contract and warranty claims, "ar[ose] out of" the contract.[198] However, the court would have refused to enforce this agreement to arbitrate antitrust claims because such enforcement would violate "public policy." In other words, courts held that antitrust claims were inarbitrable (non-arbitrable).

Antitrust claims were not alone in this regard. Other claims that courts held to be inarbitrable included: securities,[199] RICO,[200] patent,[201] copyright,[202] "non-core" bankruptcy proceedings,[203] Title VII,[204] ADEA,[205] and ERISA.[206] With such a long list of inarbitrable claims, arbitration was basically confined to resolving breach-of-contract claims.

In the 1980's, the Supreme Court revolutionized arbitration law to require enforcement of agreements to arbitrate regardless of the claims asserted. The Court drastically increased the variety of claims that are arbitrable.[207] The Court now holds that the FAA

> mandates enforcement of agreements to arbitrate statutory claims. Like any statutory directive, the [FAA]'s mandate may be overridden by a contrary congressional command. The burden is on the party opposing arbitration, however,

---

[198]   See §§ 30–31.

[199]   See Wilko v. Swan, 346 U.S. 427, 438 (1953).

[200]   See Page v. Moseley, Hallgarten, Estabrook & Weeden, Inc., 806 F.2d 291, 298–300 (1st Cir.1986). "RICO" is an abbreviation for "Racketeer Influenced and Corrupt Organizations." 18 U.S.C. §§ 1961–68.

[201]   See Beckman Instruments, Inc. v. Technical Dev. Corp., 433 F.2d 55, 63 (7th Cir.1970).

[202]   See Kamakazi Music Corp. v. Robbins Music Corp., 522 F.Supp. 125, 137 (S.D.N.Y.1981), aff'd, 684 F.2d 228 (2d Cir.1982).

[203]   See Zimmerman v. Continental Airlines, 712 F.2d 55, 59 (3rd Cir.1983). But see Hays and Co. v. Merrill Lynch, Pierce, Fenner & Smith, Inc., 885 F.2d 1149, 1155 (3d Cir.1989) (overruling Zimmerman and holding that non-core bankruptcy proceedings are arbitrable). Since Hays, courts have generally held that non-core bankruptcy proceedings are arbitrable. See, e.g., In re Gandy, 299 F.3d 489, 495 (5th Cir.2002) ("it is generally accepted that a bankruptcy court has no discretion to refuse to compel the arbitration of matters not involving "core" bankruptcy proceedings under 28 U.S.C. § 157(b)"). A core proceeding involves "the administration of the estate; the allowance of claims against the estate; the voidance of preferences or fraudulent transfers; determinations as to dischargeability of debts; priorities of liens; or the confirmation of a plan." Id. at 1156 n.9.

[204]   See Utley v. Goldman Sachs & Co., 883 F.2d 184, 187 (1st Cir.1989).

[205]   See Nicholson v. CPC Int'l Inc., 877 F.2d 221, 231 (3rd Cir.1989). "ADEA" is an abbreviation for the Age Discrimination in Employment Act. See 29 U.S.C. §§ 621–634.

[206]   See Barrowclough v. Kidder, Peabody & Co., 752 F.2d 923, 941 (3d Cir.1985). "ERISA" is an abbreviation for the Employment Retirement Income Security Act. 29 U.S.C. §§ 1001 et seq.

[207]   See Macneil, Speidel & Stipanowich, supra note 22, ch.16.

to show that Congress intended to preclude a waiver of judicial remedies for the statutory rights at issue * * * . If Congress did intend to limit or prohibit waiver of a judicial forum for a particular claim, such an intent will be deducible from [the statute's] text or legislative history, * * * or from an inherent conflict between arbitration and the statute's underlying purposes.[208]

Since first making a statement to this effect in 1985,[209] the Supreme Court has yet to discover a single instance in which "Congress intended to preclude a waiver of judicial remedies for the statutory rights at issue." In other words, the Supreme Court has for decades consistently found that statutory claims are arbitrable.[210]

§ 28   Current Inarbitrability (Non-Arbitrability)

(a) Simple Inarbitrability

(1) Labor Arbitration

While the previous paragraphs explain how the Supreme Court began in the 1980's holding virtually all claims arbitrable under the FAA, the Court did not until 2009 hold employment discrimination claims arbitrable in labor arbitration, which is governed not by the FAA but the Labor Management Relations Act. Prior to 2009, when employees represented by a labor union asserted federal discrimination claims in court they were allowed to proceed with litigation despite arbitration clauses in their collective bargaining agreements.[211] Courts allowing this generally relied on the Supreme Court's 1974 case, *Alexander v. Gardner-Denver* Co.[212] However, in the 2009 case of *14 Penn Plaza LLC v. Pyett*,[213] the Supreme Court

---

[208]   Shearson/American Express Inc. v. McMahon, 482 U.S. 220, 226–27 (1987)(citations omitted).

[209]   Mitsubishi Motors Corp. v. Soler Chrysler-Plymouth, Inc., 473 U.S. 614, 628 (1985)("Having made the bargain to arbitrate, the party should be held to it unless Congress itself has evinced an intention to preclude a waiver of judicial remedies for the statutory rights at issue.")

[210]   Mitsubishi Motors Corp. v. Soler Chrysler-Plymouth, Inc., 473 U.S. 614 (1985)(antitrust); Shearson American Express, Inc. v. McMahon, 482 U.S. 220 (1987)(Securities Exchange Act and RICO); Rodriguez de Quijas v. Shearson/American Express, Inc., 490 U.S. 477 (1989)(Securities Act); Gilmer v. Interstate/Johnson Lane Corp., 500 U.S. 20 (1991)(employment discrimination); CompuCredit Corp. v. Greenwood, 132 S.Ct. 665 (2012) (Credit Repair Organization Act).

[211]   Pyett v. Pennsylvania Bldg. Co., 498 F.3d 88, 90 (2d Cir.2007) ("mandatory arbitration clauses in collective bargaining agreements are unenforceable to the extent they waive the rights of covered workers to a judicial forum for federal statutory causes of action"), rev'd and remanded sub nom. 14 Penn Plaza LLC v. Pyett, 556 U.S. 247 (2009).

[212]   415 U.S. 36 (1974).

[213]   556 U.S. 247 (2009).

criticized *Gardner-Denver*,[214] and distinguished it to enforce collective bargaining arbitration clauses that "clearly and unmistakably require[ ] union members to arbitrate" statutory discrimination claims.[215] Since *Penn Plaza*, courts have routinely enforced such clauses to require arbitration, rather than litigation, of discrimination claims brought by employees represented by a labor union.[216]

(2)   Mortgages, Automobile Dealers, and the Military

The previous section explained that the Supreme Court has for decades, consistently held that the FAA makes arbitrable every claim that has come before the Court.[217] However, the Court recognizes the authority of Congress to make federal claims inarbitrable,[218] and several bills have been introduced in Congress to make various federal claims inarbitrable, that is, to carve out certain claims from the FAA's mandate to enforce arbitration agreements.[219] A few such bills have become law. Perhaps the most significant is the Dodd Frank Wall Street Reform Act,[220] which generally banned the use of pre-dispute arbitration agreements in connection with residential mortgages and home-equity loans.[221] Other statutes prohibiting

---

[214]   See, e.g., id. at 265 ("We recognize that apart from their narrow holdings, the *Gardner-Denver* line of cases included broad dicta that were highly critical of the use of arbitration for the vindication of statutory antidiscrimination rights. That skepticism, however, rested on a misconceived view of arbitration that this Court has since abandoned."); see also id. ("The suggestion in *Gardner-Denver* that the decision to arbitrate statutory discrimination claims was tantamount to a substantive waiver of those rights, therefore, reveals a distorted understanding of the compromise made when an employee agrees to compulsory arbitration.").

[215]   *Id.* at 274.

[216]   *See, e.g.*, Savant v. APM Terminals, 776 F.3d 285, 291–92 (5th Cir. 2014) (dismissing unionized employee's age discrimination suit due to collective bargaining agreement's supplement providing that "Any complaint that there has been a violation of any employment law, such as * * * [the] ADEA, * * * shall be resolved solely by the grievance and arbitration provisions of the collective bargaining agreement."); Thompson v. Air Transp. Int'l L.L.C., 664 F.3d 723, 727 (8th Cir. 2011) (enforcing collective bargaining arbitration agreement to dismiss unionized employee's suit and compel arbitration of claims under the Arkansas Civil Rights Act and the Family Medical Leave Act).

[217]   See § 27.

[218]   While Congress can make federal claims inarbitrable, a *state* legislature cannot make state-law claims inarbitrable. Any state law attempting to do so would be preempted by the FAA's command that arbitration agreements be enforced. See § 12.

[219]   *See, e.g.*, Karen Halverson Cross, Letting the Arbitrator Decide Unconscionability Challenges, 26 Ohio St.J. on Disp.Resol. 1, 72–73 (2011); Marcia Coyle, Anti-arbitration bills set off a classic brawl, Nat'l L.J., Aug.12, 2002, at A8.

[220]   Pub.L. 111–203, 124 Stat. 1376 (2010).

[221]   15 U.S.C. § 1639c. The Dodd Frank Act also authorized the Securities and Exchange Commission and the newly created Consumer Financial Protection Bureau to "prohibit or impose conditions or limitations on the use of" pre-dispute arbitration clauses in many consumer financial services contracts. 12 U.S.C. § 5518, 15 U.S.C.

enforcement of pre-dispute arbitration agreements reach motor vehicle franchise agreements between automobile manufacturers and dealers,[222] employment agreements of military contractors,[223] and agreements extending credit to military personnel.[224]

Also, some courts refuse to enforce agreements to arbitrate claims under the Magnuson-Moss Warranty Act,[225] although the only federal appellate courts to address the question found such claims arbitrable.[226]

---

§ 78o. The Dodd Frank Act also prohibited enforcement of pre-dispute arbitration agreements in the context of certain whistleblowers. 7 U.S.C. § 26(n)(2).

[222]   15 U.S.C. § 1226(a)(2) ("Notwithstanding any other provision of law, whenever a motor vehicle franchise contract provides for the use of arbitration to resolve a controversy arising out of or relating to such contract, arbitration may be used to settle such controversy only if after such controversy arises all parties to such controversy consent in writing to use arbitration to settle such controversy.") Courts have considered whether this statute governs arbitration clauses in documents related to a motor vehicle franchise contract. Arciniaga v. General Motors Corp., 460 F.3d 231 (2d Cir.2006) (stockholders agreement was not a "motor vehicle franchise contract" within the meaning of the Motor Vehicle Franchise Contract Arbitration Fairness Act (MVFCAFA)); Pride v. Ford Motor Co., 341 F.Supp.2d 617, 619 (N.D.Miss.2004)(an automobile dealership investment and employment contract was not a "motor vehicle franchise contract").

[223]   Defense Appropriations Act, Pub. L. No. 111–118, § 8116, 123 Stat. 3409, 3454 (2009) (uncodified); 48 C.F.R. § 222.7402.

[224]   10 U.S.C. § 987(f)(4) ("Notwithstanding section 2 of title 9, or any other Federal or State law, rule, or regulation, no agreement to arbitrate any dispute involving the extension of consumer credit shall be enforceable against any covered member or dependent of such a member, or any person who was a covered member or dependent of that member when the agreement was made.")

For another possible exception, also relating to military personnel, compare Lopez v. Dillard's Inc., 382 F.Supp.2d 1245 (D.Kan.2005) (claims under Uniformed Services Employment and Reemployment Rights Act of 1994 (USERRA) are inarbitrable), with Garrett v. Circuit City Stores, Inc., 449 F.3d 672 (5th Cir.2006)(claims under USERRA are arbitrable), Landis v. Pinnacle Eye Care, LLC, 537 F.3d 559, 563 (6th Cir.2008)(same); Ernest v. Lockheed Martin Corp., 2008 WL 2958964, at *9 (D.Colo.2008) (same).

[225]   See Breniser v. Western Recreational Vehicles, Inc., 2008 WL 5234528, at *6 (D.Or.2008); Rickard v. Teynor's Homes, Inc., 279 F.Supp.2d 910 (N.D.Ohio 2003); Browne v. Kline Tysons Imports, Inc., 190 F.Supp.2d 827 (E.D.Va.2002); Pitchford v. Oakwood Mobile Homes, Inc., 124 F.Supp.2d 958 (W.D.Va.2000); Koons Ford of Baltimore, Inc. v. Lobach, 919 A.2d 722, 732–35 (Md.2007); Parkerson v. Smith, 817 So.2d 529 (Miss.2002).

[226]   Davis v. Southern Energy Homes, Inc., 305 F.3d 1268 (11th Cir.2002); Walton v. Rose Mobile Homes LLC, 298 F.3d 470 (5th Cir.2002). See also Jones v. General Motors Corp., 640 F.Supp.2d 1124, 1138–43 (D.Ariz.2009); Borowiec v. Gateway 2000, Inc., 808 N.E.2d 957 (Ill.2004); Stacy David, Inc. v. Consuegra, 845 So.2d 303 (Fla.Ct.App.2003); Abela v. General Motors Corp., 669 N.W.2d 271 (Mich.Ct.App.2003); Southern Energy Homes, Inc. v. Ard, 772 So.2d 1131 (Ala.2000); In re American Homestar of Lancaster, Inc., 50 S.W.3d 480 (Tex.2001); Results Oriented Inc. v. Crawford, 538 S.E.2d 73 (Ga.Ct.App.2000).

(3) Bankruptcy

Core bankruptcy proceedings[227] are sometimes inarbitrable as federal appellate courts generally hold that bankruptcy courts may decline to enforce arbitration agreements if enforcement would conflict with a purpose of the Bankruptcy Code,[228] such as its purpose of coordinating in a single forum resolution of all of the debtor's disputes with its various creditors.[229]

(4) Family Law: Child Custody

Courts review child-custody agreements between divorcing spouses to ensure that such agreements adequately serve the interests of children; courts will void, as against public policy, those agreements that do not meet this standard.[230] Similarly, courts "cannot adopt an arbitration award that concerns the beneficial interests of children without first exercising independent judgment to determine whether the best interests of the children are met by that award."[231] Accordingly, some courts flatly refuse to enforce

---

[227] A core proceeding involves "the administration of the estate; the allowance of claims against the estate; the voidance of preferences or fraudulent transfers; determinations as to dischargeability of debts; priorities of liens; or the confirmation of a plan." Hays and Co. v. Merrill Lynch, Pierce, Fenner & Smith, Inc., 885 F.2d 1149, 1156 n.9 (3d Cir.1989).

[228] Moses v. CashCall, Inc., 781 F.3d 63, 88 (4th Cir. 2015) ("[T]he refusal to send a non-core claim to arbitration requires more than a finding that arbitration would potentially conflict with the purposes of the Bankruptcy Code. Rather, the conflict must be inherent and 'sufficient to override by implication the presumption in favor of arbitration."): In re Electric Machinery Enterprises, Inc., 479 F.3d 791, 799 (11th Cir.2007) ("Only if the bankruptcy court actually makes a sufficient finding that enforcing an arbitration agreement would inherently conflict with the Bankruptcy Code does it have the discretion to deny enforcement of the arbitration agreement").

[229] In re Thorpe Insulation Co., 671 F.3d 1011, 1022 (9th Cir. 2012)("Because Congress intended that the bankruptcy court oversee all aspects of a § 524(g) reorganization, only the bankruptcy court should decide whether the debtor's conduct in the bankruptcy gives rise to a claim for breach of contract. Arbitration in this case would conflict with congressional intent."); In re White Mountain Mining Co., L.L.C., 403 F.3d 164, 169–70 (4th Cir. 2005)("Congress intended to centralize disputes about a debtor's assets and legal obligations in the bankruptcy courts. Arbitration is inconsistent with centralized decision-making because permitting an arbitrator to decide a core issue would make debtor-creditor rights contingent upon an arbitrator's ruling rather than the ruling of the bankruptcy judge assigned to hear the debtor's case.") (internal citations omitted); In re U.S. Lines, Inc., 197 F.3d 631, 640 (2d Cir.1999)("there will be occasions where a dispute involving both the Bankruptcy Code and the Arbitration Act presents a conflict of near polar extremes: bankruptcy policy exerts an inexorable pull towards centralization while arbitration policy advocates a decentralized approach towards dispute resolution.") (internal quotations omitted).

[230] See Stephen J. Ware, Principles of Alternative Dispute Resolution § 3.39(b) (3d ed.2016). See also Restatement (Second) of Contracts § 191 (1981)("A promise affecting the right of custody of a minor child is unenforceable on grounds of public policy unless the disposition as to custody is consistent with the best interest of the child.")

[231] Kovacs v. Kovacs, 633 A.2d 425, 431–32 (Md.Ct.Spec.App.1993).

agreements to arbitrate child custody disputes.[232] This refusal respecting child custody "is in contrast to the clear majority position holding that arbitration agreements respecting property division and spousal support upon divorce are enforceable."[233]

(b) Arbitrability with Strings Attached: The "Effectively Vindicate" Doctrine

While nearly all claims are now arbitrable,[234] the Supreme Court holds that some federal statutory claims are arbitrable only when certain conditions are met. As the Court explained in the 2000 case, *Green Tree Financial Corp.-Alabama v. Randolph*:

> we have recognized that federal statutory claims can be appropriately resolved through arbitration, and we have enforced agreements to arbitrate that involve such claims. We have likewise rejected generalized attacks on arbitration that rest on suspicion of arbitration as a method of weakening the protections afforded in the substantive law to would-be complainants. These cases demonstrate that even claims arising under a statute designed to further important social policies may be arbitrated because *so long as the prospective litigant effectively may vindicate his or her statutory cause of action* in the arbitral forum, the statute serves its functions.[235]

---

[232] Compare Cohen v. Cohen, 600 N.Y.S.2d 996, 996–97 (App.Div.1993) (refusing to compel arbitration of custody before rabbinical tribunal because "[d]isputes over custody and visitation are not subject to arbitration"); Schechter v. Schechter, 881 N.Y.S.2d 151, 152 (App.Div.2009) (reversing confirmation of arbitration award on custody and visitation); Pulfer v. Pulfer, 673 N.E.2d 656, 659 (Ohio Ct.App.1996) (holding that "matters of child custody may only be decided by the trial court and are not subject to arbitration despite any agreement entered into by the parties"), with Fawzy v. Fawzy, 973 A.2d 347, 360–61 (N.J.2009) ("the constitutionally protected right to parental autonomy includes the right to submit any family controversy, including one regarding child custody and parenting time, to a decision maker chosen by the parents. * * * [T]he review of an arbitration award is to take place within the confines of the Arbitration Act, unless there is a claim of adverse impact or harm to the child. Only in that case will further review be required"); In re Marriage of Popack, 998 P.2d 464, 469 (Colo.Ct.App.2000); Wojnar v. Wojnar, 2006 WL 473789, at *1 (Mich.App.2006) (pursuant to state statute, "parties in a divorce action may consent to binding arbitration through a signed agreement providing for an award on disputed matters, including property division, child custody, child support, parenting time, and spousal support."); Miller v. Miller, 620 A.2d 1161, 1163–64 (Pa.Super.1993).

[233] E. Gary Spitko, Reclaiming the "Creatures of the State": Contracting for Child Custody Decisionmaking in the Best Interests of the Family, 57 Wash. & Lee L.Rev. 1139, 1165–66 n.98 (2000) (citing cases). "Given that agreements to arbitrate child support issues also strongly and directly implicate the interests of a child who is not a party to the arbitration agreement, * * *[m]ost courts * * * have held that arbitration awards of child support should be subject to a high level of judicial review." Id.

[234] See § 27.

[235] Green Tree Fin. Corp.-Alabama v. Randolph, 531 U.S. 79, 89–90 (2000) (quotations omitted) (emphasis added). The Court previously used the "effectively

The *Randolph* Court went on to hold that courts should not enforce agreements to arbitrate when enforcement would prevent the prospective litigant from "*effectively vindicating* his or her statutory cause of action."[236] Cases applying the "effectively vindicate" doctrine typically involve federal employment discrimination claims or claims arising under federal legislation regulating consumer finance. These cases have refused to enforce arbitration agreements due to the amount of arbitration fees the claimant is required to pay, although courts differ on how to determine when the fees are too high.[237] To the extent these cases render unenforceable agreements requiring the employee or consumer to pay an arbitration organization's filing fee plus half of the arbitrator's fees,[238] they have departed from the custom in many arbitration contexts, where the claimant (plaintiff) pays the arbitration organization's filing fee and each of the two parties pays half the arbitrator's fee.[239] While this arrangement is customary and has been enforced in a variety of contexts, this arrangement is now doubtful when federal employment or consumer claims are involved.

The "effectively vindicate" doctrine has also been used to render unenforceable arbitration agreement provisions prohibiting class actions.[240] However, the Supreme Court rejected this use of the "effectively vindicate" doctrine in *American Express Co. v. Italian Colors Restaurant.*[241] Plaintiffs in *American Express* pursued class litigation despite an agreement requiring individual (as opposed to class) arbitration.[242] While the district court dismissed the suits and ordered individual arbitrations, the Second Circuit reversed, based in part on a declaration from an economist who estimated that the cost of an expert analysis necessary to prove the antitrust claims would be "at least several hundred thousand dollars, and might

---

vindicate" phrase in Gilmer v. Interstate/Johnson Lane Corp., 500 U.S. 20 (1991) (Age Discrimination in Employment Act), Shearson/American Exp., Inc. v. McMahon, 482 U.S. 220 (1987) (Securities Exchange Act), and Mitsubishi Motors Corp. v. Soler Chrysler-Plymouth, Inc., 473 U.S. 614 (1985) (Sherman Act).

[236]   Green Tree, 531 U.S. at 90 (emphasis added).

[237]   Compare Morrison v. Circuit City Stores, Inc., 317 F.3d 646 (6th Cir.2003), with Bradford v. Rockwell Semiconductor Sys., Inc., 238 F.3d 549 (4th Cir.2001); Muriithi v. Shuttle Exp., Inc. 712 F.3d 173, 181–83 (4th Cir.2013).

[238]   Shankle v. B-G Maintenance Mgmt., Inc., 163 F.3d 1230 (10th Cir.1999); Paladino v. Avnet Computer Tech., Inc., 134 F.3d 1054, 1062 (11th Cir.1998)(finding that this "does not comport with the statutory policy" of Title VII). Contra Arakawa v. Japan Network Group, 56 F.Supp.2d 349, 351 (S.D.N.Y.1999) (rejecting *Paladino* and comparing authorities from various courts).

[239]   See §§ 36(a) & (c).

[240]   Kristian v. Comcast Corp., 446 F.3d 25, 45–61 (1st Cir.2006)(agreement also required each party to pay its own attorney's fees and limited remedies). See also § 34.

[241]   133 S.Ct. 2304 (2013).

[242]   Id. at 2308.

exceed $1 million," while the maximum recovery for an individual plaintiff would be $38,549.[243] The Second Circuit stated that because "the class action waiver in this case precludes plaintiffs from enforcing their statutory rights, we find the arbitration provision unenforceable."[244] The Supreme Court disagreed.

> [T]he fact that it is not worth the expense involved in proving a statutory remedy does not constitute the elimination of the right to pursue that remedy. The class-action waiver merely limits arbitration to the two contracting parties. It no more eliminates those parties' right to pursue their statutory remedy than did federal law before its adoption of the class action for legal relief in 1938. Or, to put it differently, the individual suit that was considered adequate to assure "effective vindication" of a federal right before adoption of class-action procedures did not suddenly become "ineffective vindication" upon their adoption.[245]

While *American Express* confines the effectively-vindicate doctrine, the Court left open the possibility that the doctrine still applies to cases in which the "filing and administrative fees attached to arbitration [ ] are so high as to make access to the forum impracticable."[246]

To the extent the effectively-vindicate doctrine survives *American Express*,[247] the doctrine extends only to *federal* statutory claims, not to claims arising under *state* law. The reasoning underlying the doctrine is that the policy of the federal statute in question would be undermined by enforcement of claimants' promises to arbitrate under the procedures in the arbitration agreement[248] because enforcing such promises would deter some claimants from seeking to vindicate their claims. That policy clashes with the FAA's command that arbitration agreements be enforced.[249] The holding of cases applying the effectively-vindicate doctrine is

---

[243]   Id.

[244]   In re American Express Merchants' Litigation, 634 F.3d 187, 199 (2d Cir.2011).

[245]   133 S.Ct. 2304, 2310–11 (2013).

[246]   Id.

[247]   For a post-American Express application of the doctrine, see Nesbitt v. FCNH, Inc., No. 14–1502, 2016 WL 53816, at *2 (10th Cir. Jan. 5, 2016) (affirming hold that agreement requiring arbitration in accordance with the Commercial Rules of the American Arbitration Association and requiring each party to bear its own expenses "effectively deprived [employee] of her rights" under the Fair Labor Standards Act and thus was unenforceable).

[248]   Claimants make such promises when they agree to arbitrate under rules of an organization that requires such fees.

[249]   9 U.S.C. § 2 (arbitration agreements enforced "save upon such grounds as exist at law or in equity for the revocation of any contract.")

that the FAA must yield to the other federal statute with which it is in tension. But the FAA does not yield to a state statute or state common law doctrine with which it is tension because the Supremacy Clause of the United States Constitution makes federal law supreme over state law.[250]

---

[250]   See U.S. Const. art. VI, cl. 2; Coneff v. AT & T Corp., 673 F.3d 1155, 1158 n.2 (9th Cir. 2012) ("Plaintiffs assert primarily state statutory rights, but Mitsubishi, Gilmer, Green Tree and similar decisions are limited to federal statutory rights."); Green Tree Fin.Corp. of AL v. Wampler, 749 So.2d 409, 416 (Ala.1999)("Unlike *Paladino*, in which competing federal policies were in play, this present case arises under common-law principles governed solely by Alabama law and involves only one federal policy, that being a policy favoring arbitration.")

Chapter 5

TERMS OF ARBITRATION AGREEMENTS

Table of Sections

§ 29   Introduction

The previous chapter (sections 19–28) discussed the formation of arbitration agreements. This chapter (sections 29–38) discusses the terms of arbitration agreements. Just as contract law generally allows parties to choose the terms of their contracts, arbitration law generally allows parties to choose the terms of their arbitration agreements. The "FAA lets parties tailor some, even many features of arbitration by contract, including the way arbitrators are chosen, what their qualifications should be, which issues are arbitrable, along with procedure and choice of substantive law."[1] But just as freedom of contract is not absolute outside the arbitration context, it is not absolute with respect to arbitration agreements either. Parties have wide, but not unlimited, latitude with the terms of their arbitration agreements.

1.   CONTRACTUAL ARBITRABILITY (SCOPE OF ARBITRATION AGREEMENT)
Table of Sections

Sec.

§ 30   Presumptively Decided by Courts

If a party seeks to litigate, rather than arbitrate, a particular claim, the court will send that claim to arbitration only if the parties agreed to arbitrate that claim.[2] That the parties agreed to arbitrate *some* claim is not enough. They must have agreed to arbitrate *that* claim.[3] Whether or not they did so is a question of contract

---

[1]   Hall Street Associates v. Mattel, 552 U.S. 576, 585 (2008).

[2]   See § 3(a)–(b).

[3]   "[A] court may order arbitration of a particular dispute only where the court is satisfied that the parties agreed to arbitrate *that dispute*." Granite Rock Co. v. Int'l Bhd. of Teamsters, 561 U.S. 287 (2010) (emphasis in original).

interpretation about the scope of the arbitration agreement, the question of "contractual arbitrability."

Contractual arbitrability should be distinguished from "statutory arbitrability," which is discussed in earlier sections.[4] Even if the parties did agree to arbitrate a particular claim, the court will still allow a party to litigate, rather than arbitrate, that claim if that claim is created by a federal statute that overrides the FAA's rule of enforcing arbitration agreements. Such claims are few.[5] The discussion below assumes that no such claims are involved. If such claims are involved then the reader should consult both the following sections and the sections on statutory arbitrability.[6]

The threshold issue regarding contractual arbitrability is who— court or arbitrator—decides whether a claim is arbitrable. Consider, for example, a contract between Buyer and Seller obligating each party to arbitrate any "controversy or claim arising out of or relating to this contract, or the breach thereof." Suppose that Buyer sues Seller, alleging antitrust violations, and Seller moves to stay the litigation and to compel arbitration. Buyer may argue that the parties agreed to arbitrate breach-of-contract claims but not antitrust claims. Therefore, Seller's motion to compel arbitration should be denied. In other words, Buyer may argue contractual in-arbitrability, the scope of the agreement is not broad enough to include antitrust claims.

If Buyer sues outside the United States the foreign court is likely to grant Seller's motion. Most nations' laws give arbitrators, not courts, the initial power to rule on the agreement's scope, that is, questions of contractual arbitrability.[7] Under such laws, Buyer would have to go to arbitration to persuade the arbitrator that the parties did not agree to arbitrate antitrust claims. Only after getting a ruling from the arbitrator to that effect, or successfully challenging an arbitrator's contrary ruling in court,[8] could Buyer to litigate the antitrust claim.

---

[4]   See §§ 27–28.

[5]   Id.

[6]   See id.

[7]   See Thomas E. Carbonneau, Beyond Trilogies: A New Bill of Rights and Law Practice Through the Contract of Arbitration, 6 Am.Rev.Int'l Arb. 1, 17 (1995) (most nations' laws "contain the *kompetenz-kompetenz* doctrine, under which arbitral tribunals are given the authority to rule initially at least upon questions of contractual inarbitrability. These determinations are subject to judicial review * * * at the stage of enforcement when a final award can be challenged on the basis of an invalid or non-existent arbitration agreement or for excess of arbitral authority.") See also § 68.

[8]   See id. See also Gary B. Born, International Commercial Arbitration 85–86 (2d ed.2001) (discussing variations of the competence-competence doctrine).

In contrast, the FAA sends disputes about an arbitration agreement's scope (contractual arbitrability) to courts, rather than to arbitrators.[9] In the United States, a court will interpret the arbitration agreement between Buyer and Seller. If the court interprets the arbitration clause to cover Buyer's antitrust claim, then the court will grant Seller's motion and send the claim to arbitration. If the court finds that the arbitration clause does not cover Buyer's antitrust claim, the court will deny Seller's motion. This approach follows from FAA § 3, which provides:

> If any suit or proceeding be brought in any of the courts of the United States upon any issue referable to arbitration under an agreement in writing for such arbitration, the court in which such suit is pending, *upon being satisfied that the issue involved in such suit or proceeding is referable to arbitration under such an agreement*, shall on application of one of the parties stay the trial of the action until such arbitration has been had in accordance with the terms of the agreement, providing the applicant for the stay is not in default in proceeding with such arbitration.[10]

FAA § 3 requires the court to satisfy itself that the issue involved in the suit is covered by the arbitration agreement before compelling arbitration. While the FAA is not the primary law governing labor arbitration,[11] the rule that courts, rather than arbitrators, resolve contractual arbitrability disputes applies to labor arbitration, too.[12]

The rule that courts, rather than arbitrators, resolve disputes about the scope of the agreement (contractual arbitrability disputes) is merely a default rule. The parties can contract around this rule by using an arbitration agreement that says such disputes shall be resolved by the arbitrator rather than the court, provided that they do so "clearly."[13] For example, an agreement can incorporate the

---

[9]   First Options of Chicago, Inc. v. Kaplan, 514 U.S. 938 (1995). See also Howsam v. Dean Witter Reynolds, Inc., 537 U.S. 79, 83 (2002) ("the question whether the parties have submitted a particular dispute to arbitration, i.e., the 'question of arbitrability,' is an issue for judicial determination unless the parties clearly and unmistakably provide otherwise. * * * Similarly, a disagreement about whether an arbitration clause in a concededly binding contract applies to a particular type of controversy is for the court.")

[10]   9 U.S.C. § 3 (emphasis added).

[11]   See §§ 50 & 52.

[12]   See § 52(d). AT & T Technologies, Inc. v. Communications Workers of Am., 475 U.S. 643 (1986).

[13]   First Options of Chicago, Inc. v. Kaplan, 514 U.S. 938, 946–47 (1995). See § 21(a) (discussing facts and reasoning of *First Options*). See also Howsam v. Dean Witter Reynolds, Inc., 537 U.S. 79, 83 (2002) ("the question whether the parties have submitted a particular dispute to arbitration, i.e., the 'question of arbitrability,' is an issue for judicial determination unless the parties clearly and unmistakably provide

American Arbitration Association's Commercial Arbitration Rules, which provide that "[t]he arbitrator shall have the power to rule on his or her own jurisdiction, including any objections with respect to the existence, *scope* or validity of the arbitration agreement or to the arbitrability of any claim or counterclaim."[14] Had Buyer and Seller, in the example above, used such an agreement then the court would grant Seller's motion to compel arbitration.[15] Buyer would have to go to arbitration to persuade the arbitrator that the arbitration agreement should be interpreted not to cover Buyer's antitrust claim.

---

otherwise."); AT & T Technologies, Inc. v. Communications Workers of Am., 475 U.S. 643 (1986).

For cases holding that the parties did contract around the default rule, that is, did agree that the arbitrator should decide arbitrability, see Allen v. Regions Bank, 2010 WL 3168217, at *4 (5th Cir.2010) ("the Regions Agreement was clear: 'Any dispute regarding whether a particular controversy is subject to arbitration . . . shall be decided by the arbitrator(s).' The Allens accepted this agreement by continuing to use their deposit accounts with Regions and by signing signature cards. This was sufficient clarity to demand arbitration of arbitrability."); Sadler v. Green Tree Servicing, LLC, 466 F.3d 623 (8th Cir.2006); Ex parte Waites, 736 So.2d 550 (Ala.1999).

[14]   Am.Arbitration Ass'n, Commercial Arbitration Rules, R–7(a) (2013) (emphasis added).

[15]   See Terminix Int'l Co., LP v. Palmer Ranch Ltd. P'ship, 432 F.3d 1327, 1332–33 (11th Cir.2005) (holding that by incorporating AAA Rules into arbitration agreement, parties clearly and unmistakably agreed that arbitrator should decide whether arbitration clause was valid); Contec Corp. v. Remote Solution, Co., 398 F.3d 205, 208 (2d Cir.2005) ("[W]hen . . . parties explicitly incorporate rules that empower an arbitrator to decide issues of arbitrability, the incorporation serves as clear and unmistakable evidence of the parties' intent to delegate such issues to an arbitrator."); Citifinancial, Inc. v. Newton, 359 F.Supp.2d 545, 549–52 (S.D.Miss.2005) (holding that by agreeing to be bound by procedural rules of AAA, including rule giving arbitrator power to rule on his or her own jurisdiction, defendant agreed to arbitrate questions of jurisdiction before arbitrator); Sleeper Farms v. Agway, Inc., 211 F.Supp.2d 197, 200–03 (D.Me.2002)(since the AAA rules constitute "a clear and unmistakable delegation of scope-determining authority to an arbitrator," the court "refers this dispute" to the arbitrator "to determine * * * what issues * * * are covered by the arbitration clause.")

See also JAMS Comprehensive Arbitration Rules and Procedures, Rule 11(c) ("Jurisdictional and arbitrability disputes, including disputes over the formation, existence, validity, interpretation or scope of the agreement under which Arbitration is sought, and who are proper Parties to the Arbitration, shall be submitted to and ruled on by the Arbitrator. The Arbitrator has the authority to determine jurisdiction and arbitrability issues as a preliminary matter."), available at http://www.jamsadr.com/rules-comprehensive-arbitration/#Rule 11; Monex Deposit Co. v. Gilliam, 616 F.Supp.2d 1023, 1025 (C.D.Cal.2009) (granting motion to compel arbitration and noting that agreement "incorporates JAMS Rules providing that the arbitrator decides scope and validity disputes with respect to particular claims."); Greenspan v. Ladt, LLC, 111 Cal.Rptr.3d 468, 494–95 (Ct.App.2010)("LADT interprets the concluding language of Rule 11(c) to mean the arbitrator makes an initial decision on arbitrability, and, later, the courts independently make the final decision. Not so. For one thing, LADT's interpretation would conflict with JAMS Rule 11(a), which provides that "[t]he resolution of the issue by the Arbitrator shall be final." * * * [T]he arbitrator decides arbitrability issues at the outset, and his decision is final.")

Only after getting a ruling from the arbitrator to that effect could Buyer litigate the antitrust claim.[16]

The question discussed in the previous paragraphs (whether parties to an arbitration agreement delegated to their arbitrator issues about the scope of that agreement) is different from the question whether parties delegated to an arbitrator issues about who are the parties to the arbitration agreement. That latter question asks whether a particular party even formed an arbitration agreement at all, and thus is generally for the court (rather than arbitrator) to decide under the Supreme Court's 2002 *First Options* case and more recent authority, which hold that although the arbitrator may initially determine his or her own jurisdiction, courts should review that determination de novo.[17]

§ 31   Contractual and Non-Contractual Approaches

(a) Contractual   Approaches   to   Interpreting   an Arbitration Agreement's Scope

The previous section explained the default rule in the United States that courts, as opposed to arbitrators, resolve disputes about the scope of arbitration agreements.[18] In other words, courts interpret arbitration agreements to determine whether the parties did or did not agree to arbitrate a particular claim. One might suppose that interpreting arbitration clauses is the same as interpreting any other contract terms: in each case the court's job is to enforce the parties' apparent intentions by interpreting the contract's terms as those terms would ordinarily be understood by reasonable people in the positions of the parties.[19] A court taking this approach would apply the usual techniques of contract interpretation to the arbitration agreement. Such courts sometimes begin by classifying the arbitration clause as "broad" or "narrow."

> [R]ecognizing there is some range in the breadth of arbitration clauses, a court should classify the particular clause as either broad or narrow * * * . Where the arbitration clause is narrow, a collateral matter will generally be ruled beyond its purview. Where the arbitration clause is broad, there arises a presumption of

---

[16]   While agreements sending contractual arbitrability disputes to the arbitrator are enforceable, there may in some cases be a dispute about whether the agreement does or does not do so. This dispute is also one of contract interpretation. Who resolves it, the court or the arbitrator? This question leads one into an infinite regression, a metaphysical quandary without end.

[17]   First Options of Chicago, Inc. v. Kaplan, 514 U.S. 938 (1995). See § 21(a).

[18]   See § 30.

[19]   Restatement (Second) of Contracts § 202(3) (1981).

arbitrability and arbitration of even a collateral matter will be ordered if the claim alleged implicates issues of contract construction or the parties' rights and obligations under it.[20]

Tort claims, for example, are often covered by broad arbitration clauses.[21]

Of course, the classifications "broad" and "narrow" are just generalizations and will often be insufficiently precise.[22] Rather than just mechanically placing an arbitration clause in one of two categories, the task of contract interpretation requires a court to be sensitive to the particular language and context of the arbitration agreement in that case.[23]

---

[20]   Louis Dreyfus Negoce S.A. v. Blystad Shipping & Trading Inc., 252 F.3d 218, 224 (2d Cir.2001) (internal quotation marks and citations omitted). As one court put it, " 'broad' arbitration clauses (which contain language submitting to arbitration all disputes 'arising under' or 'relating to' an agreement) have been held to encompass a variety of extra-contractual claims, [while] 'restrictive' or 'narrow' arbitration clauses reflect an intent to arbitrate only a limited range of disputes and * * * the phrase 'arising under' is intended to cover only those disputes relating to the interpretation and performance of a contract." Wilson v. Olathe Bank, 1998 WL 596739, at *2 (D.Kan. July 31, 1998)(citations omitted).

[21]   CD Partners, L.L.C. v. Grizzle, 424 F.3d 795 (8th Cir.2005) (tort claims covered by broad arbitration clause); Sears Authorized Termite and Pest Control, Inc. v. Sullivan, 816 So.2d 603 (Fla.2002) (same); Accomazzo v. CEDU Education Services, Inc. 15 P.3d 1153 (Idaho 2000) (intentional tort claims arose out of contract and thus covered by clause). See also Hicks v. Cadle Co., 355 Fed.Appx. 186, 189, 193 (10th Cir.2009) (clause which required arbitration of, among other claims, "any claim based on or arising from an alleged tort," broad enough to require arbitration of defamation and intentional infliction of emotional distress claims). Some broad clauses are even written to expressly cover claims based on "statutory law, common law, equitable claims, or claims for breach of fiduciary duty or other wrongful acts." Herrington v. Union Planters Bank, 2000 WL 424232, *2 (S.D.Miss.Jan.21, 2000).

[22]   Ian R. Macneil, Richard E. Speidel & Thomas J. Stipanowich, Federal Arbitration Law § 20.2.1 (1994) ("the form of an arbitration agreement may assume an unfortunate talismanic function, going somewhat beyond simply looking at the language to ascertain party intention."). See, e.g., Local 827, Intern. Broth. of Elec. Workers, AFL-CIO v. Verizon New Jersey, Inc., 458 F.3d 305, 306 (3d Cir.2006)("In this appeal, we must decide between the conflicting conclusions reached by two district judges in the same court regarding the interpretation of the same collective bargaining contract. One has held that the contract's arbitration clause is narrow, while the other has held that it is broad."); id. at 309 ("The District Court in this case stated that there was some ambiguity in the CBA's arbitration clause, as evidenced by the fact that several arbitrators had held that the clause was broad, while others had found it narrow.")

[23]   Neither the FAA nor Supreme Court precedent suggests that courts should classify arbitration clauses as broad or narrow. Ivax Corp. v. B. Braun of Am., 286 F.3d 1309, 1320 n.23 (11th Cir.2002) ("It appears to us . . . that the [Supreme] Court in Moses Cone made no such distinction" between broad and narrow clauses.); Chelsea Family Pharmacy, PLLC v. Medco Health Solutions, Inc., 567 F.3d 1191 (10th Cir.2009)(Gorsuch, J., concurring) ("I write separately only to question this business of classifying arbitration clauses as 'broad' or 'narrow.' ")

(b) Non-Contractual Approaches to Interpreting an Arbitration Agreement's Scope

While courts often apply the usual techniques of contract interpretation to the interpretation of arbitration agreements, there are also recurring departures from these usual techniques. To put it more directly, courts often seem to have an agenda, other than just effectuating the apparent intentions of the parties, when interpreting arbitration agreements. Courts often seem to have a finger on the scale.

Sometimes the court's agenda is to favor arbitration, that is, to interpret the arbitration clause broadly. This is the avowed policy of the Supreme Court. Its holdings establish that "in applying general state-law principles of contract interpretation to the interpretation of an arbitration agreement * * *, due regard must be given to the federal policy favoring arbitration, and ambiguities as to the scope of the arbitration clause itself [are] resolved in favor of arbitration."[24] The Court reaffirmed this requirement that interpretation give "give 'due regard . . . to the federal policy favoring arbitration' " as recently as its 2015 decision in *DIRECTV, Inc. v. Imburgia.*[25]

This interpretive agenda to favor arbitration is especially prominent in labor arbitration cases. Courts have long favored a broad interpretation of collective bargaining agreements' arbitration clauses.[26] In nearly all cases, a broader interpretation benefits the employee and union rather than the employer. That is because nearly all labor arbitration cases are grievances (claims) by the employee against the employer,[27] and if the arbitration clause is interpreted to cover the dispute, then the employee may win in arbitration. In contrast, if the arbitration clause is interpreted not to cover the dispute, then there will probably not be any adjudication of the dispute.[28] So in the labor context, a broad interpretation of the arbitration clause is nearly always favored by the employee and union. That broad interpretation is often provided by courts who make statements like this oft-quoted one by the Supreme Court: "[a]n order to arbitrate the particular grievance should not be denied

---

[24]   Volt Information Sciences, Inc. v. Board of Trustees of the Leland Stanford Junior University, 489 U.S. 468, 475–76 (1989). See, e.g., Simula, Inc. v. Autoliv, Inc., 175 F.3d 716 (9th Cir.1999)(agreement to arbitrate "all disputes arising in connection with this agreement" includes antitrust, defamation and trade secret claims).

[25]   136 S.Ct. 463 (2015).

[26]   See, e.g., AT & T Technologies, Inc. v. Communications Workers of America, 475 U.S. 643, 649–51 (1986); United Steelworkers of America v. Warrior & Gulf Navigation Co., 363 U.S. 574, 582–83 (1960).

[27]   See § 59(b).

[28]   See id. Adjudication is a process by which somebody (the adjudicator) decides the result of a dispute. See supra § 1, n.1.

unless it may be said with positive assurance that the arbitration clause is not susceptible of an interpretation that covers the asserted dispute. Doubts should be resolved in favor of coverage."[29]

In other cases, by contrast, the court's agenda is to confine arbitration by interpreting the arbitration clause narrowly. This occurs when the court strains its interpretation to favor an employee or consumer plaintiff who seeks to litigate, rather than arbitrate, her claims despite having signed a take-it-or-leave-it arbitration agreement. For example, a New Jersey case interpreted an arbitration clause not to cover statutory employment discrimination claims because it did not, in "clear and unmistakable" language, include them.[30]

While a court's agenda in interpreting arbitration clauses affects the outcome in some cases, most cases are not controversial because the scope of the arbitration agreement (contractual arbitrability) is clear. The typical arbitration clause is written broadly to cover any "controversy or claim arising out of or relating to this contract, or the breach thereof."[31] In the bulk of cases, all claims do plainly arise out of or relate to the contract or its breach, so any fair-minded court (or arbitrator) will hold that the parties agreed to arbitrate the claims.

A complaint may include multiple claims, some of which are covered by the arbitration agreement and others of which are not. If this occurs and a party moves to compel arbitration, the FAA requires courts to grant the motion with respect to the arbitrable claims "even where the result would be the possibly inefficient maintenance of separate proceedings in different forums."[32]

2. MULTI-PARTY AGREEMENTS AND DISPUTES
Table of Sections

---

[29]   United Steelworkers of America v. Warrior & Gulf Navigation Co., 363 U.S. 574, 582–83 (1960).

[30]   Alamo Rent A Car, Inc. v. Galarza, 703 A.2d 961 (N.J.1997). See also Wright v. Universal Maritime Service Corp., 525 U.S. 70 (1998)(requiring "clear and unmistakable" language encompassing statutory discrimination claims in labor arbitration context).

[31]   Macneil, Speidel & Stipanowich, supra note 22, § 20.2.2.1.

[32]   KPMG LLP v. Cocchi, 132 S.Ct. 23 (2011) (quoting Dean Witter Reynolds Inc. v. Byrd, 470 U.S. 213 (1985)).

§ 32   Claims by or Against Those Not Party to the Arbitration Agreement

The previous sections discuss contractual arbitrability, the question of whether a particular arbitration agreement covers a particular claim.[33] This is a question of contract interpretation—interpreting the scope of the arbitration agreement. A specific application of that question is whether a particular arbitration agreement covers claims against a particular person who is not a party to the arbitration agreement.[34]

(a) Party Plaintiff vs. Non-Party Defendant

Consider, for example, an arbitration clause in a contract between Buyer and Seller for the sale of goods. If Buyer sues Seller, Seller will be able to obtain a stay of the litigation and an order compelling Buyer to arbitrate.[35] But what if Buyer also sues the manufacturer of the goods, the lender who financed Buyer's purchase, an insurance company involved in the transaction, or the individual salesperson who actually made the sale? Must Buyer arbitrate its claims against those third parties even though they are not parties to the arbitration agreement?

These are primarily questions of contract law, particularly the law of third-party beneficiaries. Contracts often confer rights on those who are not party to it, "intended beneficiaries."[36] To qualify as an intended beneficiary, one must show that "recognition of a right to performance in the beneficiary is appropriate to effectuate the intention of the parties."[37] In other words, whether a particular party may enforce a promise to arbitrate is a question of contract interpretation. Accordingly, if the arbitration clause in the agreement between Buyer and Seller is written broadly to cover "all disputes, claims, or controversies arising from or relating to this Contract or the relationships which result from this Contract," then Buyer is required to arbitrate its claims against defendants (such as the manufacturer or salesperson) who are not party to the arbitration

---

[33]   See §§ 30–31.

[34]   Those not party to the arbitration agreement are often called "non-signatories" but this usage should be avoided if it misleads some into believing that the only way to be a party to an arbitration agreement is to sign it. Other methods of manifesting assent are also effective to make one a party to an arbitration agreement. See § 22.

[35]   See § 3(b).

[36]   See generally E. Allan Farnsworth, Contracts ch.10 (4th ed.2004).

[37]   Restatement (Second) of Contracts § 302(1) (1981).

agreement.[38] In contrast, if the arbitration clause is expressly limited to disputes between Buyer and Seller then Buyer may sue other defendants.[39] Some courts phrase the issue as whether Buyer's claims against defendants other than Seller are "intertwined with" or have a "significant relationship with" the agreement containing the arbitration clause.[40]

Note that intended third-party beneficiaries of another party's promise to arbitrate can compel arbitration but, without more, cannot be compelled to arbitrate.[41] In other words, the beneficiaries have the right, but not the duty, to arbitrate. This follows from the consensual nature of contracts generally and arbitration agreements in particular. Parties to a contract can grant rights to non-parties but cannot impose duties on non-parties. Contractual duties belong only to parties who agree to them and the non-party to an arbitration agreement, by definition, did not agree to arbitrate.[42] So third-party beneficiary law, as a part of contract law, understandably confers on a non-party the right, but not the duty, to arbitrate.

In contrast, legal doctrines outside of contract law do impose duties, including the duty to arbitrate, on parties who did not directly

---

[38]   Sherer v. Green Tree Servicing, LLC, 548 F.3d 379, 383 (5th Cir.2008) ("the language of the Loan Agreement demonstrates that Sherer has agreed to arbitrate his claims that arise against nonsignatories whose 'relationships . . . result from th[e] [a]greement.' Sherer is bound by the language of the Loan Agreement, and Green Tree, as a nonsignatory whose relationship resulted from the Loan Agreement, may therefore compel Sherer to arbitrate his claims."); Blinco v. Green Tree Servicing LLC, 400 F.3d 1308, 1311 (11th Cir.2005); Ex Parte Gates, 675 So.2d 371, 374 (Ala.1996).

The Supreme Court held that "third-party beneficiary theories" could be applied to arbitration because they are "traditional principles' of state law allow[ing] a contract to be enforced by or against nonparties to the contract." Arthur Andersen LLP v. Carlisle, 556 U.S. 624, 630–31 (2009).

[39]   Monsanto Co. v. Benton Farm, 813 So.2d 867 (Ala.2001); Ex parte Martin, 703 So.2d 883, 888 (Ala.1996). The same is true of an arbitration clause expressly limited to disputes between general contractor and subcontractor; it does not cover disputes between subcontractor and a third party. In re Application of Diesel Constr. Co., Inc., 234 N.Y.S.2d 349 (N.Y.Sup.Ct., Special Term 1962).

[40]   Long v. Silver, 248 F.3d 309 (4th Cir.2001); Bimota SPA v. Rousseau, 628 F.Supp.2d 500, 504 (S.D.N.Y.2009) ("A non-signatory may compel arbitration on an estoppel theory, where (i) there is a close relationship between the parties and controversies involved and (ii) the signatory's claims against the non-signatory are intimately founded in and intertwined with the underlying agreement containing the arbitration clause.") (internal citations and quotations omitted). See also CD Partners, L.L.C. v. Grizzle, 424 F.3d 795, 798 (8th Cir.2005)("[a] nonsignatory can enforce an arbitration clause against a signatory to the agreement * * * [w]hen each of a signatory's claims against a nonsignatory makes reference to or presumes the existence of the written agreement").

[41]   Macneil, Speidel & Stipanowich, supra note 22, § 18.3.1.6 (Supp.1999).

[42]   Although one may later become a party to an earlier arbitration agreement by assuming the duties (including the duty to arbitrate) of one of the parties to the earlier agreement. See, e.g., Trippe Mfg.Co. v. Niles Audio Corp., 401 F.3d 529, 531–33 (3d Cir.2005); Employers Ins. of Wausau v. Bright Metal Specialties, Inc., 251 F.3d 1316 (11th Cir.2001).

assent to the arbitration agreement. Such non-contractual doctrines include estoppel,[43] agency,[44] and corporate veil-piercing.[45] The Supreme Court held in its 2009 *Arthur Andersen LLP v. Carlisle* case that "assumption, piercing the corporate veil, alter ego, incorporation by reference, third-party beneficiary theories, waiver and estoppel," could be applied to arbitration because they are "traditional principles' of state law allow[ing] a contract to be enforced by or against nonparties to the contract."[46]

(b)　Non-Party Plaintiff vs. Party Defendant

Plaintiffs, like defendants, can be intended third-party beneficiaries of another party's promise to arbitrate.[47] For example, a plaintiff injured while test driving an auto dealer's car "could be considered" a third-party beneficiary of the dealer's insurance policy—the contract between the dealer and its insurer.[48] If that plaintiff brings a breach-of-contract claim against the dealer's insurer then the insurer may rely on the policy's arbitration clause to require the plaintiff to arbitrate, rather than litigate, his claims against the insurer. In other words, if the plaintiff wants to enforce some of the policy's terms (by suing on them) then he "cannot pick and choose the portions of the contract that he wants to apply."[49]

---

[43]　Am. Bureau of Shipping v. Tencara Shipyard S.P.A., 170 F.3d 349, 352–53 (2d Cir.1999); Deloitte Noraudit A/S v. Deloitte Haskins & Sells, U.S., 9 F.3d 1060 (2d Cir.1993); Amknor Tech., Inc. v. Alcatel Bus. Sys., 278 F. Supp. 2d 519, 521–22 (E.D.Penn. 2003).

[44]　See § 22(b)(1).

[45]　Bridas S.A.P.I.C. v. Government of Turkmenistan, 447 F.3d 411 (5th Cir.2006)(alter ego); Thomson-CSF, S.A. v. American Arbitration Ass'n, 64 F.3d 773 (2d Cir.1995)(endorsing veil-piercing but not applying it in this case); Laborers' Int'l Union v. Foster Wheeler Corp., 26 F.3d 375 (3d Cir.1993)(alter ego).

[46]　Arthur Andersen LLP v. Carlisle, 556 U.S. 624, 630–31 (2009).

[47]　Topolski v. Helena Ass'n of Realtors, Inc., 15 P.3d 414 (Mont.2000)(client sought arbitration against real estate broker and court ordered broker to arbitrate, even though client's contract with broker lacked an arbitration clause, because broker had assented to association rules requiring broker to arbitrate client's claims).

[48]　Ex Parte Dyess, 709 So.2d 447, 449–50 (Ala.1997). "Dyess is suing American Hardware under the uninsured motorist provision in the policy American Hardware issued to Jack Ingram Motors. In effect, Dyess is a third-party beneficiary of the policy between American Hardware and Jack Ingram Motors." Id. at 450.

[49]　Id. at 451. Washington Mut.Fin.Group, LLC v. Bailey, 364 F.3d 260 (5th Cir.2004); Int'l Paper Co. v. Schwabedissen Maschinen & Anlagen GMBH, 206 F.3d 411 (4th Cir.2000); Friedman v. Yula, 679 F.Supp.2d 617, 628 (E.D.Pa.2010) ("having embraced the written agreement between Robert and Defendants to prove his claims and his damages, Allan cannot now walk away from the arbitration clauses in the Agreements. * * * Therefore, Plaintiff Allan Friedman must be compelled to arbitration claims under the Joinder Agreement."); Benton v. Vanderbilt University, 137 S.W.3d 614, 618–19 (Tenn.2004); Cook's Pest Control, Inc. v. Boykin, 807 So.2d 524, 526 (Ala.2001); Johnson v. Pennsylvania National Insurance Cos., 594 A.2d 296, 298–99 (Pa.1991); District Moving & Storage Co. v. Gardiner & Gardiner, Inc., 492 A.2d 319, 322–23 (Md.App.1985). But see City of Peru v. Ill. Power Co., 630 N.E.2d 454 (Ill.1994). An exception is where the arbitration clause is expressly limited to

However, several courts hold that this reasoning applies only to plaintiffs whose claims rest on the contract containing the arbitration clause. These courts hold that an arbitration clause in a contract to which the plaintiff could be considered a third-party beneficiary is no obstacle to that plaintiff's desire to litigate, rather than arbitrate, non-contract claims, such as tort claims.[50] Of course, such a plaintiff might be required to arbitrate due to non-contractual doctrines such as those noted at the end of the previous subsection: estoppel, agency, and corporate veil-piercing.[51]

§ 33 Consolidation of, and Stays Pending, Related Proceedings

In litigation, rules of civil procedure encourage courts to consolidate related cases and to join multiple parties in a single action if their disputes arise out of the same transaction or occurrence.[52] Consolidation or joinder can avoid multiple litigation over the same facts, thus saving time and money and helping to avoid inconsistent results. These same goals also argue for arbitrators to consolidate cases and to join parties. The obstacle to doing so, however, is the contractual nature of arbitration. Parties who have not agreed to arbitrate have a right to litigate rather than arbitrate.[53] And parties who have agreed to arbitrate have a right to arbitrate rather than litigate.[54]

Consider a construction project in which the owner of the land has a contract with the general contractor and a separate contract with the architect.[55] Suppose that Owner's contract with Contractor has an arbitration clause but Owner's contract with Architect does not. Owner claims that Contractor breached the construction contract because the work had defects. Contractor replies that any

---

disputes among the contracting parties, as opposed to disputes involving the third party. Lewis v. CEDU Educational Services, Inc., 15 P.3d 1147, 1150—52 (Idaho 2000).

The principle that one ought not be able to "pick and choose" some portions of a contract, but not others, also applies to a non-party who "steps into the shoes" of a party to the arbitration agreement because the non-party is the executor or receiver of the party's estate. Isp.com LLC. v. Theising, 805 N.E.2d 767 (Ind.2004); Briarcliff Nursing Home, Inc. v. Turcotte, 894 So.2d 661 (Ala.2004).

[50]   Fleetwood Enters., Inc. v. Gaskamp, 280 F.3d 1069 (5th Cir.2002); E.I. DuPont de Nemours & Co. v. Rhone Poulenc Fiber & Resin, 269 F.3d 187 (3d Cir.2001); Infiniti of Mobile, Inc. v. Office, 727 So.2d 42 (Ala.1999).

[51]   See § 32(a).

[52]   See, e.g., Fed.R.Civ.P. 14 (third-party practice), 19 (joinder of persons needed for just adjudication), 20 (permissive joinder of parties), 22 (interpleader), 23 (class actions), and 24 (intervention).

[53]   See § 3(a).

[54]   See § 3(b).

[55]   These facts are loosely based on Moses H. Cone Memorial Hospital v. Mercury Construction Corp., 460 U.S. 1 (1983).

defects are due to negligence by Architect in specifying the wrong materials, for example. Assume that either Architect or Contractor must be liable to Owner and the only question is to determine which one is liable.

Owner could pursue separate proceedings, suing Architect and asserting a claim in arbitration against Contractor. But this imposes on Owner the cost of two proceedings and the risk of inconsistent results. A court might rule for Architect on the belief that Contractor (who is not a party to the litigation) is liable, while the arbitrator might rule for Contractor on the belief that Architect (who is not a party to the arbitration) is liable. So Owner would lose both cases even though, as assumed above, one of the defendants must be liable to Owner.[56]

Under the FAA, Owner is stuck with these problems.[57] Owner may not compel the other two parties into a single proceeding. Owner may not compel Architect to arbitrate because Architect never agreed to arbitrate. And Owner may not compel Contractor to litigate because Contractor has a contractual right to arbitrate its disputes with Owner. The FAA "requires piecemeal resolution when necessary to give effect to an arbitration agreement."[58]

In contrast, Owner's situation is more favorable under the arbitration law of certain states, such as California. A California statute allows a court to refuse enforcement of an arbitration agreement if one of the parties to it is also a party to pending litigation with a third party arising out of the same transaction.[59] So

---

[56]   Owner is not saved from this result by ordinary principles of claim preclusion (*res judicata*) and issue preclusion (collateral estoppel) because preclusion may only be asserted against a party to the prior proceeding. See Jack H. Friedenthal, Mary Kay Kane & Arthur R. Miller, Civil Procedure § 14.14 (4th ed.2005). Contractor is not bound by the court's ruling because Contractor was not a party to the litigation. Architect is not bound by the arbitrator's ruling because Architect was not a party to the arbitration.

[57]   Moses H. Cone Memorial Hospital v. Mercury Construction Corp., 460 U.S. 1 (1983).

[58]   Id. at 20. The Court went on to say:

Under the Arbitration Act, an arbitration agreement must be enforced notwithstanding the presence of other persons who are parties to the underlying dispute but not to the arbitration agreement. If the dispute between [Contractor] and [Owner] is arbitrable under the Act, then [Owner's] two disputes will be resolved separately—one in arbitration, and the other (if at all) in state-court litigation.

Id. Accord Reliance Ins. Co. v. Raybestos Prods. Co., 382 F.3d 676 (7th Cir.2004)(insured had arbitration clause in contracts with some, but not all, of its insurers); MPACT Constr. Group v. Superior Concrete Constructors, Inc., 802 N.E.2d 901 (Ind.2004) (enforcing arbitration agreement between owner and contractor but refusing to force sub-contractors to arbitrate when they had not agreed to do so).

[59]   Cal.Civ.Proc.Code § 1281.2(c) (West 2007). This provision provides, in pertinent part, that when a court determines that

under California law, a court could order Contractor to litigate in one proceeding with Owner and Architect to prevent conflicting rulings.

Ordinarily, state law (such as California's) on consolidation is irrelevant because the FAA governs nearly all arbitration and preempts inconsistent state law.[60] But in *Volt Information Sciences, Inc. v. Board of Trustees of the Leland Stanford Junior University*,[61] the Supreme Court held that the parties were governed by California arbitration law, rather than the FAA, because of a provision in their agreement to that effect.[62]

If consolidation (of related cases only one of which is subject to arbitration) does not occur, the question arises which proceeding (arbitration or litigation) will reach a decision first.[63] The FAA does not directly address whether: (1) arbitration should be stayed until litigation concludes, (2) litigation should be stayed until arbitration concludes, or (3) neither should be stayed. The Supreme Court has

---

[a] party to the arbitration agreement is also a party to a pending court action or special proceeding with a third party, arising out of the same transaction or series of related transactions and there is a possibility of conflicting rulings on a common issue of law or fact [,] * * * the court (1) may refuse to enforce the arbitration agreement and may order intervention or joinder of all parties in a single action or special proceeding; (2) may order intervention or joinder as to all or only certain issues; (3) may order arbitration among the parties who have agreed to arbitration and stay the pending court action or special proceeding pending the outcome of the arbitration proceeding; or (4) may stay arbitration pending the outcome of the court action or special proceeding.

Id.

[60] Film Finances, Inc. v. Superior Court, 2002 WL 228205 (Cal.Ct.App.2002) (unpublished opinion). See generally §§ 6–14.

[61] 489 U.S. 468 (1989).

[62] See § 16. For more recent cases on whether choice-of-law clauses opt out of FAA preemption and into Cal.Civ.Proc.Code Ann. § 1281.2(c), compare Wolsey, Ltd. v. Foodmaker, Inc., 144 F.3d 1205 (9th Cir.1998)("we are bound by *Mastrobuono*, not by *Volt*. Because *Mastrobuono* dictates that general choice-of-law clauses do not incorporate state rules that govern the allocation of authority between courts and arbitrators, the district court erred in applying Cal.Civ.Proc.Code Ann. § 1281.2(c)"); Stone & Webster, Inc. v. Baker Process, Inc., 210 F.Supp.2d 1177 (S.D.Cal.2002)(general choice-of-law clause did not choose California over FAA); Nissan World, LLC v. Mkt. Scan Info. Sys., 2007 WL 1657350, at *5 (D.N.J.2007) ("this Court's decision as to whether the choice of law clause includes California arbitration law is not bound by Volt"); Olathe Senior Apts., LP v. Ace Fire Underwriters Ins. Co., 2005 WL 2416005, at *7 (D.Kan.2005) ("absent a provision that specifically provides that the California arbitration rules will govern the issues subject to arbitration, the court finds that the FAA controls and plaintiffs' claims . . . are subject to arbitration without application of the stay provisions in § 1281.2."), with Cronus Investments, Inc. v. Concierge Servs., 107 P.3d 217 (Cal.2005)(general choice-of-law clause did choose California over FAA); Security Ins.Co. of Hartford v. TIG Ins.Co., 360 F.3d 322, 326 (2d Cir.2004)(same); Mount Diablo Medical Center v. Health Net of California, Inc., 124 Cal.Rptr.2d 607 (Ct.App.2002) (same).

[63] The parties may care about this even when issues resolved in the first proceeding will not have preclusive effect on the second proceeding under the doctrine of collateral estoppel. See § 41.

not directly addressed this question. The Supreme Court has held, in a two-party dispute, that arbitrable claims should not be stayed until litigation of non-arbitrable claims concludes.[64] In a multi-party dispute, a stay of arbitration pending litigation might "violate[ ] the spirit if not the letter" of this holding.[65] In contrast, a California statute allows a court to stay arbitration until litigation concludes.[66]

§ 34 Class Actions

The previous section explained that rules of civil procedure encourage courts to join multiple parties in a single action because this tends to save time and money and helps to avoid inconsistent results.[67] Taking this reasoning further is the class action, which can effectively join millions of parties in one case. While class action litigation can be controversial, it is also widespread and well-established. By contrast, class action arbitration rests on a much less secure foundation.

Before the 21st Century, classwide arbitration was rare.[68] In 2003, though, the Supreme Court seemed to bless class arbitration in *Green Tree Financial Corp. v. Bazzle.*[69] The *Bazzle* case involved an

---

[64] See KPMG LLP v. Cocchi, 132 S.Ct. 23 (2011) (per curiam); Dean Witter Reynolds Inc. v. Byrd, 470 U.S. 213 (1985).

[65] Macneil, Speidel & Stipanowich, supra note 22, § 10.9.1, at 10:107. See AgGrow Oils, Inc. v. Nat. Union Fire Ins.Co., 242 F.3d 777 (8th Cir.2001)(district court should consider whether to stay litigation until completion of arbitration involving one of the parties to litigation).

> There is now arbitration pending, and it should be given priority to the extent it is likely to resolve issues material to this lawsuit. On the other hand, the lawsuit involves more parties and claims than the arbitration. In a complex, multi-party dispute of this type, issues such as the risk of inconsistent rulings, the extent to which parties will be bound by the arbitrators' decision, and the prejudice that may result from delays must be weighed in determining whether to grant a discretionary stay, and in fashioning the precise contours of any stay.

Id. at 783. Sunopta, Inc. v. Abengoa Bioenergy New Technologies, Inc., 2008 WL 782656, at *5–6 (E.D.Mo.2008) (staying litigation until completion of arbitration involving one of the parties to litigation).

[66] Cal.Civ.Proc.Code § 1281.2(c) (West 2007). This provision is quoted supra note 59.

[67] See § 33.

[68] Jean R. Sternlight, As Mandatory Binding Arbitration Meets the Class Action, Will the Class Action Survive?, 42 Wm. & Mary L.Rev. 1, 38 & n.135 (2000).

[69] 539 U.S. 444 (2003). *Bazzle* involved Green Tree's form consumer loan contract, which contained an arbitration clause. Id. at 447. Plaintiffs sued Green Tree in South Carolina state court and asked the court to certify a class action. Id. at 449. Green Tree sought to stay the court proceedings and compel arbitration. Id. The trial court both (1) certified a class action and (2) entered an order compelling arbitration. Id. Green Tree then selected an arbitrator with the plaintiffs' consent and the arbitrator, administering the proceeding as a class arbitration, awarded the class $10,935,000 in statutory damages, along with attorney's fees. Id. The trial court confirmed the award, and Green Tree appealed claiming, among other things, that class arbitration was legally impermissible. Id. On appeal, the South Carolina

arbitration agreement that neither permitted nor prohibited class arbitration, but rather was silent on that question. *Bazzle* decided that it was for the arbitrator, rather than a court, to interpret this silence,[70] and many arbitrators after *Bazzle* interpreted "silent" contracts to permit class arbitration.[71] Some of the major arbitration organizations developed special rules for handling the growing number of demands for class arbitration.[72]

This trend toward class arbitration began to reverse, however, with the Supreme Court's 2010 decision in *Stolt-Nielsen S.A. v. AnimalFeeds International Corp.*,[73] which interpreted arbitration agreement silence on class arbitration as a prohibition of it. While the arbitrators in *Stolt-Nielsen* "imposed class arbitration even though the parties concurred that they had reached 'no agreement' on that issue," the Court said "the differences between bilateral and class-action arbitration are too great for arbitrators to presume, consistent with their limited powers under the FAA, that the parties' mere silence on the issue of class-action arbitration constitutes consent to resolve their disputes in class proceedings."[74] The *Stolt-Nielsen* Court held that "a party may not be compelled under the FAA to submit to class arbitration unless there is a contractual basis for concluding that the party agreed to do so."[75]

Supreme Court held that the contracts were silent with respect to class arbitration, that they consequently authorized class arbitration, and that arbitration had properly taken that form. Id. at 450. The Supreme Court granted certiorari to consider whether that holding is consistent with the FAA. Id.

While three dissenting justices thought the arbitration clause prohibited class arbitration, id. at 458–59, the Court agreed with the South Carolina Supreme Court that the clause was silent on whether class arbitration was permitted. Id. at 450–51. Rather than affirming the South Carolina Supreme Court, however, the Court held that the arbitrator, rather than a court, should decide whether this silent contract should be interpreted to permit or prohibit class arbitration. Id. at 451–52. Therefore, the Court remanded for further proceedings. Id. at 454.

[70] See id.

[71] P. Christine Deruelle & Robert Clayton Roesch, Gaming the Rigged Class Arbitration Game: How We Got Here and Where We Go Now—Part I, Metropolitan Corp. Counsel, Aug. 2007, at 9 ("As of June 15, 2007, AAA arbitrators have rendered 51 Clause Construction Awards concerning otherwise silent arbitration agreements, and in all but two of those decisions, the arbitrators have allowed class wide proceedings.")

[72] Am.Arbitration Ass'n, AAA Policy on Class Arbitration (2005), available at https://www.adr.org/aaa/ShowPDF?doc=ADRSTG_003840 (last visited Jan. 24, 2016); JAMS, JAMS Class Action Procedures (2009), http://www.jamsadr.com/rules-class-action-procedures/ (last visited Dec. 13, 2010).

[73] 559 U.S. 662 (2010).

[74] Id. at 1775–76.

[75] Id. at 1775. For cases applying Stolt-Nielsen, see Oxford Health Plans LLC v. Sutter, 133 S.Ct. 2064, 2067 (2013) ("The parties agreed that the arbitrator should decide whether their contract authorized class arbitration, and he determined that it did."); In re Checking Account Overdraft Litig., 2010 WL 3361127, at *2 (S.D.Fla.Aug.23, 2010) ("Here, since the Agreement does not discuss class action

With *Stolt-Nielsen* interpreting arbitration agreement silence on class arbitration as a prohibition of it, both silent clauses and clauses expressly prohibiting class arbitration raise the same question: whether parties can use arbitration agreements to prevent all class actions, both litigation or arbitration. For many years, arbitration agreements' "class waivers" split state and lower federal courts. Some courts enforced arbitration agreements precluding both litigation and classwide arbitration, thus leaving only individual arbitration to resolve the claims,[76] while other courts refused, often on unconscionability grounds, to enforce such agreements.[77] For

---

arbitration, the parties did not agree to submit to class action arbitration. * * * Plaintiff must proceed to arbitration as an individual."); Jock v. Sterling Jewelers, Inc., 2010 WL 2898294, at *4 (S.D.N.Y.July 26, 2010) (vacating arbitration award that "started from the premise that an arbitration clause silent on class arbitration may be construed to permit such arbitration"). However, parties in some cases may not agree on whether the agreement is, in fact, silent. See Fisher v. Gen. Steel Domestic Sales, LLC, 2010 WL 3791181, at *3 (D.Colo.2010) (distinguishing *Stolt-Nielsen* because these parties contested whether the agreement was silent).

76   Jenkins v. First Am. Cash Advance of Ga., LLC, 400 F.3d 868, 877–78 (11th Cir. 2005); Johnson v. West Suburban Bank, 225 F.3d 366, 373–74 (3rd Cir.2000); Livingston v. Associates Fin., Inc., 339 F.3d 553, 557 (7th Cir.2003); Snowden v. Checkpoint Check Cashing, 290 F.3d 631, 638 (4th Cir. 2002); Borrero v. Travelers Indem. Co., 2010 WL 4054114, at *1 (E.D.Cal.2010); Green v. SuperShuttle Intern., Inc., 2010 WL 3702592, at *3 (D.Minn.2010); Johnson v. Carmax, Inc., 2010 WL 2802478, at *3–4 (E.D.Va.2010) Sanders v. Comcast Cable Holdings, LLC, 2008 WL 150479, at *10 (M.D.Fla.2008); Jackson v. Payday Loan Store of Ill., Inc., 2010 WL 1031590, at *5 (N.D.Ill.2010); Deaton v. Overstock.com, Inc., 2007 WL 4569874, at *3 (S.D.Ill.2007); Med Center Cars, Inc. v. Smith, 727 So.2d 9, 20 (Ala.1998); Maiorano v. Prof'l Cmty. Mgmt., Inc., 2010 WL 3786721, at *2 (Cal.App.Dep't Super.Ct.2010); Rains v. Foundation Health Systems Life & Health, 23 P.3d 1249, 1253 (Colo.App.2001); Edelist v. MBNA Am. Bank, 790 A.2d 1249, 1260–61 (Del.Super.Ct.2001); Walther v. Sovereign Bank, 872 A.2d 735, 750 (Md.Ct.App.2005); Gras v. Associates First Capital Corp., 786 A.2d 886, 892 (N.J.Super.Ct.App.Div.2001); Ranieri v. Bell Atlantic Mobile, 759 N.Y.S.2d 448 (2003); Strand v. U.S. Bank Nat. Ass'n ND, 693 N.W.2d 918 (N.D. 2005); Autonation USA Corp. v. Leroy, 105 S.W.3d 190, 201 (Tex.App.2003); Bandler v. Charter One Bank, 2010 WL 3617115 (Super.Ct.Vt.2010). See also Utah Code Ann. § 70C–4–105(1) (West Supp.2009) (stating that "a creditor may contract with the debtor of an open-end consumer credit contract for a waiver by the debtor of the right to initiate or participate in a class action related to the open-end consumer credit contract.").

77   Dale v. Comcast Corp., 498 F.3d 1216 (11th Cir.2007); Ting v. AT & T, 319 F.3d 1126, 1150 (9th Cir. 2003); Ingle v. Circuit City Stores, Inc., 328 F.3d 1165 (9th Cir. 2003); Omstead v. Dell, Inc., 594 F.3d 1081 (9th Cir.2010); Jones v. DirecTV, Inc., 667 F.Supp.2d 1379 (N.D.Ga.2009); Knepp v. Credit Acceptance Corp. (In re Knepp), 229 B.R. 821, 842 (Bankr. N.D. Ala. 1999); Discover Bank v. Superior Court, 30 Cal.Rptr.3d 76 (Cal.2005); Armendariz v. Foundation Health Psychcare Services, Inc., 99 Cal.Rptr.2d 745 (Cal.2000); Cohen v. DirecTV, Inc., 48 Cal.Rptr.3d 813 (Ct.App.2006); Aral v. EarthLink, Inc., 36 Cal.Rptr.3d 229 (Ct.App.2005); Muhammad v. County Bank of Rehoboth Beach, 2006 WL 2273448 (N.J.2006); Powertel v. Bexley, 743 So.2d 570 (Fla.App.1999); Whitney v. Alltel Communications, Inc., 173 S.W.3d 300 (Mo.App.2005); Kinkel v. Cingular Wireless, LLC, 828 N.E.2d 812, 820 (Ill.App.2005); Leonard v. Terminix International Company, LP, 854 So.2d 529, 538–39 (Ala. 2003); Williams v. Aetna Fin. Co., 700 N.E.2d 859, 866–67 (Ohio 1998); State of West Virginia ex rel. Dunlap v. Berger, 567 S.E.2d 265 (W.Va. 2002).

instance, in *Discover Bank v. Superior Court*,[78] the California Supreme Court said:

> We do not hold that all class action waivers are necessarily unconscionable. But when the waiver is found in a consumer contract of adhesion in a setting in which disputes between the contracting parties predictably involve small amounts of damages, and when it is alleged that the party with the superior bargaining power has carried out a scheme to deliberately cheat large numbers of consumers out of individually small sums of money, then, at least to the extent the obligation at issue is governed by California law, the waiver becomes in practice the exemption of the party "from responsibility for [its] own fraud, or willful injury to the person or property of another." (Civ.Code, § 1668.) Under these circumstances, such waivers are unconscionable under California law and should not be enforced.[79]

This "*Discover Bank* rule is preempted by the FAA," according to the 2011 U.S. Supreme Court decision in *AT & T Mobility LLC v. Concepcion*.[80] The *AT & T* case involved a federal court's application of the *Discover Bank* rule to hold unconscionable an arbitration clause in a cell phone contract. The Ninth Circuit held that the *Discover Bank* rule was not preempted by the FAA because that rule was simply "a refinement of the unconscionability analysis applicable to contracts generally in California,"[81] and thus fell within the savings clause at the end of FAA § 2, which states that arbitration agreements "shall be valid, irrevocable, and enforceable, save upon such grounds as exist at law or in equity for the revocation of any contract."[82]

The Supreme Court's majority[83] disagreed. It said "[t]he overarching purpose of the FAA, evident in the text of §§ 2, 3, and 4, is to ensure the enforcement of arbitration agreements according to their terms so as to facilitate streamlined proceedings."[84] The Court's reasoning built on this premise that an important purpose of the FAA was to enforce agreements in which parties choose the more

---

[78]   30 Cal.Rptr.3d 76 (Cal.2005).

[79]   Id. at 87.

[80]   563 U.S. 333 (2011).

[81]   Laster v. AT & T Mobility LLC, 584 F.3d 849, 857 (9th Cir.2009).

[82]   9 U.S.C. § 2.

[83]   Four justices joined the opinion with Justice Thomas concurring in the result. AT & T Mobility LLC v. Concepcion, 563 U.S. 333, 343 (2011). (Thomas, J., concurring). (FAA § 2 "does not include all defenses applicable to any contract but rather some subset of those defenses").

[84]   Id. at 1748.

streamlined process (arbitration) over the more elaborate process (litigation). The Court suggested that the FAA would preempt (hypothetical) state law deeming unconscionable arbitration agreements lacking "judicially monitored discovery,"[85] "adherence to the Federal Rules of Evidence,"[86] or "arbitration-by-jury"[87] because requiring arbitration to include these aspects of litigation would effectively convert the more streamlined process into the more elaborate process so it would no longer be "arbitration," as that process was envisioned by those who enacted the FAA.[88] Similarly, the Court concluded "Requiring the availability of classwide arbitration interferes with fundamental attributes of arbitration and thus creates a scheme inconsistent with the FAA."[89] Quoting its decision in *Stolt-Nielsen*, the *AT & T* Court said:

> "[C]hanges brought about by the shift from bilateral arbitration to class-action arbitration" are "fundamental." * * * The conclusion follows that class arbitration, to the extent it is manufactured by *Discover Bank* rather than consensual, is inconsistent with the FAA.
>
> First, the switch from bilateral to class arbitration sacrifices the principal advantage of arbitration—its informality—and makes the process slower, more costly, and more likely to generate procedural morass than final judgment. * * *
>
> * * *
>
> Second, class arbitration requires procedural formality. The AAA's rules governing class arbitrations mimic the Federal Rules of Civil Procedure for class litigation. * * *
>
> [I]t is at the very least odd to think that an arbitrator would be entrusted with ensuring that third parties' due process rights are satisfied.

---

[85]   Id. at 1748.

[86]   Id.

[87]   Id. at 1751, n.7.

[88]   In fact, arbitration is generally less elaborate than litigation; arbitration agreements commonly provide for less discovery and motion practice than is typical of litigation and commonly provide for fewer rules of evidence than are typical of litigation. But the parties are free to draft their agreement almost any way they like. See § 36–37. The *AT & T* Court said that "Parties could agree to arbitrate pursuant to the Federal Rules of Civil Procedure, or pursuant to a discovery process rivaling that in litigation. Arbitration is a matter of contract, and the FAA requires courts to honor parties' expectations. * * * But what the parties in the aforementioned examples would have agreed to is not arbitration as envisioned by the FAA, lacks its benefits, and therefore may not be required by state law." 563 U.S. 333 (2011).

[89]   Id. at 1748.

* * *

Third, class arbitration greatly increases risks to defendants. Informal procedures do of course have a cost: The absence of multilayered review makes it more likely that errors will go uncorrected. * * *

* * * We find it hard to believe that defendants would bet the company with no effective means of review, and even harder to believe that Congress would have intended to allow state courts to force such a decision.[90]

In sum, *AT & T* and *Stolt-Nielsen* see "bilateral" arbitration—the simple type of arbitration contemplated by the FAA—as the norm, and see class arbitration as a strange process that a few parties might choose, but which should not be imposed on parties who have agreed to arbitrate without specifically addressing class arbitration. And *AT & T* strongly suggests that courts may not consider it a strike against the enforceability of an arbitration agreement that the agreement provides only for arbitration, and not for class arbitration. *AT & T* reads the FAA as preempting state law—even state law categorized as "unconscionability" or some other ground for the revocation of any contract—that "[r]equir[es] the availability of classwide arbitration."[91]

However, the Securities Exchange Commission prohibits agreements forbidding both class arbitration and class litigation, so such agreements are not enforceable in securities brokers' contracts with their customers and employees.[92] The Consumer Financial

---

[90] Id. at 1750–52.

[91] Id. at 1748. See also American Express Co. v. Italian Colors Restaurant, 133 S.Ct. 2304 (2013). Shortly after *AT & T*, the Supreme Court vacated the judgments of lower courts that had found arbitration agreement class waivers unconscionable and had then permitted class litigation. Fensterstock v. Educ. Fin. Partners, 611 F.3d 124, 141 (2d Cir.2010) (concluding that the arbitration agreement was unconscionable and that, under Stolt, the court could not force class arbitration when the arbitration agreement was silent), cert. granted, judgment vacated, Affiliated Computer Services, Inc. v. Fensterstock, 564 U.S. 1001 (2011) (NO. 10–987); Brewer v. Missouri Title Loan, Inc., 323 S.W.3d 18 (Mo.Aug.31, 2010) (striking a consumer title loan class arbitration waiver and the arbitration agreement requiring arbitration on an individual basis, leaving the consumer with the option of bringing a class action in court), cert. granted, judgment vacated, Missouri Title Loans, Inc. v. Brewer, 561 U.S. 1001 (U.S.Mo. 2011) (NO. 10–1027). For post-*AT & T* cases, see Noohi v. Toll Bros., Inc., 708 F.3d 599, 606–07 (4th Cir.2013) (*AT & T* "prohibited courts from altering otherwise valid arbitration agreements by applying the doctrine of unconscionability to eliminate a term barring classwide procedures."); Coneff v. AT & T Corp., 673 F.3d 1155 (9th Cir.2012) (FAA preempts Washington state law invalidating class-action waiver as substantively unconscionable).

[92] See FINRA Rule 13204.

Protection Bureau seeks a similar prohibition for agreements within its jurisdiction.[93]

3. ARBITRATION PROCEDURE
Table of Sections

---

[93]   "Today the Consumer Financial Protection Bureau (CFPB) announced it is considering proposing rules that would ban consumer financial companies from using 'free pass' arbitration clauses to block consumers from suing in groups to obtain relief." CFPB Considers Proposal to Ban Arbitration Clauses that Allow Companies to Avoid Accountability to Their Customers, Oct. 7, 2015. http://www.consumerfinance.gov/newsroom/cfpb-considers-proposal-to-ban-arbitration-clauses-that-allow-companies-to-avoid-accountability-to-their-customers/

§ 35 Overview

Arbitration, like any *adjudication*,[94] involves the presentation of evidence and argument to the adjudicator. The presentation of evidence and argument in litigation is governed by rules of procedure and evidence enacted by government. In contrast, the rules of procedure and evidence in arbitration are, with few exceptions, whatever the parties' arbitration agreement says they are. The procedures of arbitration are largely determined by contract. According to the Supreme Court,

> The point of affording parties discretion in designing arbitration processes is to allow for efficient, streamlined procedures tailored to the type of dispute. It can be specified, for example, that the decisionmaker be a specialist in the relevant field, or that proceedings be kept confidential to protect trade secrets. And the informality of arbitral proceedings is itself desirable, reducing the cost and increasing the speed of dispute resolution.[95]

Arbitration is generally less elaborate than litigation; arbitration agreements commonly provide for less discovery and motion practice than is typical of litigation, and commonly provide for fewer rules of evidence than are typical of litigation. But the parties are free to draft their agreement almost any way they like. Arbitration privatizes procedural law by allowing parties to create their own customized rules of procedure and evidence.

There are, however, limits on the parties' freedom of contract. If the arbitration occurs and does not meet a court's definition of a "fundamentally fair hearing" then the court will grant a motion to vacate the arbitration award.[96] Also, courts have refused to send employment and consumer disputes to arbitration when persuaded that the agreed-upon procedures for arbitration would have been unfair. These cases rest on contract law's unconscionability doctrine,[97] or special concerns regarding the vindication of federal statutory rights.[98] For example, an oft-cited case is *Cole v. Burns Int'l Security Services*,[99] enforced an employee's agreement to arbitrate statutory employment discrimination claims, but only because:

---

[94] See Stephen J. Ware, Principles of Alternative Dispute Resolution § 1.5(a) (3d ed.2016).

[95] AT & T Mobility LLC v. Concepcion, 563 U.S. 333, 343 (2011).

[96] See § 43(c).

[97] See § 25.

[98] See § 28.

[99] 105 F.3d 1465 (D.C.Cir.1997).

the arbitration arrangement (1) provides for neutral arbitrators, (2) provides for more than minimal discovery, (3) requires a written award, (4) provides for all of the types of relief that would otherwise be available in court, and (5) does not require employees to pay either unreasonable costs or any arbitrators' fees or expenses as a condition of access to the arbitration forum.[100]

While other courts use different words, the substance of this list is generally typical. The more of these five factors that are present, the more likely a court is to enforce the arbitration agreement.

These five factors, along with other aspects of arbitration procedure, are discussed in the following three sections.

§ 36   Pre-Hearing

(a) Selection of Arbitrator(s)

(1)   Methods of Selection

Arbitration requires at least one arbitrator. Selection of the arbitrator or arbitrators typically occurs through agreement of the parties. If the parties cannot agree on an arbitrator, however, the court will appoint one. The FAA gives courts the authority to do so:

> If in the agreement provision be made for a method of naming or appointing an arbitrator or arbitrators or an umpire, such method shall be followed; but if no method be provided therein, or if a method be provided and any party thereto shall fail to avail himself of such method, or if for any other reason there shall be a lapse in the naming of an arbitrator or arbitrators or umpire, or in filling a vacancy, then upon the application of either party to the controversy the court shall designate and appoint an arbitrator or arbitrators or umpire, as the case may require, who shall act under the said agreement with the same force and effect as if he or they had been specifically named therein; and unless otherwise provided in the agreement the arbitration shall be by a single arbitrator.[101]

Many states have similar provisions.[102] Court appointment of an arbitrator is rarely necessary because the parties usually agree on an arbitrator.

---

[100]   Id. at 1482 (quoting Gilmer v. Interstate/Johnson Lane Corp., 500 U.S. 20, 28 (1991)).

[101]   9 U.S.C. § 5. See, e.g., Astra Footwear Indus. v. Harwyn Int'l, Inc., 442 F.Supp. 907 (S.D.N.Y.1978).

[102]   Unif. Arbitration Act § 11 (2000); NY C.P.L.R. 7504 (CONSOL.2012).

Agreements for selecting an arbitrator fall into three categories. First, the parties can name an arbitrator (*e.g.*, "Donald Salvia") in their arbitration agreement. While this is fairly common in post-dispute arbitration agreements,[103] it is rare in pre-dispute arbitration agreements. At the time a pre-dispute agreement is formed, the parties probably hope and expect that no dispute will ever occur. Why take the time to negotiate agreement on who the arbitrator should be when arbitration is so unlikely? Even if the parties consider the possibility of a dispute, they do not know what that dispute will involve. Maybe Donald Salvia would be the best arbitrator for one sort of dispute but not for another. Finally, at the time a pre-dispute agreement is formed, the parties do not know *when* a dispute will occur. Perhaps by then, Donald Salvia will be unavailable or unwilling to serve as an arbitrator. For all these reasons, pre-dispute agreements rarely name an arbitrator.

What pre-dispute agreements typically do is specify a procedure for selecting an arbitrator. Many pre-dispute agreements commit the parties to arbitrate according to the rules of an arbitration organization, like the American Arbitration Association ("AAA"). AAA rules, like the rules of other arbitration organizations, contain procedures for selecting an arbitrator. The AAA Commercial Arbitration Rules serve as an example.

Under its Commercial Rules, the AAA sends the parties a list of ten potential arbitrators with some information about each person.[104] Then each party can strike the potential arbitrators to which that party objects.[105] Each party also ranks the remaining people in order of that party's preference.[106] The AAA invites those people with the highest combined ranking to serve as arbitrators.[107] If this process does not produce an arbitrator willing to serve then the AAA picks an arbitrator.[108]

An alternative to using the rules of an arbitration organization for selecting arbitrators is to agree to *tripartite* arbitration. The agreement specifies that there will be three arbitrators: each party picks one arbitrator and those two arbitrators agree on the third.[109]

---

[103] See e.g., Smith v. DHL Express (USA) Inc., 2005 WL 3111013 (N.D.Cal.2005); DeOliveira v. Liberty Mutual Ins.Co., 2003 WL 21101303 (Conn.2003).

[104] Am.Arbitration Ass'n, Commercial Arbitration Rules, R–12(a) (2013).

[105] Id., R–11(b).

[106] Id.

[107] Id.

[108] Id.

[109] See, e.g., Delta Mine Holding Co. v. AFC Coal Properties, Inc., 280 F.3d 815, 817 (8th Cir.2002)("Paragraph 8.2 provided that disputes over this provision were subject to arbitration by a panel of three arbitrators, one selected by Delta Mine, one by AFC, 'and a third selected by the other two arbitrators in accordance with the then

Tripartite arbitration, which also occurs under the auspices of arbitration organizations,[110] raises legal and ethical issues, addressed below, about the extent to which the party-appointed arbitrator may be partial, rather than neutral.[111] In some circumstances the party-appointed arbitrators are expected to be neutral; in other, they function as partisans, representing the interests of the party that appointed them. Because additional arbitrators tend to make arbitration more expensive and slower, tripartite arbitration is normally used only in high-value disputes.

Nearly all arbitrations have either one or three arbitrators, or more rarely five, but any number is possible.

(2) Arbitrator Fees

Arbitrators are normally paid market rates for their work.[112] Some arbitrators get paid a lot. One thousand dollars per day is common and some arbitrators earn much more than that.[113] Particularly in high-dollar cases, disputing parties are willing to pay high arbitrator fees to get high-quality arbitrators. But few arbitrators outside the labor context are in such demand that they can make a living arbitrating. Even well-respected arbitrators may be asked to arbitrate only one or two cases a year. Most arbitrators have full-time jobs and arbitrate only as a sideline.

Labor arbitration is a distinct and quite different market. Because almost all collective bargaining agreements include arbitration clauses, the nation's 15 million unionized workers

---

applicable rules of the American Arbitration Association.' "); U.S. Life Ins. Co. v. Superior Nat. Ins. Co., 591 F.3d 1167, 1170–71 (9th Cir.2010)(arbitration panel "consisted of an arbitrator appointed by each party and a neutral arbitrator selected by the parties' arbitrators").

[110]   See, e.g., Am.Arbitration Ass'n, Commercial Arbitration Rules, R–16 (2013).

[111]   See § 43(b). See also David J. McLean & Sean-Patrick Wilson, Is Three a Crowd? Neutrality, Partiality and Partisanship in the Context of Tripartite Arbitrations, 9 Pepp.Disp.Resol.L.J. 167 (2008).

[112]   In contrast, some arbitrators provide their services on a pro bono basis as a way of serving others. These volunteer arbitrators range from merchant members of a trade association (who arbitrate disputes among members of that association) to a local lawyer who arbitrates consumer disputes for the Better Business Bureau. See Sasha A. Carbone & Jeffrey T. Zaino, Increasing Diversity Among Arbitrators, 84 N.Y.St.B.J. 33 (2012) ("Getting the first arbitration case can be difficult for the new practitioner, but there are opportunities to serve on a pro bono basis or on reduced fee cases that may provide future opportunities."); Samuel Estreicher & Matt Ballard, Affordable Justice Through Arbitration, 57 Disp.Resol.J. 8, 11 (2003) ("[T]he AAA has formalized the process for a claimant to receive a waiver or deferral of the AAA administration fee based on financial hardship. And now it has a roster of over 3,000 arbitrators who have volunteered to serve pro bono where an individual would otherwise be financially unable to pursue his or her rights in the arbitral forum.")

[113]   See, e.g., Eric Berkowitz, Is Justice Served?, L.A. Times Mag., Oct. 22, 2006 (one arbitrator charges $7500 per day).

produce enough grievances to make it possible for experienced labor arbitrators to make a full-time career out of arbitrating.[114]

In many contexts, the parties agree that the arbitrator's fee will be split equally between the parties.[115] In some cases, however, courts refuse to enforce consumer and employment arbitration agreements unless the business or employer relieves the consumer or employee of any obligation to pay significant arbitrator fees.[116]

(3) Judicial and Regulatory Constraints on Party Selection of Arbitrator(s)

Courts place limits on the arbitrators the parties may select. Courts place these limits in two ways. First, courts have refused to enforce arbitration awards on the ground that the parties (perhaps unknowingly) selected an arbitrator who had a previous relationship with one of the parties. This topic, discussed in a later section,[117] is a judicial limit on the arbitrators the parties may select for legally-binding arbitration insofar as it denies legal force to their choice to have their dispute resolved by certain arbitrators.

Second, courts have refused to enforce executory arbitration agreements when dissatisfied with the agreement's method of selecting an arbitrator. This is a distinct possibility when parties to a take-it-or-leave-it form contract select an arbitrator closely connected to the party drafting the contract. Some drafting parties even write contracts that reserve to themselves complete discretion over the selection of the arbitrator.[118] Only slightly less one-sided are

---

[114] The National Association of Arbitrators' membership consists of about 600 individuals who arbitrate the majority of labor arbitration cases. Dennis R. Nolan, Labor and Employment Arbitration in a Nutshell 24–25 (2007).

[115] Linda J. Demaine & Deborah R. Hensler, "Volunteering" to Arbitrate Through Predispute Arbitration Clauses: The Average Consumer's Experience, 67 Law & Contemp. Probs. 55, 70 (2004) (of a sample of arbitration clauses in consumer contracts, "[t]he most common overarching rule (found in thirteen of the thirty clauses that mention expenses) is that the parties will divide the expenses of arbitration equally."); Andrew Kramer, et al., Mandatory Arbitration as an Alternative Method of Resolving Workplace Disputes, 1999 ALI-ABA Course of Study: Hot Issues in Employment and Litigation 177, 216 (There is a "nearly universal custom" in favor of equal cost-splitting).

[116] See § 25(a).

[117] See § 43(b).

[118] Compare Murray v. United Food and Commercial Workers Intern.Union, 289 F.3d 297 (4th Cir.2002)(employment arbitration agreement unconscionable, where, though the parties ostensibly engaged in an alternate strike method to select the single arbitrator from a list of prospective arbitrators, they were to exercise these alternate strikes from a list of arbitrators provided by the employer); Hooters of America, Inc. v. Phillips, 173 F.3d 933, 938–39 (4th Cir.1999)(decided under duty of good faith and fair dealing, rather than unconscionability); Ditto v. Re/Max Preferred Properties, Inc., 861 P.2d 1000, 1004 (Okla.App.1993)(independent contractor's arbitration agreement was unconscionable because it "would exclude [her] from any voice in selection of the arbitrators."); Rodriguez v. Windermere Real Estate/Wall Street, Inc., 175 P.3d 604,

agreements naming a close affiliate of the drafting party to be the arbitrator.[119] More debatable are agreements requiring the arbitrators to share a profession or membership in an organization with the drafting party. As Judge Easterbrook wrote for the Seventh Circuit:

> Industry arbitration, the modern law merchant, often uses panels composed of industry insiders, the better to understand the trade's norms of doing business and the consequences of proposed lines of decision. See Lisa Bernstein, Private Commercial Law in the Cotton Industry: Creating Cooperation Through Rules, Norms, and Institutions, 99 Mich.L.Rev. 1724, 1728 (2001). The more experience the [arbitration] panel has, and the smaller the number of repeat players, the more likely it is that the panel will contain some actual or potential friends, counselors, or business rivals of the parties. Yet all participants may think the expertise-impartiality tradeoff worthwhile; the Arbitration Act does not fasten on every industry the model of the disinterested generalist judge.[120]

Other courts may be less deferential to party autonomy in making that "expertise-impartiality tradeoff," especially in contracts of adhesion.[121]

---

607 (Wash.App.2008) (same), with Greenwald v. Weisbaum, 785 N.Y.S.2d 664 (N.Y.2004)(Arbitration provision of accounting firm's partnership agreement, which required that arbitration panel be comprised exclusively of partners and members of firm's board of directors, did not create situation in which one of parties to dispute adjudicated its own cause, so as to make provision invalid and unenforceable); Hottle v. BDO Seidman LLP, 846 A.2d 862 (Conn.2004).

119   See, e.g., Sehulster Tunnels/Pre-Con v. Traylor Brothers, Inc./Obayashi Corp., 4 Cal.Rptr.3d 655 (Ct.App.2003); Graham v. Scissor Tail, Inc., 171 Cal.Rptr. 604 (Cal.1981) (refusing to enforce arbitration agreement between musician and concert promoter where agreement named musician's union as arbitrator). For a more subtle fact pattern in which the party drafting the agreement encouraged the non-drafting party to select among arbitrators who attended an "orientation" conducted by the drafting party, see Pokorny v. Quixtar, Inc., 601 F.3d 987, 1002–03 (9th Cir.2010).

120   Sphere Drake Ins. Ltd. v. All Am. Life Ins. Co., 307 F.3d 617, 620 (7th Cir.2002).

121   For example, the drafting party in Broemmer v. Abortion Services of Phoenix, Ltd., 840 P.2d 1013 (Ariz.1992), was an abortion clinic. The court did not enforce the arbitration clause requiring arbitration before "licensed medical doctors who specialize in obstetrics/gynecology." Id. at 104. *Compare* State ex rel. Vincent v. Schneider, 194 S.W.3d 853, 859 (Mo.2006) (holding unconscionable provision stating that "the arbitrator shall be selected by the President of the Homebuilders Association of Greater St. Louis"), with Lynes v. Calcagni Associates, 2006 WL 894913 (Conn.Super.2006) (enforcing clause providing that "If any dispute arises out of or in connection with this Agreement * * * such dispute shall be submitted to arbitration * * *. Only licensed architects, home inspectors, ASHI members, engineers or professional contractors will be eligible to serve as an arbitrator."); Brown v. Wells Fargo Bank, NA, 85 Cal.Rptr.3d 817, 832 (Ct.App.2008) (rejecting investors' argument that National Association of Securities Dealers "arbitration is substantively

Courts are no longer the only branch of government to regulate arbitrators. By statute, California now requires extensive disclosures by neutral arbitrators of potential conflicts of interest,[122] and California statutes regulate organizations that administer consumer arbitrations.[123] California even has a statute responding to the phenomenon of judges, still on the bench, talking with arbitration organizations about becoming arbitrators after the judge leaves the bench.[124] All of these statutes are, among other things, limits on the arbitrators certain parties may select for legally-binding arbitration insofar as they deny legal force to the parties' pre-dispute choice to have their dispute resolved by certain arbitrators.

(b) Pleadings

Litigation generally begins with a complaint filed and served by the plaintiff, followed by an answer filed and served by the defendant. Arbitration is analogous but the terminology may be different. Arbitration typically begins with a *demand* for arbitration filed and served by the *claimant*, followed by an answer filed and served by the *respondent*. However, respondents seem to omit answers more often in arbitration than in litigation. Perhaps that is because in litigation

---

unconscionable because under the NASD Code, a minority of arbitrators may be affiliated with the securities industry").

[122] Cal.Civ.Proc.Code §§ 1281.9, 1281.91 (West 2007). At least some of these statutory rules have been interpreted to override contrary language in the arbitration agreement or applicable arbitration organization rules. Azteca Const., Inc. v. ADR Consulting, Inc., 18 Cal.Rptr.3d 142 (Ct.App.2004) (statute permitting party uncomfortable with the disclosures of any proposed arbitrator to disqualify him or her within 15 days overrides AAA rule giving AAA sole power to disqualify arbitrator). See also Judicial Council of California, Ethics Standards for Neutral Arbitrators in Contractual Arbitration (Jan. 1, 2016), available at http://www.courts.ca.gov/26582. htm. Courts have held that these state standards, as applied in securities arbitrations, are preempted by the federal securities laws. Credit Suisse First Boston Corp. v. Grunwald, 400 F.3d 1119 (9th Cir.2005); Jevne v. Superior Court, 111 P.3d 954 (Cal.2005).

[123] Cal.Civ.Proc.Code § 1281.92 (prohibiting private arbitration companies from administering consumer arbitrations for parties in which they have financial interest); id. § 1281.96 (requiring disclosures by private arbitration companies administering consumer arbitrations); id. § 1284.3 (regulating fees charged in consumer arbitrations).

Some of these state statutes may be preempted by the FAA. Compare Arbitration between Lemoine Skinner III v. Donaldson, Lufkin & Jenrette, 2003 WL 23174478, at *8–9 (N.D.Cal.Dec.29, 2003) (FAA preempts Cal.Civ.Proc.Code 1281.92(b) to the extent it creates a ground, not found in the FAA, for vacating an arbitration award), with Ovitz v. Schulman, 35 Cal.Rptr.3d 117, 130–32 (Cal.App.2005)(rejecting FAA preemption challenge to Cal.Civ.Proc.Code 1286.2(a)(6)(A), which requires vacatur for arbitrator's failure to comply with state disclosure requirements). See § 44(d).

[124] Cal.Civ.Proc.Code § 170.1(a)(8) (West 2006).

not answering a claim typically has the effect of admitting it,[125] while under many arbitration rules a claim not answered is denied.[126]

Omitting answers is one way arbitration can be less elaborate than litigation. Another way is that arbitration complaints tend to be more concise and less legalistic than complaints in litigation.[127] An arbitration complaint typically includes only basic factual allegations, the nature or source of the claims and defenses, the remedies sought, and the adjudicator's jurisdiction.[128] While a court's jurisdiction is often shown by citing a statute, the arbitrator's jurisdiction is shown by the agreement to arbitrate.[129]

(c) Filing Fees (and Un-Administered Arbitration)

In litigation, parties do not pay the judge directly and generally pay small court fees insufficient to cover the full cost of the judge, jury, court clerk, other administrative personnel, and the courthouse itself. By contrast, parties to arbitration generally must pay in full the analogous costs: the arbitrator's fee and the administrative costs of the arbitration organization and any cost of the hearing room. Most arbitration is administered by an organization, such as the American Arbitration Association. The administering organization generally charges the parties an arbitrator's fee (which the organization pays

---

[125] Fed.R.Civ.P. 8(b)(6) ("An allegation—other than one relating to the amount of damages—is admitted if a responsive pleading is required and the allegation is not denied."); Fed.R.Civ.P. 12(a)(1)(A)(i) (defendant must serve an answer within 21 days after being served with the summons and complaint).

[126] See, e.g., Am. Arb. Ass'n, Commercial Arbitration Rules, R–4(c) ("If no answering statement is filed within the stated time, respondent will be deemed to deny the claim. Failure to file an answering statement shall not operate to delay the arbitration.")

[127] Richard Chernick, et al., How to Conduct a Complex Financial Arbitration Part 1: Matters To Consider Prior to the Hearings, 1440 Practicing Law Institute Corporate Law and Practice Course Handbook 453, 456 (2004) ("A statement of Claim or Demand for Arbitration is a far different document than a Complaint in litigation. A claim is much more informal than a pleading and is usually much shorter. There are virtually no 'rules of pleading' in arbitration [and] technical pleading rules need not be followed.")

[128] See, e.g., Am. Arb. Ass'n, Commercial Arbitration Rules, R–4(a)(i).

> The initiating party (the "claimant") shall, within the time period, if any, specified in the contract(s), give to the other party (the "respondent") written notice of its intention to arbitrate (the "demand"), which demand shall contain a statement setting forth the nature of the dispute, the names and addresses of all other parties, the amount involved, if any, the remedy sought, and the hearing locale requested.

Id.

[129] See, e.g., id. R–4(a)(ii) ("The claimant shall file at any office of the AAA two copies of the demand and two copies of the arbitration provisions of the contract, together with the appropriate filing fee as provided in the schedule included with these rules.")

to the arbitrator) and a separate administrative fee, which the organization keeps.

Parties can arbitrate without an arbitration organization. This un-administered arbitration saves the parties from paying the fees of an arbitration organization. But it also requires the parties to agree on their own to an arbitrator and to conduct the arbitration with the help of only the arbitrator. That requires the arbitrator to perform administrative tasks that an organization would otherwise handle. Because the arbitrator's hourly rate may be high,[130] the parties may find it cheaper to pay the fees of an arbitration organization.

Arbitration organization fees, like court filing fees, are generally imposed at the time a case is filed. Arbitration filing fees vary widely and often depend on the size of the case, as measured by the remedy sought by the claimant.[131] Filing fees required of consumers in small arbitrations are generally modest, usually no more than a court fee.[132] In contrast, filing fees for larger commercial cases can run into the thousands of dollars, far exceeding court fees.[133] And after the initial filing fee additional administrative fees (along with an arbitrator's fee) may be required of the parties to hold a hearing or otherwise complete the arbitration.[134] In short, arbitration organizations and arbitrators generally receive higher payments from parties who require more work by the arbitration organization and arbitrator, while courts generally charge parties who consume a lot of the court system's resources about the same as parties who consume little of those resources.

(d) Discovery

"Limitations on discovery, particularly judicially initiated discovery, remain one of the hallmarks of American commercial

---

[130] See § 36(a)(2).

[131] See, e.g., Am.Arbitration Ass'n, Commercial Arbitration Rules, Administrative Fee Schedules (2015), available at http://www.adr.org/feeschedule.

[132] "Under the AAA's rules, the business is responsible for paying all the administrative fees and the remaining arbitrator's fees for small consumer claims, both for claims brought by the consumer as well as claims brought by the business." Christopher R. Drahozal & Samantha Zyontz, An Empirical Study of AAA Consumer Arbitrations, 25 Ohio St. J.on Disp.Resol. 843, 864 (2010). "In cases with claims seeking less than $10,000, consumer claimants paid an average of $96 ($1 administrative fees + $95 arbitrator fees)." Id. at 845. See also Am.Arbitration Ass'n, Consumer Arbitration Rules (2014).

[133] See, e.g., Am.Arbitration Ass'n, Commercial Arbitration Rules, Administrative Fee Schedules (2015).

[134] See, e.g., Am.Arbitration Ass'n, Commercial Arbitration Rules, Administrative Fee Schedules (2015) ("An Initial Filing Fee is payable in full by a filing party when a claim, counterclaim, or additional claim is filed. A Final Fee will be incurred for all cases that proceed to their first hearing and is payable in advance at the time the first hearing is scheduled.")

arbitration."[135] Discovery in most arbitrations is minimal, but in some cases it is substantial. Discovery, like other aspects of arbitration, is primarily determined by the arbitration agreement.[136] Some arbitration agreements provide that discovery may be had in accordance with the Federal Rules of Civil Procedure.[137] Arbitration pursuant to these agreements is unlikely to have significantly less discovery than litigation.

Many arbitration agreements incorporate the rules of an arbitration organization, such as the American Arbitration Association. These rules typically do not grant the parties rights to broad discovery but rather grant the arbitrator wide discretion in authorizing discovery. For example, the AAA Commercial Rules provide:

R–22. Pre-Hearing Exchange and Production of Information

(a) *Authority of arbitrator.* The arbitrator shall manage any necessary exchange of information among the parties with a view to achieving an efficient and economical resolution of the dispute, while at the same time promoting equality of treatment and safeguarding each party's opportunity to fairly present its claims and defenses.

(b) *Documents.* The arbitrator may, on application of a party or on the arbitrator's own initiative:

    i.   require the parties to exchange documents in their possession or custody on which they intend to rely;

---

[135] Macneil, Speidel & Stipanowich, supra note 22, § 34.1, at 34:2. See also 3 Thomas H. Oehmke, Commercial Arbitration §§ 89.1–89.3 (3d ed. 2009); Bruce A. McAllister & Amy Bloom, Evidence in Arbitration, 34 J. Mar.L. & Com. 35, 42 (2003)("It is axiomatic that discovery is not as available in arbitration as it may be in court litigation.")

[136] See, e.g., Robert A. Weiner & B. Ted Howes, Arbitration Discovery: When should discovery provisions be included in an arbitration agreement?, Disp.Resol.Mag., Summer 1999, at 30, 30–32; John Wilkinson, Arbitration Contract Clauses: A Potential Key to a Cost-Effective Process, Disp.Resol.Mag. Fall 2009, at 9 (many parties are expanding their arbitration clauses to "place meaningful limits on discovery").

[137] See, e.g., Medicine Shoppe International, Inc. License Agreement, in Christopher R. Drahozal, "Unfair" Arbitration Clauses, 2001 U.Ill.L.Rev. 695, 776, App. II; Scott Atlas & Nancy Atlas, Potential ADR Backlash, Disp.Resol.Mag., Summer 2004, 14, 16 ("parties increasingly have attempted to build into their contracts procedural safeguards akin to rules of civil procedure. Arbitrators are now charged with judge-like ethical and procedural duties. They must * * * allow more discovery * * * and increasingly conduct hearings under rules of procedure * * *. [T]hese protections have made the arbitration process more like, and sometimes as expensive as, court proceedings.")

ii.   require the parties to update their exchanges of the documents on which they intend to rely as such documents become known to them;

iii.   require the parties, in response to reasonable document requests, to make available to the other party documents, in the responding party's possession or custody, not otherwise readily available to the party seeking the documents reasonably believed by the party seeking the documents to exist and to be relevant and material to the outcome of disputed issues; and

iv.   require the parties, when documents to be exchanged or produced are maintained in electronic form, to make such documents available in the form most convenient and economical for the party in possession of such documents, unless the arbitrator determines that there is good cause for requiring the documents to be produced in a different form. The parties should attempt to agree in advance upon, and the arbitrator may determine, reasonable search parameters to balance the need for production of electronically stored documents relevant and material to the outcome of disputed issues against the cost of locating and producing them.

R–23 Enforcement Powers of the Arbitrator

The arbitrator shall have the authority to issue any orders necessary to enforce the provisions of rules R–21 and R–22 and to otherwise achieve a fair, efficient and economical resolution of the case, including, without limitation:

(a) conditioning any exchange or production of confidential documents and information, and the admission of confidential evidence at the hearing, on appropriate orders to preserve such confidentiality;

(b)   imposing reasonable search parameters for electronic and other documents if the parties are unable to agree;

(c)   allocating costs of producing documentation, including electronically stored documentation;

(d)   in the case of willful non-compliance with any order issued by the arbitrator, drawing adverse inferences, excluding evidence and other submissions, and/or making special allocations of costs or an interim award of costs arising from such non-compliance; and

(e) issuing any other enforcement orders which the arbitrator is empowered to issue under applicable law.[138]

The arbitrator's preferences may strongly influence the amount of discovery in a particular case. And arbitrators seem to be authorizing more discovery in recent years.[139] Perhaps this is a result of the increasing variety of parties and claims going to arbitration,[140] as arbitration has broadened beyond disputes over commercial and labor agreements to statutory claims brought by consumers, employees, and other parties.[141]

Some courts, especially in the employment discrimination context, have indicated that they will not enforce arbitration agreements unless they have confidence that there will be sufficient discovery to allow claimants to gather necessary evidence.[142] On the other hand, the Supreme Court has suggested that the FAA would preempt (hypothetical) state law holding arbitration agreements unconscionable unless they provide for as much discovery as is available in litigation.[143]

FAA § 7 authorizes the arbitrators to "summon in writing any person to attend before them or any of them as a witness and in a proper case to bring with him or them any book, record, document, or paper which may be deemed material as evidence in the case."[144] Courts are split on whether this provision authorizes subpoenas of non-parties for pre-hearing discovery or only for the hearing itself.[145]

---

[138] See, e.g., Am.Arbitration Ass'n, Commercial Arbitration Rules, R–22 and R–23 (2013).

[139] Thomas J. Stipanowich, Arbitration: The "New Litigation", 2010 U.Ill.L.Rev. 1, 12; John Wilkinson, Arbitration Contract Clauses: A Potential Key to a Cost-Effective Process, Disp. Resol.Mag. at 9 (Fall 2009) (in response to this trend, many parties are expanding their arbitration clauses to "place meaningful limits on discovery").

[140] See Edward Brunet, Replacing Folklore Arbitration with a Contract Model of Arbitration, 74 Tul.L.Rev. 39 (1999)(connecting increased discovery with broader changes in arbitration law and practice).

[141] See § 27–28.

[142] See, e.g., Cole v. Burns Int'l Security Services, 105 F.3d 1465 (D.C.Cir.1997); Armendariz v. Foundation Health Psychcare Services, Inc., 99 Cal.Rptr.2d 745 (Cal.2000). See Arreguin v. Global Equity Lending, Inc., 2008 WL 4104340, at *7 (N.D.Cal.2008) (finding that American Arbitration Association Commercial Arbitration Rules satisfy requirement of sufficient discovery).

[143] AT & T Mobility LLC v. Concepcion, 563 U.S. 333, 343 (2011).

[144] 9 U.S.C. § 7.

[145] Compare In re Security Life Insurance Co. of America, 228 F.3d 865, 870–71 (8th Cir.2000)("We thus hold that implicit in an arbitration panel's power to subpoena relevant documents for production at a hearing is the power to order the production of relevant documents for review by a party prior to the hearing."); American Federation of Television and Radio Artists, AFL-CIO v. WJBK-TV, 164 F.3d 1004, 1009 (6th Cir.1999) (under LMRA, "a labor arbitrator is authorized to issue a subpoena duces tecum to compel a third party to produce records he deems material to the case either before or at an arbitration hearing."); Meadows Indemnity Co. v. Nutmeg Insurance

Therefore, some parties seeking to enforce arbitral subpoenas of non-parties for pre-hearing discovery do so in state courts.[146] The Revised Uniform Arbitration Act (RUAA) authorizes subpoenas of non-parties for pre-hearing discovery for testimony and specifically authorizes depositions, which traditionally are rare in arbitration.[147] However, these provisions of RUAA "can be waived or varied by agreement of the parties"[148] so presumably have no effect on arbitration arising out of an arbitration agreement that, expressly or by incorporating arbitration organization rules, limits discovery.

If the arbitration agreement or the applicable arbitration organization rules authorize it, arbitrators may impose sanctions on parties (or lawyers) who fail to comply with the arbitrators' discovery orders. Courts will enforce those sanctions like any other arbitration award.[149]

§ 37   Hearing

(a)   General Comparison with Trial

A hearing is to arbitration what a trial is to litigation. Hearings look like trials in some respects: adversaries trying to persuade a neutral adjudicator by presenting evidence and making arguments. Like trials, arbitrations typically proceed with opening statements,

---

Co. 157 F.R.D. 42 (M.D.Tenn.1994)(enforcing pre-hearing discovery subpoena of non-parties); Stanton v. Paine Webber Jackson & Curtis, Inc. 685 F.Supp. 1241 (S.D.Fla.1988)(same), with Life Receivables Trust v. Syndicate 102 at Lloyd's of London 549 F.3d 210, 216–17 (2d Cir.2008) ("we join the Third Circuit in holding that section 7 of the FAA does not authorize arbitrators to compel pre-hearing document discovery from entities not party to the arbitration proceedings."); Hay Group, Inc. v. E.B.S. Acquisition Corp., 360 F.3d 404 (3d Cir.2004) (no authority for pre-hearing discovery subpoena); COMSAT Corp. v. National Science Foundation, 190 F.3d 269, 275 (4th Cir.1999)("Nowhere does the FAA grant an arbitrator the authority to order non-parties to appear at depositions, or the authority to demand that non-parties provide the litigating parties with documents during prehearing discovery."); Ware v. C.D. Peacock, Inc., 2010 WL 1856021 (N.D. Ill.2010); Empire Fin. Group v. Pension Fin. Servs., Inc., 2010 WL 742579 (N.D. Tex.2010). See also Alliance Healthcare Services, Inc. v. Argonaut Private Equity, LLC, 804 F.Supp.2d 808, 811 (N.D.Ill.2011) (quotation omitted) ("permitting an arbitrator to hold a preliminary hearing that is not a hearing on the merits does not transform the preliminary hearing into a prohibited discovery device.")

[146]   Charles E. Harris II, Enforcing Arbitral Subpoenas: Reconsidering Federal Question Jurisdiction Under FAA Section 7, 66 Disp. Resol. J. 24, 25 (2011).

[147]   "If an arbitrator permits discovery under subsection (c), the arbitrator may order a party to the arbitration proceeding to comply with the arbitrator's discovery-related orders, issue subpoenas for the attendance of a witness and for the production of records and other evidence at a discovery proceeding, and take action against a noncomplying party to the extent a court could if the controversy were the subject of a civil action in this State." Unif. Arbitration Act § 17(d) (2000).

[148]   Id. cmt.1.

[149]   McDaniel v. Bear Stearns & Co., 196 F. Supp. 2d 343, 364 (S.D.N.Y. 2002); Superadio Ltd. Partnership v. Winstar Radio Productions, LLC, 844 N.E.2d 246, 252–54 (Mass.2006).

presentation of witnesses by the claimant for examination and cross-examination, followed by similar presentation of the respondent's witnesses, and concluding with closing statements by counsel. But arbitration hearings differ from trials in other respects. While juries may consist of twelve people, an arbitration panel rarely consists of more than three. While judges sit up high, wear black robes and expect to be called "Your Honor," arbitrators do not.

(b) Confidentiality

In contrast to trials, which are usually in government buildings open to the public and the press, arbitration hearings are generally on private property and closed to non-participants.[150] A few state statutes even protect arbitration materials from discovery or admissibility in litigation.[151] Absent such a statute, however, the evidence and arguments produced in arbitration may discoverable and admissible in litigation,[152] even if there is an explicit confidentiality provision in the arbitration agreement.[153] One study found confidentiality provisions in only 13.5% of arbitration agreements studied.[154] In some contexts, a confidentiality provision may support a finding that the agreement to arbitrate is unconscionable.[155]

While litigation typically has a transcript or other record of the hearing, arbitration often does not.[156]

---

[150] See, e.g., Am.Arbitration Ass'n, Commercial Arbitration Rules, R–25 (2013) ("The arbitrator and the AAA shall maintain the privacy of the hearings unless the law provides to the contrary. Any person having a direct interest in the arbitration is entitled to attend hearings. The arbitrator shall otherwise have the power to require the exclusion of any witness, other than a party or other essential person, during the testimony of any other witness. It shall be discretionary with the arbitrator to determine the propriety of the attendance of any other person.") However, "[t]he presumption of privacy and confidentiality in arbitration proceedings shall not apply in class arbitrations. All class arbitration hearings and filings may be made public, subject to the authority of the arbitrator to provide otherwise in special circumstances." Am.Arbitration Ass'n, Supplementary Rules for Class Arbitrations, 9(a) (2003).

[151] See, e.g., Ark.Code Ann. § 16–7–206 (1999); Cal.Evid.Code § 703.5 (West 1995); Mo.Ann.Stat. § 435.014 (West 2010); Tex.Civ.Prac. & Rem. Code Ann. § 154.073(b) (Vernon 2005). See also Group Health Plan, Inc. v. BJC Health Sys., Inc., 30 S.W.3d 198 (Mo.Ct.App.2000).

[152] United States v. Panhandle Eastern Corp., 118 F.R.D. 346 (D.Del.1988); Contship Containerlines, Ltd. v. PPG Industries, Inc., 2003 WL 1948807 (S.D.N.Y. Apr.23, 2003).

[153] Lawrence E. Jaffee Pension Plan v. Household Int'l, Inc., 2004 WL 1821968 (D.Colo.Aug.13, 2004); Urban Box Office Network v. Interfase Managers, 2004 WL 2375819 (S.D.N.Y.Oct.21, 2004).

[154] Demaine & Hensler, supra note 115, at 69.

[155] See § 25(a).

[156] John S. Murray, Alan Scott Rau, & Edward F. Sherman 640–641 (2nd ed. 1996). Macneil, Speidel & Stipanowich, supra note 22.

(c) Role of Lawyers

Lawyers in many arbitration hearings do what they do at trial: make opening statements, call witnesses who testify under oath, cross-examine opposing witnesses, submit briefs, and make closing arguments.[157] But not all hearings look like this. In some arbitration contexts, such as trade association arbitration, lawyers often are not present.[158] In labor arbitration, employees are often represented by a union representative, rather than a lawyer,[159] although the Rhode Island Supreme Court questioned whether some of these representatives might be engaged in the unlicensed practice of law.[160] Going further, the Florida Supreme Court prohibited the practice of having a non-lawyer representative in securities arbitration on the ground that it did constitute the unlicensed practice of law.[161] The same argument has been used to challenge the representation of

---

The FAA contains no provisions respecting maintenance or records of hearings or of records being furnished to the parties. Nor has any requirement that records of hearings be maintained or furnished to the parties been established by judicial decision. The maintenance of a record, if any, is strictly a matter for the agreement of the arbitrating parties.

Id. § 32.7.1, at 32:53. See, e.g., Am.Arb.Ass'n, Commercial Arbitration Rules, Rule R–28 (2013) ("Any party desiring a stenographic record shall make arrangements directly with a stenographer and shall notify the other parties of these arrangements at least three days in advance of the hearing. The requesting party or parties shall pay the cost of the record. * * *)

[157] See Jay E. Grenig & R. Wayne Estes, Arbitration Advocacy, §§ 2.4, 4.18–4.19, & 4.21 (2000).

[158] See Macneil, Speidel & Stipanowich, supra note 22, § 32.5.5, at 32:49–32:50 ("[S]ome trade groups have long followed the practice of requiring that parties appear without counsel.") The law of many states provides that a pre-hearing waiver of the right to an attorney is void. See Unif. Arbitration Act § 6 (1956), 7 U.L.A. 383 (2009); Unif. Arbitration Act § 4(b)(4) (2000), 7 U.L.A. 19 (2009). FAA § 2, by contrast, may require enforcement of an agreement to proceed without an attorney, provided that enforcement would not be unconscionable, see § 25, or deprive the parties of a fundamentally fair hearing. See § 43(c). For an employment arbitration agreement providing that employer will not hire a lawyer if employee does not hire one, see Johnson v. Long John Silver's Restaurants, Inc., 320 F.Supp.2d 656 (M.D.Tenn.2004).

[159] Laura J. Cooper et al., ADR in the Workplace 23 & n.17 (2nd ed. 2005); Judith A. McMorrow, The Advocate as Witness: Understanding Context, Culture and Client, 70 Fordham L. Rev. 945, 973 (2001) ("The formal structure of labor arbitration involves a union representative and management representative making presentations to the neutral person. The representatives need not be lawyers. Figures vary, but somewhere between twenty-five and thirty-five percent of the union advocates are lawyers.").

[160] In re Town of Little Compton, 37 A.3d 85, 95 (R.I.2012) ("although the conduct involved in this case may be the practice of law pursuant to the language of § 11–27–2, because of the long-standing involvement of nonlawyer union employees at public grievance arbitrations, we will not limit this involvement at this time. We may in the future, however".)

[161] The Florida Bar Re: Advisory Opinion on Nonlawyer Representation in Securities Arbitration, 696 So.2d 1178 (Fla.1997).

parties in arbitration by out-of-state lawyers.[162] ABA Model Rule of Professional Conduct 5.5(c) provides that

A lawyer admitted in another United States jurisdiction, and not disbarred or suspended from practice in any jurisdiction, may provide legal services on a temporary basis in this jurisdiction that:

* * *

(3)   are in or reasonably related to a pending or potential arbitration, mediation, or other alternative dispute resolution proceeding in this or another jurisdiction, if the services arise out of or are reasonably related to the lawyer's practice in a jurisdiction in which the lawyer is admitted to practice and are not services for which the forum requires pro hac vice admission.[163]

If lawyers are present at the arbitration hearing, they may be well-advised to behave somewhat differently than they do at trial. Depending on context, the rules of evidence in arbitration can be minimal.[164] Lawyers making objections may find that doing so

---

[162]   Compare Birbrower, Montalbano, Condon & Frank v. Superior Court, 949 P.2d 1 (Cal.1998)(New York lawyers barred from recovering fees for work performed in California in connection with an impending California arbitration, because they had done so in violation of the California Business and Professions Code § 6125 which states "No person shall practice law in California unless the person is an active member of the State Bar."), with Williamson v. John D. Quinn Constr. Corp., 537 F.Supp. 613, 616 (S.D.N.Y.1982) (rejecting claim that out-of-State attorney and firm were foreclosed from recovery obtained in connection with services rendered in arbitration proceeding because not authorized to practice law in that State); Siegel v. Bridas Sociedad Anonima Petrolera Industrial Y Comercial, 1991 WL 167979, at *5 (S.D.N.Y.1991) (quoting and following Williamson "representation of a party in an arbitration proceeding by a non-lawyer or a lawyer from another jurisdiction is not the unauthorized practice of law."); Prudential Equity Group, LLC v. Ajamie, 538 F.Supp.2d 605, 607–08 (S.D.N.Y.2008)(following Williamson); Colmar, Ltd. v. Fremantlemedia North America, Inc., 801 N.E.2d 1017, 1026 (Ill.App.2003)(relying on Model Rule of Professional Responsibility 5.5(c) as persuasive authority that "an out-of-state attorney's representation of a client during arbitration does not violate the rules prohibiting the unlicensed practice of law"). See also Cal.Civ.P. Code § 1282.4 (West 2007) (allows non-resident lawyers to participate in California arbitrations, creating limited exception to Birbrower); Fla.Bar Rule 1–3.11 (permitting out-of-state attorneys to participate in arbitrations taking place in Florida under limited circumstances); Doctor's Associates, Inc. v. Jamieson, 2006 WL 2348849 (Ct.App.Conn.2006)(holding that the absence of a specific statute or rule concerning an out-of-state attorney's participation in private arbitration proceeding is not a bar to the authority of the court to allow such an out-of-state attorney to represent client in Connecticut, as long as attorney otherwise complies with Connecticut requirements); Disciplinary Counsel v. Alexicole, Inc., 822 N.E.2d 348 (Ohio 2004) (A non-attorney who was not licensed to practice law in Ohio cannot represent his or her client in an arbitration taking place in Ohio); In re Creasy, 12 P.3d 214, 217 (Ariz.2000) (examining witness in arbitration constitutes practice of law).

[163]   Model Rules of Professional Conduct R.5.5(c) (2013).

[164]   See § 37(d).

accomplishes nothing other than irritating the arbitrator. If the arbitrator has some expertise on the subject matter of the dispute, the lawyer may not need to lay the sort of factual and evidentiary foundations required in court. Also, lawyers may find that certain personal styles successful in front of a jury are less successful in front of an arbitrator. Many lawyers who succeed in arbitration remain seated and businesslike throughout the hearing, without the sort of movement or drama that might be effective in capturing a jury's attention.

(d) Rules of Evidence

Rules of evidence are historically intertwined with the jury.[165] Understandable then, that arbitration (without a jury) nearly always has less elaborate rules of evidence than those used in jury trials. Some arbitrations have no rules of evidence so the parties may present whatever evidence they like and the arbitrators can give to it whatever weight they like.[166]

Arbitrators' general openness to admitting evidence is due in part to the fact that "refusing to hear evidence pertinent and material to the controversy" is one of the few grounds for vacating the arbitration award,[167] while hearing evidence that would not be admissible in court is not a ground for vacatur.[168]

Evidentiary rules, like other aspects of arbitration, are primarily determined by the arbitration agreement. Many agreements incorporate the rules of an arbitration organization such as the American Arbitration Association. The AAA's Commercial Arbitration Rules allow the parties to offer into evidence whatever is

---

[165]   Ellen E. Sward, The Decline of the Civil Jury 82–84, 243–60 (2001).

[166]   Macneil, Speidel & Stipanowich, supra note 22, §§ 35.1.2.1. & 35.1.2.4.

[167]   9 U.S.C. § 10(a)(3). "To too many arbitrators, [this provision] has meant one thing: let everything remotely relevant in, no matter how prejudicial, cumulative, incredible, suspect or otherwise useless, for fear that ruling out anything may lead to vacatur." McAllister & Bloom, supra note 135, at 36. See § 43(c).

[168]   Bowles Fin. Group, Inc. v. Stifel, Nicolaus & Co., 22 F.3d 1010, 1013 (10th Cir.1994) (refusing to vacate award won by lawyer who introduced evidence that would not have been admissible in litigation; "This court has no power to judicially impose our rules of evidence on an arbitration proceeding."); U.S. ex rel. Nat'l Roofing Services, Inc. v. Lovering-Johnson, Inc., 53 F. Supp. 2d 1142, 1145–47 (D.Kan.1999)(extending Bowles rule to case where arbitrator may well have relied on evidence—of settlement offer—that would not have been admissible in litigation); A.G. Edwards & Sons, Inc. v. McCullough, 764 F. Supp. 1365, 1368 (D.Ariz.1991)("evidence of settlement offer, while inadmissible in court, was admissible in arbitration where rules of evidence are inapplicable"); WHD, LP. v. Mayflower Capital, LLC, 673 S.E.2d 168, 2009 WL 368335 at *5 (N.C.App.2009) (refusing to vacate arbitration award where arbitrator may have relied on evidence that would not have been admissible in litigation).

relevant and material.[169] These rules also say that the parties *shall* produce evidence the arbitrator deems necessary.[170] This is typical of most arbitration in that it contemplates a more active role by the arbitrator than is typical of judges and juries. In the United States, judges and juries are typically passive triers-of-fact, receiving only the evidence presented by the parties. In contrast, some arbitrators are more inquisitorial, sometimes questioning witnesses,[171] or making other investigations into evidence.[172]

If evidence is required from someone other than the parties, the arbitrator may obtain it through subpoena. Those who fail to comply with an arbitrator's subpoena may be compelled to do so by a court.[173]

(e) No Hearing; Dispositive Motions

Much litigation ends on a grant of a motion to dismiss or for summary judgment. Such motions are generally less likely to succeed in arbitration than in litigation,[174] perhaps because the lesser pleadings and discovery typical of arbitration make it less likely that all factual issues can be resolved without a hearing. That said, arbitrators generally do have the power to grant dispositive motions.[175] Courts have enforced awards by arbitrators who decided

---

[169]   Am.Arbitration Ass'n, Commercial Arbitration Rules, R–34(a) (2013) ("The parties may offer such evidence as is relevant and material to the dispute and shall produce such evidence as the arbitrator may deem necessary to an understanding and determination of the dispute. Conformity to legal rules of evidence shall not be necessary. All evidence shall be taken in the presence of all of the arbitrators and all of the parties, except where any of the parties is absent, in default or has waived the right to be present.").

[170]   See id.

[171]   Macneil, Speidel & Stipanowich, supra note 22, § 35.4.5; Stanley Weinstein, An Arbitrator's Wish List, 58 Disp. Resol.J., July 2003, 54, 57.

[172]   See, e.g., Am.Arbitration Ass'n, Commercial Arbitration Rules, R–36 (2013).

[173]   9 U.S.C. § 7. In contrast, the law on discovery subpoenas is more complicated. See § 36(d).

[174]   See, e.g., Eastern Air Lines, Inc., 79 Lab.Arb.Rep. 61, 64, n.3 (BNA 1982) ("a summary judgment is extraordinary (although not unheard of) in arbitration proceedings"); Jennifer J. Johnson, Wall Street Meets the Wild West: Bringing Law and Order to Securities Arbitration, 84 N.C.L.Rev. 123, 175 (2005)("There is an unspoken bias in [securities] arbitrations that panels should view dispositive motions with much skepticism and proceed as a matter of course to a hearing."); Gary W. Jackson, Prosecuting Class Actions in Arbitration, Assoc. of Trial Lawyers of Am., ATLA Annual Convention Reference Materials, 829 (2006); Harold M. Brody & Anthony J. Oncidi, Careful What You Wish For: Is Arbitration the Employer's Panacea? Perhaps There is a Better Alternative, 9 HR Advisor: Legal & Practical Guidance, Nov./Dec. 2003, at 7.

[175]   Sheldon v. Vermonty, 269 F.3d 1202, 1206 (10th Cir.2001) (holding that arbitrators can dispose of legal issues on dispositive motions); Warren v. Tacher, 114 F.Supp.2d 600, 602 (W.D.Ky.2000)("the arbitrators had the authority to decide and grant a pre-hearing motion to dismiss.") See also Unif. Arbitration Act § 15(b) ("An arbitrator may decide a request for summary disposition of a claim or particular issue: (1) if all interested parties agree; or (2) upon request of one party to the arbitration proceeding if that party gives notice to all other parties to the proceeding, and the

to forgo live testimony and decide the case on the documentary evidence submitted.[176] This is often called "desk arbitration." And just as litigation may result in a judgment against a party who does not participate,[177] the same is true in arbitration,[178] and is sometimes called an "ex parte award."

---

other parties have a reasonable opportunity to respond."); Am.Arbitration Ass'n, Commercial Arbitration Rules, R–33 (2013) ("The arbitrator may allow the filing of and make rulings upon a dispositive motion only if the arbitrator determines that the moving party has shown that the motion is likely to succeed and dispose of or narrow the issues in the case.")

[176] British Ins. Co. of Cayman v. Water Street Ins. Co., Ltd., 93 F.Supp.2d 506 (S.D.N.Y.2000).

> Oral argument is not a necessary component of due process in all circumstances. While hearings are advisable in most arbitration proceedings, arbitrators are not compelled to conduct oral hearings in every case. The lack of oral hearings does not amount to the "denial of fundamental fairness" required to warrant vacating the award. As long as an arbitrator's choice to render a decision based solely on documentary evidence is reasonable, and does not render the proceeding "fundamentally unfair," the arbitrator is acting within the liberal sphere of permissible discretion.

Id. at 517 (citations omitted). See also Weizmann Institute of Science v. Neschis, 421 F.Supp.2d 654, 681 (S.D.N.Y.2005) ("the Tribunal's decision to forego live testimony in favor of affidavits from some witnesses is common practice"); Intercarbon Bermuda Ltd. v. Caltex Trading & Transport Corp., 146 F.R.D. 64 (S.D.N.Y.1993) (confirming award after arbitrator refused to conduct oral hearing despite party's repeated requests); Burdette v. FSC Sec. Corp., 1993 WL 593997, at *4 (W.D.Tenn.1993) (confirming arbitral award in nature of summary judgment); Schlessinger v. Rosenfeld, Meyer & Susman, 47 Cal.Rptr. 2d 650 (Ct.App.1995) (upholding AAA arbitral award based on summary adjudications); Unif.Arbitration Act (2000) § 15(b), 7 U.L.A. 53 (2005) ("An arbitrator may decide a request for summary disposition of a claim or particular issue" "if all interested parties agree" or "upon request of one party to the arbitration proceeding if that party gives notice to all other parties to the proceeding, and the other parties have a reasonable opportunity to respond"); Am.Arbitration Ass'n, Commercial Arbitration Rules, E–6 (2013) ("Where no party's claim exceeds $25,000, exclusive of interest, attorneys' fees and arbitration costs, and other cases in which the parties agree, the dispute shall be resolved by submission of documents, unless any party requests an oral hearing, or the arbitrator determines that an oral hearing is necessary. Where cases are resolved by submission of documents, the following procedures may be utilized at the agreement of the parties or the discretion of the arbitrator. (a) Within 14 calendar days of confirmation of the arbitrator's appointment, the arbitrator may convene a preliminary management hearing, via conference call, video conference, or internet, to establish a fair and equitable procedure for the submission of documents * * * .")

[177] Fed.R.Civ.P. 55(a)("When a party against whom a judgment for affirmative relief is sought has failed to plead or otherwise defend, and that failure is shown by affidavit or otherwise, the clerk must enter the party's default."); N.Y.C.P.L.R. § 3215 (McKinney 2007). Like other judgments, default judgments can be set aside for various reasons including "excusable neglect." Fed.R.Civ.P. 60(b). See generally Arthur J. Park, Fixing Faults in the Current Default Judgment Framework, 34 Campbell L.Rev. 155 (2011). The requirements for obtaining a default judgment vary by state. For example, in many cases California requires a "prove-up hearing" at which "The court shall hear the evidence offered by the plaintiff, and shall render judgment in the plaintiff's favor for that relief, not exceeding the amount stated in the complaint * * * , as appears by the evidence to be just." Cal.C.Civ.P. § 585(b).

[178] Val-U Construction Co. v. Rosebud Sioux Tribe, 146 F.3d 573, 575 (8th Cir.1996)("The AAA held an arbitration hearing and Val-U presented its case. The

(f) Written Awards, Reasoned Opinions, and the Role of Precedent

Arbitrator's decisions, called arbitration awards, generally are written.[179] But in some types of arbitration, awards can be very brief,[180]—perhaps consisting of just two sentences finding for the claimant and ordering the respondent to pay a particular dollar amount. Such an award, which resembles the typical general verdict rendered by a jury rather than the opinion of a trial judge, is unlikely to cite much precedent or to serve as precedent for future decisions by arbitrators or courts. In contrast, the sort of reasoned, written opinions commonly issued by judges are also issued by arbitrators in several contexts including: (1) employment,[181] (2) labor, (3) international commercial and maritime.[182]

While commercial arbitration awards in the United States are generally not published,[183] awards in some other fields are often published. For example, many labor arbitration opinions, especially the more important ones, are published in the Bureau of National Affairs' *Labor Arbitration Reports*.[184] "[A]rbitral precedent plays a

---

Tribe was not represented at the hearing."); id. at 579 ("the Tribe never requested that the AAA postpone the hearing until the issue of sovereign immunity was resolved."); AAA Employment Arbitration Rules and Mediation Procedures, Rule 29 ("Unless the law provides to the contrary, the arbitration may proceed in the absence of any party or representative who, after due notice, fails to be present or fails to obtain a postponement. An award shall not be based solely on the default of a party. The arbitrator shall require the party who is in attendance to present such evidence as the arbitrator may require for the making of the award.")

[179] See, e.g., Am.Arbitration Ass'n, Commercial Arbitration Rules, R–46 (2013).

[180] W. Mark C. Weidemaier, Judging-Lite: How Arbitrators Use and Create Precedent, 90 N.C. L. Rev. 1091, 1104 (2012)("Securities awards are published, and securities arbitrators may and sometimes do issue reasoned awards. But historically, norms in securities arbitration have disfavored reasoned awards, and the available evidence suggests that securities arbitrators do not often issue them."); FINRA Customer Code 12904(g), (h). Securities arbitration awards are published. Id.

[181] Weidemaier, supra note 180, at 1102–03 ("The AAA's employment arbitration rules provide that arbitrators will provide "written reasons for the award unless the parties agree otherwise." Since 2000, the AAA has published these awards, and current rules require that awards be made available to the public at cost. These awards are also available online through LexisNexis in fully searchable format. Under current practice, however, the names of parties and witnesses are redacted before publication.")

[182] "Only in a few, specialized types of arbitrations do arbitrators routinely craft written decisions—labor arbitrations, international commercial arbitrations, and maritime arbitrations." Edward Brunet & Charles B. Craver, Alternative Dispute Resolution: The Advocate's Perspective 316, 319, 327–28 (2001).

[183] See Macneil, Speidel & Stipanowich, supra note 22, § 3.2.3, at 3:13 & § 37.4.1, at 37:10–37:13; Amy J. Schmitz, Untangling the Privacy Paradox in Arbitration, 54 U.Kan.L.Rev. 1211, 1216 (2006) ("arbitration awards generally are not published").

[184] Brunet & Craver, supra note 182, at 319; Weidemaier, supra note 180, at 1106 ("most labor arbitration awards are unpublished, and awards that are submitted to the BNA for publication are published only if the BNA decides the award is of sufficiently 'general interest.' ")

major role [in] labor arbitration, where arbitrators are engaged primarily in building a 'common law of the workplace.' "[185] Similarly, the rules of several leading international arbitration organizations require that arbitration awards be supported by reasoned opinions.[186] In some international fields, arbitrators often cite earlier arbitration awards as precedent.[187]

§ 38   Remedies

(a) Determined by Contract, Within Limitations

(1) Generally Determined by Contract; the Mastrobuono Case

Remedies, like other aspects of arbitration, are primarily determined by the arbitration agreement.[188] For example, the Supreme Court used a contractual analysis to determine whether the arbitrator could award punitive damages in *Mastrobuono v. Shearson Lehman Hutton, Inc.*[189] As the Court said, "the case before us comes down to what the contract has to say about the arbitrability of petitioners' claim for punitive damages."[190]

Mastrobuono stated that this contractual analysis is mandated by the FAA and that it preempts any state law requiring a non-contractual analysis. New York law, at the time, required a non-contractual analysis. New York law prohibited arbitrators from awarding punitive damages regardless of the arbitration agreement's terms.[191] *Mastrobuono* found that the FAA preempted that New York law.[192] The Court pointed out that the contract authorized

---

[185]   Weidemaier, supra note 180, at 1116. "[L]abor arbitrators often justify their decisions by citing only other arbitration awards." Id. at 1095.

[186]   See Born, supra note 8, at 794.

[187]   Christopher S. Gibson & Christopher R. Drahozal, Iran-United States Claims Tribunal Precedent in Investor-State Arbitration, 23 J. Int'l Arb. 521, 537–44 (2006)("extensive reliance on [Iran-United States Claims] Tribunal precedents" in investor-state arbitration); Gabrielle Kaufmann-Kohler, Arbitral Precedent: Dream, Necessity, or Excuse?, 23 Arb. Int'l 357 (2007).

[188]   Parties can get creative. For instance, "baseball" arbitration limits the arbitrator to two remedies: each party's final settlement offer. The arbitrator must pick one of those two options (usually a dollar amount) as the award. See, e.g., Alan Scott Rau, Edward F. Sherman & Scott R. Peppet, Processes of Dispute Resolution: The Role of Lawyers 935–39 (4th ed.2006); David Hechler, "Baseball" Arbitration, Nat'l L. J., Jan.23, 2002.

[189]   514 U.S. 52 (1995).

[190]   Id. at 58.

[191]   See Garrity v. Lyle Stuart, Inc., 40 N.Y.2d 354, 386 N.Y.S.2d 831 (1976).

[192]   The Court said its "decisions in Allied-Bruce, Southland, and Perry make clear that if contracting parties agree to include claims for punitive damages within the issues to be arbitrated, the FAA ensures that their agreement will be enforced according to its terms even if a rule of state law would otherwise exclude such claims from arbitration." 514 U.S. at 58. "[I]n the absence of contractual intent to the contrary, the FAA would pre-empt the Garrity rule." Id. at 59.

arbitration in accordance with the rules of the National Association of Securities Dealers ("NASD") and a NASD manual provided to NASD arbitrators contained this provision: "The issue of punitive damages may arise with great frequency in arbitrations. Parties to arbitration are informed that arbitrators can consider punitive damages as a remedy."[193] Thus the Court found that the arbitration clause "contradicts * * * the conclusion that the parties agreed to foreclose claims for punitive damages."[194] The Court then went on to cite two further reasons for interpreting the contract to permit arbitrators to award punitive damages: (1) "the federal policy favoring arbitration,"[195] which means that "ambiguities as to the scope of the arbitration clause itself are resolved in favor of arbitration," and (2) "the common-law rule of contract interpretation that a court should construe ambiguous language against the interest of the party that drafted it."[196] These final two points suggest that the Court favors interpretations of arbitration agreements that preserve the full remedies of the parties, especially parties who sign form arbitration agreements presented to them on a take-it-or-leave-it basis.

(2) Limitations on Contract; the Book Case

Some courts have gone beyond interpretation of arbitration agreements to hold that certain contractual remedy-limitations are unenforceable. These cases tend to arise in the context of take-it-or-leave-it arbitration agreements presented to employees and consumers. These cases rest on contract law's unconscionability doctrine,[197] special concerns regarding the vindication of federal statutory rights,[198] or a combination of the two.[199] However, the 2003 Supreme Court case of *Pacificare Health Systems, Inc. v. Book*,[200] indicates that in at least some cases involving contractual remedy-limitations, courts should send to the arbitrators the question whether to enforce those limitations.[201]

---

[193] Mastrobuono, 514 U.S. at 61 (quoting Mastrobuono v. Shearson Lehman Hutton, Inc., 20 F.3d 713, 717 (7th Cir.1994)).

[194] Mastrobuono, 514 U.S. at 61.

[195] Id. at 62.

[196] Id.

[197] See § 25.

[198] See §§ 27–28.

[199] See Graham Oil Co. v. Arco Products Co., 43 F.3d 1244 (9th Cir.1994).

[200] 538 U.S. 401 (2003).

[201] In *Book*, physicians brought claims under a statute (RICO) that provides for treble damages. The defendants' motion to compel arbitration was denied by the district court because the arbitration agreement prohibited the arbitrators from awarding "punitive damages." Id. at 403. The Supreme Court found the agreement ambiguous. Id. at 405. "[W]e should not, on the basis of 'mere speculation' that an arbitrator might interpret these ambiguous agreements in a manner that casts their

(b) Typical Contract Terms

Many arbitration agreements provide that the arbitrator may order any remedy that a court could order.[202] And this seems to be the usual default interpretation of arbitration agreements that are silent on remedies. For example, arbitrators order parties to pay punitive damages[203] and issue injunctions[204] even though the arbitration agreement may not expressly authorize those remedies.

In contrast, arbitration is generally less suited than litigation as a forum for an emergency remedy, such as a temporary restraining order. This is because arbitration cannot award any remedy until an arbitrator has been appointed. The party against whom a restraining order is sought likely can delay that appointment until it does whatever the other party sought to restrain. For this reason, the American Arbitration Association maintains an emergency panel of arbitrators that can quickly rule on requests for provisional remedies before the appointment of the arbitrators who will hear the rest of the case,[205] "but that option appears to be used only rarely."[206]

Suppose a party to an arbitration agreement asks a court to issue preliminary injunctive relief in disputes that are ultimately to be resolved by an arbitration panel. Most courts are willing to do

---

enforceability into doubt, take upon ourselves the authority to decide the antecedent question of how the ambiguity is to be resolved." Id. at 406–07. "Since we do not know how the arbitrator will construe the remedial limitations," the Court concluded "the proper course is to compel arbitration." Id. at 407.

Arbitrators may decide the enforceability of remedy-limitations not only when the arbitration agreement is ambiguous (as in *Book*) but also when the arbitration agreement provides that the arbitrator shall decide the enforceability of the arbitration agreement. Id. at 406–07. See Terminix International Co. v. Palmer Ranch Ltd.Partnership, 432 F.3d 1327, 1331–32 (11th Cir.2005) (by incorporating AAA Rules—including rule that "[t]he arbitrator shall have the power to rule on his or her own jurisdiction, including any objections with respect to the existence, scope or validity of the arbitration agreement"—into their agreement, the parties agreed that the arbitrator should decide the validity of the arbitration clause, including its provisions on remedies.)

[202] See, e.g., Am.Arbitration Ass'n, Commercial Arbitration Rules, R–47(a) (2013) ("The arbitrator may grant any remedy or relief that the arbitrator deems just and equitable and within the scope of the agreement of the parties, including, but not limited to, specific performance of a contract.")

[203] See Bosack v. Soward, 586 F.3d 1096 (9th Cir.2009); Todd Shipyards Corp. v. Cunard Line, 943 F.2d 1056 (9th Cir.1991); Raytheon Co. v. Automated Business Sys., Inc., 882 F.2d 6 (1st Cir.1989); Bonar v. Dean Witter Reynolds, Inc., 835 F.2d 1378 (11th Cir.1988).

[204] Saturday Evening Post Co., v. Rumbleseat Press, Inc., 816 F.2d 1191 (7th Cir.1987); Western Tech. Services Intern., Inc. v. Caucho Industriales S.A., 2010 WL 1848949 (N.D.Tex.2010); Matter of Sprinzen (Nomberg), 415 N.Y.S.2d 974, 977 (N.Y.1979).

[205] See Am.Arbitration Ass'n, Commercial Arbitration Rules, R–38 (2013).

[206] Christopher R. Drahozal & Quentin R. Wittrock, Is There a Flight from Arbitration?, 37 Hofstra L. Rev. 71, 78–79 (2008).

this,[207] but some hold that "courts should not grant injunctive relief unless there is 'qualifying contractual language' which permits it."[208]

(c) Consequences of Limiting Remedies in Arbitration

An arbitration agreement limiting the remedies available to an arbitrator may be unenforceable.[209] But if it is enforceable, an additional issue arises: may a court issue a remedy that the arbitrator may not, or have the parties waived that remedy altogether? This issue has arisen in the context of agreements that prohibit arbitrators from awarding punitive damages. May a court award punitive damages on a claim covered by such an arbitration agreement?

At least one court answers no.[210] The alternative would require arbitration of liability and other non-punitive damages issues, followed by judicial resolution of claims for punitive damages. At least one court has severed a claim for punitive damages to send the rest of the dispute to arbitration.[211] This bifurcation is inefficient. If, however, this bifurcation is chosen by the parties, courts are likely to

---

[207] See, e.g., Performance Unlimited, Inc. v. Questar Publishers, Inc., 52 F.3d 1373, 1380 (6th Cir.1995) (concluding that district court erred as a matter of law when it concluded that it could not enter preliminary injunctive relief because the parties' dispute was the subject of mandatory arbitration); Merrill Lynch, Pierce, Fenner & Smith v. Salvano, 999 F.2d 211, 214 (7th Cir.1993) ("the weight of federal appellate authority recognizes some equitable power on the part of the district court to issue preliminary injunctive relief in disputes that are ultimately to be resolved by an arbitration panel"); Ortho Pharmaceutical Corp. v. Amgen, Inc., 882 F.2d 806, 812 (3rd Cir.1989) ("we hold that a district court has the authority to grant injunctive relief in an arbitrable dispute, provided that the traditional prerequisites for such relief are satisfied"). Merrill Lynch, Pierce, Fenner & Smith, Inc. v. Bradley, 756 F.2d 1048, 1052 (4th Cir.1985) (A district court has jurisdiction to preserve the status quo pending the arbitration of the parties' dispute if the enjoined conduct would render the arbitration process a "hollow formality", i.e., "the arbitral award when rendered could not return the parties substantially to the status quo ante.")

[208] Manion v. Nagin, 255 F.3d 535, 538–39 (8th Cir.2001)(quoting Merrill Lynch, Pierce, Fenner & Smith, Inc. v. Hovey, 726 F.2d 1286, 1292 (8th Cir.1984)). See also Simula, Inc. v. Autoliv, Inc., 175 F.3d 716, 726 (9th Cir.1999) (affirming denial of preliminary injunction because plaintiff's claims were arbitrable and arbitral panel was authorized to grant provisional remedies). For an example of "qualifying contractual language," see Peabody Coalsales Co. v. Tampa Elec. Co., 36 F.3d 46, 47 n.3 (8th Cir.1994).

[209] See Merrill Lynch, Pierce, Fenner & Smith, Inc. v. Salvano, 999 F.2d 211, 214 (7th Cir.1993).

[210] Waltman v. Fahnestock & Co., 792 F.Supp. 31, 33–34 (E.D.Pa.1992), aff'd, 989 F.2d 490 (3d Cir.1993).

[211] See DiCrisci v. Lyndon Guar.Bank, 807 F.Supp. 947, 953 (W.D.N.Y.1992) (severing claim for punitive damages pending completion of arbitration). See also Mulder v. Donaldson, Lufkin & Jenrette, 611 N.Y.S.2d 1019, 1021 (Sup.Ct.1994) (plaintiff's "appropriate recourse was to wait for a favorable award from the arbitrators, and then bring a plenary action in this court for punitive damages"); Singer v. Salomon Bros.Inc., 593 N.Y.S.2d 927, 930 (Sup.Ct.1992) ("At the conclusion of the arbitration, this court may award punitive damages, if proper.")

enforce it to effectuate the FAA's primary command to enforce arbitration agreements.[212]

---

[212]   9 U.S.C. § 2.

Chapter 6

ENFORCEMENT AND VACATUR OF ARBITRATION AWARDS

Table of Sections

      (2)   State Grounds for Vacatur Narrower than Federal Grounds

1.   ENFORCEMENT OF ARBITRATION AWARDS
Table of Sections

§ 39 Confirmation

As a general rule, arbitration awards are final and binding on the parties with only very limited grounds for judicial review. If the losing party complies with the award, that ends the dispute. If the losing party refuses to comply, however, the prevailing party may seek court enforcement of the award. One option is for the prevailing party to seek a court order *confirming* the award.[1] A confirmed award in favor of the plaintiff (or "claimant") is enforced in the same manner as other court judgments: through orders to turn over property, judicial liens, garnishment, etc.[2] In addition, arbitration awards generally have preclusive effect—that is, the arbitrator's ruling precludes re-litigating or re-arbitrating the claims resolved in arbitration.

---

[1]   9 U.S.C. § 9.

[2]   FAA § 13 provides:

    The party moving for an order confirming, modifying, or correcting an award shall, at the time such order is filed with the clerk for the entry of judgment thereon, also file the following papers with the clerk:

    (a) The agreement; the selection or appointment, if any, of an additional arbitrator or umpire; and each written extension of the time, if any, within which to make the award.

    (b) The award.

    (c) Each notice, affidavit, or other paper used upon an application to confirm, modify, or correct the award, and a copy of each order of the court upon such an application.

    The judgment shall be docketed as if it was rendered in an action.

    The judgment so entered shall have the same force and effect, in all respects, as, and be subject to all the provisions of law relating to, a judgment in an action; and it may be enforced as if it had been rendered in an action in the court in which it is entered.

    9 U.S.C. § 13.

§ 40 Claim Preclusion (*Res Judicata*)

(a) Generally Applicable

The doctrine of claim preclusion (or *res judicata*) bars *adjudication*[3] of claims that have already been adjudicated in a prior proceeding. Arbitration awards have claim-preclusive effect in that they preclude later claims covered by the award.[4] This is true whether or not a court has confirmed the award.[5]

Suppose Ann asserts a claim in arbitration against Bob and the arbitrator rules for Bob. If Ann then asserts the same claim in litigation, a court will grant Bob's motion to dismiss the case. The court treats the prior arbitration award in Bob's favor just as it would treat a prior court decision in Bob's favor, as precluding further litigation of that claim. Finality is central to binding adjudication, whether that adjudication be litigation or arbitration.

(b) Labor Arbitration

The claim-preclusive effect of arbitration awards can be less clear in labor arbitration because many collective bargaining agreements prohibit discrimination that is also prohibited by statute. A collective bargaining agreement may, for example, prohibit discrimination on the basis of race and sex so an employee with a discrimination claim could sue for violation of Title VII of the Civil Rights Act of 1964 or file a grievance for violation of the collective bargaining agreement. If the employee goes to arbitration and loses, the arbitration award precludes the employee from litigating her claim for violation of the collective agreement, but would the award

---

[3] See § 1, n.1.

[4] Restatement (Second) of Judgments § 84 (1982); Charles Alan Wright, et al., Federal Practice and Procedure § 4475.1 (2005). For cases giving claim-preclusive effect to arbitration awards, see, e.g., Myer v. Americo Life Inc., 469 F.3d 731, 733 (8th Cir.2006); IDS Life Ins. Co. v. Royal Alliance Assocs., Inc., 266 F.3d 645 (7th Cir.2001); Century Int'l Arms, Ltd. v. Fed. State Unitary Enter.State Corp., 172 F.Supp.2d 79, 95–96 (D.D.C.2001); Fink v. Golenbock, 680 A.2d 1243, 1252 (Conn.1996); Sartor v. Superior Court, 187 Cal.Rptr. 247 (Cal.Ct.App.1982) (award in favor of architectural firm is *res judicata* barring homeowner's identical causes of action against firm's employees).

[5] Val-U Const. Co. v. Rosebud Sioux Tribe, 146 F.3d 573, 581 (8th Cir.1998) ("[t]he fact that the award in the present case was not confirmed by a court * * * does not vitiate the finality of the award."); Jacobson v. Fireman's Fund Ins. Co., 111 F.3d 261, 267 (2d Cir.1996) ("[the] contention that only a judicially confirmed arbitration award may form the basis for the defenses of *res judicata* and collateral estoppel is without merit * * * [These] doctrines are applicable to issues resolved by arbitration where there has been a final determination on the merits, notwithstanding a lack of confirmation of the award."); Camp v. Kollen, 567 F.Supp.2d 170 (D.D.C.2008) (unconfirmed award given claim preclusive effect); Thibodeau v. Crum, 6 Cal.Rptr.2d 27 (Cal.Ct.App.1992) (unconfirmed award in arbitration between homeowner and general contractor is *res judicata* barring homeowner's identical claim against subcontractor).

preclude the employee from litigating her Title VII claim? Not according to the Supreme Court's 1974 *Alexander v. Gardner-Denver Co.*, decision, which allowed such a Title VII suit to proceed.[6] *Alexander* was also understood by lower courts to prohibit enforcement of executory collective bargaining agreement provisions requiring employees to arbitrate, rather than litigate, statutory discrimination claims.[7]

However, in the 2009 case of *14 Penn Plaza LLC v. Pyett*,[8] the Supreme Court criticized *Gardner-Denver*,[9] and distinguished it to enforce collective bargaining arbitration clauses that "clearly and unmistakably require[ ] union members to arbitrate" statutory discrimination claims.[10] Since *Penn Plaza*, courts have routinely enforced such clauses to require arbitration, rather than litigation, of discrimination claims brought by employees represented by a labor union.[11] Similarly, since *Penn Plaza*, courts have held that an arbitration *award* on an employee's statutory discrimination claim precludes suit on that claim if the collective bargaining agreement clearly and unmistakably required employees to arbitrate, rather than litigate, statutory claims, or the employee in fact arbitrated

---

[6]   Alexander v. Gardner-Denver Co., 415 U.S. 36, 50 (1974). The *Gardner-Denver* Court did suggest that the arbitrator's findings could be admitted "as evidence" at trial and "accorded such weight as the court deems appropriate." Id. at 60 n.21.

[7]   Pyett v. Pennsylvania Bldg. Co., 498 F.3d 88, 90 (2d Cir.2007) ("mandatory arbitration clauses in collective bargaining agreements are unenforceable to the extent they waive the rights of covered workers to a judicial forum for federal statutory causes of action"), rev'd and remanded sub nom. 14 Penn Plaza LLC v. Pyett, 556 U.S. 247 (2009).

[8]   556 U.S. 247 (2009).

[9]   See, e.g., id. at 265 ("We recognize that apart from their narrow holdings, the *Gardner-Denver* line of cases included broad dicta that were highly critical of the use of arbitration for the vindication of statutory antidiscrimination rights. That skepticism, however, rested on a misconceived view of arbitration that this Court has since abandoned."); *see also id.* ("The suggestion in *Gardner-Denver* that the decision to arbitrate statutory discrimination claims was tantamount to a substantive waiver of those rights, therefore, reveals a distorted understanding of the compromise made when an employee agrees to compulsory arbitration.").

[10]   Id. at 274.

[11]   See, e.g., Savant v. APM Terminals, 776 F.3d 285, 291–92 (5th Cir. 2014) (dismissing unionized employee's age discrimination suit due to collective bargaining agreement's supplement providing that "Any complaint that there has been a violation of any employment law, such as * * * [the] ADEA, * * * shall be resolved solely by the grievance and arbitration provisions of the collective bargaining agreement."); Thompson v. Air Transp. Int'l L.L.C., 664 F.3d 723, 727 (8th Cir. 2011) (enforcing collective bargaining arbitration agreement to dismiss unionized employee's suit and compel arbitration of claims under the Arkansas Civil Rights Act and the Family Medical Leave Act). See also Safrit v. Cone Mills Corp., 248 F.3d 306, 308 (4th Cir.2001) (rejecting unionized employee's argument "that her good-faith compliance with the grievance provisions of the governing CBA should preserve her right to pursue claims in a federal forum").

statutory claims.[12] However, courts strictly construe the "clear and unmistakable" requirement, which has resulted in several cases where litigation of the statutory discrimination claim was not precluded, typically because the arbitration agreement did not specifically cite the statutory claims covered.[13] Also, courts continue to permit litigation of statutory discrimination claims after arbitration awards rejecting employees' contract claims (for violation of the collective bargaining agreement) but not addressing their statutory claims.[14]

§ 41   Issue Preclusion (Collateral Estoppel)

The doctrine of issue preclusion bars adjudication of issues that have been decided in a prior case. The doctrine of issue preclusion can apply if that prior case was an arbitration,[15] but issue preclusion

---

[12]   Watkins v. Duke Med. Ctr., No. 1:13CV1007, 2014 WL 4442936, at *8 (M.D.N.C. Sept. 9, 2014) (dismissing plaintiff's discrimination claims "to the extent they were the subject of the binding Arbitration Award at issue. . . ."); Driskell v. Macy's Dep't Store Downtown Sacramento, No. CIV S–10–2033 KJM GGH PS, 2011 WL 1636242 (E.D. Cal. Apr. 29, 2011) (precluding employee's suit on statutory discrimination claim after arbitration award denied that claim).

[13]   See, e.g., St. Aubin v. Unilever HPC NA, No. 09 C 1874, 2009 WL 1871679, at *4 (N.D. Ill. June 26, 2009) (holding that the employee's claim was not precluded because the collective bargaining agreement did not contain a "'clear and unmistakable' requirement to arbitrate employment discrimination claims," because the arbitration clause did not specifically refer to discrimination claims); Nichols v. Androscoggin County, No. 2:14–cv–421–NT, 2015 WL 2189844, at *3 (D. Maine May 11, 2015) (holding the waiver was not clear and unmistakable because it did not cite the statutory rights being waived); Pulkkinen v. Fairpoint Commc'ns., Inc., No. 09–CV–99–P–H, 2010 WL 716109, at *5 (D. Maine Feb. 23, 2010) (same). See also Cavallaro v. Univ. of Mass. Mem'l Healthcare, Inc., 678 F.3d 1, 7 n.7 (1st Cir.2012) ("A broadly-worded arbitration clause such as one covering 'any dispute concerning or arising out of the terms and/or conditions of [the CBA] . . .' will not suffice [to establish waiver]; rather, something closer to specific enumeration of the statutory claims to be arbitrated is required."); Kovac v. Superior Dairy, Inc., 930 F. Supp. 2d 857, 865 (N.D. Ohio 2013) ("Sixth Circuit case law shows that the 'clear and unmistakable' standard is not easily met.")

[14]   Fitzgerald v. Shore Mem'l Hosp., Civil No. 12–6221 (JBS/AMD), 2015 WL 1137817, at *7–8 (D.N.J. Mar. 1, 2015) (holding an employee's FMLA claim was not precluded because the arbitrator chose not to address the FMLA issue during arbitration); Mathews v. Denver Newspaper Agency LLP, 649 F.3d 1199, 1207–08 (10th Cir. 2011) (employee's suit on statutory claims not precluded by arbitration award denying contract claim, but not addressing statutory claim; "Because the arbitration agreement empowered the arbitrator to resolve only the dispute submitted, and because the dispute submitted made no mention of statutory claims, the arbitral decision could in no way determine the question of Mathews's statutory rights").

[15]   Witkowski v. Welch, 173 F.3d 192, 199–200 (3d Cir.1999); Universal American Barge Corp. v. J-Chem, Inc., 946 F.2d 1131, 1137 (5th Cir.1991); Coffey v. Dean Witter Reynolds, Inc., 961 F.2d 922, 925 (10th Cir.1989); Tremont LLC v. Halliburton Energy Services, Inc., 696 F.Supp.2d 741(S.D.Tex.2010); Barackman v. Anderson, 84 P.3d 830 (Or.Ct.App.2004). See also Restatement (Second) of Judgments § 84 cmt. c (1982) ("When arbitration affords opportunity for presentation of evidence and argument substantially similar in form and scope to judicial proceedings, the award should have the same effect on issues necessarily determined as a judgment has.")

from arbitration awards is a matter of judicial discretion,[16] and is applied less in labor arbitration than in other arbitration.[17]

While issue preclusion can only be asserted *against* one who was a party to the prior case, it can be asserted *by* one who was a stranger to that prior case.[18] When issue preclusion is asserted by one who was a stranger to the prior case, it is called "non-mutual" issue preclusion. Suppose that Ann asserts a claim in arbitration against Bob and the arbitrator rules that certain conduct by Bob was negligent. If Claire then sues Bob for damages arising out of the same conduct, the court hearing Claire's case may hold, under the doctrine of non-mutual issue preclusion, that Claire does not have to re-prove Bob's negligence. The court adopts the arbitrator's ruling regarding Bob's negligence and moves on to the other issues of Claire's suit, such as whether her damages were caused by Bob's negligence. The court treats the prior arbitration ruling against Bob just as it would treat a prior court ruling against Bob, as precluding further litigation of that issue, even against a new party.[19]

In practice, however, a challenge for Claire will be proving to the court that the arbitrator really did rule that Bob was negligent. Some arbitration awards are not accompanied by reasoned opinions.[20] If the arbitration award for Ann contained no reasoning, a court may not be able to learn *why* the arbitrator ruled against Bob. Perhaps the arbitrator concluded that Bob was negligent or perhaps the arbitrator concluded that Bob was not negligent but was liable to Ann for some other reason. If the latter, Bob is not precluded from arguing the negligence issue in Claire's suit. Courts have denied issue-preclusive effect from arbitration awards because the court could not infer the factual basis for the arbitrator's decision.[21] In addition,

---

[16]   Universal American Barge Corp. v. J-Chem, Inc., 946 F.2d 1131, 1137–38 (5th Cir.1991) (courts must "carefully consider whether procedural differences between arbitration and the district court proceeding might prejudice the party challenging the use of offensive collateral estoppel. The district court specifically must determine whether procedural opportunities available to the party in the subsequent action might be likely to cause a different result.")

[17]   Ian R. Macneil, Richard E. Speidel & Thomas J. Stipanowich, Federal Arbitration Law § 39.3.1.2 (1994).

[18]   Macneil, Speidel & Stipanowich, supra note 17, § 39.1.1; Jack H. Friedenthal, Mary Kay Kane & Arthur R. Miller, Civil Procedure § 14.14 (4th ed.2005); Bouriez v. Carnegie Mellon Univ., 2010 WL 569564, at *4 (W.D.Pa.2010).

[19]   See, e.g., Riverdale Dev. Co. v. Ruffin Bldg. Sys. Inc., 146 S.W.3d 852, 854 (Ark.2004) ("a third party * * * is entitled to rely upon an arbitration award such as [the one] here under the doctrines of collateral estoppel or *res judicata*").

[20]   See § 37(f).

[21]   See, e.g., Postlewaite v. McGraw-Hill, Inc., 333 F.3d 42, 49 (2d Cir. 2003) ("[T]he party asserting preclusion bears the burden of showing with clarity and certainty what was determined by the prior judgment."; "issue preclusion will apply only if it is quite clear that this requirement has been met."); Hybert v. Shearson Lehman/American Express, Inc. 688 F.Supp. 320 (N.D.Ill.1988); Sports Factory, Inc.

under the law of some states, arbitration awards have non-mutual issue-preclusive effect only if the arbitration agreement provides that they will have such effect.[22]

2.   VACATUR OF ARBITRATION AWARDS
Table of Sections

---

v. Chanoff, 586 F.Supp. 342, 346 (E.D.Pa.1984); Lee L. Saad Constr. Co. v. DPF Architects, P.C., 851 So.2d 507 (Ala.2003).

[22]   Buckner v. Kennard, 99 P.3d 842, 846 (Utah 2004) ("a private arbitration award does not have nonmutual collateral estoppel effect unless the parties expressly provide for such preclusive effect beforehand"); Vandenberg v. Superior Court, 88 Cal.Rptr.2d 366, 377–81 (Cal.1999) ("a private arbitration award, even if judicially confirmed, may not have nonmutual collateral estoppel effect under California law unless there was an agreement to that effect in the particular case.")

§ 42   Introduction

(a) Vacatur of Award Contrasted with Appellate Reversal of Trial Court

A party disappointed with an arbitrator's decision may ask a court to vacate the arbitration award. In some ways, a court considering whether to vacate an arbitration award is like an appellate court considering whether to reverse the decision of a trial court. But "the grounds on which courts review arbitration awards are much narrower than the grounds on which appeals courts review decisions of trial courts."[23] In particular, when appellate courts reverse trial courts they generally do so on the ground that the trial court has erred in its findings of fact or conclusions of law. Appellate courts usually give some deference to trial courts' factual findings—reversing only those that are "clearly erroneous"—but give no deference to trial courts' legal rulings, reviewing them de novo.[24] So the typical appeal of a trial court's decision centers on the appellant's argument that the trial court made an error of law.

By contrast, arbitrators' legal rulings are rarely given de novo review by courts considering a motion to vacate an arbitration award.[25] In fact, the FAA may not allow courts to review arbitrators' legal rulings at all because "error of law" by the arbitrator is not even a ground for vacating an arbitration award. The FAA only permits courts to vacate:

(1) Where the award was procured by corruption, fraud, or undue means;

(2) Where there was evident partiality or corruption in the arbitrators, or either of them;

(3) Where the arbitrators were guilty of misconduct in refusing to postpone the hearing, upon sufficient cause shown, or in refusing to hear evidence pertinent and

---

[23] Christopher R. Drahozal, Commercial Arbitration: Cases and Problems 494 (2d ed.2006).

[24] "For purposes of standard of review, decisions by judges are traditionally divided into three categories, denominated questions of law (reviewable de novo), questions of fact (reviewable for clear error), and matters of discretion (reviewable for 'abuse of discretion')." Pierce v. Underwood, 487 U.S. 552 (1988).

[25] The FAA's "grounds are narrower than the standards for appellate review in a judicial case where a court reviews a lower court's legal rulings de novo and factual findings for clear error." Maureen A. Weston, The Other Avenues of Hall Street and Prospects for Judicial Review of Arbitral Awards, 14 Lewis & Clark L. Rev. 929, 933–34 (2010).

material to the controversy; or of any other misbehavior by which the rights of any party have been prejudiced; or

(4) Where the arbitrators exceeded their powers, or so imperfectly executed them that a mutual, final, and definite award upon the subject matter submitted was not made.[26]

Why are the FAA's grounds for vacating arbitration awards so narrow that they do not even include "error of law" by the arbitrator? The following two subsections summarize two common explanations.

(b) Narrow Grounds for Vacatur Save Time and Money

One explanation of why the FAA's grounds for vacating arbitration awards are so narrow that they do not even include "error of law" by the arbitrator is that such a ground would reduce the efficiency of arbitration. As the Supreme Court's 2008 opinion in *Hall Street Associates, L.L.C. v. Mattel, Inc.*,[27] recognized, arbitration's propensity to save time and money is strengthened by the narrowness of the FAA's grounds for vacatur. *Hall Street* described the FAA's provisions on confirmation and vacatur of arbitration awards

> as substantiating a national policy favoring arbitration with just the limited review needed to maintain arbitration's essential virtue of resolving disputes straightaway. Any other reading opens the door to the full-bore legal and evidentiary appeals that can render informal arbitration merely a prelude to a more cumbersome and time-consuming judicial review process and bring arbitration theory to grief in post-arbitration process.[28]

In other words, the FAA's narrow grounds for vacatur reduce the likelihood that a court will vacate an award and thus reduce the likelihood that a party disappointed with an award will incur the expenses necessary to challenge it in court.[29] The FAA's narrow

---

[26] 9 U.S.C. § 10(a).

[27] 552 U.S. 576 (2008).

[28] 552 U.S. 576 (internal quotation omitted).

[29] Courts do not vacate arbitration awards very often. See Macneil, Speidel & Stipanowich, supra note 17, § 40.1.4. Courts do grant a significant minority of motions to vacate awards. Michael H. Leroy & Peter Feuille, The Revolving Door of Justice: Arbitration Agreements That Expand Court Review of an Award, 19 Ohio St.J.on Disp.Resol. 861, tbl.1 (2004) (at first-level of court review, 139 (92.1%) arbitration awards were confirmed, while 12 (7.9%) were vacated. 118 of initial court decisions were appealed. At higher levels of court review, 102 (86.4%) awards were confirmed, while 16 (13.6%) were vacated); Lawrence R. Mills et al., Vacating Arbitration Awards, Disp.Resol.Mag., Summer 2005, at 23, 24 (20% vacatur rate). However, there is no data indicating the number of awards that never become the subject of a motion to vacate.

grounds for vacatur increase the finality of the arbitrator's decision and thus reduce costs to both parties and to the court system.[30]

In contrast, if the FAA had listed "error of law" among the grounds for vacating an arbitration award, more parties disappointed with their arbitration awards could be expected to challenge those awards in court.[31] In addition to the costs of those challenges themselves, attempts to vacate awards on that basis might also make the underlying arbitration process more expensive. Currently, arbitrators in many cases do not write reasoned opinions explaining their decisions,[32] nor is there typically a transcript or other record of the arbitration hearing.[33] These cost-saving aspects of arbitration might have to change if courts vacated awards lacking a basis on which the court could assure itself that the arbitrator correctly applied the law. The Supreme Court has said that "A prime objective of an agreement to arbitrate is to achieve 'streamlined proceedings and expeditious results.' "[34] These goals of saving time and money are advanced by the FAA's narrow grounds for vacatur and would be hindered if courts reviewed arbitrators' legal rulings as closely as appellate courts review trial courts' legal rulings.

(c) Arbitration Award as Contract Term

The second explanation of why the FAA's grounds for vacating arbitration awards are so narrow that they do not even include "error of law" by the arbitrator is that such a ground would conflict with the contractual core of arbitration law. As Judge Richard Posner wrote for the Seventh Circuit:

For a discussion focused on labor arbitration, see Dennis R. Nolan, Labor and Employment Arbitration in a Nutshell 172–201 (2d ed.2007).

[30] See also Henry S. Noyes, If You (Re)Build It, They Will Come: Contracts to Remake the Rules of Litigation in Arbitration's Image, 30 Harv.J.L. & Pub.Pol'y 579, 592 (2007) ("limited appellate review encourages finality and discourages parties from pursuing dubious, costly appeals"); Jackson Williams & Morgan Lynn, Public Citizen Releases the Costs of Arbitration, PIABA B.J., Summer 2002, at 52 ("Public Citizen agrees that proponents of arbitration are undoubtedly correct that the limited, narrow grounds upon which an arbitration award can be appealed will reduce litigation costs. Parties will avoid paying court reporters to record or transcribe hearings or appellate attorneys to write briefs.")

[31] Abbott v. Mulligan, 647 F.Supp.2d 1286,1291–92 (D.Utah 2009) ("If a misinterpretation or misapplication of the law was a sufficient basis upon which a district court could overturn an arbitration panel's ruling, district courts would become routine avenues for appeal every time a plausible argument could be made that the arbitration panel got the law wrong. An appeal to the district court would be virtually guaranteed if one of the parties felt they had grounds to argue that the arbitrators got the law *really* wrong. Such review would defeat the rationale and purposes behind the FAA.")

[32] See § 37(f).

[33] See § 37(b).

[34] Preston v. Ferrer, 552 U.S. 346, 357 (2008).

> It is tempting to think that courts are engaged in judicial review of arbitration awards under the Federal Arbitration Act, but they are not. When parties agree to arbitrate their disputes they opt out of the court system, and when one of them challenges the resulting arbitration award he perforce does so not on the ground that the arbitrators made a mistake but that they violated the agreement to arbitrate, * * * conduct to which the parties did not consent when they included an arbitration clause in their contract.[35]

In other words, the FAA does not make "error of law" a ground for vacatur because arbitrators are not necessarily supposed to apply the law. They are supposed to apply the contract.

This understanding of arbitrators bound by contract, rather than by law "external" to the contract, has two main features. First, courts have long acknowledged that arbitrators are not obligated to apply the law and may, without fear of vacatur, decide the case by applying something other than "law," such as industry custom or the arbitrator's own sense of equity.[36]

Second, the understanding that arbitrators are bound by contract, rather than by law "external" to the contract, generally leads courts and commentators to see issues of vacatur through a contractual lens. Although arbitrators, like courts, are adjudicators issuing legally-binding rulings, an arbitrator's power to issue such a ruling comes from the parties' contract. As the Supreme Court said in a labor arbitration case, "we must treat the arbitrator's award as if it represented an agreement between" the parties themselves.[37] And as Judge Frank Easterbrook wrote for the Seventh Circuit, "In the main, an arbitrator acts as the parties' agent and as their delegate may do anything the parties may do directly."[38] In short, a court enforcing an arbitration award is a court enforcing a contract. The parties agreed to comply with the arbitrator's decision and if a party refuses to do so then that party is in breach of contract. Just as courts routinely enforce most other sorts of contracts without assessing the wisdom of the contract's terms, so courts routinely

---

[35]　Wise v. Wachovia **Sec.**, LLC, 450 F.3d 265, 269 (7th Cir.2006).

[36]　See § 44(c).

[37]　Eastern Associated Coal Corp. v. United Mine Workers, 531 U.S. 57, 62 (2000). See also United Paperworkers Int'l Union v. Misco, Inc., 484 U.S. 29, 42 (1987) ("A court's refusal to enforce an arbitrator's award * * * because it is contrary to public policy is a specific application of the more general doctrine, rooted in the common law, that a court may refuse to enforce contracts that violate law or public policy."); Seymour v. Blue Cross/Blue Shield, 988 F.2d 1020, 1023 (10th Cir.1993) ("The public policy exception is rooted in the common law doctrine of a court's power to refuse to enforce a contract that violates public policy or law.")

[38]　George Watts & Son, Inc. v. Tiffany and Co., 248 F.3d 577, 580 (7th Cir.2001) (Easterbrook, J.).

enforce arbitration awards without assessing the wisdom of the award's terms.

However, not all contracts are enforceable and, similarly, not all arbitration awards are enforceable. Just as contract law has long recognized defenses to contract enforcement, arbitration law has long recognized defenses to the enforcement of an arbitration award. Contract law's defenses include misrepresentation, mistake, duress, undue influence, unconscionability, and illegality. These contract defenses generally resemble the FAA's grounds for vacating an arbitration award. FAA § 10(a) permits courts to vacate:

(1)   Where the award was procured by corruption, fraud, or undue means;

(2)   Where there was evident partiality or corruption in the arbitrators, or either of them;

(3)   Where the arbitrators were guilty of misconduct in refusing to postpone the hearing, upon sufficient cause shown, or in refusing to hear evidence pertinent and material to the controversy; or of any other misbehavior by which the rights of any party have been prejudiced; or

(4)   Where the arbitrators exceeded their powers, or so imperfectly executed them that a mutual, final, and definite award upon the subject matter submitted was not made.[39]

Subsection 1's "corruption, fraud, or undue means" resembles contract law's defenses of illegality, misrepresentation, undue influence, and duress. Subsection 2's "partiality or corruption" and subsection 3's "misconduct" or "misbehavior" resemble contract law's defenses of unconscionability, illegality, and undue influence. Subsection 4's "exceeded * * * powers" or "imperfectly executed them" resembles contract law's defenses of illegality and mistake.

These "statutory" grounds for vacatur—the grounds expressly stated in FAA § 10(a)—are discussed next.

§ 43   Statutory Grounds for Vacatur

(a)   Corruption, Fraud or Undue Means

FAA § 10(a)(1) permits courts to vacate an arbitration award where the "award was procured by corruption, fraud, or undue means."[40] To vacate, there must be a close causal connection between

---

[39]   9 U.S.C. § 10(a).

[40]   9 U.S.C. § 10(a)(1). "The best reading of the terms 'undue means' * * * is that it describes underhanded or conniving ways of procuring an award that are similar to corruption or fraud, but do not precisely constitute either." Nat'l Casualty Co. v. First State Ins. Group, 430 F.3d 492, 499 (1st Cir.2005). "Ex parte contact [between the

the wrongdoing—corruption, fraud (including perjury) or undue means—and the award.[41] The party seeking vacatur must also show that the wrongdoing was "(1) not discoverable upon the exercise of due diligence prior to the arbitration, (2) materially related to an issue in the arbitration, and (3) established by clear and convincing evidence."[42] If the alleged wrongdoing was brought to the attention of the arbitrators then the award will not be vacated on this ground.[43] Vacatur under FAA § 10(a)(1) is not common but does happen occasionally. For example, the Eleventh Circuit vacated an award due to perjury by an expert witness as to his qualifications.[44]

(b) Evident Partiality or Corruption

(1) Arbitrator's Conduct

FAA § 10(a)(2) permits courts to vacate an arbitration award where "there was evident partiality or corruption in the arbitrators."[45] While arbitrator partiality is a ground for vacating an award, issues of partiality may arise long before an award is rendered. During the arbitrator-selection process,[46] a party may challenge the appointment of an arbitrator on the ground that the arbitrator is partial to the opposing party. "The primary remedy sought at this early stage is disqualification of the partial arbitrator and the appointment of a substitute."[47] While this remedy can be ordered by a court, "there is little FAA case law dealing with challenges to arbitrator impartiality before an award."[48] Such pre-award disputes over arbitrator partiality tend to be resolved by the parties themselves, by the arbitrator (perhaps by resigning her appointment), or by the organization administering the arbitration.

With respect to post-award disputes over arbitrator partiality, the Fourth Circuit explained:

> The party asserting evident partiality has the burden of proof. The alleged partiality must be direct, definite, and capable of demonstration rather than remote, uncertain or

---

arbitrator and a party] involving disputed issues raises a presumption that the arbitration award was procured by fraud, corruption, or other undue means." Rosenthal-Collins Group, L.P. v. Reiff, 748 N.E.2d 229, 232 (Ill.Ct.App.2001) (vacating award) (applying state law rather than FAA).

[41] See Macneil, Speidel & Stipanowich, supra note 17, § 40.2.2.

[42] A.G. Edwards & Sons, Inc. v. McCullough, 967 F.2d 1401, 1404 (9th Cir.1992). Accord Bauer v. Carty & Co., Inc., 246 Fed.Appx. 375, 377 (6th Cir.2007).

[43] Barahona v. Dillard's, Inc., 2010 WL 1655322, at *2 (5th Cir.2010)

[44] Bonar v. Dean Witter Reynolds, Inc., 835 F.2d 1378 (11th Cir.1988).

[45] 9 U.S.C. § 10(a)(2).

[46] See § 36(a).

[47] Macneil, Speidel & Stipanowich, supra note 17, § 28.1.1.

[48] Id.

speculative. Therefore, the burden on a claimant for
vacation of an arbitration award due to "evident partiality"
is heavy, and the claimant must establish specific facts that
indicate improper motives on the part of an arbitrator.[49]

As this passage suggests, courts are not quick to find arbitrator
partiality and few awards are vacated because arbitrators showed
"evident partiality" in their conduct of the arbitration. Parties have
alleged that evident partiality was demonstrated by an arbitrator
who "appeared disinterested" during one party's presentation,[50] an
arbitrator who made "several comments" indicating "empathy" for
the opposing party,[51] an arbitrator who called a party's lawyer "bitter
and irresponsible,"[52] and an arbitrator who used the term "young
lady" in addressing a party's lawyer.[53] But in none of these cases did
the court vacate the award. Courts have also rejected the "structural
bias" argument that arbitrators of industry associations are biased
against claims brought against the industry.[54]

The topic of arbitrator partiality gains another layer of
complexity when the arbitrator alleged to be partial is a party-
appointed arbitrator in tripartite arbitration. For example, conduct
that would be a troubling indicator of partiality in a single
arbitrator—speaking with one party beyond the presence of the other
party—is common of party-appointed arbitrators. As the Ninth
Circuit said in one case, "before the submission of the parties' pre-
hearing briefs * * * , each party had ex parte contact with its party
arbitrator. This is customary in tripartite arbitration panels."[55]
Accordingly, Judge Easterbrook, writing for the Seventh Circuit,
suggested that very different partiality standards be applied to
party-appointed arbitrators "because in the main party-appointed
arbitrators are *supposed* to be advocates. In labor arbitration a union
may name as its arbitrator the business manager of the local union,
and the employer its vice-president for labor relations. Yet no one

---

[49]   Peoples Sec. Life Ins. Co. v. Monumental Life Ins. Co., 991 F.2d 141, 146 (4th
Cir.1993).

[50]   Austin South I, Ltd. v. Barton-Malow Co., 799 F.Supp. 1135, 1143
(M.D.Fla.1992).

[51]   Remmy v. Paine Webber, Inc., 32 F.3d 143, 148 (4th Cir.1994).

[52]   InterChem Asia 2000 Pte. Ltd. v. Oceana Petrochemicals AG, 373 F.Supp.2d
340, 348 (S.D.N.Y.2005).

[53]   Smith v. Prudential Securities, Inc., 846 F.Supp.978, 980 (M.D.Fla.1994).

[54]   Harter v. Iowa Grain Co., 220 F.3d 544 (7th Cir.2000) (National Grain & Feed
Association arbitration); Scott v. Prudential **Sec.**, Inc., 141 F.3d 1007, 1015–16 (11th
Cir. 1998) (National Futures Trading Association arbitration).

[55]   U.S. Life Ins.Co. v. Superior Nat.Ins.Co., 591 F.3d 1167, 1171 n.1 (9th
Cir.2010).

believes that the predictable loyalty of these designees spoils the award."[56]

On the other hand, the Wisconsin Supreme Court "prescrib[ed] presumptive impartiality as the appropriate role for the party-appointed arbitrator, unless the parties contract for non-neutral arbitrators or the arbitration rules otherwise provide for non-neutral arbitrators."[57] Similarly, the American Arbitration Association's Commercial Arbitration Rules provide:

> Where the parties have agreed that each party is to name one arbitrator, the arbitrators so named must meet the standards of Section R–18 [quoted infra in the text at note 73] with respect to impartiality and independence unless the parties have specifically agreed pursuant to Section R–18(b) that the party-appointed arbitrators are to be non-neutral and need not meet those standards.[58]

The AAA and American Bar Association in 2004 approved a "Code of Ethics for Arbitrators in Commercial Disputes." It "establishes a presumption of neutrality for all arbitrators, including party appointed arbitrators, which applies unless the parties' agreement, the arbitration rules agreed to by the parties or applicable laws provide otherwise."[59]

(2) Arbitrator's Disclosure

As noted above, few arbitration awards are vacated because arbitrators showed "evident partiality" in their conduct of the arbitration.[60] Perhaps more awards are vacated due to partiality in the arbitrator's failure to make disclosures. The leading non-disclosure partiality case is *Commonwealth Coatings Corp. v. Continental Casualty Co.*,[61] decided by the Supreme Court in 1968. In *Commonwealth Coatings*, a subcontractor sued a surety on the

---

[56]   Sphere Drake Ins., Ltd. v. All Am.Life Ins.Co., 307 F.3d 617, 620 (7th Cir.2002) (emphasis in original).

[57]   Borst v. Allstate Ins.Co., 717 N.W.2d 42, 48 (Wis.2006). See also Metro. Prop. & Cas.Ins.Co. v. J.C. Penney Cas.Ins.Co., 780 F. Supp. 885, 892 (D.Conn.1991) (expressing concern about party-appointed arbitrator's ex parte meetings party to discuss the merits of the case prior to his appointment as arbitrator, "The fact that party selected arbitrators are not expected to be 'neutral', however, does not mean that such arbitrators are excused from their ethical duties and the obligation to participate in the arbitration process in a fair, honest and good-faith manner.")

[58]   Am.Arbitration Ass'n, Commercial Arbitration Rules, R–13(b) (2013). See also Macneil, Speidel & Stipanowich, supra note 17, § 44.28.4 ("On the international arbitration scene party-arbitrators are generally expected to be as independent as neutral arbitrators.")

[59]   The Code of Ethics for Arbitrators in Commercial Disputes, Mar. 1, 2004.

[60]   FAA § 10(a)(2) permits courts to vacate an arbitration award where "there was evident partiality or corruption in the arbitrators."

[61]   393 U.S. 145 (1968).

prime contractor's bond to recover money due for a painting job.[62] Each party appointed an arbitrator and the two party-appointed arbitrators appointed a third, neutral arbitrator.[63] The arbitrators unanimously ruled for the surety.[64] Then the subcontractor learned for the first time that the neutral arbitrator, an engineering consultant, had a business relationship with the prime contractor.[65] The prime contractor had paid the arbitrator consulting fees of about $12,000 over a period of four or five years.[66] Although there was no evidence of actual bias or prejudice, the Supreme Court reversed the lower courts and vacated the arbitration award. The Court's opinion held that non-disclosure of "any dealings that might create an impression of possible bias" or creating "even an appearance of bias" would warrant vacating.[67] The concurring opinion required disclosure of substantial relationships only.[68]

What particular dealings or relationships trigger a duty to disclose can only be determined case-by-case in a fact-intensive inquiry.[69] Nevertheless, the Fourth Circuit has identified four factors to be considered:

---

[62]   Id. at 146.

[63]   Id.

[64]   Id.

[65]   Id.

[66]   Id.

[67]   Id. at 149.

[68]   393 U.S. at 150 (White, J., concurring). See Nationwide Mut. Ins. Co. v. Home Ins. Co., 429 F.3d 640 (6th Cir. 2005).

> [T]he party seeking invalidation must demonstrate more than an amorphous institutional predisposition toward the other side; a lesser showing would be tantamount to an 'appearance of bias' standard. The alleged partiality must be direct, definite, and capable of demonstration, and the party asserting [it] * * * must establish specific facts that indicate improper motives on the part of the arbitrator.

Id. at 645 (internal quotation marks and citations omitted).

[69]   Compare, e.g., Positive Software Solutions, Inc. v. New Century Mortgage Corp., 436 F.3d 495 (5th Cir.2006) (vacating award where arbitrator failed to disclose that seven years before the arbitration, he and his former law firm were co-counsel in a lengthy litigation matter with law firm and particular lawyer representing winning party in arbitration); Schmitz v. Zilveti, 20 F.3d 1043, 1044 (9th Cir.1994) (vacating award where the arbitrator failed to disclose that his law firm had represented the corporate parent of the defendant corporation involved in the arbitration in 19 matters over a 35-year period ending some 21 months before the arbitration.); Neaman v. Kaiser Found. Hosp., 11 Cal.Rptr.2d 879 (Ct.App.1992) (failure of neutral arbitrator to reveal that he had served as a party-arbitrator for one of the parties required the award to be set aside); Wages v. Smith Barney Harris Upham Co., 937 P.2d 715 (Ariz.Ct.App.1997) (vacating award when arbitrator failed to disclose that he had represented investors with similar claims against predecessor-in-interest to respondent), with Lucent Techs. Inc. v. Tatung Co., 379 F.3d 24 (2d Cir.2004) (arbitrator's prior service as expert witness for one of the parties does not constitute evident partiality when that service involved matter unrelated to dispute at issue and engagement concluded prior to arbitration); Freeman v. Pittsburgh Glass Works, LLC, 709 F.3d 240, 254–55 (3d Cir.2013) (party's undisclosed campaign contributions to

(1) the extent and character of the personal interest, pecuniary or otherwise, of the arbitrator in the proceeding; (2) the directness of the relationship between the arbitrator and the party he is alleged to favor; (3) the connection of that relationship to the arbitration; and (4) the proximity in time between the relationship and the arbitration proceeding.[70]

Courts may even vacate an award by an arbitrator who did not know of his relationship with a party if he would have discovered the relationship had he engaged in a reasonable investigation.[71]

Many arbitration agreements incorporate the rules of organizations such as the American Arbitration Association. "In most cases such contractual mechanisms, which permit issues of partiality and personal interest to be addressed as they arise, play a significant role in policing such conflicts and make recourse to the courts less likely."[72] For example, the AAA's Commercial Arbitration Rules say:

R–17.   Disclosure

(a) Any person appointed or to be appointed as an arbitrator, as well as the parties and their representatives, shall disclose to the AAA any circumstance likely to give

---

arbitrator's election campaign not evidence of partiality because they are on the public record and because opposing party's lawyers contributed more); Apusento Garden (Guam) Inc. v. Superior Court of Guam, 94 F.3d 1346, 1352 (9th Cir.1996) (confirming award of arbitrator who failed to disclose that he and Apusento Garden's expert witness were both limited partners in a partnership unrelated to the arbitration); Woods v. Saturn Distribution Corp., 78 F.3d 424 (9th Cir.1996) (no evident partiality arising from arbitrators' financial dependence on Saturn where arbitrators, like Woods, were Saturn auto dealers); Casden Park La Brea Retail LLC v. Ross Dress For Less, Inc., 75 Cal.Rptr.3d 763 (Ct.App.2008) (neutral arbitrator had no duty to disclose employer's prior dealings with a party because the arbitrator did not participate in or have a pecuniary interest in those transactions); Guseinov v. Burns, 51 Cal.Rptr.3d 903 (Ct.App.2006) (declining to vacate award despite arbitrator's nondisclosure of prior service as a pro bono mediator in an unrelated case involving a party's attorney).

[70]   ANR Coal Co., Inc. v. Cogentrix of North Carolina, Inc., 173 F.3d 493, 500 (4th Cir.1999). By statute, California requires extensive disclosures by neutral arbitrators of potential conflicts of interest. See § 36(a)(3). Gray v. Chiu, 151 Cal.Rptr.3d 791, 797 (Ct.App. 2013) (vacating award).

[71]   New Regency Productions, Inc. v. Nippon Herald Films, Inc., 501 F.3d 1101, 1107–08 (9th Cir.2007) ("an arbitrator's lack of actual knowledge of the presence of a conflict does not excuse non-disclosure where the arbitrator had a duty to investigate, and thus had constructive knowledge of, the conflict.") See also Applied Indus. Materials Corp. v. Ovalar Makine Ticaret Ve Sanayi, A.S., 492 F.3d 132, 138 (2d Cir.2007) ("where an arbitrator has reason to believe that a nontrivial conflict of interest might exist, he must (1) investigate the conflict (which may reveal information that must be disclosed under Commonwealth Coatings) or (2) disclose his reasons for believing there might be a conflict and his intention not to investigate."); id. (if an arbitrator fails to follow this rule by investigating or disclosing a potential nontrivial conflict of interest, such a failure "is indicative of evident partiality.")

[72]   Macneil, Speidel & Stipanowich, supra note 17, § 28.2.6.1, at 28:57 (Supp.1999).

rise to justifiable doubt as to the arbitrator's impartiality or independence, including any bias or any financial or personal interest in the result of the arbitration or any past or present relationship with the parties or their representatives. Such obligation shall remain in effect throughout the arbitration. Failure on the part of a party or a representative to comply with the requirements of this rule may result in the waiver of the right to object to an arbitrator in accordance with Rule R–41.

(b)   Upon receipt of such information from the arbitrator or another source, the AAA shall communicate the information to the parties and, if it deems it appropriate to do so, to the arbitrator and others.

(c)   Disclosure of information pursuant to this Section R–17 is not an indication that the arbitrator considers that the disclosed circumstance is likely to affect impartiality or independence.

R–18.   Disqualification of Arbitrator

(a)   Any arbitrator shall be impartial and independent and shall perform his or her duties with diligence and in good faith, and shall be subject to disqualification for:

   i.   partiality or lack of independence,

   ii.   inability or refusal to perform his or her duties with diligence and in good faith, and

   iii. any grounds for disqualification provided by applicable law.

(b) The parties may agree in writing, however, that arbitrators directly appointed by a party pursuant to Section R–13 shall be non-neutral, in which case such arbitrators need not be impartial or independent and shall not be subject to disqualification for partiality or lack of independence.

(c)   Upon objection of a party to the continued service of an arbitrator, or on its own initiative, the AAA shall determine whether the arbitrator should be disqualified under the grounds set out above, and shall inform the parties of its decision, which decision shall be conclusive.[73]

---

[73]   Am.Arbitration Ass'n, Commercial Arbitration Rules, R–17, 18 (2013).

(c) Fundamentally Fair Hearing

FAA § 10(a)(3) permits courts to vacate an arbitration award where "the arbitrators were guilty of misconduct in refusing to postpone the hearing, upon sufficient cause shown, or in refusing to hear evidence pertinent and material to the controversy; or of any other misbehavior by which the rights of any party have been prejudiced."[74] This provision has been summarized by courts as requiring arbitrators to provide the parties with a "fundamentally fair hearing," which requires only notice and an opportunity to be heard.[75] An arbitration award may be rendered against a party who does not participate after receiving notice.[76]

Courts are cautious about vacating an award due to an arbitrator's ruling on a procedural or evidentiary issue. Most hold that "a challenge to an arbitrator's evidentiary rulings or limitations on discovery should not provide a basis for vacating an award unless the error substantially prejudiced a party's ability to present material evidence in support of its case."[77] An award has been vacated, however, where the arbitrator misled a party about what evidence had been admitted.[78] Also, ex parte evidence received by arbitrators has triggered vacatur.[79]

---

[74]   9 U.S.C. § 10(a)(3). See, e.g., Tempo Shain Corp. v. Bertek, Inc., 120 F.3d 16 (2d Cir.1997); Goldfinger v. Lisker, 500 N.E.2d 857 (N.Y.Ct.App.1986) (vacating award due to arbitrator's ex parte contacts).

[75]   See Macneil, Speidel & Stipanowich, supra note 17, § 32.4.1.1 (fundamental fairness requires that each party have an opportunity to present its case and offer its evidence to the arbitrator). See, e.g., Legacy Trading Co., Ltd. v. Hoffman, 2010 WL 325893, at *3 (10th Cir.2010) ("a fundamentally fair arbitration hearing requires only notice, opportunity to be heard and to present relevant and material evidence and argument before the decision makers, and that the decision-makers are not infected with bias") (citation omitted); Nationwide Mut. Ins. Co. v. Home Ins. Co., 278 F.3d 621, 625 (6th Cir.2002) ("Fundamental fairness requires only notice, an opportunity to present relevant and material evidence and arguments to the arbitrators, and an absence of bias on the part of the arbitrators."); FDIC v. Air Florida Sys., 822 F.2d 833 (9th Cir.1987) (upholding decision of arbitrator to deny one party's request to hold an oral evidentiary hearing and to require all evidence to be submitted in writing where sole issue involved valuation of corporate stock.).

[76]   See § 37(e) (discussing dispositive motions).

[77]   Schlessinger v. Rosenfeld, Meyer & Susman, 47 Cal.Rptr.2d 650, 659 (Ct.App.1995). See also U.S. Life Ins. Co. v. Superior Nat. Ins. Co., 591 F.3d 1167, 1174 (9th Cir.2010) ("the phrase 'refusing to hear evidence pertinent and material to the controversy' necessarily implies prejudice to the rights of a party"); Nat'l Casualty Co. v. First State Ins. Group, 430 F.3d 492, 499 (1st Cir.2005) (vacatur only where "the exclusion of relevant evidence so affects the rights of a party that it may be said that he was deprived of a fair hearing.").

[78]   Gulf Coast Industrial Workers Union v. Exxon Co., USA, 70 F.3d 847 (5th Cir.1995).

[79]   Macneil, Speidel & Stipanowich, supra note 17, § 32.4.1.2 ("In the absence of waiver, reliance by the arbitrators entirely on ex parte hearings is fundamentally unfair."). Compare, e.g., Pac. Reins. Mgmt. Corp. v. Ohio Reins. Corp., 935 F.2d 1019, 1025 (9th Cir.1991); Totem Marine Tug & Barge, Inc. v. N. Am. Towing, Inc., 607 F.2d

Rules of evidence in arbitration are discussed in an earlier section.[80]

(d) Exceeded Powers

FAA § 10(a)(4) permits courts to vacate an arbitration award where, among other things, "the arbitrators exceeded their powers."[81] These powers are, basically, whatever the arbitration agreement says they are.[82] Courts vacate awards under this provision "in cases where the arbitrators somehow alter the parties' contractual obligations" or "fail to meet their obligations, as specified in a given contract, to the parties."[83]

In *Stolt-Nielsen S.A. v. AnimalFeeds International Corp.,*[84] the Supreme Court relied on FAA § 10(a)(4) to vacate an award permitting classwide arbitration where the arbitration agreement did not authorize it. The Court said "an arbitration decision may be vacated under § 10(a)(4) of the FAA on the ground that the arbitrator 'exceeded [his] powers,' for the task of an arbitrator is to interpret and enforce a contract, not to make public policy. In this case, we must conclude that what the arbitration panel did was simply to impose its own view of sound policy regarding class arbitration."[85] By contrast, in the 2013 case of *Oxford Health Plans LLC v. Sutter*, "[t]he parties agreed that the arbitrator should decide whether their contract authorized class arbitration" so the Supreme Court affirmed denial of a motion to vacate the award permitting classwide

---

649, 653 (5th Cir.1979) ("[a]rbitrators cannot conduct ex parte hearings or receive evidence except in the presence of each other and of the parties, unless otherwise stipulated"); Goldfinger v. Lisker 500 N.E.2d 857 (N.Y.1986) (private communication between arbitrator and party constitutes misconduct sufficient to vacate award), with U.S. Life Ins. Co. v. Superior Nat. Ins. Co., 591 F.3d 1167, 1176 (9th Cir.2010) ("Ex parte conduct by an arbitration panel requires vacatur of an award only if the ex parte contact constitutes misbehavior that prejudices the rights of a party.")

[80] See § 37(d).

[81] 9 U.S.C. § 10(a)(4).

[82] Macneil, Speidel & Stipanowich, supra note 17, § 40.5. Vaughn v. Leeds, Morelli & Brown, PC, 315 Fed.Appx. 327, 330 (2d Cir.2009) ("this Court has consistently accorded the narrowest of readings to this statutory ground [§ 10(a)(4)], focusing on whether the arbitrators had the power, based on the parties' submissions or the arbitration agreement, to reach a certain issue, not whether the arbitrators correctly decided that issue"); Bull NH Infor. Sys., Inc. v. Hutson, 229 F.3d 321, 330 (1st Cir.2000) ("To determine whether an arbitrator has exceeded his authority under § 10 * * * , courts do not sit to hear claims of factual or legal error by an arbitrator as an appellate court does in reviewing decisions of lower courts * * * and even where such error is painfully clear, courts are not authorized to reconsider the merits of the arbitration awards.")

[83] Western Employers Ins. Co. v. Jefferies & Co., Inc., 958 F.2d 258, 262 (9th Cir.1992).

[84] 559 U.S. 662 (2010).

[85] Id. at 1767–68.

arbitration.[86] The *Oxford* Court said "A party seeking relief under [§ 10(a)(4)] bears a heavy burden. It is not enough to show that the arbitrator committed an error—or even a serious error. Because the parties bargained for the arbitrator's construction of their agreement, an arbitral decision even arguably construing or applying the contract must stand, regardless of a court's view of its (de)merits."[87]

FAA § 10(a)(4)'s "exceeded powers" ground for vacatur relates to the "contractual arbitrability" or "scope of arbitration agreement" topic discussed earlier.[88] As explained there, if a party seeks to litigate rather than arbitrate a particular claim, the court will send that claim to arbitration only if the parties agreed to arbitrate that claim. That the parties agreed to arbitrate *some* claim is not enough. They must have agreed to arbitrate *that* claim. This point about the enforcement of executory arbitration agreements has its counterpart with respect to enforcement of arbitration awards. Courts will enforce an arbitrator's award on a claim only if the parties agreed to arbitrate that claim. That the parties agreed to arbitrate *some* claim is not enough. They must have agreed to arbitrate *that* claim. If the parties used a broad arbitration agreement, such as one covering all disputes "relating to" the parties' relationship, then the arbitrator likely had the power to rule on all claims between the parties. But when parties use narrower arbitration agreements, the possibility arises of an arbitration award that exceeds the arbitrator's power by ruling on claims not properly before the arbitrator. However, even if the arbitrator ruled on a claim not covered by the arbitration agreement, the arbitrator may have received the power to rule on that claim by the parties' conduct—if they argued the merits of that claim in arbitration without either party objecting that it was beyond the scope of the arbitration. In other words, a party's right to object to the arbitrator's ruling on a claim beyond the scope of the arbitration agreement may be waived by the party arguing the merits of that claim without clearly objecting to the arbitrator's power to reach those merits.[89] In contrast, parties who do object in arbitration

---

[86]   133 S.Ct. 2064, 2067 (2013).

[87]   Id. at 2068.

[88]   See §§ 29–31.

[89]   Environmental Barrier Co., LLC v. Slurry Systems, Inc., 540 F.3d 598, 606 (7th Cir.2008) (rejecting SSI's argument that arbitrator exceeded his powers because "SSI never told the arbitrator that it thought this dispute was nonarbitrable. To the contrary, it voluntarily submitted to the arbitrator's authority, filed a counterclaim, and confined its objections to EBC's standing to arbitrate. Only after the arbitrator issued an award unfavorable to SSI and the case wound up in court did SSI raise an objection to the arbitrator's authority to decide the dispute."); Fortune, Alsweet & Eldridge, Inc. v. Daniel, 724 F.2d 1355, 1356–57 (9th Cir.1983) ("[a]n agreement to arbitrate an issue need not be express; * * * it may be implied from the conduct of the parties"; appellant's "conduct demonstrated he agreed to submit this conflict to

to the arbitrator's power to reach the merits presumably do not waive their right to make this argument in a motion to vacate under FAA § 10(a)(4) because the Supreme Court has held that "merely arguing the arbitrability issue to an arbitrator does not indicate a clear willingness to arbitrate that issue."[90]

Broader questions about arbitrators exceeding their powers are discussed next.

§ 44   Formerly Non-Statutory Grounds for Vacatur

(a) Introduction

In addition to the statutory grounds for vacating arbitration awards,[91] courts until recently also recognized additional grounds for vacatur. These *non-statutory* grounds could be divided into two categories: *contractually-created* grounds for vacatur and *judicially-created* grounds for vacatur. Both categories of non-statutory grounds for vacatur were undermined by the Supreme Court's 2008 opinion in *Hall Street Associates v. Mattel*,[92] which stated that the FAA's four grounds for vacatur are "exclusive."[93] Nevertheless, important

---

arbitration and waived any right to object."); Tristar Pictures, Inc. v. Director's Guild of America, Inc., 160 F.3d 537, 540 (9th Cir.1998) ("Tristar's challenge to the arbitrator's jurisdiction fails, not only because of the broad language of the arbitration clause, but also because of Tristar's prior actions. Although Tristar did suggest at the arbitration hearing that the arbitrator had no authority to decide certain issues, it chose to argue that the arbitrator lacked authority rather than simply refusing to come to the table.") (internal quotations omitted); Metzler Contracting Co. LLC v. Stephens, 774 F.Supp.2d 1073 (D.Haw.2011) ("the Stephenses voluntarily submitted their argument concerning these issues to the arbitrator, and cannot now claim that the arbitrator had no authority to decide them"); Data Mountain Solutions, Inc. v. Giordano, 680 F.Supp.2d 110, 124 (D.D.C.2010) ("If a party has not consented to arbitration of a given issue, then an arbitrator 'exceed[s][his] powers' by reaching that issue, and any consequent award may be vacated by a court upon judicial review. 9 U.S.C. § 10(a)(4)."); id. at 131 ("Mr. Giordano has failed utterly to demonstrate that he made a "clear and explicit" objection to the presentation of the fee-splitting dispute to the arbitrator. He therefore consented to the arbitration of that issue and may not challenge the arbitrator's authority").

90   First Options of Chicago v. Kaplan, 514 U.S. 938, 946 (1995). See also Dedon GmbH v. Janus et Cie, 411 Fed.Appx. 361, 364 (2d Cir.2011); Opals on Ice Lingerie v. Bodylines Inc., 320 F.3d 362, 368–69 (2d Cir.2003).

91   See § 43.

92   552 U.S. 576 (2008).

93   Id. at 1403. Those four grounds are:

(1) Where the award was procured by corruption, fraud, or undue means;

(2) Where there was evident partiality or corruption in the arbitrators, or either of them;

(3) Where the arbitrators were guilty of misconduct in refusing to postpone the hearing, upon sufficient cause shown, or in refusing to hear evidence pertinent and material to the controversy; or of any other misbehavior by which the rights of any party have been prejudiced; or

questions remain about the extent to which formerly non-statutory grounds for vacatur can be re-characterized to fit within the four statutory grounds and thus continue to apply notwithstanding *Hall Street*. In other words, *Hall Street* clearly requires some changes in the labels given to some grounds for vacatur but *Hall Street* leaves much uncertainty about the extent to which the substance of these grounds must also change.

To provide a context for these issues and the impact of *Hall Street*, consider two types of arbitration agreements: those that require the arbitrator to apply the law correctly and those that do not.[94] When the FAA was enacted in 1925 (and, to a lesser extent, still today), agreements that required the arbitrator to apply the law correctly were called "restricted submissions" because the agreement submitting the dispute to arbitration[95] imposed an important restriction on the manner in which the arbitrator was authorized to decide the case.[96] In contrast, an "unrestricted submission" allows the arbitrator to decide the case according to law or according to some other source of norms, such as the customs in a particular industry or the arbitrator's own sense of equity. The next two subsections discuss arbitration arising out of restricted and unrestricted submissions, respectively, and the state of the law governing each of them after *Hall Street*.

(b) Agreements Requiring Arbitrators to Apply the Law Correctly

(1) Hall Street *and Interpretation of the FAA*

One way to require the arbitrator to apply the law correctly is to authorize a court to vacate an arbitration award that does not apply

---

(4) Where the arbitrators exceeded their powers, or so imperfectly executed them that a mutual, final, and definite award upon the subject matter submitted was not made.

9 U.S.C. § 10(a).

[94]   By "the law" in this context we mean the substantive law governing the merits of the parties' dispute, as opposed to arbitration law governing the formation, terms and enforcement of agreements to arbitrate.

[95]   Today, the term "submission agreement" is perhaps used more often to describe *post-dispute* arbitration agreements than pre-dispute arbitration agreements, see § 3, because a post-dispute agreement clearly submits a particular dispute to arbitration, while the parties to a pre-dispute agreement probably hope at the time of the agreement that they will not have a dispute at all, let alone one requiring arbitration. Prior to the FAA, pre-dispute arbitration agreements were generally not enforceable so presumably a higher percentage of arbitration in that era than today arose out of post-dispute "submission" agreements.

[96]   As Professor Drahozal points out, "submissions can be restricted in any number of ways. But in this context, the most relevant restriction is one that requires the arbitrators to follow the law." Christopher R. Drahozal, Contracting Around Hall Street, 14 Lewis & Clark L.Rev. 905, 914 n.50 (2010).

the law correctly. For example, one arbitration agreement said "The Court shall vacate, modify or correct any award: (i) based upon any of the grounds referred to in the Federal Arbitration Act, (ii) where the arbitrators' findings of fact are not supported by substantial evidence, or (iii) where the arbitrators' conclusions of law are erroneous."[97] This language purports to create, by contract, grounds for vacatur—numbers ii and iii—not otherwise found in the law. Prior to *Hall Street*, courts were split on whether to enforce such contractually-created grounds for vacatur.[98] *Hall Street* resolved this split against enforcement. The Court refused to enforce a clause providing that "[t]he [District] Court shall vacate, modify or correct any award: (i) where the arbitrator's findings of facts are not supported by substantial evidence, or (ii) where the arbitrator's conclusions of law are erroneous."[99] The Court rejected such contractually-created grounds for vacatur, which the Court called "expandable judicial review authority."[100] *Hall Street* stated that the FAA's four grounds for vacatur are "exclusive" and cannot be "supplemented by contract."[101]

While *Hall Street* generally prevents parties from adding to the FAA's four grounds for vacatur, one of those grounds can be read to enforce certain agreements requiring arbitrators to apply the law correctly. FAA § 10(a)(4) permits courts to vacate an arbitration award where "the arbitrators exceeded their powers."[102] Suppose an arbitration agreement says "the arbitrators have the power to render an award that correctly applies the law of Wisconsin but lack the power to render any other award." The arbitrators arguably exceed their powers if they render an award that does not apply the law of Wisconsin correctly.[103] Along these lines, the Seventh Circuit vacated an award on the ground that the arbitrator had exceeded his authority by failing to apply the law when the arbitration clause included an " 'express stipulation that the arbitrator shall strictly

---

[97] Kyocera Corp. v. Prudential-Bache Trade Services, Inc., 341 F.3d 987, 990–91 (9th Cir. 2003).

[98] Hall Street, 552 U.S. at 583 n.5.

[99] Hall Street Associates v. Mattel, 552 U.S. 576, 579 (2008).

[100] Id. at 584.

[101] Id. at 1403.

[102] 9 U.S.C. § 10(a)(4).

[103] Professor Drahozal cites modern scholars supporting this view, as well as commentators from the era in which the FAA was enacted. Christopher R. Drahozal, Contracting Around Hall Street, 14 Lewis & Clark L.Rev. 905, 915 (2010). See e.g., Wesley A. Sturges, A Treatise on Commercial Arbitrations and Awards § 366, at 793–94 (1930) ("With respect to matters of law, it is frequently said that, if arbitrators are required by the terms of a given submission to decide 'according to law,' an award may be vacated as for mistake of law if the arbitrators decide contrary to law. * * * Their award may fall even though they have misjudged the law, for they depart, it is said, from their authority under the submission.")

abide by the terms of this [contract] and shall strictly apply rules of law applicable thereto,' namely the rules of Wisconsin law."[104] The Seventh Circuit opinion, by Judge Posner, which was decided while *Hall Street* was pending before the Supreme Court, distinguished the issues in the two cases, stating that "[t]he question in our case is different. It is whether the arbitrator can be directed to apply specific substantive norms and held to the application."[105] However, post-*Hall Street* cases have not agreed with Judge Posner. Since *Hall Street*, most courts have refused to enforce agreements requiring arbitrators to apply the law correctly.[106]

(2) State Courts and FAA Preemption

In contrast, a few state supreme court decisions since *Hall Street* have enforced agreements requiring arbitrators to apply the law correctly.[107] For example, the 2011 Texas Supreme Court decision in

---

[104]   Edstrom Industries, Inc. v. Companion Life Insurance Co., 516 F.3d 546, 550 (7th Cir.2008) (Posner, J.)

[105]   Id.

[106]   Francis v. Landstar Sys. Holdings, Inc., 2009 WL 4350250 (M.D. Fla. Nov. 25, 2009) (citing *Hall Street* in refusing to enforce agreement that the "Arbitrator's authority is strictly limited to resolving the Dispute on the basis of such applicable state or federal law"); Wood v. Penntex Res. LP, 2008 WL 2609319 (S.D. Tex. June 27, 2008) (citing *Hall Street* in refusing to enforce agreement providing that "this Agreement confers no power or authority upon the arbitrators to render any decision that is based on clearly erroneously findings of fact, that manifestly disregards the law, or exceeds of the powers of the arbitrator, and no such decision will be eligible for confirmation"); In re Raymond Prof'l Group, Inc., 397 B.R. 414, 431 (Bankr. N.D. Ill. 2008) ("Until *Hall Street* was decided, the Seventh Circuit panel opinion in *Edstrom Indus.* could have been read to expand the standard of review for vacating an arbitration award. However, after *Hall Street*, the *Edstrom Indus.* opinion must be read more narrowly."); Brookfield Country Club, Inc. v. St. James-Brookfield, LLC, 696 S.E.2d 663, 667 (Ga.2010); HL 1, LLC v. Riverwalk, LLC,15 A.3d 725 (Me.2011); Pugh's Lawn Landscape Co., Inc. v. Jaycon Dev.Corp., 320 S.W.3d 252, 260 (Tenn.2010).

[107]   Raymond James Financial Services, Inc. v. Honea, 55 So.3d 1161, 1169 (Ala.2010). ("Under the Alabama common law, courts must rigorously enforce contracts, including arbitration agreements, according to their terms in order to give effect to the contractual rights and expectations of the parties. Applying that principle in this case requires us to give effect to the provision in the arbitration agreement authorizing a court having jurisdiction to conduct a de novo review of the award entered as a result of arbitration proceedings conducted pursuant to that same agreement."); Cable Connection, Inc. v. DirectTV, Inc., 190 P.3d 586, 589 (Cal. 2008) (discussing *Hall Street* and concluding that FAA does not preempt state law enforcing arbitration agreement providing that "The arbitrators shall not have the power to commit errors of law or legal reasoning, and the award may be vacated or corrected on appeal to a court of competent jurisdiction for any such error."); Nafta Traders, Inc. v. Quinn, 339 S.W.3d 84 (Tex.2011) (enforcing restricted submission).

In contrast, several states' courts hold that their state law does not enforce contractually-created grounds for vacatur. Brookfield Country Club, Inc. v. St. James-Brookfield, LLC, 696 S.E.2d 663, 667 (Ga.2010); HL 1, LLC v. Riverwalk, LLC, 2011 WL 816811 (Me.2011); Brucker v. McKinlay Transp., Inc., 557 N.W.2d 536, 540 (Mich.1997); John T. Jones Constr. Co. v. City of Grand Forks, 665 N.W.2d 698, 704

Nafta Traders, Inc. v. Quinn,[108] enforced an arbitration agreement that said "The arbitrator does not have authority (i) to render a decision which contains a reversible error of state or federal law, or (ii) to apply a cause of action or remedy not expressly provided for under existing state or federal law."[109] The Texas Supreme Court recognized the similarity between this clause and the arbitration clause in *Hall Street*.

> [W]hile the Supreme Court and the parties in *Hall Street* framed the issue as "expandable judicial review authority", the flip-side is limited arbitral decision-making authority * * *. The parties in *Hall Street* attempted to accomplish indirectly the same end that Quinn and Nafta sought directly—a limit on the arbitrator's authority.[110]

In other words, directing the court to vacate "where the arbitrator's conclusions of law are erroneous" (as the *Hall Street* agreement did) is just an indirect way of doing what the *Nafta Traders* agreement did directly, that is, deprive the arbitrator of "authority * * * to render a decision which contains a reversible error of state or federal law." Further highlighting the similarities between the two cases, the Texas Supreme Court noted that the Texas Arbitration Act (TAA), much like FAA § 10(a)(4), instructs courts to vacate arbitration awards if the arbitrators "exceeded their powers."[111] With such strong similarities between the cases, how did the Texas Supreme Court reach a different result from *Hall Street*?

It did so by interpreting the TAA differently than *Hall Street* interpreted the FAA. "We must, of course, follow *Hall Street* in applying the FAA, but in construing the TAA, we are obliged to examine *Hall Street*'s reasoning and reach our own judgment."[112] The Texas Supreme Court said that *Hall Street* "did not discuss [FAA] section 10(a)(4)" and this

> omission appears to us to undercut the Supreme Court's textual analysis. When parties have agreed that an arbitrator should not have authority to reach a decision based on reversible error—in other words, that an arbitrator should have no more power than a judge—a motion to vacate for such error as exceeding the arbitrator's authority is firmly grounded in the text of section 10. The

---

(N.D.2003); Pugh's Lawn Landscape Co., Inc. v. Jaycon Dev.Corp., 320 S.W.3d 252, 260 (Tenn.2010).

[108]   339 S.W.3d 84 (Tex.2011).

[109]   Id. at 88.

[110]   Id. at 92.

[111]   Id. at n.15 (citing Tex. Civ. Prac. & Rem.Code § 171.088(a)(3)(A)).

[112]   Id. at 91–92.

Supreme Court's reasoning that an arbitrator's merely legal errors are not the kind of "egregious departures from the parties' agreed-upon arbitration" section 10 addresses loses force when such errors directly contradict the parties' express agreement and deprive them of the benefit of their reasonable expectations.[113]

Accordingly, the Texas Supreme Court interpreted the TAA to enforce agreements requiring arbitrators to apply the law correctly and thus require courts to vacate awards in which arbitrators exceed their powers by failing to apply the law correctly.

So interpreted, the TAA differs from the FAA as interpreted by the U.S. Supreme Court in *Hall Street*. In a conflict between state and federal *substantive* law, the federal law prevails under the Supremacy Clause of the United States Constitution.[114] However, federal *procedural* law does not preempt state law. For instance, the Federal Rules of Civil Procedure do not preempt inconsistent state law because the Federal Rules of Civil Procedure only apply in federal court and the "inconsistent" state law—the state rules of civil procedure—only apply in state court. There is no conflict because each governs in its own forum. While the U.S. Supreme Court's 1984 decision in *Southland Corp. v. Keating*,[115] established that section 2 of the FAA is substantive law that preempts inconsistent state law,[116] the Court has never extended that holding to the FAA's provisions on confirmation and vacatur of awards, FAA §§ 9–11.[117] These FAA provisions do not, the Texas Supreme Court held, preempt the TAA, although the TAA (as interpreted in *Nafta Traders*) recognizes a ground for vacatur not found in the FAA.[118] Moreover, *Hall Street* itself said:

> In holding that [FAA] §§ 10 and 11 provide exclusive regimes for the review provided by the statute, we do not purport to say that they exclude more searching review

---

[113]   Id. at 92–93.

[114]   See §§ 6–7.

[115]   465 U.S. 1, 11 (1984).

[116]   See § 7.

[117]   The Supreme Court of Alabama said "in Hall Street, the Supreme Court of the United States acknowledged that state statutory or common law might permit arbitration awards to be reviewed under standards different from those enumerated in [FAA] § 10, thus effectively stating that § 10 represents procedural as opposed to substantive law." Raymond James Financial Services, Inc. v. Honea, 55 So.3d 1161, 1168 (Ala.2010).

[118]   339 S.W.2d at 100–01. See also Ovitz v. Schulman, 35 Cal.Rptr.3d 117, 130–32 (Cal.App.2005) (rejecting FAA preemption challenge to Cal.Civ.Proc.Code 1286.2(a)(6)(A), which requires vacatur for arbitrator's failure to comply with state disclosure requirements). See § 44(a) (FAA preemption of state grounds for vacatur); § 36(a)(3) (discussing California's disclosure requirements).

based on authority outside the statute as well. The FAA is not the only way into court for parties wanting review of arbitration awards: they may contemplate enforcement under state statutory or common law, for example, where judicial review of different scope is arguable. But here we speak only to the scope of the expeditious judicial review under §§ 9, 10, and 11, deciding nothing about other possible avenues for judicial enforcement of arbitration awards.[119]

So *Hall Street* may support *Nafta Traders'* holding that the FAA does not preempt the TAA's additional grounds for vacatur.

In contrast, some federal courts prior to *Hall Street* held that the FAA preempts state grounds for vacatur not found in federal law.[120] Perhaps these holdings will be reconsidered after *Hall Street*, which suggests that federal (as well as state) courts might review awards "under state statutory or common law," as opposed to the FAA, at least when the parties "contemplate" that.[121]

(c) Agreements Not Requiring Arbitrators to Apply the Law Correctly

(1) Tension in the Law

As noted above, arbitration agreements can be divided into two types: those that require the arbitrator to apply the law correctly and those that do not.[122] The latter agreements ("unrestricted submissions") give the arbitrator discretion whether to decide the case according to law or according to some other source of norms, such as the customs in a particular industry[123] or the arbitrator's own

---

[119]   Hall St. Assocs., L.L.C. v. Mattel, Inc., 552 U.S. 576, 590 (2008).

[120]   See infra § 44(d).

[121]   Or perhaps these words from *Hall Street* merely reiterate the Supreme Court's 1989 holding that parties can make an enforceable agreement that state arbitration law will govern at least some aspects of their arbitration that would, in the absence of such an agreement, be governed by the FAA. See § 16 (discussing Volt Info. Sciences, Inc., v. Board of Trustees of the Leland Stanford Junior Univ., 489 U.S. 468, 479 (1989)).

[122]   See § 44(a).

[123]   Some industries have developed their own bodies of law applied by their own arbitrators, who are often merchants rather than lawyers. See Lisa Bernstein, Merchant Law in a Merchant Court: Rethinking the Code's Search for Immanent Business Norms, 144 U. Pa. L. Rev. 1765 (1996) (grain); Lisa Bernstein, Opting Out of the Legal System: Extralegal Contractual Relations in the Diamond Industry, 21 J. Legal Stud. 115 (1992) (diamonds); Lisa Bernstein, Private Commercial Law in the Cotton Industry: Creating Cooperation Through Rules, Norms, and Institutions, 99 Mich. L. Rev. 1724 (2001) (cotton); see also Lisa Bernstein, Private Commercial Law, in 3 Palgrave Dictionary of Economics and the Law 108, 108 (Peter Newman ed., 1998) ("Private commercial law exists in over fifty industries including diamonds, grain,

sense of equity.[124] Courts have long stated their commitment to enforce such agreements by enforcing arbitration awards arising out of them without considering whether the award rests on a correct application of law. For example, the California Supreme Court said:

> As early as 1852, this court recognized that, 'The arbitrators are not bound to award on principles of dry law, but may decide on principles of equity and good conscience, and make their award ex aequo et bono [according to what is just and good].' As a consequence, arbitration awards are generally immune from judicial review.[125]

In this century, the Connecticut Supreme Court said "[u]nder an unrestricted submission, the arbitrators' decision is considered final and binding; thus the courts will not review the evidence considered by the arbitrators nor will they review the award for errors of law or fact."[126] And the Second Circuit quoted New York's highest court for the proposition that "absent provision in the arbitration clause itself, an arbitrator is not bound by principles of substantive law."[127]

---

feed, independent films, printing, binding, peanuts, rice, cotton, burlap, rubber, hay and tea.").

[124]   A small number of arbitration agreements call for application of the arbitrator's own sense of equity. Christopher R. Drahozal, Contracting Out of National Law: An Empirical Look at the New Law Merchant, 80 Notre Dame L.Rev. 523, 538–39 (2005); Christopher R. Drahozal, Is Arbitration Lawless?, 40 Loy. L.A. L. Rev. 187, 206–07 (2006).

[125]   Moncharsh v. Heily & Blase, 832 P.2d 899, 904 (Cal.1992) (citations omitted).

[126]   Industrial Risk Insurers v. Hartford Steam Boiler Inspection & Ins. Co., 779 A.2d 737, 744 (Conn.2001).

[127]   State Farm Mut. Automobile Ins. Co. v. Mallela, 372 F.3d 500, 507 n.5 (2d Cir.2004) (quoting Silverman v. Benmor Coats, Inc., 61 N.Y.2d 299, 308 (N.Y.1984)). See also T.Co. Metals, LLC v. Dempsey Pipe & Supply, Inc., 592 F.3d 329, 339 (2d Cir.2010) (vacating an award requires more than error or misunderstanding of the law); Puerto Rico Tel. Co. v. U.S. Phone Mfg. Corp., 427 F.3d 21, 32 (1st Cir.2005) ("a mere mistake of law by an arbitrator cannot serve as the basis for judicial review.");Wallace v. Buttar, 378 F.3d 182, 189–90 (2d Cir.2004) ("A federal court cannot vacate an arbitral award merely because it is convinced that the arbitration panel made the wrong call on the law."); Univ. Commons-Urbana, Ltd. v. Universal Constructors Inc., 304 F.3d 1331, 1337 (11th Cir.2002) ("Only a manifest disregard for the law, in contrast to a misinterpretation, misstatement, or misapplication of the law, can constitute grounds to vacate an arbitration decision."); Todd Shipyards Corp. v. Cunard Line, 943 F.2d 1056, 1060 (9th Cir.1991) ("[C]onfirmation is required even in the face of erroneous* * * misinterpretations of law* * *. It is not enough that the Panel may have failed to understand or apply the law * * *. An arbitrator's decision must be upheld unless it is completely irrational, or it constitutes a manifest disregard for the law.") (internal citations omitted); Advest, Inc. v. McCarthy, 914 F.2d 6, 8 (1st Cir.1990) (courts are not authorized to reconsider the merits of arbitration awards "[e]ven where such error is painfully clear"); Miller v. Prudential Bache Secs., 884 F.2d 128, 130 (4th Cir.1989) ("mere" error of law is insufficient to set aside arbitrator's award); Miller v. Prudential Bache Secs., 884 F.2d 128, 130 (4th Cir.1989) ("mere" error of law is insufficient to set aside arbitrator's award); Moseley, Hallgarten, Estabrook & Weeden, Inc. v. Ellis, 849 F.2d 264, 272 (7th Cir.1988) ("mistake" of law is insufficient to vacate arbitration award); WHD, LP. v. Mayflower Capital, LLC, 673

On the other hand, the Supreme Court has repeatedly said that "judicial scrutiny of arbitration awards * * * is sufficient to ensure that arbitrators comply with the requirements of the statute"[128] giving rise to the claim asserted in arbitration, e.g., the Securities Exchange Act or the Age Discrimination in Employment Act. Is this an assurance from the Supreme Court that courts will scrutinize arbitration awards closely enough to ensure that arbitrators correctly apply the law? If so, can this assurance be reconciled with recurring statements by many courts that they will not consider whether arbitration awards correctly apply the law because arbitrators are not bound to decide cases according to law? The following history may explain this tension in the law.[129]

(2) Historical Context

Prior to the 1980's, the claims courts sent to arbitration were primarily breach-of-contract claims. As late as 1985, a United States Supreme Court Justice could refer to "the undisputed historical fact that arbitration has functioned almost entirely in either the area of labor disputes or in 'ordinary disputes between merchants as to questions of fact.' "[130] Arbitrators in these two contexts hear almost nothing but breach-of-contract claims. In the labor context, a union or employee asserts breach of a collective bargaining agreement. In the commercial context, merchants allege breach of contracts for the sale of goods and raise "questions of fact—quantity, quality, time of delivery, compliance with terms of payment, excuses for non-performance, and the like."[131]

When hearing breach-of-contract claims, the arbitrator is not so much applying the law as applying the contract. Put another way, the arbitrator is resolving questions that the parties could have resolved when they formed the contract. The arbitrator is resolving questions that arise because the parties chose to draft a contract in

---

S.E.2d 168, 2009 WL 368335, at *4 (N.C.App.2009) (table) ("our Courts have long held that if an arbitrator makes a mistake, either as to law or fact, it is the misfortune of the party, and there is no help for it.") (internal quotations omitted).

[128] Shearson/American Express, Inc. v. McMahon, 482 U.S. 220, 232 (1987). Accord 14 Penn Plaza LLC v. Pyett, 556 U.S. 247, n.10 (2009); Gilmer v. Interstate/Johnson Lane Corp., 500 U.S. 20, 32 n.4 (1991). These statements followed the Supreme Court's earlier consideration of the issue in an international arbitration context. Mitsubishi Motors Corp. v. Soler Chrysler-Plymouth, Inc., 473 U.S. 614, 637 n.19 (1985).

[129] The following history is largely based on Stephen J. Ware, Interstate Arbitration: Chapter 1 of the Federal Arbitration Act, in Edward Brunet, Richard E. Speidel, Jean R. Sternlight & Stephen J. Ware, Arbitration Law in America: A Critical Assessment 111–112 (2006).

[130] Mitsubishi Motors Corporation v. Soler Chrysler-Plymouth Inc., 473 U.S. 614, 650 (1985) (Stevens, J. dissenting).

[131] Id. at 646, n.11 (quoting Cohen & Dayton, The New Federal Arbitration Law, 12 Va. L. Rev. 265, 281 (1926)).

broad, general terms, rather than detailed, specific terms. For example, a collective bargaining agreement might say the employer must have "just cause" before terminating an employee, and the labor arbitrator may be called upon to decide whether shouting obscenities at a supervisor is "just cause." The parties could have resolved this question themselves by specifically defining "just cause" in the agreement to include "using foul language" or "shouting at a supervisor." But the parties' broad language left a gap in the agreement and it is the arbitrator's job, as the parties' agent, to fill that gap by interpreting or applying the agreement.

The Supreme Court emphasizes that courts should not substitute their own judgment for that of the arbitrators on such questions of contract interpretation. "[A]s long as the arbitrator is even arguably construing or applying the contract and acting within the scope of his authority, that a court is convinced he committed serious error does not suffice to overturn his decision."[132] On this view, which prevails in the law, contracts are private matters between the parties and the parties have hired the arbitrator as their agent to interpret and apply their contract.[133] Arbitration is private, contractual self-governance by which parties hire their agent, the arbitrator, to resolve their disputes.[134] As the Supreme Court put it,

---

[132]   United Paperworkers Int'l Union v. Misco, Inc., 484 U.S. 29, 38 (1987). See also Oxford Health Plans LLC v. Sutter, 133 S.Ct. 2064 (2013).

A party seeking relief under [§ 10(a)(4)] bears a heavy burden. It is not enough to show that the arbitrator committed an error—or even a serious error. Because the parties bargained for the arbitrator's construction of their agreement, an arbitral decision even arguably construing or applying the contract must stand, regardless of a court's view of its (de)merits. Only if the arbitrator acts outside the scope of his contractually delegated authority— issuing an award that simply reflects his own notions of economic justice rather than drawing its essence from the contract—may a court overturn his determination. So the sole question for us is whether the arbitrator (even arguably) interpreted the parties' contract, not whether he got its meaning right or wrong.

Id. at 2068 (quotations and citations omitted).

[133]   "In the main, an arbitrator acts as the parties' agent and as their delegate may do anything the parties may do directly." George Watts & Son, Inc. v. Tiffany and Co., 248 F.3d 577, 580 (7th Cir.2001) (Easterbrook, J.).

[134]   See, e.g., United Steelworkers of America v. Warrior & Gulf Nav. Co., 363 U.S. 574 (1960).

A collective bargaining agreement is an effort to erect a system of industrial self government. . . . Gaps may be left to be filled in by reference to the practices of the particular industry and of the various shops covered by the agreement. Many of the specific practices which underlie the agreement may be unknown, except in hazy form, even to the negotiators . . . [The arbitration] grievance machinery under a collective bargaining agreement is at the very heart of the system of industrial self government. Arbitration is the means of solving the unforeseeable by molding a system of private law for all the problems which may arise and to provide for their solution in a way which will generally accord with the variant needs and desires of the parties. The processing of disputes through the grievance machinery is actually a

"we must treat the arbitrator's award as if it represented an agreement between" the parties themselves.[135]

In short, the arbitration of most breach-of-contract claims fits comfortably with recurring statements by many courts that they will not consider whether arbitration awards correctly apply the law because arbitrators are not bound to decide the case according to law. If the arbitrator is resolving a contract-interpretation issue, the arbitrator is reaching a result that the parties could have reached themselves (by simply contracting for it) when they agreed to arbitrate, and thus the arbitrator is acting within her powers derived solely from the parties. The same is true when the arbitrator is deciding many other issues of contract and commercial law because these bodies of law consist largely of default rules, that is, rules the parties can alter or avoid by contract.[136]

By contrast, the same is not necessarily true when arbitrators are deciding claims based on other areas of law. Some claims arise out of law consisting of mandatory rules, as opposed to default rules.[137] For example, statutes designed to protect consumers and employees often consist of rules parties cannot alter or avoid by pre-

---

vehicle by which meaning and content are given to the collective bargaining agreement.

Id. at 580–1.

[135] Eastern Associated Coal Corp. v. United Mine Workers, 531 U.S. 57, 62 (2000).

[136] See Alan Scott Rau, The Culture of American Arbitration and the Lessons of ADR, 40 Tex.Int'l L.J. 449 (2005).

Of course, in thinking about judicial review [of arbitration] on matters of "law" we should distinguish between mere rules of construction, which come into play in the absence of a contrary agreement, and mandatory rules. After all, most "rules" of contract or commercial law are nothing more than "gap-fillers." They supply a term where the parties have not expressly supplied one themselves; modern commercial law looks in particular to industry custom and course of dealing to furnish the "framework of common understanding controlling any general rules of law which hold only when there is no such understanding." But where the parties have bargained for dispute resolution through arbitration, the method they have chosen to fill any gaps in the agreement is the arbitrator's interpretation. His interpretation is their bargain. In contrast, legal "rules" in other areas may reflect stronger and overriding governmental or societal interests. In such cases, obviously, some greater degree of arbitral deference should be expected.

Id. at 521.

[137] A default rule is one that governs unless the parties contract out of it. In contrast, a mandatory rule is one that governs despite a contract term to the contrary, i.e., a rule that cannot be avoided by contract. One can identify which laws are default and which are mandatory by examining the sorts of contract terms that are, and are not, enforceable. For example, the legal rule that the place for delivery in a sale of goods is the seller's place of business is a default rule because parties can make an enforceable contract requiring delivery at some other location. In contrast, the legal rule giving a consumer the right that goods purchased not be "in a defective condition unreasonably dangerous to the user" is mandatory because it applies no matter what the contract terms say.

dispute contract.[138] Indeed, an important purpose of these statutes is often to protect consumers and employees from contract terms unfavorable to them. When arbitrators resolve such claims (e.g., securities law or employment discrimination,) they are not resolving questions the parties could have resolved themselves when the parties formed their contract. And it was in the context of these sorts of statutory claims—which the Supreme Court began sending to arbitration in the 1980's—that the Court said that "judicial scrutiny of arbitration awards * * * is sufficient to ensure that arbitrators comply with the requirements of the statute"[139] giving rise to the claim asserted in arbitration. This is significant because it may be in cases involving statutes designed to protect consumers, investors, and employees that it is most controversial for courts to confirm and enforce arbitration awards that do not apply the law correctly. It may be in these sorts of cases that it would be most controversial for the Supreme Court to say, as other courts have said, "arbitration awards are generally immune from judicial review"[140] and "courts will not * * * review the award for errors of law."[141] Instead of saying this, the Supreme Court's 1980's opinions enforcing pre-dispute agreements to arbitrate statutory claims suggested that courts could review awards for errors of law.[142] Perhaps the Court suggested judicial review of arbitrators' errors of law because the Court was trying to make its new enforcement of pre-dispute agreements to arbitrate statutory claims less controversial by calming fears that claims in areas such as employment discrimination and investor protection would be sent to "lawless" arbitration.[143]

---

[138]   For the relevance of the pre-dispute/post-dispute distinction, see Stephen J. Ware, Interstate Arbitration: Chapter 1 of the Federal Arbitration Act, in Edward Brunet, Richard E. Speidel, Jean R. Sternlight & Stephen J. Ware, Arbitration Law in America: A Critical Assessment 111–112 (2006).

[139]   Shearson/American Express, Inc. v. McMahon, 482 U.S. 220, 232 (1987). Accord 14 Penn Plaza LLC v. Pyett, 556 U.S. 247, n.10 (2009); Gilmer v. Interstate/Johnson Lane Corp., 500 U.S. 20, 32 n.4 (1991). These statements followed the Supreme Court's earlier consideration of the issue in an international arbitration context. Mitsubishi Motors Corp. v. Soler Chrysler-Plymouth, Inc., 473 U.S. 614, 637 n.19 (1985).

[140]   Moncharsh v. Heily & Blase, 832 P.2d 899, 904 (Cal.1992) (citations omitted).

[141]   Industrial Risk Insurers v. Hartford Steam Boiler Inspection & Ins. Co., 779 A.2d 737, 744 (Conn.2001).

[142]   See § 27–28.

[143]   See Stephen J. Ware, Default Rules From Mandatory Rules: Privatizing Law Through Arbitration, 83 Minn.L.Rev. 703 (1999).

A crucial step in the reasoning of the Court's decisions expanding arbitrability is that "the streamlined procedures of arbitration do not entail any consequential restriction on substantive rights." This point is essential to the Court's conclusion that claims such as antitrust, securities, and employment discrimination are arbitrable. If an agreement to arbitrate one of these claims did entail a "restriction on substantive rights," the Court would not enforce the agreement because the statutes conferring the rights

(3) Manifest Disregard of Law

Following the Supreme Court's cue, some federal appellate courts began tightening judicial review of arbitrators' legal rulings on statutory claims. While many courts had held out the possibility that they could vacate awards in cases of "manifest disregard of the law" by the arbitrator,[144] the manifest-disregard doctrine was very narrow[145] so it was nearly impossible, until about 1997, to find a case vacating an arbitration award in reliance on it.[146] But then some courts began expanding the "manifest disregard" doctrine to conform more closely to the Supreme Court's repeated statement that "judicial scrutiny of arbitration awards * * * is sufficient to ensure that arbitrators comply with the requirements of the statute" giving rise to the claim. Perhaps the leading case was *Cole v. Burns International Security Services*,[147] which held that agreements to arbitrate statutory employment discrimination claims were enforceable "only if judicial review under the 'manifest disregard of the law' standard is sufficiently rigorous to ensure that arbitrators have properly interpreted and applied statutory law."[148] The opinion went on to assert that "the courts are empowered to review an arbitrator's award to ensure that its resolution of public law issues is correct."[149] *Cole*, in essence, called for the "manifest disregard of law" standard to become a *de novo* "error of law" standard, at least with respect to claims under statutory or public law.

---

are indisputably mandatory, not default, rules. For example, in Mitsubishi Motors Corporation v. Soler Chrysler-Plymouth Inc., the Court held that antitrust claims were arbitrable. The Court explicitly rested its holding on the premise that the arbitrators would apply federal antitrust statutes to the dispute and that a court would grant a motion to vacate the arbitration award if the arbitrators did not apply them.

Id. at 715–16.

[144] Every United States Court of Appeals and many state appellate courts have adopted some version of the "manifest disregard" doctrine, Birmingham News Co. v. Horn, 901 So.2d 27, 48–50 (Ala.2004) (citing cases), and the Supreme Court apparently endorsed it in First Options of Chicago, Inc. v. Kaplan, 514 U.S. 938, 942 (1995) (citing Wilko v. Swan, 346 U.S. 427, 436–37 (1953)). See also Ga.Code Ann. § 9–9–13(b)(5) (Supp.2006) ("The award shall be vacated * * * if the court finds that the rights of that party were prejudiced by: * * * The arbitrator's manifest disregard of the law.")

[145] An oft-cited Second Circuit opinion said that an error of law should lead to vacatur for "manifest disregard" only if the error is "obvious and capable of being readily and instantly perceived by the average person qualified to serve as an arbitrator. Moreover, the term 'disregard' implies that the arbitrator appreciates the existence of a clearly governing legal principle but decides to ignore or pay no attention to it." Merrill, Lynch, Pierce, Fenner & Smith, Inc. v. Bobker, 808 F.2d 930, 933 (2d Cir.1986).

[146] See Macneil, Speidel & Stipanowich, supra note 17, § 40.7.1, at 40:84–40:85; Cole v. Burns Int'l Security Services, 105 F. 3d 1465 (D.C.Cir.1997).

[147] 105 F.3d 1465 (D.C.Cir.1997). This case is also discussed in § 35.

[148] 105 F.3d. at 1487.

[149] Id.

Along these lines, the following year the Second Circuit in *Halligan v. Piper Jaffray, Inc.*,[150] reversed a district court's denial of a motion to vacate for manifest disregard of employment discrimination law. *Halligan* said that "when a reviewing court is inclined to hold that an arbitration panel manifestly disregarded the law, the failure of the arbitrators to explain the award can be taken into account."[151] *Halligan* seemed to challenge the longstanding practice (in many sorts of cases) of arbitrators not to write reasoned opinions justifying their decisions.[152] That practice has largely ensured that parties challenging arbitration awards have little to point to and, consequently, little chance of persuading a court to vacate the award.[153] If the law had continued moving in the direction exemplified by *Cole* and *Halligan*, arbitrators might have been required to write reasoned opinions, giving parties more opportunity to identify manifest disregard of the law by arbitrators.[154]

(4)   Current Uncertainty About "Manifest Disregard"

The law did not, however, continue moving in that direction— the direction of greater judicial scrutiny of arbitrators' legal rulings. To the contrary, some federal appellate courts weakened the "manifest disregard" ground for vacatur,[155] with the Seventh Circuit even suggesting that it could be eliminated.[156] This view received support from the Supreme Court's 2008 opinion in *Hall Street Associates v. Mattel*.[157]

---

[150]   148 F.3d 197 (2d Cir.1998).

[151]   Id. at 204.

[152]   See § 37(f).

[153]   Trivisonno v. Metropolitan Life Ins.Co., 39 Fed.Appx. 236, 241 (6th Cir.2002) ("The Sixth Circuit has continued to hold that arbitrators are not required to explain their decisions. That remains the law in this circuit, however desirable it might be, despite the recognition that should arbitrators choose not to explain their decisions it becomes all but impossible to determine whether they acted with manifest disregard for the law.")

[154]   See generally Stephen L. Hayford, A New Paradigm for Commercial Arbitration: Rethinking the Relationship Between Reasoned Awards and the Judicial Standards for Vacatur, 66 Geo.Wash.L.Rev. 443, 445 (1998).

[155]   See Sarofim v. Trust Company Of The West, 440 F.3d 213, 217 (5th Cir.2006) (confining manifest disregard doctrine to cases in which enforcement of the award would "result in significant injustice.").

[156]   Wise v. Wachovia Securities, LLC, 450 F.3d 265, 268–69 (7th Cir.2006) (Posner, J.) ("we have defined 'manifest disregard of the law' so narrowly that it fits comfortably under the first clause of the fourth statutory ground—'where the arbitrators exceeded their powers.' For we have confined it to cases in which arbitrators 'direct the parties to violate the law.'")

[157]   552 U.S. 576 (2008).

In *Hall Street*, the Supreme Court stated that the FAA's four grounds for vacatur are "exclusive."[158] The Court viewed the FAA's provisions on confirmation and vacatur of arbitration awards

> as substantiating a national policy favoring arbitration with just the limited review needed to maintain arbitration's essential virtue of resolving disputes straightaway. Any other reading opens the door to the full-bore legal and evidentiary appeals that can render informal arbitration merely a prelude to a more cumbersome and time-consuming judicial review process and bring arbitration theory to grief in post-arbitration process.[159]

This rationale, along with *Hall Street's* statement that the FAA's four grounds for vacatur are "exclusive," led some courts and commentators to conclude that *Hall Street* prohibits judicially-created grounds for vacatur, including "manifest disregard."[160] By contrast, some other courts still use "manifest disregard" to vacate awards,[161] reasoning that so-called "non-statutory" grounds, such as "manifest disregard," are better characterized as *statutory* grounds because they are shorthand to define what constitutes arbitrators' "exceed[ing] their powers" under FAA § 10(a)(4).[162]

---

158   Id. at 1403.

159   552 U.S. 576 (2008) (internal quotation omitted).

160   Medicine Shoppe Int'l, Inc. v. Turner Investments, Inc., 614 F.3d 485, 489 (8th Cir.2010) (citing *Hall Street* for the proposition that a "claim that the arbitrator disregarded the law" is "not included among those specifically enumerated in § 10 and [ ] therefore not cognizable"); Frazier v. CitiFinancial Corp., LLC, 604 F.3d 1313, 1322–24 (11th Cir.2010) ("Although our prior precedents have recognized these three non-statutory grounds for vacatur [arbitrary and capricious, public policy, and manifest disregard] * * * We hold that our judicially-created bases for vacatur are no longer valid in light of Hall Street"); Citigroup Global Markets, Inc. v. Bacon, 562 F.3d 349, 358 (5th Cir.2009); Robert Lewis Rosen Assocs., Ltd. v. Webb, 566 F.Supp.2d 228, 233 (S.D.N.Y.2008) (due to *Hall Street,* "manifest disregard of the law standard is no longer good law."); Carey Rodriguez Greenberg & Paul, LLP v. Arminak, 583 F.Supp.2d 1288, 1290 (S.D.Fla.2008) (citing *Hall Street* and stating that "An allegation that the Award violates public policy is not one of the four exclusive statutory grounds upon which the Award may be vacated."); Hereford v. D.R. Horton, Inc., No. 1070396, 2008 WL 4097594, at *5 (Ala.2008) ("we hereby overrule our earlier statement * * * that manifest disregard of the law is a ground for vacating * * * an arbitrator's award"); Ancor Holdings, LLC v. Peterson, Goldman & Villani, Inc., 294 S.W.3d 818 (Tex.Ct.App.2009) ("manifest disregard of the law and gross mistake are not grounds for vacating an arbitration award under the FAA").

161   Comedy Club, Inc. v. Improv West Assocs., 553 F.3d 1277, 1283 (9th Cir. 2009) (vacating an award on manifest disregard grounds post-*Hall Street*); Stolt-Nielsen SA v. AnimalFeeds Int'l Corp., 548 F.3d 85, 93–95 (2d Cir.2008), rev'd on other grounds, 559 U.S. 662 (2010); Sharp v. Downey, 13 A.3d 1, 21 (Md.Ct.App.2010) (vacating award due to manifest disregard of law, which continues to be a ground for vacatur under Maryland Arbitration Act).

162   Comedy Club, Inc. v. Improv West Assocs., 553 F.3d 1277, 1290 (9th Cir. 2009); Chase Bank USA, N.A. v. Hale, 859 N.Y.S.2d 342, 349 (Sup.Ct.2008) ("this court will view 'manifest disregard of law' as judicial interpretation of the section 10

The Supreme Court left uncertainty in the post-*Hall Street* case of *Stolt-Nielsen S.A. v. AnimalFeeds International Corp.*[163] in which it said "We do not decide whether 'manifest disregard' survives our decision in [Hall Street], as an independent ground for review or as a judicial gloss on the enumerated grounds for vacatur set forth at 9 U.S.C. § 10."[164] With this uncertainty in the law, we do not know whether courts will vacate awards on the ground that arbitrators did not apply the law correctly. The Supreme Court left unresolved the very important question of whether arbitrators are bound to apply the law in all, some, or none of the cases they hear, not to mention the subsidiary question of whether they must do so correctly. Until these question are resolved, some mystery will surround the Supreme Court's repeated statement that "judicial scrutiny of arbitration awards * * * is sufficient to ensure that arbitrators comply with the requirements of the statute"[165] giving rise to the claim asserted in arbitration.

(d) Federal Preemption of State Law on Vacatur

State courts sometimes cite to their own state statutes when discussing the grounds for vacating arbitration awards.[166] State law regarding vacatur is generally similar to federal law.[167] But if a

---

requirement, rather than as a separate standard of review"); id. at 351 ("public policy" ground for vacatur is an interpretation of § 10(a)(4)); Macneil, Speidel & Stipanowich, supra note 17, § 40.5.1.3. See also Sands v. Menard, Inc., 787 N.W.2d 384, 397 (Wis.2010) ("a court must overturn an arbitrator's award when the panel exceeds its powers. Wis. Stat. § 788.10(1)(d). An arbitration panel exceeds its powers when it engages in perverse misconstruction or positive misconduct, when the panel manifestly disregards the law, or where the award itself is illegal or violates strong public policy."); Broom v. Morgan Stanley DW Inc., 236 P.3d 182, 184 (Wash.2010) ("in Boyd v. Davis, * * * we approved of facial legal error as an accepted basis for vacating an arbitral award. In Boyd, we suggested that such error indicates that the arbitrators exceeded their powers.").

163   559 U.S. 662 (2010).

164   Stolt-Nielsen S.A. v. AnimalFeeds International Corp., 559 U.S. 662 (2010). The fourth circuit reads this passage "to mean that manifest disregard continues to exist either 'as an independent ground for review or as a judicial gloss on the enumerated grounds for vacatur set forth at 9 U.S.C. § 10.' Therefore, we decline to adopt the position of the Fifth and Eleventh Circuits that manifest disregard no longer exists." Wachovia Securities, LLC v. Brand, 671 F.3d 472, 483 (4th Cir.2012).

165   Shearson/American Express, Inc. v. McMahon, 482 U.S. 220, 232 (1987). Accord 14 Penn Plaza LLC v. Pyett, 556 U.S. 247, n.10 (2009); Gilmer v. Interstate/Johnson Lane Corp., 500 U.S. 20, 32 n.4 (1991). These statements followed the Supreme Court's earlier consideration of the issue in an international arbitration context. Mitsubishi Motors Corp. v. Soler Chrysler-Plymouth, Inc., 473 U.S. 614, 637 n.19 (1985).

166   See, e.g., Cal.Civ.Proc.Code § 1286.2 (West 1982 & Supp.2005) (containing many pages of case annotations).

167   See Unif. Arbitration Act (1956) § 12, 7 U.L.A. 497–500 (2005) (grounds for vacating the award); 7 U.L.A. 95 (2005)(table of jurisdictions adopting the act); Unif. Arbitration Act (2000) § 23, 7 U.L.A. 73–74, 81–83 (2005) (grounds for vacating the award); 7 U.L.A. 1 (2005) (table of jurisdictions adopting the act).

particular state law does differ from federal law, the question arises whether the FAA preempts the state law. State law might differ in one of two ways. It might add additional grounds for vacatur not found in federal law. Or it might recognize fewer grounds for vacatur than recognized by federal law.

(1) State Grounds for Vacatur Broader than Federal Grounds

As noted above,[168] the Supreme Court's 2008 decision in *Hall St. Assocs., L.L.C. v. Mattel, Inc.*,[169] may suggest that the FAA does not preempt state law adding at least some grounds for vacatur beyond those in FAA § 10. In contrast, some federal courts before *Hall Street* held that the FAA preempts state grounds for vacatur not found in federal law.[170] The Washington Supreme Court apparently disagrees, believing some state grounds for vacatur can survive FAA preemption. In the 2010 case of *Broom v. Morgan Stanley DW Inc.*,[171] it affirmed a lower court order vacating an award on the ground that the award contained facial legal error.[172] The dissent argued that this is not a ground for vacatur under the FAA and that the FAA preempts Washington law to the extent it has this ground.[173] The

---

[168] See § 44(b)(2).

[169] 552 U.S. 576, 590 (2008).

[170] See Alston v. UBS Fin. Services, Inc., 2006 WL 20516, n.3 (D.D.C.2006) ("The Alstons attempt to rely on Virginia law as a basis for vacatur as well [as the FAA]. The court, however, need not analyze the Alstons' motion under Virginia law because, to the extent that the FAA and Virginia law conflict, state law is preempted"); In re Arbitration between Lemoine Skinner III v. Donaldson, Lufkin & Jenrette Secs. Corp., 2003 WL 23174478, at *8 (N.D.Cal.Dec.29, 2003) ("the [FAA] sets out exclusive grounds upon which an arbitration award may be vacated. * * * Any state law that allows for additional grounds for dismissal of an arbitration award would be preempted by the FAA."); Jacada (Europe) Ltd. v. Int'l Mktg.Strategies, Inc., 255 F.Supp. 2d 744, 750–51 (W.D.Mich.2003); M & L Power Servs., Inc. v. Am.Networks Int'l, 44 F. Supp. 2d 134, 141–42 (D.R.I.1999) ("the FAA only preempts state law to the extent that said state law provides lesser protection for arbitration agreements and awards than does federal law. * * * In this case, the 'complete irrationality' ground for vacating an arbitration award violates Congress' policy as set forth in the FAA. As such, it is preempted and may not be applied to any case to which the FAA applies"); Collins v. Blue Cross Blue Shield of Michigan, 916 F.Supp. 638, 640–42 (E.D.Mich.1995) (as between Michigan's standard and federal "manifest disregard of law" standard, "the federal standard of review must prevail"), vacated on other grounds, 103 F.2d 35 (6th Cir.1996)(no federal jurisdiction); Macneil, Speidel & Stipanowich, supra note 17, § 40.1 ("the FAA preempts any state grounds for vacation unless the parties have clearly agreed to be bound by them.")

[171] 236 P.3d 182 (Wash.2010).

[172] "[T]he arbitration panel ruled that all of the Brooms' claims except for the CPA claim were barred by state and federal statutes of limitations." Id. at 183–84. "The Brooms filed a complaint in superior court and moved to vacate the arbitration award. They argued that the award contained facial legal error because state statutes of limitations do not apply to arbitration. The trial court agreed and vacated the award." Id. at 184.

[173] · Broom v. Morgan Stanley DW Inc., 236 P.3d 182, 192 (2010) (Madsen, C.J., dissenting).

majority did not respond to this argument or otherwise mention the FAA.

(2) State Grounds for Vacatur Narrower than Federal Grounds

While the FAA may preempt state grounds for vacatur not found in federal law,[174] little support can be found for the argument that the FAA preempts state law recognizing *fewer* grounds for vacatur than are found in federal law. For example, federal law used to (and may still) recognize a ground for vacatur, "manifest disregard of law," not found in California law.[175] If a California court confirms an arbitration award notwithstanding the court's finding that the arbitrator manifestly disregarded the law, the party seeking to vacate the arbitration award may argue that FAA preemption of state arbitration law requires an order vacating the award. This argument was rejected by the California Court of Appeals in *Siegel v. Prudential Ins. Co.*[176]

> California's rule precluding on the merits review of an arbitration award does not stand as an obstacle to full effectuation of the purpose of the [FAA]—enforcement of arbitration agreements * * * . California's rule evidences no hostility towards arbitration. In fact, California's rule furthers the use of arbitration by somewhat more strictly limiting judicial review of the merits of an award. California's rule against on the merits review furthers rather than defeats full effectuation of the federal law's objectives.[177]

Similarly, a Kentucky appellate court applied state, rather than federal, law of vacatur to a case involving interstate commerce because Kentucky law recognized narrower grounds for vacatur than were found in federal law and thus did not "frustrate" Congress' purpose in enacting the FAA.[178]

---

[174]   See § 44(d)(1).

[175]   Moncharsh v. Heily & Blase, 10 Cal.Rptr.2d 183, 190 (Cal.1992). This ground is discussed in § 44(c).

[176]   79 Cal.Rptr.2d 726 (Ct.App.1999).

[177]   Id. at 735.

[178]   Strausbaugh v. H & R Block Fin. Advisors, Inc., 2007 WL 3122257, at *4–5 (Ky.Ct.App.2007) ("Based on our analysis of federal and state law, we hold that Kentucky courts are not compelled by federal preemption to substitute and apply 9 U.S.C. § 10 (2002), and the federal case law interpreting it, in place of the [Kentucky Uniform Arbitration Act], even when reviewing arbitration awards involving interstate commerce.")

Chapter 7

EMPLOYMENT AND LABOR ARBITRATION

Table of Sections

1. EMPLOYMENT ARBITRATION

---

1.   EMPLOYMENT ARBITRATION
Table of Sections

---

§ 45   The Conventional Distinction Between "Employment" and "Labor"

Law governing employment is often divided into two categories: "employment law" which applies to employees as individuals, and "labor law" which regulates employees in their collective activities— for example, forming a labor union and negotiating a "collective bargaining agreement" between the union and employer. Like other fields, labor law has its own specialized terminology.[1] For instance, claims alleging breach of collective bargaining agreements are called "grievances."

The categories of "employment law" and "labor law" carry over into the terminology of arbitration. "Employment arbitration" arises out of a contract between an employer and an individual employee, while "labor arbitration" arises out of a collective bargaining agreement between an employer and a union. Employment arbitration, both in its practice and in the law governing it, is very much within the mainstream of arbitration. In contrast, labor arbitration is practiced quite differently from other arbitration and is governed by its own unique set of laws.

§ 46   The FAA's Exclusion of Certain "Contracts of Employment"

The FAA applies to an arbitration agreement "in any maritime transaction or a contract evidencing a transaction involving commerce."[2] FAA § 1 defines "commerce" to mean interstate or international commerce.[3] The Supreme Court interprets this language broadly to reach all transactions affecting interstate or international commerce.[4] So interpreted, FAA § 1's definition of commerce is extremely broad, bringing the vast majority of arbitration agreements within the coverage of the FAA.[5] There is, however, an exception to this extremely broad reach of the FAA. FAA § 1 says "nothing herein contained shall apply to contracts of employment of seamen, railroad employees, or any other class of workers engaged in foreign or interstate commerce."[6] Arbitration agreements falling within this "employment exclusion" are not governed by the FAA.

The case law interpreting the employment exclusion is somewhat complicated. First, the Supreme Court holds that *labor*

---

[1]   For an introduction to labor law, see Douglas E. Ray, et al., Understanding Labor Law (3d ed.2011).

[2]   9 U.S.C. § 2.

[3]   "Commerce" is defined as

commerce among the several States or with foreign nations, or in any Territory of the United States or in the District of Columbia, or between any such Territory and another, or between any such Territory and any State or foreign nation, or between the District of Columbia and any State or Territory or foreign nation, but nothing herein contained shall apply to contracts of employment of seamen, railroad employees, or any other class of workers engaged in foreign or interstate commerce.

9 U.S.C. § 1.

[4]   See § 4(d).

[5]   Id.

[6]   9 U.S.C. § 1.

arbitration is not primarily governed by the FAA but, rather, is governed by the Labor Management Relations Act.[7] In contrast, most *employment* arbitration is governed by the FAA. In the 2001 decision of *Circuit City Stores, Inc. v. Adams*,[8] the Supreme Court held that the FAA applies to all employment contracts except for those of "seamen, railroad employees, or any other class of workers engaged in foreign or interstate commerce," which the Supreme Court interpreted as those workers involved with the actual transportation of goods.[9] Lower courts have followed *Circuit City* in not applying the FAA to such "transportation workers," while applying it to other employees.[10]

Employment arbitration of those transportation workers is governed by state arbitration law.[11] Some states treat employment arbitration agreements differently from other arbitration agreements,[12] while many other states treat employment arbitration no differently from other arbitration. For example, employment arbitration agreements are enforceable under California law,[13] the

---

[7] See § 4(d). Labor arbitration is the subject of § 48–61.

[8] 532 U.S. 105 (2001).

[9] Id. at 119. This strange result of a *federal* statute governing employees *less* closely connected to interstate commerce, while *state* law governs employees *most* closely connected to it is explained and critiqued in Richard A. Epstein, Fidelity Without Translation, 1 Green Bag 2d 21, 27–29 (1997).

[10] Compare, e.g., Lenz v. Yellow Transp., Inc., 431 F.3d 348, 351–52 (8th Cir.2005) (customer service representative for interstate trucking company, who fielded calls from customers regarding their shipment orders, was not a transportation worker and thus was governed by FAA); Hill v. Rent-A-Center, Inc., 398 F. 3d 1286, 1289–90 (11th Cir.2005) (an account manager who as part of his job duties transports merchandise across the Georgia/Alabama border was not a transportation worker), with Palcko v. Airborne Express, Inc., 372 F.3d 588, 593 (3d Cir.2004)(employee was a "transportation worker" because "she was responsible for 'monitoring and improving the performance of drivers under [her] supervision to insure [sic] timely and efficient delivery of packages.' Such direct supervision of package shipments makes Palcko's work "so closely related [to interstate and foreign commerce] as to be in practical effect part of it."); In re Villanueva, 311 S.W.3d 475, 479 (Tex.Ct.App.2009) (FAA inapplicable to truck driver).

[11] Palcko v. Airborne Express, Inc., 372 F.3d 588, 595–96 (3d Cir.2004).

[12] For examples of state statutes treating it differently, see § 13.

[13] The California Code of Civil Procedure provides that "A written agreement to submit to arbitration an existing controversy or a controversy thereafter arising is valid, enforceable and irrevocable, save upon such grounds as exist for the revocation of any contract." Cal.Civ.Proc.Code § 1281 (West 1982). This provision, unlike the FAA, makes no exception for employment agreements. In contrast, an earlier California statute had provided that arbitration agreements are "valid, enforceable and irrevocable, save upon such grounds as exist at law or in equity for the revocation of any contract; provided, however, the provisions of this title shall not apply to contracts pertaining to labor." Former Cal.Civ.Proc.Code § 1280, repealed by Stats. 1961, c.461, p.1540 § 1 (emphasis added). Under ordinary principles of statutory construction, the replacement of a statute expressly excluding labor contracts by a statute silent on the question is a strong indication that such contracts are covered by the newer statute. At least one California court has cited § 1281 in enforcing an

Uniform Arbitration Act,[14] and the Revised Uniform Arbitration Act,[15] none of which contains an "employment exclusion" like that found in the FAA.

§ 47   Employment Arbitration

Unlike labor arbitration law,[16] employment arbitration law is, after *Circuit City*, very much within the mainstream of arbitration law.[17] This section collects the exceptions, the features peculiar to employment arbitration law. Most of these peculiarities seem to reflect judicial discomfort with employers conditioning employment on employees' agreements to arbitrate employment disputes, especially those involving discrimination claims.

The first peculiarity of employment arbitration law is the possibility that the employee's agreement to arbitrate will not be enforced even though the agreement would be enforceable under the standards of ordinary contract law. Courts generally use contract law's objective standard of assent to determine whether an arbitration agreement is enforceable,[18] but in employment cases some courts have required more for enforceability. For example, the Ninth Circuit has refused to enforce employees' arbitration agreements on the ground that the employees did not "knowingly" assent to the agreements.[19]

---

employment arbitration agreement. See Lee v. Technology Integration Group, 82 Cal.Rptr.2d 387, 392 (Ct.App.1999).

[14]   Unif. Arbitration Act (1956) § 1, 7 U.L.A. 102 (2005).

[15]   Unif. Arbitration Act (2000) § 6, 7 U.L.A. 22 (2005).

[16]   See §§ 45 & 48.

[17]   For an overview, see Richard A. Bales, Compulsory Arbitration: The Grand Experiment in Employment (1997).

[18]   See §§ 22–26.

[19]   *See* Prudential Ins.Co. of Am. v. Lai, 42 F.3d 1299, 1305 (9th Cir.1994)("a Title VII plaintiff may only be forced to forego her statutory remedies and arbitrate her claims if she has knowingly agreed to submit such disputes to arbitration."); Ashbey v. Archstone Prop. Mgmt., Inc., 785 F.3d 1320, 1323–24 (9th Cir. 2015) ("[N]ot only must there be a valid agreement to arbitrate that encompasses the right at issue, that agreement must also be 'knowing.' "); Simmons v. Morgan Stanley Smith Barney, LLC, 872 F. Supp. 2d 1002, 1013 (S.D. Cal.2012) (denying a motion to compel arbitration because, "[t]he Court [did] not find that Plaintiff [ ] knowingly fore[went] his statutory remedies on the statutory employment discrimination claims. . . ." (citing *Lai*, 42 F.3d 1299 (9th Cir. 1994)). *See also* Walker v. Ryan's Family Steak Houses, Inc., 400 F.3d 370, 381 (6th Cir. 2005) (holding that employees cannot be compelled to arbitrate because they did not knowingly and voluntarily waive their constitutional right to jury trial when they signed agreements to arbitrate all employment-related disputes). But see Caley v. Gulfstream Aerospace Corp., 428 F.3d 1359, 1372 (11th Cir.2005) ("general contract principles govern the enforceability of arbitration agreements" and "no heightened 'knowing and voluntary' standard applies"); Mayne v. Monaco Enterprises, Inc., No. 32978–0–III, 2015 WL 6689919, at *4 (Wash.Ct.App.Nov. 3, 2015) ("An employer can condition employment upon the employee waiving his right to a jury trial and voluntarily signing an arbitration agreement. That is easily accomplished at the onset of employment * * * where the employee knows the

The second peculiarity of employment arbitration law is that enforcement of employees' agreements to arbitrate may be conditioned on procedural features not required of arbitration generally. For example, several courts have refused to enforce agreements to arbitrate discrimination claims where the agreement required the employee to pay an arbitration organization's filing fee plus half of the arbitrator's fees.[20]

The Equal Employment Opportunity Commission, which is generally not bound by an arbitration agreement between employer and employee,[21] has sought to prevent enforcement of employment arbitration agreements. Prior to *Circuit City,* it issued a policy statement to this effect,[22] and in one case the EEOC obtained an injunction preventing a particular employer from requiring its employees to sign an arbitration agreement.[23] The EEOC's activism on employment arbitration varies among administrations, and it has not been active on this matter in recent years.

In contrast, the National Labor Relations Board has more recently held that an employer violated the National Labor Relations Act by conditioning employment on an arbitration agreement that prohibited its employees from filing class actions and other joint claims in any forum—arbitration or litigation.[24] This NLRB holding,

---

condition before agreeing to accept employment. The task is more difficult when there is already an existing at-will employment relationship.").

[20]   See § 28(b).

[21]   Equal Employment Opportunity Commission v. Waffle House, 534 U.S. 279 (2002).

[22]   See EEOC Policy Statement on Mandatory Arbitration, 133 Daily Lab.Rep.(BNA) at E–4 (July 10, 1997) http://www.eeoc.gov/policy/docs/mandarb.html. See also Richard A. Bales, Compulsory Employment Arbitration and the EEOC, 27 Pepp.L.Rev. 1 (1999).

[23]   See United States Equal Employment Opportunity Commission v. River Oaks Imaging and Diagnostic, 1995 WL 264003 (S.D.Tex.Apr.19, 1995).

[24]   Murphy Oil USA, Inc., 361 NLRB No. 72 (2014); D.R. Horton, Inc., 357 NLRB No. 184 (2012).

however, has been rejected by several appellate courts.[25] The Supreme Court has recently granted cert. to decide the issue.[26]

2. OVERVIEW OF LABOR ARBITRATION
Table of Sections

§ 48   Labor Arbitration Defined

Labor arbitration is the endpoint of a grievance process negotiated by an employer and the union representing a unit of the employer's employees.[27] Most collective bargaining agreements contain a grievance arbitration provision.[28] Unions and employers typically negotiate a collective bargaining agreement (CBA) with many provisions addressing a wide range of workplace issues, such as wages and benefits, discipline, scheduling, and job security. A grievance arbitration process provides a means to resolve conflicts

---

[25]   Compare Lewis v. Epic Sys. Corp., 823 F.3d 1147 (7th Cir. 2016) (agreeing with NLRB that requiring employees to bring wage-and-hour claims only through individual arbitration violates the National Labor Relations Act), with D.R. Horton, Inc. v. NLRB, 737 F.3d 344, 362 (5th Cir.2013)("because the NLRA does not contain a congressional command exempting the statute from application of the FAA, the Mutual Arbitration Agreement must be enforced according to its terms"); Sutherland v. Ernst & Young LLP, 726 F.3d 290, 297 n.8 (2d Cir.2013)("employee's ability to proceed collectively under the Fair Labor Standards Act (FLSA) can be waived in an arbitration agreement"); Owen v. Bristol Care, Inc., 702 F.3d 1050, 1054 (8th Cir.2013)("given the absence of any 'contrary congressional command' from the FLSA that a right to engage in class actions overrides the mandate of the FAA in favor of arbitration, we reject Owen's invitation to follow the NLRB's rationale in D.R. Horton and join our fellow circuits that have held that arbitration agreements containing class waivers are enforceable in claims brought under the FLSA").

[26]   Epic Sys. Corp v. Lewis, 16–285, Ernst & Young v. Morris, 16–300, NLRB v. Murphy Oil, 16–307 (cert granted Jan. 13, 2017).

[27]   Ariana R. Levinson, What the Awards Tell Us About Labor Arbitration of Employment-Discrimination Claims (hereinafter Labor Arbitration), 46 Mich. J.L.Reform 789, 794 (2013). Labor arbitration is different from employment arbitration which is discussed in §§ 45–47.

[28]   Collective Bargaining Negotiations & Contract Manual, Methods of Settling Disputes, CBNC 8:3706, 9:2501 (Bloomberg BNA); Mario F. Bognanno, et al., The Conventional Wisdom of Discharge Arbitration Outcomes & Remedies: Fact or Fiction, 16 Cardozo J.Conflict Resol. 153, 154 (2014–15); Ann C. Hodges, The Americans with Disabilities Act in the Unionized Workplace, 48 U.Miami L.Rev. 567, 576 & n.56 (1994); Arnold Zack & Richard Bloch, Labor Agreement in Negotiation and Arbitration, Chapter 7, The Grievance Procedure & the Arbitration Clause, at 160 (Bloomberg BNA 1995).

about interpretation and application of the CBA that arise during the term of the agreement. Most CBAs provide that the union, rather than an employee with a grievance, decides whether to file a grievance and whether to pursue arbitration.[29] Union control assures that employees are aided by a union representative and that the CBA is interpreted in a consistent manner that is fair to all represented employees.[30] Labor arbitration in both the public and private sector functions similarly as the end-point of a grievance process controlled by the union. While different labor laws govern the private and public sector, the grievance arbitration process is substantially similar. Section 301 of the Labor Management Relations Act and the National Labor Relations Act apply to most private sector employers while the Railway Labor Act governs private-sector railway and airline employers. In the public sector, state law governs state employers, and the Federal Labor Relations Act governs federal employers.[31]

§ 49   Relationship Between the National Labor Relations Act and Labor Arbitration

The National Labor Relations Board (NLRB) is the federal administrative agency responsible for administering the National Labor Relations Act (NLRA). Section 7 of the NLRA protects employees' right "to self-organization, to form, join or assist labor organizations," to collectively bargain and to engage in other concerted activities regarding terms and conditions of employment. (It also protects employees' right to refrain from these activities.) The NLRA prohibits certain employer conduct, such as interfering with protected Section 7 rights, discriminating against employees for engaging in Section 7 rights, and refusing to bargain with the employees' union.

When a union and an employer have a CBA, the CBA often grants parallel protections. For instance, a CBA may include a no-discrimination provision that prohibits the employer from discriminating against employees, such as a shop steward, who engage in union activity. A CBA may also prohibit the employer from making certain changes to employment conditions that would violate the CBA provisions. This protection may be similar to the protection provided by the NLRA for collective bargaining. In instances where these parallel claims arise, a union may file both a grievance (in arbitration) and an unfair labor practice charge with the NLRB. An

---

[29]   Dennis Nolan, Labor and Employment Arbitration: What's Justice Got to Do with It?, 53 Nov.Disp.Resol.J. 40, 44 (1998).

[30]   See Nolan, supra note 29, at 44.

[31]   Sections 52–54 of this book focus on LMRA Section 301. Sections 49 and 55 explain the relevance of the NLRA to labor arbitration. Section 56 addresses the RLA. Section 61 describes the laws governing labor arbitration in the public sector.

unfair labor practice charge initiates a process whereby a Regional Office of the NLRB investigates the claimed violation and determines whether to issue a complaint. If there is a parallel arbitration pending, the NLRB may decide to defer a decision until after the arbitrator has ruled. Once there has been an arbitration award, the NLRB may decide to defer to the award rather than issuing a complaint. The NLRB law and policies change with different administrations, so lawyers should check the most recent NLRB cases and general counsel memorandum to determine current practice.

§ 50   Relationship Between Section 301 and the FAA

Traditionally, private sector parties brought actions to enforce CBA agreements to arbitrate and to confirm or vacate awards solely under Section 301 of the Labor Management Relations Act (Section 301).[32] The Supreme Court has applied the FAA to agreements to arbitrate in individual employment contracts. So confusion has arisen over whether the FAA applies to grievance-arbitration agreements as well.[33] Some parties continue to seek enforcement of a CBA agreement to arbitrate or confirmation or vacatur of labor arbitration awards only under Section 301, while others seek enforcement under both 301 and the FAA.[34] The Second Circuit has held that the FAA does not provide grounds for enforcing labor arbitration agreements or enforcing or vacating labor awards, but has recognized that courts look to the FAA for guidance in labor arbitration cases.[35] Indeed, the Supreme Court and some Circuit

---

[32]   Margaret L. Moses, The Pretext of Textualism: Disregarding Stare Decisis in 14 Penn Plaza v. Pyett, 14 Lewis & Clark L.Rev. 825, 852 (2010) (noting that pre-Pyett most lower courts held that CBA's were covered by Section 301 and "not within the scope of the FAA.").

[33]   Arthur T. Carter, Edward F. Berbarie & Sean M. McCrory, The Principle Differences Between Labor and Employment Arbitration, 69 The Advoc.(Texas) 85, 87 (2014) (noting that it is unclear whether labor arbitration agreements are covered by the FAA); Moses, supra note 32, 852 (questioning whether Pyett intended to merge 301 and the FAA); Mark S. Mathison & Bryan M. Seiler, What 14 Penn Plaza LLC v. Pyett Means for Employers: Balancing Interests in a Landscape of Uncertainty, 25 ABA J.Lab.&Emp.L. 173, 185 (2010) ("The Supreme Court has never attempted to reconcile these two strands of judicial review, leaving uncertain the extent to which the two standards may differ and which of them would be applicable to those parts of a labor arbitrator's award adjudicating statutory claims."); Elkouri & Elkouri, How Arbitration Works, at 2–6 (8th ed. Kenneth May ed. 2016); Circuit City Stores, Inc. v. Adams, 532 U.S. 105 (2001); Seth Galanter & Jeremy M. McLaughlin, Does the Supreme Court Decision in 14 Penn Plaza Augur Unification of the FAA and Labor Arbitration Law?, 64 Disp.Res.J. 2 (May–July 2009) (noting that the Supreme Court repeatedly discussed the FAA in the 14 Penn Plaza opinion).

[34]   Carter, supra note 33, at 87 (noting labor arbitration awards are enforced through the FAA and Section 301).

[35]   Elkouri, supra note 33, at 2–6; Coca-Cola Bottling Co. v. Teamsters Local 812, 242 F.3d 52, 54 (2d Cir. 2001).

Courts have regularly looked to the FAA for guidance.[36] And in the Supreme Court's 2009 case, *14 Penn Plaza v. Pyett*, the Court permitted the petitioners to file a motion to compel labor arbitration of a discrimination claim under the FAA, and the Court cited to FAA precedent.[37] The issue in the case, however, was not whether the FAA and Section 301 provide grounds to compel, enforce, or vacate a labor arbitration award, so the Court did not explicitly address the issue.[38] The issue could be resolved to use only Section 301 for contractual disputes but to permit use of the FAA when statutory disputes have been subject to labor arbitration pursuant to a clear and unmistakable waiver in the CBA. The FAA is discussed in depth throughout the first 47 sections of this book.[39]

§ 51 Sources of Law

Labor arbitration is compelled by state and federal courts, and awards are also enforced and vacated by the courts.[40] The body of law governing labor arbitration is federal common law developed under Section 301.[41] State courts must apply federal law,[42] and most often a defendant will remove a labor arbitration case to federal court,[43] so most cases are decided by the federal courts. The United States Supreme Court is the final authority for labor arbitration law. As mentioned above in § 51, the National Labor Relations Board (NLRB) sometimes defers to labor arbitration or an arbitration award and has developed law regarding when it will defer. The sections that follow cover labor arbitration law on enforcing arbitration agreements, enforcing, or vacating an award, the relationship between statutory and contract claims, and the relationship between the NLRB and labor arbitration. The sections also describe the grievance-arbitration process and introduce the private law of

---

[36] United Steel Union v. Wise Alloys, LLC, 642 F.3d 1344, 1353 n. 4 (11th Cir. 2011) (applying time limits from FAA to labor arbitration case); Paperworkers v. Misco, Inc., 484 U.S. 29, 40 & n.9 (1987) (considering FAA as guidance to determine whether arbitrator engaged in misconduct by refusing to hear certain evidence); Granite Rock Co. v. IBT, 561 U.S. 287, 299 n.6 (2010) (applying FAA precedent to determine whether a labor dispute is arbitrable).

[37] 14 Penn Plaza v. Pyett, 556 U.S. 247, 254, 266 (2009).

[38] Carter, supra note 33, at 87 (noting the Court "relied primarily on the LMRA" although "the issue in the lower courts was whether the FAA required arbitration of the claim . . ."); Moses, supra note 32, at 852; Mathison, supra note 33, at 185.

[39] See §§ 1–47.

[40] Douglas E. Ray, Calvin William Sharpe, & Robert N. Strassfeld, Understanding Labor Law, at 293 (4th ed. 2014).

[41] Ray, supra note 40, at 292; Lincoln Mills, 353 U.S. 448 (1957).

[42] Ray, supra note 40, at 292.

[43] Ann C. Hodges, Judicial Review of Arbitration Awards on Public Policy Grounds: Lessons from the Case Law, 16 OhioSt.J.onDisp.Resol. 91, 139 (2000); William E. Smith, Judicial Review of Labor Arbitration Awards in Rhode Island, 3 RogerWilliamsU.L.Rev. 165, 167 (1998).

arbitration, including the substance of opinions and awards in discharge and discipline cases and in contract interpretation cases. Finally, two types of labor arbitration other than private-sector grievance arbitration are discussed, interest arbitration and public sector arbitration.

3.   LABOR ARBITRATION LAW

Table of Sections

Sec.

---

§ 52   Enforcing Labor Arbitration Agreements

(a) Section 301

Labor arbitration had traditionally been considered a substitute for the strike, rather than a substitute for litigation like other arbitration.[44] The traditional wisdom is that employers agree to enter

---

[44]   A CBA creates contract claims that probably would not have been litigated in court the way, for example, a statutory anti-trust violation would be litigated in court or a commercial contract dispute would be litigated in court if the companies had not entered into an arbitration agreement. Instead, workplace disputes might be settled through strikes, lock-outs, and other economic pressure brought to bear by the

into a collective bargaining agreement and to include an arbitration provision because the union promises not to strike. Employers, however, also agree for many other reasons, such as employee involvement and satisfaction resulting in less turn-over, the ability of unions to provide benefits like health insurance, training, retirement, and legal plans, the spelled-out agreement insuring that managers are doing their job as they should, the ability of unions to provide well-trained competent employees, and to settle workplace disputes early and avoid litigation.[45]

Historically, private sector parties would compel arbitration by invoking Section 301 of the Labor Management Relations Act. Currently, as discussed in § 50 parties may invoke the FAA in addition to or instead of Section 301, but Section 301 remains the primary basis upon which arbitration is compelled. Several significant Supreme Court cases developed federal common law permitting parties to compel labor arbitration. This section discusses Section 301, the *Lincoln Mills* case interpreting that section, and the *Steelworkers Trilogy* which remains the basis upon which labor arbitration is compelled today. It concludes with a brief discussion of additional principles used to determine whether a dispute is subject to arbitration, termed "arbitrability."

The Labor Management Relations Act was part of the Taft-Hartley Act passed in 1947. Generally, the Act was a management-friendly bill intended to curb the power of unions that were engaging in strike activity that some viewed as disruptive to industrial peace.[46] Section 301 was intended to enable unions to be sued, and particularly, to compel unions to comply with no-strike clauses in CBAs.[47] Section 301 authorizes suing for violation of a CBA in federal district court. It also establishes that a union can be sued as an entity and may sue as an entity and on behalf of its members. Before enactment of Section 301, the legal status of unions was uncertain, and different state courts had ruled differently as to whether unions

---

employer and union, rather than through litigation. See Stephen J. Ware, Principles of Alternative Dispute Resolution, at 196–98 (3d ed. 2016).

[45]   See Ray, et al., supra note 40, at 290 (identifying reasons arbitration provisions are included as 1) informality of hearing, 2) inexpensive nature of arbitration compared to litigation, 3) neutrality of third party expert, and 4) "defusing potential employee unrest.").

[46]   Theodore J. St. Antoine, Charles B. Craver, & Marion G. Crain, Labor Relations Law: Cases and Materials, 16–17 (12th ed. 2011); Diversity Jurisdiction Under 303(B) of the Taft-Hartley Act, 59 Yale L.J. 575, 575, 579–80 (1950); Alan I. Horowitz, The Applicability of Boys Markets Injunctions to Refusals to Cross a Picket Line, 76 Colum.L.Rev. 113, 114 (1976).

[47]   Archibald Cox, Grievance Arbitration in the Federal Courts, 67 Harv.L.Rev. 591, 602, 606 (1954). James E. Pfander, Federal Jurisdiction Over Union Constitutions After Wooddell, 37 Vill.L.Rev. 443, 465–66 (1992).

could sue or be sued.[48] Monetary judgments are enforceable "only against the organization as an entity and against its assets" and not against "any individual member,"[49] similar to how owners of a business are protected by a corporate structure. Section 301 does not explicitly mention arbitration, but made it possible to enforce CBAs.

(b) Lincoln Mills

In *Textile Workers v. Lincoln Mills*,[50] the union and employer had entered into a CBA wherein the union agreed not to strike, and the parties agreed to use a grievance-arbitration process to resolve disputes arising under the CBA. When the employer refused to arbitrate a grievance, the union sued to compel arbitration. The Supreme Court explained that Section 301 granted unions the ability to sue and be sued. The Supreme Court also held that federal common law, rather than state law, should be used by all courts, state and federal, determining whether to enforce a CBA agreement to arbitrate.[51] The Court reasoned that federal common law was necessary to insure consistency in labor-management relations across state lines and to foster industrial peace. The Court explained that the union had given up the right to strike in return for the employer's promise to arbitrate, so the promise must be enforceable.

(c) Steelworkers Trilogy

The *Steelworkers Trilogy* was a series of three related cases decided by the Supreme Court together that sets out the rules governing enforcing agreements to arbitrate in CBAs. In *United Steelworkers of America v. American Mfg. Co.*,[52] a disabled employee attempted to return to work, and the employer refused to permit it. The CBA contained a no-strike clause and an arbitration provision. The union argued that under a seniority provision in the CBA the grievant should be returned to work and sought arbitration. The employer argued that the claim was frivolous because the employer could not return the grievant to work. The employer asserted the grievant was unable to physically perform his job and had entered a workers' compensation settlement agreeing he was permanently partially disabled. The Court determined that even where a grievance is frivolous it must be determined in the first instance by the arbitrator. The Court reasoned that the union had agreed not to strike so the employer's return promise to arbitrate disputes must be

---

48   Ray, et al., supra note 40, at 291.

49   Labor Management Relations Act, Section 301(b), 29 U.S.C. § 185(b).

50   Textile Workers v. Lincoln Mills of Alabama, 353 U.S. 448 (1957).

51   Local 174, Teamsters v. Lucas Flour, 369 U.S. 95 (1962) (state courts should apply federal common law).

52   363 U.S. 564 (1960).

honored. The Court recognized that "processing of even frivolous claims may have therapeutic value of which those who are not part of the [work] environment may be quite unaware."[53] Finally, the Court reasoned that the courts should not remove the case from the bargained for decision maker—the arbitrator.

The second case in the trilogy, *United Steelworkers of America v. Warrior & Gulf Nav. Co.*,[54] established a presumption of arbitrability. The union filed a grievance because the employer subcontracted out unit work. The arbitration clause included disputes about the meaning and application of the CBA and about "local trouble of any kind." It excluded matters which are "strictly a function of management." Citing the exclusion, the employer refused to arbitrate the subcontracting grievance. The Supreme Court held that whether subcontracting was a management function was for the arbitrator, and not the courts, to decide. The language of the CBA excluding management functions from arbitration was unclear and created ambiguity better resolved by the arbitrator. Under the presumption of arbitrability, only in the narrowest of circumstances, when there is "forceful evidence" of excluding the particular type of dispute from the arbitration clause, should a court refrain from enforcing a labor arbitration agreement. Otherwise courts would become involved in labor cases, creating inefficiency and removing the cases from the expertise provided by the parties' mutually selected arbitrator. Thus, courts must compel arbitration "unless it may be said with positive assurance that the arbitration clause is not susceptible of an interpretation that covers the asserted dispute."

The last case in the trilogy, *United Steelworkers of America v. Enterprise Wheel & Car. Corp.*,[55] dealt with enforcing an arbitrator's award, and is discussed below in § 51. The court reasoned that as long as the award "draws its essence" from the CBA, the courts should not vacate the award.

(d) Arbitrability

Arbitrability is the question of whether a dispute should be submitted to arbitration for determination or not. Because labor arbitration is contractual, the issue is focused on whether the dispute is covered by the CBA and falls within the coverage of the arbitration provision. Courts, following the premise of the *Steelworkers Trilogy*, will only decide questions of substantive arbitrability and will leave

---

[53]   363 U.S. at 568.

[54]   363 U.S. 574 (1960).

[55]   363 U.S. 593 (1960).

questions of procedural arbitrability to the arbitrator.[56] As discussed in § 30, substantive arbitrability, also termed "contractual arbitrability," focuses on the determination of whether the arbitration clause encompasses the dispute,[57] whereas procedural arbitrability focuses on whether procedures provided for in the arbitration provision have been followed.[58] Thus, the arbitrator, rather than the courts, generally decides whether or not an arbitration is barred by the failure to comply with grievance time limits or other procedural requirements in the grievance-arbitration process.[59] This division of substantive and procedural arbitrability is analogous to that in the commercial arbitration process, discussed in depth in § 21(c).

Sometimes parties disagree over whether the conduct underlying the dispute arose under the CBA. The courts will compel arbitration even when the specific dispute arose after termination of the agreement if the decision requires interpretation of the CBA. For instance, when a union sought arbitration over an employer's failure to pay severance and argued the severance pay accrued to the workers while working under the CBA, the Supreme Court compelled arbitration.[60] But if a dispute arises after the CBA expired and does not involve conduct arising before the CBA expiration, then the CBA does not arguably govern the dispute, and the dispute is not arbitrable.[61]

The courts will decide issues concerning formation of the CBA[62] but will not decide whether the overall CBA is valid. Courts will, thus, address issues about whether the parties entered into, or formed, an agreement to arbitrate.[63] For example, in *Granite Rock*

---

[56]   John Wiley & Sons v. Livingston, 376 U.S. 543, 546–47 (1964); Oil, Chem. & Atomic Workers Local 4–447 v. Chevron Chem. Co., 815 F.2d 338, 340 (5th Cir. 1987). Some parties contract for the arbitrator to decide questions of substantive as well as procedural arbitrability. To do so requires a clear and unmistakable waiver of the right to go to a court to determine substantive arbitrability. The Common Law of the Workplace: The Views of Arbitrators, § 2.23, at 94–95 (Theodore St. Antoine 2d ed. 2005).

[57]   Granite Rock Co. v. IBT, 561 U.S. 287, 300 (2010) (noting courts must determine the arbitration agreement was validly formed, covered the dispute in question, and was legally enforceable); Litton Financial Printing Division 501 U.S. 190, 207 (1991).

[58]   Wiley, 376 U.S. at 556.

[59]   Elkouri, supra note 33, at 2–14, 6–8; John Wiley & Sons v. Livingston, 376 U.S. 543, 557 (1964) (whether preliminary steps of grievance process were exhausted); Oil, Chem. & Atomic Workers Local 4–447 v. Chevron Chem. Co., 815 F.2d 338, 340 (5th Cir. 1987) (whether grievance timelines were met).

[60]   Nolde Bros. v. Bakery & Confectionery Workers Local 358, 430 U.S. 243, 255 (1977).

[61]   Litton Financial Printing Division 501 U.S. 190, 206 (1991).

[62]   Granite Rock Co. v. IBT, 561 U.S. 287, 297 (2010).

[63]   Id.

Co. v. IBT, the Supreme Court determined that a dispute over when a CBA was ratified by the union members should be determined by a court because the date of ratification determined whether the parties agreed to arbitrate the strike conduct at issue. If the CBA was ratified before the strike, then the strike was subject to the arbitration clause, but if the CBA was ratified after the strike, then no agreement to arbitrate the strike was formed.[64] The issue of validity of the overall CBA, however, is for the arbitrator.[65] The distinction between issues of contract validity, which are decided by the arbitrator, and contract formation, which is decided by the court is further discussed in § 21(a). Issues involving arbitrability are complex, and lawyers should thoroughly research arbitrability if it will be an issue in a particular case.

§ 53   Enforcement and Vacatur of Labor Arbitration Awards

(a) Reasons for Vacatur

In most cases, the parties voluntarily comply with the arbitration award, but in some a party seeks confirmation, modification, or vacatur of the award.[66] *Enterprise Wheel* established that a court must confirm any arbitration award that "draws its essence from the" CBA, even if the award is in error.[67] Only under narrow circumstances should an award be vacated. These circumstances are: 1) the award results from procedural unfairness, such as fraud, corruption, or bias. 2) The arbitrator "clearly exceeded" the authority granted "by contravening a clear provision of the" CBA. 3) The award violates a fundamental and well-defined public policy.[68] For extensive discussion of vacatur and the rationale behind the narrow grounds for review see § 42–44. Parties likely cannot contract for any different standard of court review.[69] Since the *Steelworkers*

---

[64]   Granite Rock, 561 U.S. at 303–04. Often a CBA must be voted on by the union members to be effective, and this process is called ratification of the CBA.

[65]   Granite Rock, 561 U.S. at 301; See Nitro-Lift Technologies, L.L.C. v. Howard, 133 S.Ct. 500, 503 (2012) (employment arbitration case stating that under the FAA "attacks on the validity of the contract, as distinct from attacks on the validity of the arbitration clause itself, are to be resolved 'by the arbitrator in the first instance, not by a federal or state court.' ").

[66]   Elkouri, supra note 33, at 2–3 (citing LeRoy & Feuille, Final and Binding, But Appealable to Courts: Empirical Evidence of Judicial Review of Labor and Employment Arbitration Awards, in Arbitration 2001: Arbitrating in an Evolving Legal Environment, Proceedings of the 54th Annual Meeting of NAA 49, 62 (Grenig & Briggs eds., BNA Books 2002)).

[67]   For a general discussion of confirmation of arbitration awards, see § 39.

[68]   Ray, supra note 40, at 296.

[69]   See Chicago Typographical Union No. 16 v. Chicago Sun-Times, Inc., 935 F.2d 1501, 1505 (7th Cir. 1991) (stating in labor arbitration case that parties cannot contract for judicial review of an arbitration award); Hall Street Associates, LLC v.

Trilogy, different courts have interpreted the standards for confirmation and enforcement and vacatur of labor arbitration awards differently.[70] This section discusses each of the three most recognized grounds for vacatur of a labor arbitration award as well as other possible grounds and explains a narrow exception that permits an employee to sue an employer for a violation of a CBA when the union has breached its duty of fair representation to the employee. It then discusses modification of awards.

As to ground one, procedural unfairness (fraud, corruption, or bias), an arbitration award will be vacated because of bias if the arbitrator had a "personal stake" in the arbitration.[71] In one case, where the arbitrator was the son of an officer of an international union to which the local union bringing the grievance belonged, a court determined that bias sufficient to vacate the award was shown simply because of the particular family relationship.[72] One court found, however, that when an employer sued an arbitrator post-award and the arbitrator filed for Rule 11 sanctions against the employer's lawyer, that action did not demonstrate bias undermining the award.[73] Even situations that raise an appearance of impropriety, which would require recusal of a federal judge, do not amount to sufficient bias to vacate a labor arbitration award.[74] In one case, for instance, the court permitted an employer-appointed co-arbitrator to determine a case involving his former law partners' actions during the partnership.[75]

Similar to cases of bias resulting in vacatur, where an employer and union purposefully select an arbitrator they believe will be biased against a grievant, the award will be vacated.[76] The procedural unfairness in the process justifies vacating the award regardless of whether the arbitrator was actually biased. Likewise, labor awards will be vacated for corruption. In a RLA case, the Ninth Circuit described corruption sufficient to merit vacatur of an award

---

Mattel Inc., 552 U.S. 576, 578 (2008) (holding parties to disputes governed by the FAA cannot contract for additional grounds of review).

[70]   While in other context confirmation and enforcement are two separate parts of the process, in labor arbitration parties tend to move for enforcement, intending to include confirmation of the award and orders to comply with it.

[71]   Pitta v. Hotel Ass'n of New York City, 806 F.2d 419, 423 (2d Cir. 1986).

[72]   Morelite Constr. Corp. v. New York City Dist. Council Carpenters Benefit Funds, 748 F.2d 79, 84 (2d Cir. 1984).

[73]   Toyota of Berkeley v. Automobile Salesmen's Union Local 1095, 834 F.2d 751, 756 (9th Cir. 1987).

[74]   Pitta v. Hotel Ass'n of New York City, 806 F.2d 419, 423 (2d Cir. 1986); Apperson v. Fleet Carrier Corp., 879 F.2d 1344, 1350, 1360 (6th Cir. 1989).

[75]   Apperson, 879 F.2d at 1360–61.

[76]   Elkouri, supra note 33, at 2–36; Allen v. Allied Plant Maint. Co., 881 F.2d 291 (6th Cir. 1989).

as including violence, threats of violence, bribery, extortion, and other acts that threaten the integrity of an arbitration proceeding, including threats of economic injury, such as an employer-appointed representative threatening to blacklist a neutral member.[77]

As to ground two, clearly exceeding authority by contravening a clear provision of the CBA, the Supreme Court has reaffirmed the narrow circumstances where an arbitrator clearly exceeds the authority granted by the CBA. A court should not vacate an award even if convinced the arbitrator "committed serious errors" when the arbitrator is "arguably construing or applying the contract and acting within the scope of his authority."[78] Most courts vacate a labor arbitration award only where the award violates the clear language of the agreement.[79] For instance, in one case an arbitrator awarded no remedy where the plain language of the CBA required awarding a remedy if a violation was found.[80] Nevertheless, the Fifth Circuit continues to more broadly interpret circumstances where the arbitrator exceeds authority. The Fifth Circuit vacates the award when the arbitrator has "failed to arguably construe" the CBA by interpreting it in such a manner as to render a term used by the CBA meaningless.[81]

Courts will also vacate an award in the limited circumstance that the arbitrator lacked jurisdiction over the dispute, a substantive arbitrability issue.[82]

In limited circumstances, a court may vacate an arbitration award because it conflicts with public policy.[83] The public policy must be an explicit, fundamental, and well-defined one ascertainable from a specific statute or law.[84] For instance, an award reinstating a truck-driver who tested positive twice for marijuana use, during random drug tests, did not violate public policy.[85] The Court recognized truck drivers, like the grievant, are extensively regulated by federal law and that random testing of truck drivers is required.[86] The Court,

---

[77]   United Transp. Union v. BNSF Ry. Co., 710 F.3d 915, 932 (9th Cir. 2013).

[78]   Major League Baseball Players Ass'n v. Garvey, 532 U.S. 504 (2001); Michigan Family Res. v. SEIU, 475 F.3d 746 (6th Cir.) (2007).

[79]   Elkouri, supra note 33, at 2–23; Michigan Family Res. v. SEIU, 475 F.3d 746, 753 (6th Cir.) (2007).

[80]   Operating Eng'rs Local 9 v. Shank-Artukovich, 751 F.2d 364 (10th Cir. 1985).

[81]   Elkouri, supra note 33, at 2–25; Continental Airlines, Inc. v. Teamsters, 391 F.3d 613, 620 (5th Cir. 2004).

[82]   Elkouri, supra note 33, at 2–22.

[83]   Paperworkers v. Misco, Inc., 484 U.S. 29, 43 (1987).

[84]   Id.

[85]   Eastern Associated Coal Corp. v. Mine Workers District 17, 531 U.S. 57, 65–66 (2000).

[86]   Id. at 63–4.

however, reasoned that the applicable federal law's "remedial aims are complex," promote rehabilitation, and do not prohibit reinstatement of an employee who fails a random drug test twice.[87] The Court noted that the federal law encouraged collective bargaining rather than requiring a certain outcome for employees who test positive.[88] The Court determined that in light of these "several policies, taken together," the award did not condone drug use or ignore the risk to public safety, but rather punished the grievant with a suspension, required substance-abuse treatment, and provided only one further last chance if the grievant again tests positive.[89] Moreover, the award did not violate any "specific provision of any law or regulation."[90]

Sometimes parties urge vacatur of a labor arbitration award on grounds of manifest disregard of the law. Courts reviewing arbitration under the FAA have occasionally vacated an award because of an arbitrator's manifest disregard of the law.[91] The Supreme Court has left open the issue about whether manifest disregard is a valid basis for vacatur under the FAA, either as an independent ground for review or as a "judicial gloss on the enumerated grounds."[92] The Supreme Court has not yet addressed the issue under Section 301.[93] Some courts have, however, applied the standard of "manifest disregard of the law" to review a labor arbitration award,[94] and some courts have traditionally used the term "manifest disregard of the CBA" to describe one circumstance when an arbitrator exceeded authority.[95] If a case implicates "manifest disregard" as a standard for review, detailed research of the governing law in that jurisdiction is required.

---

[87]   Id. at 64–65.

[88]   Id. at 66.

[89]   Id. at 66.

[90]   Id. at 66.

[91]   Elkouri, supra note 33, at 2–22; see § 50 for discussion of the relationship between Section 301 and the FAA.

[92]   Stolt-Nielsen S.A. v. AnimalFeeds Int'l Corp., 559 U.S. 662, 671 n.3 (2010).

[93]   National Football League Players Ass'n v. National Football League Management Council, 2011 WL 31068 (S.D. Ca. 2011) (noting that the Ninth Circuit has not yet decided whether the FAA applies to suits brought under Section 301 and assuming, without deciding, that the manifest disregard of the law standard applies to review a labor arbitration award).

[94]   Regional Local Union No. 846 v. Gulf Coast Rebar, Inc., 83 F.Supp.3d 997, 1010, 1012, 1014 (2015).

[95]   Major League Umpires Ass'n v. American League of Professional Baseball Clubs, 357 F.3d 272, 280 (3d Cir. 2004).

(b) Vacating Award for Union Breach of Duty of Fair Representation

Union-represented employees are generally required by the federal common law developed under Section 301 to bring grievances through the grievance-arbitration process. If they instead try to litigate a claim against their employer for breach of CBA, the court will compel grievance arbitration under Section 301 and the applicable CBA provisions.[96] In some instances, however, where union conduct has resulted in an inadequate grievance-arbitration process, an employee can sue the union and the employer. To prevail in such a suit, the employee must prove that the union breached its duty of fair representation.[97] To prove such a breach involves a high standard, and most courts hold that mere negligence on a union's part does not result in a breach of the duty. Instead the employee must prove that the union acted arbitrarily, discriminatorily, or in bad faith.[98] In some instances, a court will vacate an arbitration award due to the union's breach of the duty of fair representation during the arbitration process and permit an employee to litigate de novo the breach of CBA claim against the employer under Section 301.[99] This type of claim is termed a "hybrid 301-DFR" claim because it must be brought against both the union and the employer.[100]

(c) Modification of Awards

If a party seeks enforcement of an award that is incomplete, courts will send the case back to arbitration to complete the award.[101] For instance, the arbitrator may not have calculated the specific amount of damages, and the parties cannot agree on how to calculate them. The Court will send the issue back to the parties to resolve through arbitration.[102]

§ 54 Relationship Between Labor Arbitration and Statutory Claims

(a) Parallel Contract and Statutory Claims

In most circumstances, an employee who has a statutory employment claim and a similar claim for breach of contract can proceed both in litigation and in arbitration. For example, if a CBA

---

[96] Hines v. Anchor Motor Freight, 424 U.S. 554, 567 (1976).

[97] Vaca v. Sipes, 386 U.S. 171 (1967).

[98] Hines, 424 U.S. at 570.

[99] Id. at 567.

[100] Elkouri, supra note 33, at 2–47 & n.232.

[101] Courier-Citizen Co. v. Boston Electrotypers Union No. 11, 702 F.2d 273, 279 (1983).

[102] Elkouri, supra note 33, at 2–12.

contains a no-discrimination clause that prohibits discrimination based on sex, and an employee is denied a promotion because of her sex, then she can file a grievance, and the union can pursue the claim that she was discriminated against in violation of the no-discrimination clause to arbitration if the union and the employer are unable to resolve the grievance at lower levels of the process. The employee can also file a charge with the EEOC and hire counsel to pursue her claim for a violation of Title VII of the Civil Rights Act, which prohibits employment discrimination because of sex, in litigation. One study found that the average length of time to resolve a discrimination case in arbitration is shorter than that to receive a trial for a discrimination claim in both federal and state court. [103] In some circumstances, however, a union and an employer agree to waive employees' rights to proceed with statutory claims in litigation and to require that the claim instead be pursued in arbitration. For a more in-depth discussion of the change in jurisprudence enforcing pre-dispute agreements to arbitrate statutory claims, see § 27. This section discusses the basic paradigm under the seminal case, *Gardner-Denver*, that permits an employee to litigate a claim similar to one the union has arbitrated. It then discusses the seminal case permitting unions and employers to agree to arbitration as the only available forum for a statutory claim. For further discussion of cases where a clear and unmistakable waiver precluded litigation of a statutory employment discrimination claim, see § 28(a)(1).

(b) Gardner-Denver

In *Alexander v. Gardner-Denver Co.*,[104] the Supreme Court held that a labor-arbitration award in a case about whether a CBA no-discrimination clause was violated does not preclude a subsequent suit for violation of anti-discrimination statutes.[105] The Court distinguished between the grievance alleging a violation of a contractual right and the lawsuit alleging violation of a separate statutorily guaranteed right. The court explained that, at that time during the late 1970's, labor arbitrators were experts in interpreting contracts but not law, that labor arbitration processes were not suited to deciding discrimination claims, and that unions, which rely on majoritarian decision-making and processes, cannot adequately protect statutory rights of minorities. The Court also emphasized

---

[103]   Levinson, Labor Arbitration, supra note 27, at 852.

[104]   415 U.S. 36 (1974).

[105]   Id. at 51–52. See also McDonald v. City of W. Branch, Mich., 466 U.S. 284 (1984) (labor arbitration award in wrongful termination case does not bar a Section 1983 action); Barrentine v. Ark.-Best Freight Sys., Inc., 450 U.S. 728 (1981) (joint labor-management committee decision regarding a wage grievance does not does not bar a Fair Labor Standards Act suit).

that labor arbitration is a substitute for industrial strife, and not for litigation.[106]

The Court explained that the trial court could consider a labor-arbitration award for the weight it was worth in the discrimination case.[107] The Court set out relevant factors trial courts could consider including whether the CBA provisions conform to the statutory ones, whether the arbitration forum was procedurally fair, whether the record adequately addressed the statutory claim, and the "special competence of particular arbitrators." The Court permitted lower courts, in their discretion, to accord the labor arbitration award great weight but urged the lower courts to be mindful of Congress's decision to "provide a judicial forum for the ultimate resolution of discriminatory employment claims." Some trial courts will consider the labor award and the opinion's reasoning, and some will give an award no weight. A minority continue to give a prior award claim preclusion effect.[108]

(c) 14 Penn Plaza v. Pyett

In *14 Penn Plaza v. Pyett*,[109] the Supreme Court held that a CBA's clear and unmistakable waiver of the right to litigate requires a union-represented employee to arbitrate statutory anti-discrimination claims.[110] The Court explained that arbitration agreements concerning employment claims are within the realm of workplace terms and conditions over which unions have bargaining power.[111] The Court addressed concerns about the majoritarian union processes by noting that anti-discrimination statutes and the duty of fair representation deter unions from unfairly treating minorities and that collective strength is the central premise of labor law.[112] The Court interpreted *Gardner-Denver* as addressing only contractual claims[113] and explained that the negative view of arbitration

---

[106] Gardner-Denver, 415 U.S. at 54–55.

[107] Gardner-Denver, 415 U.S. at 60 n.21.

[108] *See* Martin H. Malin, Revisiting the Meltzer-Howlett Debate on External Public Law in Labor Arbitration: Is it Time for Courts to Declare Howlett the Winner?, 24 Lab.Law 1, 20 (2008) (suggesting that some courts rely on arbitration awards rather than providing de novo review of statutory claims); Courtney Lamont Phelps, Lifting Gardner-Denver Footnote 21: The Heavy Burden to Give "Appropriate Weight" to Arbitration Decisions on Subsequent Judicial Review (2011) (unpublished student independent study paper) (on file with author) (outlining various ways courts have treated arbitration awards in employment discrimination cases).

[109] 556 U.S. 247 (2009).

[110] Id. at 251. For a discussion that sets labor arbitration in the context of the jurisprudential change from permitting only arbitration of contract claims to also permitting arbitration of statutory claims see §§ 27 and 28(a).

[111] Id. at 255–56.

[112] Id. at 261, 270–72.

[113] Id. at 262.

portrayed by *Gardner-Denver* is outmoded.[114] The Court's current view is that many arbitrators address complex statutory issues and have the skills and expertise necessary to decide statutory discrimination issues.[115] The Court also views arbitration as a more efficient alternative for resolving employment disputes than litigation.[116] For further discussion of cases where a clear and unmistakable waiver precluded litigation of a statutory employment discrimination claim, see § 40.

The Court treated the contract language in *Pyett* as a clear and unmistakable waiver. The plaintiff had admitted the language was "sufficiently explicit" and waived any objection that it was not clear and unmistakable.[117] The CBA included a no-discrimination clause that forbid discrimination, stated the names of applicable statutes, such as Title VII and the ADEA, and concluded that "[a]ll such claims shall be subject to the grievance and arbitration procedures . . . as the sole and exclusive remedy for violations."[118] The Court stated several times that the CBA included a clear and unmistakable waiver,[119] but did not discuss the requisites for a clear and unmistakable waiver.[120] The Court had previously explained that inclusion of a general arbitration clause wherein the parties agree to arbitrate disputed matters does not preclude an employee from litigating statutory claims, particularly when the CBA contains no explicit incorporation of antidiscrimination standards.[121] Since the *Pyett* decision, courts have reaffirmed that a general provision providing for arbitration of contract disputes and a general no-discrimination clause forbidding discrimination on listed grounds, such as race or gender, does not constitute a clear and unmistakable waiver.[122]

---

[114]   Id. at 265.

[115]   Id. at 268–69.

[116]   Id. at 269.

[117]   Id. at 272–73.

[118]   Id. at 252.

[119]   Id. at 259 (stating that the CBA explicitly stated the agreement to arbitrate statutory claims), at 260 (stating the CBA clearly and unmistakably required arbitration of the age discrimination claims at issue in the case).

[120]   Mark S. Mathison & Bryan M. Seiler, What 14 Penn Plaza LLC v. Pyett Means for Employers: Balancing Interests in a Landscape of Uncertainty, 25 ABA J.Lab.&Emp.L. 173, 181 (2010) (noting Pyett provides "no additional guidance" on what constitutes a clear and unmistakable waiver because the Court "refused to consider the arguments . . . that the CBA did not clearly and unmistakably require arbitration . . .").

[121]   Wright v. Universal Maritime Serv. Corp., 525 U.S. 70, 80–81 (1998).

[122]   Kovac v. Superior Dairy, Inc., 930 F.Supp. 2d 857 (N.D. Ohio 2013); Harrell v. Kellogg Co., 892 F. Supp. 2d 716 (E.D. Pa. 2012); see Wawock v. CSI Elec. Contractors, Inc., No. 14–56810, 2016 WL 2587937, at *3 (9th Cir. April 6, 2016) (requiring arbitration of "all grievances or questions in dispute" does not constitute a clear and

Courts have enumerated two circumstances in which a clear and unmistakable waiver will be found.[123] First, a CBA clearly and unmistakably waives the right to litigate a statutory claim when the CBA explicitly incorporates the statutory claim into the CBA.[124] For instance, the Fifth Circuit found that a CBA clearly and unmistakably waived an employee's right to go to court with a Rehabilitation Act claim, but not a Family Medical Leave Act (FMLA) claim.[125] The CBA defined a grievance as "a dispute, difference, disagreement or complaint between the parties related to wages, hours, and conditions of employment.[126] The grievance/arbitration provision stated a grievance includes "but is not limited to," one involving "interpretation, application of, or compliance with" the CBA.[127] The CBA incorporated an employee handbook that provided policies for compliance with the FMLA.[128] The Court reasoned those policies did not "purport to make the FMLA a part of the agreement" and were insufficient to create a clear and unmistakable waiver.[129] On the other hand, the Court ruled that the CBA incorporated the Rehabilitation Act.[130] The CBA stated, "consistent with the other provisions of this Agreement, there shall be no unlawful discrimination against handicapped employees, as prohibited by the Rehabilitation Act."[131]

Second, a CBA clear and unmistakably waives the right to litigate a statutory claim when the CBA includes an arbitration clause that explicitly refers to arbitration as the sole forum for deciding statutory claims.[132] For example, the language "the 'grievance and arbitration provisions of this [CBA] shall be the sole and exclusive remedy for any employee who believes that he or she had been subjected to illegal discrimination in violation of applicable

---

unmistakable waiver of a claim for violation of state wage statutes); Manning v. Boston Medical Center, 725 F.3d 34, 53 (1st Cir. 2013) ("broadly-worded arbitration clause" does not constitute clear and unmistakable waiver of FLSA claim).

[123]   Lawrence v. Sol G. Atlas Realty Co., 2015 WL 5076957, at *5 (E.D.N.Y. Aug. 27, 2015).

[124]   Gilbert v. Donahoe, 751 F.3d 303, 310 (5th Cir. 2014); Montgomery v. Compass Airlines, LLC, 98 F.Supp.3d 1012, 1029 (D. Minn. 2015). Cf. Manning v. Boston Medical Center Corp., 725 F.3d 34, 52 (1st Cir. 2013) ("something closer to specific enumeration of the statutory claims to be arbitrated is required" to constitute clear and unmistakable waiver).

[125]   Gilbert, 751 F.3d at 310.

[126]   Id.

[127]   Id.

[128]   Id.

[129]   Id.

[130]   Id.

[131]   Id.

[132]   Nelson v. City of Live Oak, 2011 WL 5006472 (M.D.Fla. 2011).

law and/or this [CBA]' constitutes a clear and unmistakable waiver of a court claim under Title VII."[133]

Some courts that may previously have declined to consider arbitration awards are now giving them greater weight in discrimination cases due toward the favorable position toward arbitration taken in *Pyett*.[134] Some are even applying claim preclusion principles.[135] Three circuits have, however, confirmed that *Gardner-Denver* continues to govern statutory claims when a CBA contains no clear and explicit waiver. They have each reversed a lower court that applied issue preclusion or claim preclusion.[136] Even prior to *Pyett*, some courts were more deferential to arbitration awards than others. For instance, the Second Circuit continues to hold that an arbitration opinion and award resulting from substantial evidence presented during an evidentiary hearing will preclude a plaintiff from litigating a discrimination claim unless "evidence that the decision was wrong as a matter of fact" or "the impartiality of the" evidentiary hearing "was somehow compromised."[137]

Some questions regarding labor arbitration of discrimination claims remain post-*Pyett*. Generally, when a union and an employer reach an impasse in CBA negotiations, the employer is free to implement its last final offer.[138] If an employer includes a clear and unmistakable waiver in its contract proposal, the employer may argue for implementation of the waiver post-impasse, as part of the last final offer. Because the union did not actually agree to the clause, however, courts are unlikely to find this a true clear and unmistakable waiver and are likely to determine the requisite knowledge and intent to form an agreement are absent.

Another issue that remains is what occurs when a union and employer have entered into a clear and unmistakable waiver, but the union declines to pursue a discrimination or other employment claim

---

[133]   Nelson, at *1–2.

[134]   See e.g. Hawkins v. Leggett, 955 F.Supp.2d 474 (D. Md. 2013) (Title VII decision providing great weight to an arbitrator's just cause finding).

[135]   See Ann C. Hodges, Fallout From 14 Penn Plaza, LLC v. Pyett: Fractured Arbitration Systems in the Unionized Workplace, 2010 J.Disp.Resol. 19, 51–52 (2010) (noting that some lower courts "read Pyett broadly" and preclude litigation in deference to an arbitration award).

[136]   Grimes v. BNSF Ry. Co., 746 F.3d 184 (5th Cir. 2014); Coleman v. Donahoe, 667 F.3d 835, 854 (7th Cir. 2012); Mathews v. Denver Newspaper Agency LLP, 649 F.3d 1199, 1204–05 (11th Cir. 2011).

[137]   Attard v. City of New York, No. 10–4224–cv, 2011 WL 6225249 (2nd Cir. Dec. 15, 2011) (quoting Collins v. N.Y.C. Transit Auth., 305 F.3d 113, 119 (2d Cir.2002)).

[138]   Ray, supra note 40, at 176 ([U]nilateral changes after impasse that implement proposal consistent with final offers made to the union do not violate Section 8(a)(5)).

to arbitration.[139] Because the union, and not the grievant, normally controls the grievance arbitration process, the union need not take any particular grievance to arbitration. One solution to this problem is for unions to include a right for an individual grievant to proceed with statutory claims in arbitration.[140] A similar proposal is to let each grievant choose between arbitration or litigation post-dispute.[141] Permitting individual control of the process, however, weakens the union's ability to ensure an appropriate process is used in labor arbitration and to obtain standard treatment for all employees and opens the process to displaying conflict rather than solidarity among employees to the employer.[142] Another solution that some courts have already adopted is to require the employer to litigate the statutory claim when the union declines to pursue it to arbitration.[143]

§ 55   Relationship Between the NLRB and Labor Arbitration

(a) Deferring to Arbitration

The National Labor Relations Board (NLRB) is the federal administrative agency responsible for administering the National Labor Relations Act (NLRA), which governs most private-sector employers. This section discusses the law and practice governing when the NLRB will defer to arbitration or an arbitration award.[144] The NLRB law and policies change with different administrations, so lawyers should check the most recent NLRB cases and general counsel memorandum to determine current practice. When a union

---

[139]   Stuart M. Boyarsky, Not What They Bargained For: Directing the Arbitration of Statutory Antidiscriminatory Rights, 18 Harv.Negot.L.Rev. 221, 254 (2013).

[140]   Levinson, Labor Arbitration, supra note 27, at 806. Gildea v. BLSG Mgmt., 2011 WL 4343464, at *5 (S.D.N.Y. Aug. 16, 2011) (requiring individual to proceed to arbitration without the union).

[141]   Levinson, Labor Arbitration, supra note 27, at 854–55.

[142]   Levinson, Labor Arbitration, supra note 27, at 855; David L. Gregory & Edward McNamara, Mandatory Labor Arbitration of Statutory Claims, and the Future of Fair Employment: 14 Penn Plaza v. Pyett, 19 Cornell J.L.&Pub.Pol'y 429, 452 (2010).

[143]   See e.g., Drake v. Hyundai Rotem USA, Corp., 2013 WL 4551228) (E.D. Pa. Aug. 28, 2013); Brown v. Services for the Underserved, 2012 WL 3111903 (E.D.N.Y. 2012); Silva v. Pioneer Janitorial Services, 777 F.Supp.2d 198, 207 (D. Ma. 2011); Veliz v. Collins Bldg. Serv., Inc., No. 10 Civ. 06615 (RJH), 2011 WL 4444498, at *4 (S.D.N.Y. Sept. 26, 2011); Morris v. Temco Serv. Indus., Inc., No. 09 Civ. 6194(WHP), 2010 WL 3291810, at *6 (S.D.N.Y. Aug. 12, 2010); Borrero v. Ruppert Hous. Co., Inc., No. 08 CV 5869(HB), 2009 WL 1748060, at *2 (S.D.N.Y. June 19, 2009); Kravar v. Triangle Serv., Inc., 186 L.R.R.M. 2565 (S.D.N.Y. May 19, 2009).

[144]   Public sector employees may be governed by an agency similar to the NLRB that uses similar deferral policies or somewhat different deferral policies. Martin H. Malin, Ann C. Hodges & Joseph E. Slater, & Jeffrey M. Hirsch, Public Sector Employment Cases and Materials, at 962 (3d ed. Thomson West 2016).

and an employer have a CBA, the CBA often grants parallel protections to those provided by the NLRA. In instances where these parallel claims arise, a union may file both a grievance and an unfair labor practice charge with the NLRB. If there is a parallel arbitration pending, the NLRB may decide to defer a decision until after the arbitrator has ruled.

To defer an unfair labor practice charge to arbitration, the NLRB must determine that the grievance-arbitration process is capable of effectively resolving the dispute. The NLRB, thus, imposes five requirements before deferring to arbitration. 1) The employer must be willing to submit the dispute to arbitration. 2) There must be no evidence of the employer's "hostility towards" employees' Section 7 rights. 3) The parties must have a stable bargaining relationship. 4) The arbitration clause of the CBA covers the dispute. 5) Collective bargaining must be suitable to resolving the dispute.[145]

(1) NLRA § 8(a)(5) Unilateral Changes

When the union's charge alleges that an employer violated NLRA Section 8(a)(5), the duty to bargain in good faith, by making a unilateral change to the conditions of employment, the Board often defers to arbitration. The Board does so because the employer normally defends by arguing that the change was consistent with the contract, and, thus, the claim raises issues of contract interpretation best decided by an arbitrator.[146]

(2) NLRA §§ 8(a)(1) & (3) Monitoring for a Year

Over the years, the NLRB has often been more reluctant to defer Section 8(a)(3) and independent Section 8(a)(1) charges to arbitration, although NLRB policies switch between being more or less likely to defer. A Section 8(a)(3) charge alleges that the employer has discriminated against employees because of union activity. Section 8(a)(1) prohibits interfering, restraining, or coercing employees in the exercise of their Section 7 rights. Because of this anytime another subsection of 8(a) is violated, Section 8(a)(1) is also violated. Some violations of the NLRA, however, arise only under Section 8(a)(1), and so are termed "independent 8(a)(1) violations." These include violations like preventing employees from handing out union literature, surveilling employees engaged in union activity, or threatening plant closure because employees are engaged in union activity.

---

[145] Collyer Insulated Wire, 192 NLRB 837, 841–42 (1971); Ray, supra note 48, at 296.

[146] Ray, supra note 40, at 296; Office of the General Counsel, Memorandum GC 12–01, at *2, Jan. 20, 2012.

Currently, whether or not a union files a parallel grievance, the NLRB will not defer Section 8(a)(1) and (3) charges to arbitration "unless the parties have explicitly authorized the arbitrator to decide the unfair labor practice issue, either in the" CBA "or by agreement" as to the particular case.[147] An Acting General Counsel memo from 2012 outlines the NLRB's procedure as to deferring Section 8(a)(1) and (3) charges, and a small subset of Section 8(a)(5) charges,[148] to arbitration.[149] The NLRB will only defer charges that will be arbitrated and resolved in less than a year.[150] The NLRB monitors these cases, and revokes deferral if the process does not proceed in a timely manner. If the arbitration process will take longer than a year, then the NLRB is concerned about lost evidence, faded memories, and the passage of time undermining adequate remedies (often because workers move on to other workplaces).[151] In this circumstance, the Board will not defer to arbitration except in limited circumstances, such as when all parties prefer arbitration.[152]

(b) Deferring to the Award

As with the NLRB's policies regarding deferral to the arbitration process, its policies regarding deferring to an arbitrator's award also periodically change. An example of how the issue arises is where an employee is terminated for unsatisfactory performance, and the union grieves arguing at arbitration that the grievant's performance was satisfactory. At the same time, the union files a charge alleging that the grievant was terminated not for unsatisfactory performance but because of union activity.[153] The arbitrator finds that the employee was terminated for unsatisfactory performance. The NLRB may defer to the award or conduct its own investigation of the statutory discrimination claim.

(1) NLRA § 8(a)(5) Cases

In the seminal decision governing deferral to arbitration awards, the Board defers to an award when three conditions are met.[154] 1)

---

[147]   Babcock & Wilcox Const. Co., 361 NLRB No. 132, 2014 WL 7149039, at *17 (12/15/14).

[148]   These are Section 8(a)(5) charges that involve individual rights or serious economic harm. Office of the General Counsel, Memorandum GC 12–01, at *10, Jan. 20, 2012.

[149]   Ray, supra note 40, at 307–08; Office of the General Counsel, Memorandum GC 12–01, Jan. 20, 2012.

[150]   Office of the General Counsel, Memorandum GC 12–01, at *8, Jan. 20, 2012.

[151]   Office of the General Counsel, Memorandum GC 12–01, at *6–7, Jan. 20, 2012.

[152]   Office of the General Counsel, Memorandum GC 12–01, at *8, *10, Jan. 20, 2012.

[153]   Ray, supra note 40, at 308.

[154]   Spielberg Manf. Co., 112 NLRB 1080, 1082 (1955).

The arbitration proceedings were "fair and regular." 2) "All parties had agreed to be bound" by the award. 3) The opinion and award are not "clearly repugnant to the purposes and policies of the Act."[155] Currently, in Section 8(a)(5) cases the Board further requires that the unfair labor practice issue and the CBA issue were parallel and "the arbitrator was presented generally with the facts relevant to resolving the unfair labor practice."[156] In Section 8(a)(5) cases the burden is on the party opposing deferral (generally the union) to prove the conditions were not met.[157]

(2)   NLRA §§ 8(a)(1) & (3) Cases

In a 2014 decision,[158] the NLRB specified the current deferral policy for Section 8(a)(1) and 8(a)(3) cases.[159] The burden to prove that the NLRB should defer to the arbitration award rests on the party urging deferral (normally the employer). The party must prove three requirements. 1) The arbitrator was "explicitly authorized to decide" the unfair labor practice issue. 2) The arbitrator was presented with evidence about the unfair labor practice and "considered the statutory issue or was prevented from doing so by the party opposing deferral." 3) "Board law reasonably permits the award."[160]

§ 56   The Railway Labor Act

The RLA covers employers and unions in the transportation industry, primarily railways and airlines. Arbitration is one of the dispute resolution processes included in the RLA. The RLA categorizes grievances into two categories, labeling disputes as to rights "minor disputes" and disputes over interests "major disputes."[161] The National Railroad Adjustment Board (Adjustment Board) handles arbitration of minor disputes while the National Mediation Board (Mediation Board) handles major disputes. The Adjustment Board arbitrates grievance cases that are not resolved at lower levels of the grievance process. Because the RLA requires employers and unions to submit certain disputes to the Adjustment Board for decision,[162] it differs from the National Labor Relations Act,

---

[155]   Id.

[156]   Olin Corp., 268 NLRB 573, 574 (1981).

[157]   Id.

[158]   Babcock & Wilcox Const. Co., 361 NLRB No. 132, 2014 WL 7149039 (12/15/14).

[159]   Office of the General Counsel, Memorandum GC 15–02, at *2, Feb. 10, 2015 (explaining new deferral policy applies to only 8(a)(5) cases that are "entwined with related Section 8(a)(1) and/or (3) allegations.").

[160]   Babcock & Wilcox Const. Co., 361 NLRB No. 132, 2014 WL 7149039, at *3 (12/15/14).

[161]   Elkouri, supra note 33, 4–26.

[162]   45 U.S.C. § 153(i).

which only requires parties bargain in good faith but does not require the parties agree to a grievance-arbitration process. For arbitration to occur, the employer, union, or an individual employee must request arbitration by the Adjustment Board.[163] The Adjustment Board is bipartisan and half of the 34 members are appointed and compensated by the railway employers and half by the unions.[164] The Adjustment Board operates in four different divisions or arbitration tribunals, each covering employees in different categories of positions.[165] When cases deadlock, due to the bilateral nature of the arbitration tribunal, an additional neutral arbitrator, termed a "referee" is procured by the Mediation Board to decide the case.[166] The Adjustment Board's award is enforced in U.S. District Court.[167] Court review of the awards is very limited. The only three grounds for review are these. 1) The arbitration panel involved fraud or corruption. 2) The award failed to comply with the requirements of the RLA. 3) The arbitration panel's award is outside the scope of its jurisdiction.[168]

The parties may elect to submit a dispute to a Special Board of Adjustment (Special Board) or a Public Law Board rather than the Adjustment Board.[169] Special Boards have one member selected by each party and a third neutral member.[170] Public Law Board's consist of a representative of each party and, if they deadlock, a neutral third party.[171] These awards are enforceable in the same manner as an Adjustment Board award.[172]

Finally, the airline industry uses System Boards of Adjustment.[173] Each airline has established a System Board of Adjustment.[174] Generally, each System Board of Adjustment has an "equal number of" employer and "union-chosen members."[175] As with the Adjustment Board, when the parties deadlock, an additional

---

[163]   The individual right to pursue arbitration differs from most other grievance arbitration processes, which are normally controlled by the union.

[164]   Elkouri, supra note 33, at 4–28–29.

[165]   Elkouri, supra note 33, at 4–29.

[166]   Elkouri, supra note 33, at 4–30.

[167]   Ronald C. Henson & John M. Gilman, Airline and Railroad Labor and Employment Law, 007 ALI-ABA 343, 359 (2004).

[168]   Elkouri, supra note 33, at 4–32; RLA 45 U.S.C. § 153.

[169]   Elkouri, supra note 33, at 4–34–35; Henson, supra note 167, at 359.

[170]   Elkouri, supra note 33, at 4–34–35.

[171]   Henson, supra note 167, at 359.

[172]   Elkouri, supra note 33, at 4–34–35.

[173]   Elkouri, supra note 33, at 4–35–36.

[174]   Elkouri, supra note 33, at 4–36.

[175]   Henson, supra note 167, at 347.

neutral arbitrator is selected.[176] The procedures for enforcing or vacating labor arbitration awards by a System Board of Adjustment are similar to those for enforcement of railway labor arbitration awards,[177] although the Circuit Courts have not unanimously agreed on the applicable standard of review.[178]

The Mediation Board mediates interest disputes, those where the parties cannot agree on pay, rules, or working conditions.[179] If the parties are unable to settle a dispute even with the aid of a mediation, then the Mediation Board pressures the parties to submit to voluntary arbitration.[180] The arbitration panel consists of an equal number of employer and union selected neutrals with an additional neutral arbitrator. If the parties so agree, the arbitration panel files a labor arbitration award with a federal district court. If no party petitions the court within 10 days of the filing of the award, then the award binds the parties. The only grounds to petition to vacate the award, termed "impeach" in this context, are these. 1) The award plainly does not conform to the requirements of the RLA. 2) The proceedings were not substantially in conformity with the RLA. 3) The award exceeds the stipulated agreement to arbitrate. 4) An arbitrator engaged in fraud or corruption. 5) A party practiced fraud or corruption that affected the award.[181]

4.   THE LABOR ARBITRATION PROCESS
Table of Sections

---

[176]   Henson, supra note 167, at 347.

[177]   Elkouri, supra note 190, at 4–37.

[178]   Alvin L. Goldwin, Selecting the Correct Standard for Judicial Review of Airline Grievance Arbitration Decisions, 9 U.Pa.J.Lab.& Emp.L. 743, 744, 777–78, 800 (2007).

[179]   Elkouri, supra note 190, 4–26.

[180]   Elkouri, supra note 190, 4–26–27.

[181]   Elkouri, supra note 33, at 4–27–28; RLA, § 9, Third (a),(b),(c).

§ 57   Grievance-Arbitration Process

(a) The Grievance Process

Because the grievance process is contractual, the parties can agree to any reasonable process to address disputes that suits their needs.[182] The agreed upon procedure may limit grievances to complaints that provisions of the CBA have been violated or may permit employees to raise any type of workplace complaint. Many grievance processes resemble each other and use a stepped procedure progressively elevating a grievance to higher levels of decision makers.[183] For instance, the first step of the process may be that the employee informally brings the grievance to the attention of a supervisor. If the supervisor is unable to remedy the grievance, then the second step may require that the union shop steward file a written grievance with a manager, and that the steward and manager meet within a set short time to discuss the grievance and their interpretations of the CBA. If the manager is unable to remedy the grievance, then the third step may require that the union president and company president or director of labor relations meet. At each step, there may be an informal exchange of documents between the parties.[184] If that third step fails to resolve the grievance, then at the fourth step, the union files for arbitration. Some CBAs include time limitations at each step whereas others do not, but may require prompt movement from step to step. The period in which to file at each step is often short, varying between three to 60 days.[185] In most instances, the union, rather than the grievant, controls the process, so the union decides whether to move the grievance to each successive step and whether to invoke arbitration.[186] Having described the grievance process, this section next explains how to invoke labor arbitration, describes a typical arbitration hearing, and advises on how to prepare for the hearing.

---

[182]   A union is limited by the duty of fair representation it owes to its members. See Ray, supra note 40, at 356 (discussing how union must act with good faith and a legitimate purpose when negotiating a CBA).

[183]   Levinson, Labor Arbitration, supra note 27, at 824.

[184]   Levinson, Labor Arbitration, supra note 27, at 824.

[185]   See Collective Bargaining Negotiations & Contract Manual, Methods of Settling Disputes, CBNC 9:2106 (Bloomberg BNA) (noting that filing deadlines at the initial step vary from three to 60 days); CBNC 170:1302, 170:1303, 170:2302; 170:2601, 170:2602 (example clauses from CBAs where arbitration must be filed by deadlines ranging from five to 60 days).

[186]   Levinson, Labor Arbitration, supra note 27, at 818.

(b) Invoking Arbitration and Arbitrator Selection

Invoking labor arbitration is typically even less formal than the informal demand process used in many types of arbitration.[187] Labor arbitration is usually invoked simply by the union providing to the employer a written statement that states the union is moving to the last step of the grievance arbitration process and filing for arbitration. In some situations, the parties list the names of arbitrators in the collective bargaining agreement and rotate through those arbitrators.[188] The arbitrators listed are sometimes referred to as a permanent panel of arbitrators. In this situation, the parties call the arbitrator next in rotation to schedule the arbitration hearing.

In other situations, the CBA specifies an arbitration service, and the parties contact the service to request a list of arbitrators. The use of the AAA and the FCMS are common for labor arbitration.[189] Public sector unions may commonly use a state or local service provider.[190] The parties' lawyers or other representatives,[191] should read the applicable service rules on requesting an arbitrator list and follow those rules precisely to ensure receipt of a list. Once the parties receive the list, they research the arbitrators to decide how to rank their choices. Research involves looking at any past published decisions and contacting others in the field who have appeared before the arbitrators. Many labor arbitrators belong to the National Academy of Arbitrators (Academy), a professional organization of distinguished labor arbitrators,[192] and some may have authored a paper available from the Academy.[193] A lawyer must carefully assess how each arbitrator is likely to rule on the kind of case at issue. For instance, if the case involves an argument that a union missed a deadline for moving to the third step of the grievance process then knowing that a particular arbitrator often rules for the union is not enough information. The lawyer must also know how the arbitrator tends to rule about procedural errors and, best case scenario, about

---

[187]   See § 36(b) for discussion of arbitration pleadings.

[188]   Levinson, Labor Arbitration, supra note 27, 815.

[189]   Levinson, Labor Arbitration, supra note 27, at 814. In the railway and transportation industry, employers and unions are governed by the Railway Labor Act (RLA) and arbitration is organized through the National Mediation Board. Elkouri supra note 33, at 1–17.

[190]   Elkouri supra note 33, at 1–17.

[191]   Parties to labor arbitration are often represented by non-attorneys, such as a union representative or human resources director. This book provides advice for attorneys because law students and attorneys are the target audience, but the advice applies equally to non-attorney representatives. See § 37(c) for a discussion of the role of lawyers in arbitration.

[192]   Elkouri, supra note 33, at 1–16.

[193]   Proceedings of the Academy are available on the Academy website at http://naarb.org/proceedings/index.asp.

missing deadlines. To select an arbitrator, the parties can either send their ranking to the arbitration service and rely on the service to select the appropriate arbitrator or can determine the arbitrator themselves. The former may involve a fee so the parties, or their lawyers, often simply meet telephonically to strike names until only one remains. The parties then jointly contact the arbitrator selected to schedule a hearing date. Parties and their representatives should not contact the arbitrator ex parte without permission from the opposing party, which may be given to accomplish an administrative task such as setting a hearing date and location.[194]

In other instances, the parties have not listed arbitrators or a service in the CBA but instead must mutually agree to an arbitrator.[195] In this instance, each party may propose names until agreement is reached. A lawyer can propose names based on prior experience with a particular arbitrator or based on research, and before deciding on a particular arbitrator must also research those proposed by the opposing party. Because arbitration is contractual, a CBA may specify some other process for invoking arbitration and selecting an arbitrator. Whatever the process, a lawyer must begin by consulting the relevant CBA provisions and complying with them.

The arbitrator can be any neutral person selected by the parties but most often is someone who specializes in labor arbitration and is familiar with collective bargaining and the industry or workplace involved. Often the arbitrator is a lawyer, but many are not lawyers but other types of experts in workplace relations.[196]

(c) The Arbitration Hearing

The parties in the arbitration are normally the union, rather than the individual grievant, and the employer.[197] Because the process is contractual, the parties may agree to any reasonable type of hearing that suits their needs. For instance, some parties use a joint board composed of an equal number of representatives from the union and the employer and a decision-making process that resembles negotiation rather than arbitration. Traditional labor arbitration, however, is an adjudicatory process normally in front of a single arbitrator, but sometimes in front of a panel of three.[198]

---

[194]   St. Antoine, Common Law, supra note 56, § 1.4, at 6.

[195]   Levinson, Labor Arbitration, supra note 27, at 815.

[196]   Michel Picher, Ronald L. Sabeer & David Lipsky, Cornell/PERC Institute on Conflict Resolution, The Arbitration Profession in Transition: A Survey of the National Academy of Arbitrators, at 276 (2000) available at http://naarb.org/proceedings/synopses.asp (finding that in 1999 61.4% of NAA arbitrators had a law or JD degree).

[197]   Levinson, Labor Arbitration, supra note 27, at 818.

[198]   For a discussion of the similarities and differences of the adjudicatory process to litigation, see § 36(a).

When a panel is used, each party selects one arbitrator and the arbitrators select a third. As discussed in § 43(b), party appointed arbitrators are normally neutral, but parties to labor disputes do sometimes agree that the party appointed-arbitrators are not neutral.[199] The parties may or may not be represented by a lawyer at the arbitration hearing.[200] Parties who are not represented by a lawyer are represented by a human resource representative or a union business agent, who are generally familiar with the process.[201]

Often at the beginning of the hearing, each party provides a statement of the issues in the case to the arbitrator. The arbitrator generally desires the parties to reach agreement on the issue because the jurisdiction of the arbitrator is determined by the issue.[202] As discussed in § 30, in labor cases, like other cases, courts determine the issue of contractual arbitrability, and an award can be vacated if the parties had not agreed to arbitrate that particular type of claim.[203] For instance, a CBA may grant the arbitrator authority to determine whether an employee was disciplined for just cause, but not explicitly grant the arbitrator authority to determine the remedy if just cause is found. If the parties did not agree to have the arbitrator determine the latter issue, a court may vacate the award as to the remedy.[204] The parties may also agree to let the arbitrator determine the issues.[205] In routine cases, such as terminations, the parties generally agree to the issues. In more complex cases, however, the parties may not agree. Other preliminary matters will also be addressed before opening statements. For instance, parties may have subpoenaed documents and review those. Or parties may have stipulated to the authenticity or admissibility of certain exhibits and present those joint exhibits to the arbitrator.[206] Preliminary matters may also include simple requests such as to use a slide-show

---

[199]   See Seth H. Liebman, Something's Rotten in the State of Party Appointed Arbitration: Healing ADR's Black Eye That Is "Nonneutral Neutrals," 5 CardozoJ.ConflictResol. 215, 221–223 (2004).

[200]   Levinson, Labor Arbitration, supra note 27, at 817.

[201]   Levinson, Labor Arbitration, supra note 27, at 819, 846–47; Dennis R. Nolan, Disputatio: "Creeping Legalism" as a Declension Myth, 2010 J.Disp.Resol. 1, 7 (2010).

[202]   Ariana R. Levinson, Lawyering Skills, Principles and Methods Offer Insight as to Best Practices for Arbitration (hereinafter Lawyering Skills), 60 Baylor L.Rev. 1, 57 (2008).

[203]   St. Antoine, Common Law, supra note 56, § 1.21, at 16. ("But if no agreement is reached, the arbitration proceeds at the risk of a posthearing attack on the grounds that the resulting award exceeded the jurisdiction of the arbitrator.").

[204]   See Discharge & Discipline, at 15–17, 15–18–19 (noting that "some lower courts still reject arbitration awards in circumstances that appear inconsistent with Supreme Court standards" and citing a Fifth Circuit case vacating "an arbitration ruling reinstating" an employee discharged for negligence because the CBA "provided that discipline for proper cause was the sole responsibility of the company.").

[205]   St. Antoine, Common Law, supra note 56, § 1.21, at 16.

[206]   St. Antoine, Common Law, supra note 56, § 1.27, at 19.

or other visual in opening statement. Lawyers sometimes request sequestration of witnesses, and all the witnesses who are not entitled to remain are asked to leave and admonished by the arbitrator not to discuss the case with any other witnesses.[207] Normally, the grievant and one union and one employer representative are permitted to remain throughout the hearing.

After the issues are determined and other preliminary matters are attended to, the party representatives provide opening statements.[208] In discipline cases, the burden is on the employer, and the employer representative gives the first opening statement.[209] In contract interpretation cases, the burden is on the union, and the union representative, thus, gives the first opening statement.[210] An effective opening statement tells a compelling story, summarizes the relevant CBA provisions, and provides an overview of the conclusions that the evidence will prove.[211] Often an opening statement starts by introducing the parties, the lawyers, and the theme of the case, provides a summary of the relevant law and/or CBA provisions and the theory of the case, describes the facts via a chronological story, rebuts the anticipated case theory of the opposing side, and makes a specific request for relief.[212] Sometimes a lawyer will delay providing an opening statement until immediately before presenting the client's case.[213] Effective lawyers seldom do so because the opening statement is the best opportunity to influence the arbitrators' decision before any evidence is presented.[214] If the arbitrator hears only one side of the story, all the initial evidence will be filtered only through that perspective.[215]

After opening statements, the party with the burden of proof presents its case.[216] Normally the employer proceeds first in a discipline case, and the union proceeds first in a contract interpretation case. The witnesses are sworn to tell the truth,[217] and the arbitrator may swear all witnesses as a group before sequestration or may swear in each witness immediately before the

---

[207]   St. Antoine, Common Law, supra note 56, § 1.32, at 22.

[208]   Levinson, Labor Arbitration, supra note 27, at 818.

[209]   Elkouri, supra note 33, at 7–29, 8–13.

[210]   Elkouri, supra note 33, at 7–29, 8–104.

[211]   Levinson, Lawyering Skills, supra note 202, at 64.

[212]   John W. Cooley & Steve Lubet, Arbitration Advocacy, at 111, 115, 117 (2d ed. 2003).

[213]   Levinson, Lawyering Skills, supra note 202, at 26.

[214]   Levinson, Lawyering Skills, supra note 202, at 29–31.

[215]   Levinson, Lawyering Skills, supra note 202, at 33.

[216]   See St. Antoine, Common Law, supra note 56, § 1.33, at 22–23.

[217]   Levinson, Labor Arbitration, supra note 27, at 817.

witness testifies. The party calls witnesses[218] and directly examines them using open and closed questions that permit the witness to tell the story.[219] The lawyer will introduce relevant documents or real evidence not contained in joint exhibits through the witnesses. The opposing counsel then cross-examines the witness[220] using leading questions to emphasize significant points to the arbitrator. Sometimes cross-examination is brief or waived altogether,[221] and focusing cross-examination on only one, two, or three key points is particularly effective. Parties are permitted re-direct, and then generally re-cross or re-re-direct with permission of the arbitrator. Once the initial party rests its case, the other party calls and presents its witnesses in the same manner. In some cases, the parties may request that the arbitrator visit the site involved in the incident. For instance, if there is an allegation that a manager smelled marijuana on the grievant before the grievant was discharged, the parties may want to demonstrate where the manager was in relation to the grievant and other odors emanating from the site. As a lawyer, you should definitely consider arranging a site visit if one may be dispositive in the case.

Labor arbitration, as in most arbitration as discussed in § 37(a), is less formal than litigation, and the hearing normally takes place around a conference room table. As discussed in § 37(d), rules of evidence are used, but only loosely followed.[222] Most arbitrators tend to admit most evidence "for the weight it is worth."[223] One of the limited grounds upon which a federal district court can reverse an award is when the labor arbitrator failed to admit all relevant evidence, which explains this tilt toward admission of evidence.[224] Some arbitrators do explain how much weight they believe any objected to piece of admitted evidence holds.[225] Objecting to a piece of evidence is intended to alert the arbitrator to flaws in the evidence. For example, a lawyer might make a hearsay objection to alert the

---

[218] Levinson, Labor Arbitration, supra note 27, at 804, 818.

[219] An open question is one that leaves room for the witness to answer as the witness sees fit, such as "What happened next?" A closed question is one that narrows the options but does not suggest the answer, such as "What color was the automobile?" A leading question is one that suggests the answer, such as "that was the red car, wasn't it?" Leading questions are generally used only sparingly on direct exam, such as to establish preliminary background such as education and profession or to establish a time or date.

[220] William H. Holley, Kenneth M. Jennings & Roger S. Wolters, The Labor Relations Process 483 (10th ed. 2011).

[221] Levinson, Lawyering Skills, supra note 202, at 27.

[222] Levinson, Labor Arbitration, supra note 27, at 821.

[223] Michael Z. Green, No Strict Evidence Rules in Labor Arbitration, 15 Tex.Wesleyan L.Rev. 533, 536 (2009).

[224] Green, supra note 223, at 537.

[225] Green, supra note 223, at 537.

arbitrator that the evidence is second-hand and not verified by witnesses or documents.

Once the testimony has been given and other evidence admitted, the parties have the opportunity to make closing arguments. The order of arguments may depend on the arbitrator, who may permit the party with the burden of proof to argue first, last, or both first and last. Closing arguments are an opportunity to outline the applicable contract law, relevant arbitration awards, and any relevant statutory or case-law and to explain how the evidence presented proves the party's position. Often a closing argument begins with the theme and theory of the case, provides an overview of the conclusions on each major legal or contractual issue, proceeds to argue the outcome of each conclusion in more detail focusing on significant facts, requests specific relief, and concludes by thanking the arbitrator.[226] The parties often elect to file closing briefs rather than provide an oral closing argument.[227] They may do so because they wish to cite to arbitration opinions and awards, because they believe writing is more precise than oral argument, or because they want to insure the arbitrator has the argument available in writing to refer to while writing the opinion. Filing briefs increases the length of time until a decision, and the arbitrator may have already made a fairly firm decision about the case before the briefs arrive.[228] For these reasons, lawyers should strongly consider coming to the hearing prepared to make a precise closing statement with citation to opinions and awards.[229] Some parties use a modified process where each lawyer individually presents the argument to the reporter, who then provides a written copy to the arbitrator and opposing lawyer after both arguments have been made.[230]

Sometimes transcripts are not taken in labor arbitration hearing[231] because of the added cost of having one prepared.[232] Sometimes the arbitrator records the hearing to refer to when writing the award and opinion.[233] If a reporter is used, a lawyer should make introductions and provide a business card to insure proper spelling of names and identification. At the close of the hearing, the parties

---

[226]   Cooley, supra note 212, at 207, 208, 213, 219, 220.

[227]   See Levinson, Labor Arbitration, supra note 27, at 819.

[228]   Lawyering Skills, supra note 202, at 44.

[229]   Lawyering Skills, supra note 202, at 44–45.

[230]   Levinson, Lawyering Skills supra note 202, at 41.

[231]   Levinson, Labor Arbitration, supra note 27, at 819. For a discussion of other aspects of confidentiality of arbitration hearings, see § 37(b).

[232]   St. Antoine, Common Law, supra note 56, § 1.12, at 11.

[233]   Levinson, Labor Arbitration, supra note 27, at 819.

should thank the arbitrator and make cordial goodbyes to everyone present, including the opposing party and counsel.

A hearing may last one day or several depending upon the complexity of the issue and the number of witnesses the parties call. When scheduling the hearing, a lawyer must properly estimate the amount of time needed to avoid having to schedule an additional day of hearing at the end of the first hearing date. If the parties end up needing a day they did not anticipate, in many instances, the proceeding will be significantly delayed because of the difficulty of finding a day that the arbitrator, parties, and lawyers are all available.[234]

(d) Preparing for the Hearing

Typically, the hearing dates and location are arranged by an email to the arbitrator and a pre-hearing conference is not held. Motion practice is generally not involved in labor arbitration.[235] When preparing for an arbitration hearing, the first items that the lawyer should attend to are making a case time-line and outlining the issues, contract language and/or law, and evidence supporting each.[236] Some lawyers find using a case matrix useful for the latter tasks. A review of the pertinent CBA language is crucial. Research will also involve locating relevant prior arbitration decisions between the parties and published outcomes in similar arbitration cases confronting other parties. If the issues involve statutory or other legal issues in addition to CBA issues, the lawyer must also research the relevant law. An effective lawyer refers to the time-line and outline throughout case preparation and updates them as the case preparation progresses.

If the lawyer has not already interviewed all the witnesses during the grievance process, the lawyer must interview them. The initial interview could be by phone and involves finding out what the witness has to say about the case. A follow-up phone call or interview, focused on obtaining additional information identified as necessary after research, may sometimes be necessary. Documents and other evidence should be identified and obtained by the lawyer. The other party may have provided all relevant documents informally during the grievance process so that they are available to the client and lawyer. If documents were not produced during the grievance

---

[234] Rick Bales, Labor Arbitration: Practical Ways to Cut Costs without Sacrificing Quality, 44 ABA Section of Labor & Employment Law Newsletter 10, 11 (summer 2016).

[235] See Richard A. Bales, Normative Consideration of Employment Arbitration at Gilmer's Quinceanera, 81 Tul.L.Rev. 331, 348 (2006). For discussion of dispositive motions in other types of arbitration, see § 37(e).

[236] Levinson, Lawyering Skills, supra note 202, at 52.

process, the lawyers often exchange documents once arbitration is requested. If a party fails to produce relevant documents, the opposing lawyer can ask the arbitrator to subpoena documents to the hearing,[237] but this will likely result in a delay of the hearing to review the documents. As noted in § 36(d), courts are split on whether arbitrators have authority to subpoena documents pre-hearing or only to the hearing.

To obtain documents during the grievance process and before arbitration, parties often file a written request for information with the other party. These requests resemble a request for production of documents in litigation. In the private sector, if the opposing party fails to produce the information, the party seeking information can file a charge with the National Labor Relations Board (NLRB),[238] and, after investigation, the NLRB, through the regional general counsel, will issue a complaint. The National Labor Relations Act (NLRA) requires that parties bargain in good faith, and a refusal of an employer or union to provide information related to conditions of employment and necessary to proceed with or defend against a grievance is a violation of the NLRA. When the NLRB issues a complaint, an agent may help the parties settle and exchange information. If that does not happen, the case will proceed to a hearing in front of an Administrative Law Judge, but due to the length of time that may take, the party requesting the information may then have to rely on the arbitrator's subpoena power and delay the arbitration hearing or proceed without the information.[239] In the public sector, a state law that requires bargaining in good faith may provide a similar right to information,[240] and even if no law so provides, parties may have an established practice of exchanging information during the grievance process. Generally, litigation discovery tools, such as interrogatories and depositions, are not available in labor arbitration, and so a lawyer does not need to spend time preparing discovery beyond an information request.[241]

---

[237] Levinson, Labor Arbitration, supra note 27, at 824–25; St. Antoine, Common Law, supra note 56, § 1.14, at 12.

[238] Levinson, Labor Arbitration, supra note 27, at 824. In the public sector, a similar process may be used involving a state labor agency.

[239] Levinson, Labor Arbitration, supra note 27, at 828.

[240] See e.g., Liebert Cassidy Whitmore, Labor Relations in and Negotiations in Local Government at 6, 9 (discussing California Public Employee Relations Board requiring employers to supply relevant information to unions) available at http://www.counties.org/sites/main/files/file-attachments/153-labor_relations_course_materials_2013.pdf; 20 No. 11 Mich.Emp.L.Letter 3, 3 (2012) (discussing duty to provide information under Michigan Public Employment Relations Act).

[241] Levinson, Labor Arbitration, supra note 27, at 824. For a discussion of the minimal discovery in other types of arbitration, see § 36(d).

Once the lawyer has interviewed the relevant witnesses, obtained and reviewed relevant documents and real evidence, and modified the case time-line and outline accordingly, the lawyer prepares witness examinations. The lawyer should practice direct examination with each witness and should practice admitting or referring to exhibits with the witness. The lawyer should also prepare the witness for anticipated cross-examination as well. The lawyer should explain what to expect at the arbitration hearing to the witness and should make sure the witness understands that while the process is informal, they should act professionally and respectfully toward everyone present. The lawyer should also draft a statement of the issue or issues to submit to the arbitrator at the start of the hearing and an opening and closing statement. Even when a lawyer anticipates filing a brief in lieu of closing argument, drafting the argument in advance of the hearing will help clarify the important points the lawyer needs to make during the hearing and will provide a basis for the brief.

A lawyer should prepare the exhibits for the hearing. If it is possible to stipulate with the opposing advocate to the exhibits in advance, the exhibits can be marked. Whether or not marked, they can be three-hole punched and placed into a binder to create exhibit books. Make an exhibit book for each arbitrator and each lawyer and a witness copy. Also, place the exhibits on a flash drive to provide to the arbitrator. Providing a Microsoft Word version in addition to a PDF version permits the arbitrator to cut and paste from the exhibits into the opinion.

Lawyers should also consider creating demonstrative exhibits. While in many hearings, no demonstrative exhibits are used, an eye-catching and interesting demonstrative exhibit can help persuade the arbitrator.[242] Effective demonstrative exhibits can be large reproductions of exhibits, a time-line or map, or a Power-Point bulleting the main conclusions of the argument. If a witness will refer to a demonstrative exhibit during testimony, the lawyer should prepare the witness using the demonstrative exhibit. Providing a demonstrative exhibit, such as a time-line, map or Power-Point, in electronic form that the arbitrator can take after the hearing will enable the arbitrator to refer to it when writing the opinion.[243]

(e) Conferring with the Opposing Advocate

Although arbitrators do not typically hold pre-conference hearings,[244] sometimes the lawyers informally confer with each other

---

[242]   Cooley, supra note 212, at 104.

[243]   See Bales, Labor Arbitration, supra note 234, at 11.

[244]   Bales, Labor Arbitration, supra note 234, at 11.

before the hearing. Doing so can reduce cost and increase efficiency by minimizing the amount of time needed for preliminary matters at the hearing. Parties can stipulate to authenticity or admissibility of documents and decide which documents to mark as joint exhibits.[245] They can also stipulate to the issues submitted to arbitration. Because the issue provides an opportunity to frame the case at the start of the hearing, a lawyer should not stipulate to the issue pre-hearing unless the agreed issue persuasively frames the case. The advocates can also discuss the order of witnesses and the amount of time they estimate each witness examination will take, better enabling them to estimate when a particular witness needs to be available.[246] The parties can agree on whether a reporter will be used, and if so, who will pay.[247] They can also agree on whether closing briefs will be filed, and, if so, the deadline by which the briefs will be submitted.

(f) Payment of Fees

The employer and union generally each pay for their own lawyer fees. Because the union provides representation, the grievant generally does not pay to hire a lawyer.[248] As discussed in § 3(c), parties to arbitration must pay the arbitrator a fee for the time spent on the case. Generally, the parties split equally the arbitrator's fee. Sometimes, however, a contract provides that the losing party must pay the arbitrator's fee.[249] Lawyers should be sure to check the CBA for any provision regarding payment of fees and discuss and consider the fees with the client when determining whether to proceed to arbitration.

5. THE PRIVATE LAW OF LABOR ARBITRATION
Table of Sections

---

[245]　Bales, Labor Arbitration supra note 234, at 11.

[246]　Bales, Labor Arbitration supra note 234, at 11.

[247]　Bales, Labor Arbitration supra note 234, at 11.

[248]　Most union represented employees pay dues or an equivalent fee to enable the union to provide services, such as representation, including by an attorney, at arbitration.

[249]　Levinson, Labor Arbitration, supra note 27, at 843.

---

§ 58 Introduction

(a) Written Opinions and Awards

As discussed in § 37(f), unlike securities and other arbitration where an award is typically only a couple sentences, labor arbitrators normally provide a more extensive written opinion and award to the parties.[250] Many of these awards are published by BNA (Bloomberg) or CCH (Wolters Kluwer),[251] and AAA labor arbitration awards are available on Westlaw and LEXIS Advance. Westlaw also provides access to CCH and Federal Labor Relations Authority awards. [252]

(b) Persuasive Precedent

While an arbitrator is not bound by any previous award between different parties, many arbitrators rely on them as persuasive precedent.[253] As discussed in § 37(f), arbitration precedent plays an important role in labor arbitration. Over the years, labor arbitrators have begun predictably considering certain concepts and factors for some particular types of cases. Most cases involve discharge or some other type of discipline, but some involve other issues of contract interpretation or application. This section discusses concepts involved in discipline cases, other types of CBA interpretation cases, interesting issues addressing the use of technology in the workplace, and finally discrimination and other cases that raise statutory as well as contractual claims.

§ 59 Substance of Opinions and Awards

(a) Discharge and Discipline

An employee could be discharged or otherwise disciplined for many different reasons, including tardiness, absence, insubordination, inability to perform tasks properly, use of drugs,

---

[250] W. Mark C. Weidemaier, Toward a Theory of Precedent in Arbitration, 51 Wm.& Mary L.Rev. 1895, 1910–11 (2010) (using labor arbitration as one example of an arbitration system that generates precedent); Theodore J. St. Antoine, Gilmer in the Collective Bargaining Context, 16 Ohio St.J. on Disp.Resol. 491, 509 (2001).

[251] Levinson, Labor Arbitration, supra note 27, at 810.

[252] A comprehensive list of available arbitration awards, including labor arbitration awards, is available on Cornell Library's web page at http://guides.library.cornell.edu/c.php?g=31398&p=199822.

[253] Nolan, Disputatio, supra note 201, at 5.

theft, or possession of a weapon. Most CBAs include what is often termed a just-cause provision.[254] For instance, one CBA states in its Article for Discipline & Adverse Actions, "Discipline and adverse action must be consistent with applicable laws and regulations and will be taken only for just cause."[255] A just-cause provision requires that an employer only discipline an employee for a good reason. Another CBA states, "No employee shall receive a corrective action plan or be terminated except for Just Cause. The concept of Just Cause in union contracts (as outlined in Appendix V) is the standard that management must adhere to when disciplining or discharging an employee."[256] In the appendix, the CBA defines "just cause" as "the employer must have a reason to act in disciplining an employee and the reason must be just and fair."[257]

In the private sector, the default employment rule is that employees are employed at will. Employers can fire at-will employees for any reason or no reason at all. Many situations create exceptions to this default rule. For instance, a CEO may have an individual employment contract requiring termination only for cause or an employee may be able to show that she was fired because she is a woman, which is a prohibited reason to terminate an employee under the federal statute known as Title VII. A CBA containing a just-cause provision creates another situation where the default at-will rule does not apply.

Many arbitrators agree on the types of principles that determine whether an employer had a good reason to terminate an employee. These principles explore not only the substantive reasons for the discipline but also the process used to determine that the discipline was appropriate. The employer has the burden of proof to demonstrate that the grievant engaged in the alleged infraction.[258] Often arbitrators require the employer to prove by a preponderance

[254] Elkouri supra note 33, at 15–4; Clyde W. Summers, Individualism, Collectivism and Autonomy in American Labor Law, 5 Employee Rts.& Emp.Pol'y J. 453, 478 (2001); Basic Patterns in Union Contracts, at 7 (BNA 14th ed. 1995).

[255] CBA between Department of Interior and Federal Indian Service Employees AFT Local 4524, Article 23 Discipline and Adverse Actions, at 77, available at http://www.bie.edu/cs/groups/xbie/documents/text/idc016461.pdf.

[256] CBA between Childcare Guild of Local 925, SEIU and Association of Childcare Employers, Article 22 Corrective Disciplinary Action/Termination, at 17, (effective through August 31, 2014) available at http://www.seiu925.org/files/2012/07/Child-Care-Guild-Contract-Sept.-1-2011-through-August-31-2014-FINAL-From-Lisa-B.-July-2012.pdf.

[257] CBA between Childcare Guild of Local 925, SEIU and Association of Childcare Employers, Appendix V, at 39, (effective through August 31, 2014) available at http://www.seiu925.org/files/2012/07/Child-Care-Guild-Contract-Sept.-1-2011-through-August-31-2014-FINAL-From-Lisa-B.-July-2012.pdf.

[258] Elkouri, supra note 33, at 15–25. St. Antoine, Common Law, supra note 56, § 6.9, at 190.

of the evidence that the grievant engaged in the infraction. If the alleged infraction is criminal in nature or involves moral turpitude, then many require a higher standard of proof of "clear and convincing evidence" and a minority sometimes require "beyond a reasonable doubt."[259] And recently, arbitrators have used the "clear and convincing evidence" standard in termination cases, whether or not they involve allegations of criminal behavior.[260] Some arbitrators do not specify the quantum of proof necessary to prevail, preferring instead to focus on making factual findings.

Many arbitrators require that notice be given of the types of behavior that warrant discipline and the type of discipline that is appropriate for each type of behavior.[261] For instance, a rule may state that an employee who is absent three times receives a written warning while another warns that insubordination will result in immediate termination. Arbitrators are more likely to uphold discipline against an employee who, having previously engaged in a similar infraction, has been warned that a specific disciplinary action will result from further infractions.[262]

Most arbitrators interpret a just-cause provision to require progressive discipline. Progressive discipline means that for each transgression an employee receives a greater penalty.[263] For instance, a first absence for which an employee provides no notice to the employer may warrant an oral reprimand, a second, a written warning, a third a suspension, and a fourth termination. The purpose of progressive discipline is to enable an employee to correct the problematic behavior. Some offenses are so serious, however, that discharge without lesser preceding discipline is appropriate.[264] For instance, arbitrators have found assaulting a co-worker or selling drugs on the employer's premise to warrant discharge without progressive discipline.[265] In each instance, the discipline must "fit the

---

[259]   Elkouri, supra note 33, at 15–27; St. Antoine, Common Law, supra note 56, § 6.10, at 192–93.

[260]   Elkouri, supra note 33, at 15–29.

[261]   Ariana R. Levinson, Industrial Justice: Privacy Protection for the Employed, 18 Cornell J.L.& Pub.Pol'y, 609, 640 (2009) (hereinafter Industrial Justice); See e.g., Gaylord Container Corp., 107 Lab.Arb.Rep.(BNA) 1138 (1997) (Allen, Jr., Arb.) (overturning demotion for absenteeism when employer failed to mention that demotion could be penalty for additional infractions).

[262]   Elkouri, supra note 33, at 15–79.

[263]   Levinson, Industrial Justice, supra note 261, at 644–45.

[264]   Elkouri, supra note 33, at 15–40.

[265]   Elkouri, supra note 33, at 15–44. See e.g., Burger Iron Co., 92 Lab.Arb.Rep.(BNA) 1100, 1105 (1989) (Dworkin, Arb.) (upholding discharges for selling drugs on the employer's premise).

crime," meaning that a less significant penalty is warranted for being tardy than for assaulting a co-worker.[266]

Many arbitrators also require that the employer give notice to the employee of the reason for the discipline and an opportunity for the employee to respond before the discipline is imposed.[267] Providing this opportunity prevents employers from implementing discipline without sufficient evidence to prove the grievant committed the infraction.[268]

Some arbitrators also require that the employer use an adequate process to investigate the incident causing the discipline.[269] For instance, if an anonymous note says that an employee has liquor in a company locker provided for personal use, the company should not rely on the note, but should ask the employee for permission to open the locker and should investigate whether anyone else had access to the locker.

Generally, the discipline must be for a work-related reason and not because of an employee's actions away from the workplace during personal time.[270] For instance, if an employee is out drinking and dancing and someone posts a photo of the drunk grievant on Facebook so a manager finds out about the behavior, typically that would not warrant discipline.[271] Other examples of off-duty conduct that do not warrant discipline include flying a Nazi flag on a private house porch[272] and selling marijuana.[273] Off-duty actions must significantly and concretely harm the employer to warrant discipline.[274] Examples where a grievant engages in such off-duty conduct include directly competing with the employer's business, a role model engaging in obscene conduct of which the community becomes aware, and financially harming an employer by taking unwarranted leave.[275]

---

[266]   Levinson, Industrial Justice, supra note 261, at 646.

[267]   Levinson, Industrial Justice, supra note 261, at 656–57; Bud Indus. Inc., 124 Lab.Arb.Rep.(BNA) 908, 914 (2007) (Miles, Arb.); Penn Window Co., 120 Lab.Arb.Rep.(BNA) 298, 303 (2004) (Dissen, Arb.).

[268]   Elkouri, supra note 33, at 15–48.

[269]   Levinson, Industrial Justice, supra note 261, at 644.

[270]   Summers, supra note 254, at 478–79; Levinson, Industrial Justice, supra note 261, at 677.

[271]   Cf. Shawnee County, 123 Lab.Arb.Rep.(BNA) 1659 (2007) (Daly, Arb.) (termination relating to photo of grievant dancing at a bar posted on public web page overturned).

[272]   Dept. of Corr. Servs., 114 Lab.Arb.Rep.(BNA) 1533, 1542 (1997) (Simmelkjaer, Arb).

[273]   Lockheed Aeronautical Sys. Co., 92 Lab.Arb.Rep.(BNA) 669 (1989) (Jewett, Arb.).

[274]   Levinson, Industrial Justice, supra note 261, at 677.

[275]   Levinson, Industrial Justice, supra note 261, at 676–79.

Most arbitrators also consider whether the grievant was treated in the same way that others who committed the same infraction were.[276] For instance, if the grievant was terminated for assault on a co-worker, but in two prior instances employees were suspended for assault, the arbitrator may find no good cause for termination and reduce the penalty to a suspension. Consistent enforcement of rules is necessary if an employer wishes to discipline an employee for running afoul of a rule.[277] When rules are inconsistently enforced or not enforced at all, employees are led to believe that violations will go unsanctioned. [278] Employers must promulgate only reasonable rules necessary for safe and efficient business operations.[279] Rules must be disseminated and known to employees.[280]

Arbitrators recognize that employees have a right to privacy when being disciplined.[281] Arbitrators may find an investigation inadequate because the employer failed to interview co-worker witnesses individually in private.[282]

Some CBAs expressly limit an arbitrator's ability to lessen the level of discipline imposed by the employer when the arbitrator finds the grievant committed the alleged infraction.[283] Many CBAs provide no such limit, and arbitrators often consider mitigating factors when determining whether an employer imposed an appropriate level of discipline.[284] For instance, long seniority weighs against imposing the most severe discipline of termination.[285] Other factors that weigh against severe penalties are honesty and acceptance of responsibility for an infraction, a work record devoid of other discipline, and commendations and promotions.[286] Arbitrators will also reduce discipline when management is at least partially at fault for the infraction.[287] For instance, an arbitrator reinstated, without back pay, a severely depressed employee discharged for assaulting a supervisor who had demeaned the employee.[288] Other factors, such

---

[276]   Levinson, Industrial Justice, supra note 261, at 644.

[277]   Levinson, Industrial Justice, supra note 261, at 640.

[278]   Levinson, Industrial Justice, supra note 261, at 669.

[279]   Levinson, Industrial Justice, supra note 261, at 643.

[280]   Elkouri, supra note 33, at 15–77.

[281]   Levinson, Industrial Justice, supra note 261, at 639; Rhodia, Inc., 118 Lab.Arb.Rep.(BNA) 455, 464 (2003) (Neas, Arb.).

[282]   ESAB Welding & Cutting Prods., 115 Lab.Arb.Rep.(BNA) 79, 83 (2000) (Wolkinson, Arb.).

[283]   Elkouri, supra note 33, at 15–33 & n.165.

[284]   Levinson, Industrial Justice, supra note 261, at 645.

[285]   Elkouri, supra note 33, at 15–74.

[286]   Levinson, Industrial Justice, supra note 261, at 645.

[287]   Elkouri, supra note 33, at 15–87–88.

[288]   Bethlehem Structural Prods. Corp., 106 Lab.Arb.Rep.(BNA) 452, 456 (1995) (Witt, Arb.).

as lack of seniority or a poor work record, tend to support a high level of discipline.[289]

Arbitrators also follow the principle that employees should obey their employers' orders and grieve later, except in certain situations involving imminent safety risks, an intrusive invasion of privacy, or direction of unlawful behavior, where it is permissible for an employee to refuse a direct order.[290] Thus, employees who decide to refuse an employer's order risk being disciplined without recourse to a successful grievance.

(b) Contract Interpretation

Unions not only bring discipline cases, but also arbitrate cases involving any alleged breach of a CBA provision. These cases might involve any number of issues such as an allegation that an employer has sub-contracted work in violation of a work-preservation provision, a dispute over whether a certain scheduling system is permissible, a request to accommodate a disabled employee, or allegations that pay or break provisions are not being properly followed. Although less frequent, employers too can sometimes seek arbitration in a CBA interpretation dispute.[291]

The arbitrator will examine all relevant contract language, the intent of the parties as expressed when negotiating the provision, and the past practice of the parties.[292] For a simple dispute, the arbitrator may simply have to read the wage and hour provision, identify that it states a person in the grievant's position should be paid a certain amount, and order the employer to pay that amount. Such simple disputes, however, normally settle earlier in the grievance process. Thus, arbitrators generally confront situations where the contract language is not clear. For instance, the CBA may contain a work-preservation clause that states "employees not hired as custodians cannot perform cleaning tasks and whenever the number of custodians present is inadequate another custodian will be called in to work." The CBA also contains a management rights clause that states, "management reserves to itself all rights not explicitly curtailed by this agreement." The arbitrator presented with no specific language about sub-contracting must determine whether the

---

[289] Elkouri, supra note 33, at 15–73, 15–76.

[290] Levinson, Industrial Justice, supra note 261, at 649.

[291] Employers can sometimes grieve because the CBA makes express provision for it at some stage of the grievance procedure. Elkouri, supra note 33, at 5–17 & n.71 (stating that of 400 agreements examined in one survey, 26% provided for company grievances) (citing Basic Patterns in Union Contracts 34 (BNA Books 14th ed 1995)). Employers have, for instance, arbitrated against a union to receive damages for violation of a no-strike clause in a CBA. Elkouri, supra note 33, at 18–26.

[292] Elkouri, supra note 33, at 9–26–27.

work-preservation clause explicitly curtails the ability to use a sub-contractor not hired by the employer as a custodian. To do so, the arbitrator may turn to the parties' negotiations. The arbitrator may find that the union offered a clause that prohibited sub-contracting but it was rejected by management, which would suggest sub-contracting out all the custodial work is permissible. Or the arbitrator may find that the work-preservation clause was sought by the union in response to sub-contracting out of administrative services which the employer ceased because of the new provision. Such history would suggest that sub-contracting is not permissible. The arbitrator may also look at the past practice of the parties. If other non-custodial work has been sub-contracted out that suggests the work-preservation clause does not prohibit it. On the other hand, if no type of work has been sub-contracted out, that suggests the work-preservation clause prohibits sub-contracting the cleaning work.

Ambiguity in CBA terms and a conflict over their interpretation can arise for several different reasons. As in any contract case, it is difficult to precisely describe every concept. The parties may use inherently vague terms or create ambiguity due to grammar or typographical errors. Provisions may conflict with each other, such as in the example above with the conflict between the work-preservation clause and the management rights clause. Even within one provision, contradictory language may be used. Application of a provision to a particular situation often is not foreseen.[293] Indeed, one of the reasons parties put arbitration clauses in their CBAs is precisely to deal with that type of unanticipated situation.[294] Sometimes parties intentionally agree to ambiguous language, reasoning that leaving the interpretation to an arbitrator is preferable to failing to reach agreement on the CBA as a whole.

The intent of the parties as expressed when negotiating the agreement is often used to interpret CBA language.[295] If available, bargaining history can point strongly toward the correct interpretation in an ambiguous situation. When a party has attempted and failed to include a certain provision, arbitrators are unlikely to read the CBA as including that provision. If the party, however, offered the provision as a clarification then the arbitrator may read the CBA to include the provision even if it was not ultimately integrated into the express terms of the agreement.[296] Because the clause is presented as clarifying the parties' current

---

293 St. Antoine, Common Law, supra note 56, § 2.2, at 71 Section.
294 Elkouri, supra note 33, at 9–14–15.
295 Elkouri, supra note 33, at 9–26.
296 Elkouri, supra note 33, at 9–28.

interpretation of the CBA, failure to include it does not indicate the parties understanding differed from the offered clause. When assessing the parties' intent, many arbitrators take into consideration the level of sophistication of the negotiating parties and are more likely to hold sophisticated negotiators to the plain meaning of the drafted provision.[297]

Arbitrators also rely on past practice to interpret ambiguous CBA language,[298] and often past practice is the only evidence of intent relied upon by arbitrators.[299] Parties, both employer and union, are assumed to know what is occurring at the workplace,[300] and even practices which are not regularly occurring will be considered by arbitrators to interpret ambiguous language.[301] In reliance on past practice, arbitrators rely on prior arbitration awards between the same company and union dealing with the same issue. They also honor past grievance settlements between the parties.[302] In most instances, employer handbooks are not considered because they are simply a unilateral statement not binding on the union, but, in some instances, a longstanding handbook rule may evidence a past practice.[303] If the past practice of the parties is unclear, arbitrators may rely on industry practice or practice between the employer and another union when the same CBA language is used between them.[304]

Not all arbitrators rely on the language of the CBA, the expressed intent of the parties, and past-practice. Some rely only on the plain meaning of the terms used,[305] and interpret the terms according to their "usual and ordinary meaning."[306] Others permit extrinsic evidence, such as expressions of intent during negotiations and past practice, only to determine if the terms of the CBA are ambiguous or not, in which case the plain language would prevail.[307] Other arbitrators consider all the evidence,[308] and some will even interpret the CBA contrary to what the terms taken out of context

---

[297]   Elkouri, supra note 33, at 9–44.

[298]   Elkouri, supra note 33, at 12–1.

[299]   Elkouri, supra note 33, at 12–21.

[300]   Elkouri, supra note 33, at 12–22.

[301]   Elkouri, supra note 33, at 12–24.

[302]   Elkouri, supra note 33, at 9–32.

[303]   Elkouri, supra note 33, at 9–36–37 & n.179.

[304]   Elkouri, supra note 33, at 9–33.

[305]   Elkouri, supra note 33, at 9–8 & n.20; St. Antoine, Common Law, supra note 56, § 2.21, at 72.

[306]   St. Antoine, Common Law, supra note 56, at 69.

[307]   TriMas Corp., 125 Lab.Arb.Rep.(BNA) 911, 921 (2008) (Nolan, Arb.).

[308]   Considering all the evidence may be based on the "theory that all language is infected with ambiguity." St. Antoine, supra note 56, at 75.

suggest.[309] Generally though, arbitrators agree that a party's subjective intent which was not expressed across the table does not bear on the meaning of the CBA terms.[310]

Even in situations where an agreement is absolutely silent on a subject, an arbitrator may determine that past practices prohibits the employer from making a unilateral change.[311] While the precise test a particular arbitrator may use varies, generally arbitrators consider whether the practice was known to both parties and consistently used over a period of time rather than only sporadically.[312] For instance, if the employees have always had ten paid minutes to change into their uniforms before starting their shift, and the employer cuts it to five minutes, an arbitrator may find that violates the CBA because the practice is incorporated into the pay provision. The party urging the use of past practice bears the burden of proving the requirements.[313] Many arbitrators will find a binding past practice as to wages and benefits, but permit management to make unilateral changes to "methods of operation and direction of the workforce" reasoning the latter are generally reserved to management through a management rights clause in the CBA.[314] In other situations where a CBA is silent on a subject, arbitrators may rely on common arbitration principles, such as the requirements for just cause discussed in § 59(a), assuming they were known to the parties or may determine what the parties would have agreed had they bargained over the subject.[315] For example, if a CBA contains a description of the bargaining unit, seniority provisions, and a grievance and arbitration procedure, most arbitrators will infer "employees cannot be discharged without just cause."[316] Or if a CBA contains a grievance and arbitration procedure, an arbitrator may infer the union thereby agreed not to strike.[317] An arbitrator may also award damages when a union violates a no-strike clause in the CBA even though the clause does not mention damages.[318]

---

[309]   Elkouri, supra note 33, at 9–11.

[310]   Elkouri, supra note 33, at 9–12.

[311]   Elkouri, supra note 33, at 12–2–3; St. Antoine, Common Law, supra note 56, § 2.21, at 90–91. See Steelworkers v. Warrior & Gulf Navigation Co., 363 U.S. 574 (1960).

[312]   Elkouri, supra note 33, at 12–4–5.

[313]   Elkouri, supra note 33, at 12–5.

[314]   Elkouri, supra note 33, at 12–7.

[315]   Elkouri, supra note 33, at 9–16; St. Antoine, Common Law, supra note 194, § 2.22, at 92–94.

[316]   St. Antoine, Common Law, supra note 56, § 2.22, at 92–94.

[317]   Handsaker, Morrison & Marjorie L., Remedies & Penalties for Wildcat Strikes: How Arbitrators & Federal Courts Have Ruled, 22 Cath.U.L.Rev. 279, 292 (1972–73).

[318]   Elkouri, supra note 33, at 18–26.

Many contract interpretation principles used by labor arbitrators will be familiar to anyone involved in any type of contract interpretation.[319]

- Critically, as mentioned above, most arbitrators will determine the meaning of a particular term in light of the contract as a whole, factoring in all relevant provisions.[320]

- Words will be provided their common meanings and industry or technical terms theirs unless otherwise defined or proven that the terms should otherwise be interpreted.[321]

- The use of the same word will indicate the same concept, while the use of different words will indicate a distinction was intended by the parties.[322]

- Terms will be interpreted consisted with the underlying purpose of the relevant provision.[323]

- "The expression of one thing is the exclusion of another."[324]

- When a list of specific items is followed by a more general term, the general term includes only items similar to the specific ones.[325]

- A provision will be interpreted against the party drafting it.[326]

- An interpretation resulting in a just result is preferred to one resulting in a harsh or arbitrary result.[327]

- As with most agreements, arbitrators will prefer an interpretation that renders a CBA provision valid and enforceable over one that renders it unlawful.[328]

---

[319]   St. Antoine, Common Law, supra note 56, § 2.1, at 70.

[320]   Elkouri, supra note 33, at 9–34.

[321]   Elkouri, supra note 33, at 9–22–24.

[322]   Elkouri, supra note 33, at 9–25–26.

[323]   Elkouri, supra note 33, at 9–34.

[324]   Elkouri, supra note 33, at 9–40. This doctrine is known by the Latin phrase "*expressio unius est exclusio alterius.*"

[325]   Elkouri, supra note 33, at 9–40–41. This doctrine is known by the Latin phrase "*ejusdem generis.*"

[326]   Elkouri, supra note 33, at 9–48–49.

[327]   Elkouri, supra note 33, at 9–42.

[328]   Elkouri, supra note 33, at 9–45.

(c) Technology

As technology advances, it sometimes raises new workplace issues. For instance, the use of social media by employees has received much attention, both by human resources professionals and in the public media. New techniques to monitor employees, such as GPS or Google watches, that raise privacy concerns have also received attention.[329] Cases involving new technology generally reach labor arbitrators before they reach the courts because of the shorter time period to reach arbitration and because of the greater workplace protection granted to employees by a CBA with a just-cause provision.

Arbitrators have applied principles relating to just cause in cases involving new technologies.[330] For example, in cases involving personal use of employer-issued equipment, such as computers or cell phones, arbitrators generally uphold discipline if the employee knew of the rule prohibiting personal use and the rule was equally enforced. [331] Sometimes, even when the rule has been enforced, arbitrators mitigate the level of damage due to seniority. [332] Additionally, arbitrators require the use of progressive discipline in situations involving personal use of employer-issued equipment.[333]

Similarly, rules prohibiting use of technology to make racially or sexually offensive communications are generally considered reasonable[334] if employees are aware of the rules[335] and the rules are consistently enforced.[336] Some arbitrators have reduced discipline for such inappropriate use of technology because the communication was

---

[329]   See Ariana R. Levinson, What Hath the Twenty First Century Wrought? Issues in the Workplace Arising from New Technologies and How Arbitrators Are Dealing with Them, 11 Transactions Tn.J.Bus.L 9, 9 (2010) (hereinafter New Technologies).

[330]   Levinson, New Technologies, supra note 329, at 13.

[331]   Levinson, New Technologies, supra note 329, at 13; Conneaut Sch. Dist., 104 Lab.Arb.Rep.(BNA) 909, 914 (1995) (Talarico, Arb.); Chevron Prods. Co., 116 Lab.Arb.Rep.(BNA) 271, 2715 (2001) (Goodstein, Arb.); AlliedSignal Engines, 106 Lab.Arb.Rep.(BNA) 614, 624 (1996) (Rivera, Arb.); Co. of Sacramento, 118 Lab.Arb.Rep.(BNA) 699, 701 (2003) (Riker, Arb.).

[332]   City of El Paso, 123 Lab.Arb.Rep.(BNA) 691–92 (2001) (Greer, Arb.).

[333]   Levinson, New Technologies, supra note 329, at 15; Clatsop County, 126 Lab.Arb.Rep.(BNA) 620, 635 (2009) (Reeves, Arb.).

[334]   Levinson, New Technologies, supra note 329, at 19; MT Detroit, 118 Lab.Arb.Rep.(BNA) 1777, 1779, 1782 (2003) (Allen, Arb.); U.S. Dept. of Agric., 118 Lab.Arb.Rep.(BNA) 1212, 1216 (2003) (Cook, Arb.).

[335]   Levinson, New Technologies, supra note 329, at 22; S. Cal. Edison, 117 Lab.Arb.Rep.(BNA) 1066, 1071–72 (2002) (Prayzich, Arb.).

[336]   Levinson, New Technologies, supra note 329, at 22; Chevron Prods. Co., 116 Lab.Arb.Rep.(BNA) 271, 272 (Goodstein, Arb.); Snohomish Co. Pub. Util. Dist. No. 1, 115 Lab.Arb.Rep. (BNA) 1, 8 (2000) (Levak, Arb.).

private, [337] shared only with a few people,[338] or did not result "in loss or other harm."[339]

Generally employees cannot be disciplined for their use of technology while off-duty and away from the workplace.[340] As well stated by one arbitrator, "[a]s a general rule, once an employee is off duty and away from the workplace, there is a presumption that the employee's private life is beyond the employer's control."[341] In some instances, however, arbitrators have found the necessary significant concrete harm to the employer resulting from the off-duty conduct to justify discipline.[342] Some cases involve an employee who is competing with the employer's business,[343] some involve role models, such as teachers, engaging in publicly observed obscene conduct,[344] and some involve deleterious communications between co-workers.[345]

In discipline cases, arbitrators normally assess the reliability and accuracy of evidence.[346] When modern technology is involved, such as images stored in a computer temporary file, expert testimony may be necessary to help the arbitrator assess the evidence.[347] Additionally, evidence is considered as a whole so consistency with other evidence can boost the reliability of unclear evidence.[348]

---

[337] Levinson, New Technologies, supra note 329, at 20; City of Fort Worth, Tex., 123 Lab.Arb.Rep.(BNA) 1125, 1130 (2007) (Moore, Arb.); Snohomish Co. Pub. Util. Dist. No. 1, 115 Lab. Arb Rep. (BNA) 1, 8 (2000) (Levak, Arb.); Ga. Power Co., 123 Lab.Arb.Rep.(BNA) 936, 948 (2006) (Nolan, Arb.). Cf. City of Fort Lauderdale, 125 Lab.Arb.Rep.(BNA) 1249, 1254 (2008) (Abrams, Arb.) (reducing length of suspension when employee only accidently made communication available to others because of a printer paper jam).

[338] Levinson, Industrial Justice, supra note 261, at 676 n.392 (2009); Chevron Prods. Co., 116 Lab.Arb.Rep.(BNA) 271, 274, 280, 281 (2001) (Goodstein, Arb.).

[339] Am. Red Cross, 125 Lab.Arb.Rep.(BNA) 1969, 1715 (2008) (Ruben, Arb.).

[340] Levinson, New Technologies, supra note 329, at 24.

[341] Dep't. of Corr. Servs., 114 Lab.Arb.Rep.(BNA) 1533, 1536 (1997) (Simmelkjaer, Arb.).

[342] Levinson, New Technologies, supra note 329, at 24; Levinson, Industrial Justice, supra note 261, at 636.

[343] GFC Crane Consultants, Inc., 122 Lab.Arb.Rep.(BNA) 801, 804 (2006) (Abrams, Arb.); Fox Television Station, 118 Lab.Arb.Rep.(BNA) 641, 645 (2003) (Allen, Arb.).

[344] Warren City Bd. of Educ., 124 Lab.Arb.Rep.(BNA) 532, 535 (2007) (Skulina, Arb.); Phoenix City Bd. of Educ., 125 Lab.Arb.Rep.(BNA) 1473 (2009) (Baroni, Arb.). Cf. L'Anse Creuse Pub. Schs., 125 Lab.Arb.Rep.(BNA) 527 (2008) (Daniel, Arb.) (reducing termination to paid administrative leave where obscene photo of teacher was posted on a publicly available website).

[345] WMATA/Metro, 124 Lab.Arb.Rep.(BNA) 972, 976 (2007) (Evans, Arb.); City of Quincy, 126 Lab.Arb.Rep.(BNA) 534, 539 (2008) (Finkin, Arb.).

[346] Levinson, New Technologies, supra note 329, at 28.

[347] Levinson, New Technologies, supra note 329, at 29. See e.g., Indep. Sch. Dist. #284, 125 Lab.Arb.Rep.257, 264 (BNA) (2008); AK Steel, 125 Lab.Arb.Rep.(BNA) 903, 904 (2008) (Dean, Arb.).

[348] Levinson, Industrial Justice, supra note 261, at 656.

In discipline cases, arbitrators also address the issue of whether employer technological monitoring is appropriate. Whether an employee is provided notice of the monitoring of actions, such as by GPS, and also of the type of conduct which constitutes an infraction of the rules is sometimes a determinative factor in monitoring cases.[349] Yet, there is no consensus among arbitrators as to the validity of surreptitious on-duty monitoring by GPS or webcams.[350] As to monitoring electronic communications, many arbitration awards permit employers doing so, even without any notice of monitoring to employees, "provided the employer has a reasonable cause to believe a violation of company policy has taken place and is monitoring for that reason."[351]

Some arbitration opinions address employer monitoring of employees' off-duty conduct. For instance, cases arise where employers hire investigators to examine employees conduct while on FMLA leave. One arbitrator held surreptitious surveillance of an employee and his truck while outside a relative's home, at an ATM, and at two shopping stores was appropriate when the employer had a reasonable suspicion of misconduct. [352] Another arbitrator permitted surreptitious surveillance of an employee using FMLA leave even though the employer had no suspicion of misconduct but was concerned about the large amount of leave taken by the employee.[353] The arbitrator overturned the termination, however, because the surveillance video demonstrated the grievant would only have been able to work a portion of his shift.[354]

Some cases involving new technology arise out of CBA provisions other than the just-cause provision. In some cases, unions protest a failure to increase pay commensurate with additional duties created

---

[349]   Levinson, New Technologies, supra note 329, at 30. Cf. Orange Co., Fla. 123 Lab.Arb.Rep.(BNA) 460, 463 (2007) (Smith, Arb.) (overturning suspension for driving employer-owned vehicle home where no notice that doing so would violate company policy); Embarq, 123 Lab.Arb.Rep.(BNA) 923, 932 (2007) (Armedariz, Arb.) (upholding discipline for time misrepresentation discovered by GPS where employer previously warned employee about falsifying time records).

[350]   Levinson, New Technologies, supra note 329, at 31.

[351]   Levinson, New Technologies, supra note 329, at 33; Dep't of Veterans Affairs, 122 Lab.Arb.Rep.(BNA) 106, 108 (2006) (Hoffman, Arb.); Dep't of Veterans Affairs, 122 Lab.Arb.Rep.(BNA) 300, 306 (2005) (Peterson, Arb.); Tesoro Ref. & Mktg. Co., 120 Lab.Arb.Rep.(BNA) 1299, 1302–03 (2005) (Suntrup, Arb.); AE Staley Mfg. Co., 119 Lab.Arb.Rep.(BNA) 1371, 1375 (2004) (Nathan, Arb.); City of Ft. Worth, 123 Lab.Arb.Rep. (BNA) 1125, 1127 (2007) (Moore, Arb.); S. Cal. Edison, 117 Lab.Arb.Rep.(BNA) 1066, 1069 (2002) (Prayzich, Arb.).

[352]   Interstate Brands Crop., 121 Lab.Arb.Rep.(BNA) 1580, 1581 (2005) (Skulina, Arb.).

[353]   Bud Indus., Inc., 124 Lab.Arb.Rep.(BNA) 908, 910 (Miles, Arb.).

[354]   Id.

by new technology.[355] In others, disputes arise because employers attempt to prohibit employees from carrying or using personal devices.[356] In one case an arbitrator denied a grievance for identity theft, when two computers containing the employees' names and social security numbers were stolen from the employer's accounting firm, because the health and safety clause could not be read so broadly.[357]

Some CBAs contain principles specifically addressing the use of technology. For instance, the UPS/Teamsters contract contained a provision limiting the use of GPS data in disciplinary hearings. The data could only be used when there was also other evidence that the employee was not at the correct location at the correct time.

(d) Discrimination Cases

In some labor arbitrations, arbitrators address statutory claims in addition to claims that the CBA has been violated.[358] This may be because the CBA permits such claims to be raised, because a statute is incorporated into the CBA,[359] or, in some limited number of cases, because the union has agreed that arbitration, rather than litigation, is the only available forum.[360] Sometimes arbitrators will refuse to hear statutory claims because they consider it outside their jurisdiction, which is limited to interpreting the CBA.[361] Many arbitrators, however, are lawyers familiar with statutory interpretation and employment law. Normally the statutes at issue are employment statutes such as Title VII of the Civil Rights Act of 1964, the Americans with Disabilities Act, the Age Discrimination in Employment Act, or the Family Medical Leave Act. In these cases, most arbitrators consider the statute, administrative guidance, and case law just as a judge would in deciding such a case.[362] One study found that while in fact-specific cases arbitrators are less likely to cite court decisions, in many employment discrimination cases, arbitrators cite multiple decisions and apply appropriate standards of proof and burden shifting.[363] The American Arbitration Association (AAA) instituted a panel of labor arbitrators with

---

[355] Levinson, New Technologies, supra note 329, at 39–40; Stanford Hosp. & Clinics, 123 Lab.Arb.Rep.(BNA) 1697, 1702 (2007) (Staudohar, Arb.); Agric. Research Serv., 122 Lab.Arb.Rep.(BNA) 1469, 1472 (2006) (Feldman, Arb.).

[356] See e.g. OZinga Ill. RMC, Inc., 123 Lab.Arb.Rep.198, 200 (BNA) (Simon, Arb.).

[357] Chicago Bd. of Educ., 125 Lab.Arb.Rep.(BNA) 1168 (2008) (Goldstein, Arb.).

[358] Nolan, Disputatio, supra note 201, at 11.

[359] Levinson, Labor Arbitration, supra note 27, 812–13.

[360] See § 54(a) & (c) for a discussion of cases where the CBA waives the right to go to court.

[361] See Levinson, Labor Arbitration, supra note 27, at 811.

[362] Elkouri, supra note 33, at 10–58–60.

[363] See Levinson, Labor Arbitration, supra note 27, at 830–32.

employment law experience to select from as arbitrators in such cases.[364]

(e) Remedies

When determining a remedy, arbitrators normally strive to make the parties whole by placing them in the position they would have been had no CBA violation occurred.[365] Typical remedies in discipline cases are reinstatement[366] or elimination of the discipline, back pay, and benefits. The amount of back pay is generally mitigated by the grievant's earnings during the period of unemployment.[367] In addition to these remedies, in other types of cases arbitrators award lost wages, medical costs, promotions, pension fund contributions, and recall rights. Arbitrators may order a grievant to undergo a medical examination, drug testing, or treatment or order parties to cease and desist from certain conduct.[368] Arbitrators have awarded lost overtime and premium pay, pay for travel time,[369] reimbursement for medical and dental expenses, health insurance premiums, and tuition.[370] They have ordered employers to issue parking permits, to cease interfering with issuance of event passes,[371] to revise employee evaluations, to reopen a closed plant,[372] or to provide a grievant special training or equipment.[373] Arbitrators may issue creative remedies, dissimilar to those typically issued by courts, such as posting of an apology, requiring an employee to continue medication, or granting a union representative a meeting with employees on company time.[374] One arbitrator ordered reinstatement of a grievant with training "appropriate to polish her interpersonal skills."[375]

In one case, the union grieved a rule requiring employees to wear pagers, respond within 15 minutes, and arrive at work within an

---

[364]   Am. Arb. Ass'n, Labor, Employment and Elections Update—Issue 6(May 2011), available at http://www.adr.org/aaa/ShowPDF?doc=ADRSTG_007039; Daily Labor Report: News Archive June 1, 2011, 105–DLR C–3, available to subscribers at http://news.bna.com/dlln/display/batch_print_display.adp.

[365]   Elkouri, supra note 33, at 18–15–16.

[366]   Levinson, Labor Arbitration, supra note 27, at 852.

[367]   Elkouri, supra note 33, at 18–37.

[368]   Levinson, Labor Arbitration, supra note 27, at 839; Elkouri, supra note 33, at 18–56–57.

[369]   Elkouri, supra note 33, at 18–16

[370]   Elkouri, supra note 33, at 18–22.

[371]   Elkouri, supra note 33, at 18–17.

[372]   Elkouri, supra note 33, at 18–19.

[373]   Elkouri, supra note 33, at 18–22.

[374]   Levinson, Labor Arbitration, supra note 27, at 840–41.

[375]   Elkouri, supra note 33, at 18–22 (quoting Mount Sinai Hospital, 105 Lab.Arb.Rep.(BNA) 1047, 1050 (1995) (Duff, Arb)).

hour. The arbitrator ordered that employees disciplined under this unreasonable unilaterally-implemented rule be made whole. The remedy included rectifying "wage loss, back pay, job demotion, blemished work record, promotion denial, seniority, or any other employment related benefit loss directly attributable to any disciplinary action stemming from the violation of the on-call pager policy."[376]

Sometimes after finding a contract violation, an arbitrator will order the parties to negotiate for an appropriate remedy.[377] Generally, arbitrators do not award mental distress damages for non-statutory breach of CBA claims[378] and are reluctant to award punitive damages.[379]

While most awards benefit employee-grievants, some awards go to an employer or a union. For instance, employers have won damages from unions that violate no-strike clauses.[380] And unions and union trust funds have won damages from employers when an employer has violated a CBA provision the benefit of which inures to the union as a whole. For instance, damages have been awarded for violations of union-representational rights and union-security clauses and for plant closures and sub-contracting.[381]

6.   TYPES OF LABOR ARBITRATION OTHER THAN PRIVATE SECTOR GRIEVANCE ARBITRATION
Table of Sections

Sec.

§ 60   Interest Arbitration

While grievance arbitration describes the bulk of labor arbitration, interest arbitration is also used by unions and employers.[382] Interest arbitration is a process where the arbitrator determines what the provisions of a CBA are, rather than how the provisions should be interpreted or applied. The parties agree that if

---

[376]   Lyondell Citgo Ref., 120 Lab.Arb.Rep.(BNA) 360, 364 (2004) (Moreland, Arb.).

[377]   Elkouri, supra note 33, at 18–7.

[378]   Elkouri, supra note 33, 18–25.

[379]   Elkouri, supra note 33, 18–29–30.

[380]   Elkouri, supra note 33, 18–26.

[381]   Elkouri, supra note 33, at 18–26–27.

[382]   Dennis R. Nolan & Richard A. Bales, Labor and Employment Arbitration, at 70 (Thomson West 2017).

they reach an impasse when negotiating for a CBA, they will arbitrate rather than striking or locking out, and the arbitrator will settle the terms of the CBA. An interest arbitrator may be required to pick one party's final offer, may have authority to pick any offer that represents a compromise between the two parties' position, or may have authority to craft any sensible resolution for the parties.[383] Interest arbitrators are most often used to settle wage provisions of the CBA, but may settle any term of a CBA, ranging from leave policies, seniority rules, subcontracting restrictions, or discipline policies.[384]

Interest arbitration is often used in the public sector because many public sector employees are forbidden from striking.[385] Statutes may provide for interest arbitration in lieu of a strike or lock-out if the parties reach impasse, or the parties may voluntarily agree to use interest arbitration.[386] Statutes may also provide principles which the arbitrator should use to determine the provisions of the CBA.[387] Many statutes provide that the parties must mediate and engage in a fact-finding process before invoking arbitration.[388] In a minority of states, interest arbitration has been held unconstitutional as a delegation of the legislature's authority to private citizens.[389]

Interest arbitration is used less often in the private sector. [390] A common example of interest arbitration in the private sector is baseball arbitration.[391] In baseball, the CBA sets minimum salaries.[392] Particular salaries are negotiated between a team and a player's agent.[393] If the team and player cannot agree on the salary, they invoke arbitration.[394] Baseball arbitration is, thus, a somewhat unique form of interest arbitration because the salaries of each player

---

[383]   Cf. Malin, supra note 144, at 804 (mentioning traditional interest arbitration, final offer issue-by-issue arbitration, and final offer package arbitration).

[384]   Elkouri, supra note 33, at 22–6–8.

[385]   Elkouri, supra note 33, at 22–3; Nolan, supra note 382, at 76.

[386]   Elkouri, supra note 33, at 22–3.

[387]   Elkouri, supra note 33, at 22–5; Nolan, supra note 382, at 77.

[388]   Elkouri, supra note 33, at 22–22. Fact-finding is a process where the parties present evidence to a neutral factfinder who issues a report. The government employer and the union can then elect to adopt, or refuse to adopt, the report.

[389]   Elkouri, supra note 33, at 22–27; Malin, supra note 144, at 805.

[390]   Nolan, supra note 382, at 71, 75.

[391]   Nolan, supra note 382, at 92–93; Barry Winograd, An Introduction to the History of Interest Arbitration in the United States, 61 Lab.LawJ. 11230499 (C.C.H.) 164, 165 (2010).

[392]   Nolan, supra note 382, at 94.

[393]   Nolan, supra note 382, at 94.

[394]   Frederick N. Donegan, Examining the Role of Arbitration in Professional Baseball, 1 Sports Law.J. 183, 191 (1994).

are set forth in an individual contract that supplements the terms of the CBA.[395] Each party presents the arbitrator with its final offer and material supporting that offer.[396] The arbitrator then selects one party's salary offer as the one the player will receive.[397]

Interest arbitration is sometimes agreed upon by other private sector parties as a method to settle disputes arising in negotiating an initial or subsequent collective bargaining agreement.[398] For example, an agreement between IBEW and San Diego Gas and Electric provided that if the parties were unable to settle on amendments to the CBA after its termination, then the dispute would be submitted to an arbitration board.[399] In another instance, the UAW negotiated a letter agreement, with an employer regarding a plant they were organizing and other unorganized plants, that provided for interest arbitration of unresolved issues if the parties remained in negotiations beyond a certain time period.[400] More often, however, parties agree after reaching impasse to submit certain determinations to an interest arbitrator.[401] Private sector employers governed by the NLRA and the unions representing their employees have an obligation under the NLRA to bargain in good faith.[402] Interest arbitration is enforceable under Section 301, and courts review interest arbitration under the same highly deferential standards used in grievance arbitration award enforcement.[403]

When a statute or the parties do not specify criteria for the interest arbitrator to follow, the arbitrator has wide discretion. Parties should present the arbitrators with the data necessary to explain their position and influence the arbitrator to rule in their favor. Often the parties present evidence in written form via exhibit books that contain pertinent data, with limited or no testimony from witnesses.[404] Arbitrators may consider what, in their opinion, the parties would have agreed to and what would be reasonable and fair to the employees and the employer.[405] They will offer a workable

---

[395]   Benjamin A. Tulis, Final-Offer "Baseball" Arbitration: Contexts, Mechanics & Applications, 20 Seton Hall J.Sports & Ent.L. 85, 87 (2010) (describing baseball arbitration as a unique form of interest arbitration because it sets the terms of an individual contract rather than a CBA).

[396]   Nolan, supra note 382, at 95.

[397]   Nolan, supra note 382, at 95; Donegan, supra note 394, at 191.

[398]   St. Antoine, Craver, supra note 46, at 590 (discussing Steelworkers CBA in 1970's that required interest arbitration).

[399]   Elkouri, supra note 33, at 22–9 & n.62.

[400]   Dana Corp., 356 NLRB 256, 257 (2010).

[401]   Elkouri, supra note 33, at 22–9.

[402]   NLRA Section 8(a)(5) & (b)(3) & (d).

[403]   Elkouri, supra note 33, at 22–4; see supra § 51.

[404]   Malin, supra note 144, at 803.

[405]   Elkouri, supra note 33, at 22–12–13; Nolan, supra note 382, at 81.

solution that can be effectively implemented by the parties.[406] They may tend to take a more conservative approach and implement less than a party seeks reasoning that incremental change is best when the parties are faced with a new practice or process.[407] Arbitrators, however, do use recognizable standards in making their determinations.[408] In wage disputes, for instance, arbitrators compare the wages to those of other similarly situated employees, consider the employer's ability to pay, and factor in the cost-of-living and inflation.[409]

Reform proposals such as the Employee Free Choice Act have contemplated revising the NLRA to require interest arbitration in all first contract situations. Interest arbitration is more widely used in other countries, such as Canada.[410]

§ 61   Public Sector Arbitration

In most ways, arbitration of cases arising in the public sector, where the government is the employer, is similar to arbitration of cases arising in the private sector.[411] The primary difference is that federal, state, and local entities are often governed by constitutions, statutes, and regulations that do not apply to private sector employers.[412]

Government entities are not governed by the LRMA Section 301, and often have a particular statute, similar to the RLA, that governs.[413] Federal government arbitration is governed by the Civil Service Reform Act of 1978 and the Federal Labor Relations Authority.[414] For discussion of how the Civil Service Reform Act imposes a non-contractual duty to arbitrate, see § 65(b)(2). With some exceptions, the Civil Service Reform Act requires CBAs to include grievance-arbitration provisions.[415] CBAs and arbitrators are, however, excluded from determining wages, hours, and certain benefits by the Civil Service Reform Act.[416] Federal sector arbitrators are required to address statutes and regulations applicable to federal

---

[406]   Elkouri, supra note 33, at 22–14.

[407]   Malin, supra note 144, at 816.

[408]   Elkouri, supra note 33, at 22–31; Malin, supra note 144, at 816.

[409]   Elkouri, supra note 33, at 22–31–32.

[410]   St. Antoine, Craver, supra note 46, at 591.

[411]   See Elkouri, supra note 33, at 20–2.

[412]   Elkouri, supra note 33, at 19–2.

[413]   Jean Read, Grievance Arbitration Awards in the Public Sector: How Final in Florida?, 35 U.MiamiL.Rev. 277, 280 (1981).

[414]   5 U.S.C. § 7121(a); Nolan, supra note 382, at 86–87.

[415]   Nolan, supra note 382, at 87.

[416]   Nolan, supra note 382, at 87.

employees.[417] The Back Pay Act circumscribes the circumstances in which an arbitrator can award a grievant back pay.[418] Appeals from grievance-arbitration are taken to the Labor Relations Authority.[419] An arbitration award is final and binding, and reviewable by the Labor Relations Authority only on limited grounds. Some grounds for review are similar to those applicable under Section 301, but the grounds for review are more numerous. 1) "The award violates a law, rule, or regulation." 2) "The arbitrator exceeded" the authority granted. 3) The award fails to "draw its essence from the" CBA. 4) "Implementation of the award is impossible" because it is vague or incomplete. 5) "Gross error of fact" or law. 6) "The arbitrator was biased or partial." 7) "The arbitrator refused to hear" relevant evidence. 8) The arbitrator is self-interested in the dispute.[420] 9) The award is contrary to public policy.[421] The decision of the Labor Relations Authority is final and unreviewable unless an unfair labor practice issue is involved, in which case appeal may be taken to the Federal Circuit Court of Appeals.[422]

Grievances involving statutory discrimination issues may be brought to arbitration, appealed to the Labor Relations Authority, and then brought to the EEOC and U.S. District Court. Alternately the claimant can elect to skip arbitration and go directly to the EEOC after lodging a complaint with the employer.[423]

Certain grievances, such as discharges, lengthy suspensions, and demotions, are brought, at the election of the grievant, in front of the Merit Systems Protection Board or taken through an arbitration process not involving the Labor Relations Authority. Those arbitration awards may be appealed to the Federal Circuit Court of Appeals.[424] Similar but distinct options are available in cases involving both statutory discrimination and other issues.[425]

Federal government interest-arbitration is conducted by the Federal Service Impasse Panel.[426] The Impasse Panel is a small group of members, lawyers, and clerks and uses various methods to attempt to resolve negotiation disputes between the parties including

---

417   Elkouri, supra note 33, at 18–63.

418   Elkouri, supra note 33, at 18–63; 5 U.S.C. § 5596(b).

419   Elkouri, supra note 33, at 20–9. Certain grievances, such as discharges, lengthy suspensions, and demotions are taken through an arbitration process not involving the Labor Relations Authority.

420   Elkouri, supra note 33, at 20–29.

421   Elkouri, supra note 33, at 20–31.

422   Elkouri, supra note 33, at 20–31.

423   Elkouri, supra note 33, at 20–39.

424   Elkouri, supra note 33, at 20–39.

425   Elkouri, supra note 33, at 20–39.

426   Elkouri, supra note 33, at 20–7.

interest-arbitration, either with or without a hearing.[427] Also, instead of resolving the dispute itself, the Impasse Panel may order outside arbitration or approve of the parties' voluntary selection of an outside arbitrator to settle the dispute.[428]

State statutes that permit collective bargaining generally provide for establishing a grievance-arbitration process, and even where not specifically mentioned by statute, public sector CBAs, like private sector CBAs, often provide for grievance arbitration.[429] Many state courts follow the presumption of arbitrability set out in the *Steelworkers Trilogy*,[430] but research particular to the state is necessary for any practicing lawyer.[431] Many state courts also consider the *Steelworkers Trilogy* when determining whether to vacate a labor arbitration award, but they may use another standard in addition or instead, such as a state law modeled on the FAA or the Uniform Arbitration Act.[432] One review of awards indicates the grounds of review most often used by state courts are the following. 1) "whether the award" draws its "essence" from the CBA, 2) whether the "arbitrators exceeded the scope of their authority, 3) "[w]hether the decision is arbitrary and capricious, and 4) whether the award is rationally related . . . to the submission" and to the CBA.[433] Many state courts also vacate awards in limited instances because the award violates public policy, using a test similar to that used by the federal courts to vacate private sector arbitration awards.[434] Some state courts, however, may use a less restrictive test than that at use in the private sector that does not require the award to violate a specific law,[435] and a lawyer must conduct research on the particular state approach.

Constitutional guarantees such as freedom of speech, free exercise of religion, prohibition of unreasonable searches and seizures, due process, and equal protection apply to government employers,[436] and extensive precedent particular to employment law exists for each guarantee. Thus, lawyers representing public-sector

---

[427]   Major H. Lee Einsel & USAF Captain Frank A. Rodman, Negotiability in the Federal Sector—Focusing on Impasse Resolution, 35 A.F.L.Rev. 147, 162, 163 (1991).

[428]   Einsel, supra note 427, at 163.

[429]   Elkouri, supra note 33, at 21–4; for discussion of state and local interest arbitration see § 78(b)(3).

[430]   Elkouri, supra note 33, at 21–50; Malin, supra note 144, at 887.

[431]   Malin, supra note 144, at 887–89.

[432]   7 U.L.A.§ 1 et seq.; Elkouri, supra note 33, 21–51, 21–52–53; Malin, supra note 144, at 922.

[433]   Elkouri, supra note 33, at 21–54.

[434]   Elkouri, supra note 33, 21–58.

[435]   Malin, supra note 144, at 943.

[436]   Elkouri, supra note 33, at 19–2.

unions and employers should be knowledgeable about the relevant precedent and alert to Constitutional issues raised by grievances that land in arbitration.[437]

---

[437]   For information on Constitutional issues see Martin H. Malin, Ann C. Hodges & Joseph E. Slater, & Jeffrey M. Hirsch, Public Sector Employment Cases and Materials, Chapter 3, 3d ed. Thomson West (2016).

Chapter 8

INTERNATIONAL ARBITRATION

Table of Sections

---

1.   OVERVIEW
Table of Sections

        (4)   Awards Made in the U.S. but "Not Considered as Domestic"

   (b)   National Law

        (1)   Implementing Legislation

        (2)   The Choice of National Arbitration Law: The "Seat" of Arbitration

   (c)   Contracting for the Procedural Rules and Substantive Law to Be Applied to a Particular Case

§ 62 Introduction: Commercial Arbitration and Public Law Arbitration

International disputes are often arbitrated. That generalization includes disputes between national governments ("States"), disputes between private parties who are citizens of different States, and disputes between States and private parties who are citizens of other States. The "citizens" involved in international arbitration are often giant corporations and the disputes routinely involve large amounts of money. Rarely is an individual consumer or employee a party in international arbitration, although it does happen.[1]

International arbitration is commonly divided into commercial arbitration and public law arbitration. Of the two, international commercial arbitration is more similar to the domestic arbitration discussed in the previous sections of this book so international commercial arbitration is discussed next, before turning to international public law arbitration. The first section on international public law arbitration distinguishes it from international commercial arbitration.[2]

§ 63 International Commercial Arbitration: Sources of Law

(a) Treaties, Primarily the New York Convention

(1) Basic Provisions

The most important body of law governing international commercial arbitration is the United Nations Convention on the

---

[1]   Some seamen do find their way into international employment arbitration. See, e.g., Lim v. Offshore Specialty Fabricators, 404 F.3d 898 (5th Cir.2005). See generally Catherine A. Rogers, The Arrival of the "Have-Nots" in International Arbitration, 8 Nev. L.J. 341, 361–63 (2007).

[2]   See § 73.

Recognition and Enforcement of Foreign Arbitral Awards.[3] (See Appendix C). This treaty is called the "New York Convention" after its birthplace. It has been ratified by nearly 150 States, including those with the most significant presence in international business, such as the United States, China, Japan, India, Germany, Russia, Brazil, the United Kingdom, France, Italy, Canada, and the Netherlands.[4] States that have ratified (or "acceded to") the New York Convention are known as "Contracting States."

The New York Convention's primary purpose is to make arbitration awards rendered in one State enforceable in the courts of other States.[5] Accordingly, it begins "[t]his Convention shall apply to the recognition and enforcement of arbitral awards made in the territory of a State other than the State where the recognition and enforcement of such awards are sought."[6] The Convention provides that "[e]ach Contracting State shall recognize arbitral awards as binding and enforce them."[7] It contains a narrow list of grounds upon which "[r]ecognition and enforcement of the award may be refused."[8]

The New York Convention succeeded in making enforcement of foreign arbitration awards more routine. So it is now generally easier to enforce foreign arbitral awards than foreign court judgments.[9] This is a major reason why parties to international contracts agree to arbitrate.[10] For example, it is generally easier to persuade a United States court to enforce a foreign arbitration award than it is to persuade a United States court to enforce a foreign court's judgment. Similarly, it is generally easier to persuade a foreign court to enforce an arbitration award made in the United States than it is to persuade a foreign court to enforce a United States court's judgment.

In addition to requiring enforcement of arbitration awards rendered in another State, the New York Convention also requires

---

[3]   Convention on the Recognition and Enforcement of Foreign Arbitral Awards, June 10, 1958, 21 U.S.T. 2517, 330 U.N.T.S. 3, available at http://www.uncitral.org/pdf/english/texts/arbitration/NY-conv/XXII_1_e.pdf (last visited Aug.1, 2011).

[4]   See http://www.uncitral.org/uncitral/en/uncitral_texts/arbitration/NYConvention_status.html (last visited Aug.17, 2013).

[5]   Alan Scott Rau, Edward F. Sherman & Scott R. Peppet, Processes of Dispute Resolution: The Role of Lawyers 960 (4th ed. 2006).

[6]   New York Convention, supra note 3, art. I(1).

[7]   Id. art. III.

[8]   Id. art. V. See § 72(b).

[9]   Rau, Sherman & Peppet, supra note 5, at 961 ("Under the Convention, enforcement in other jurisdictions of a foreign arbitral award has become considerably more simple and certain than would be the enforcement of the judgment of a foreign court."); Leonard L. Riskin, et al., Dispute Resolution & Lawyers 624–626 (3rd ed.2005).

[10]   Christian Bühring-Uhle, Arbitration and Mediation in International Business 135–43 (1996).

enforcement of executory arbitration agreements.[11] The New York Convention's remedy for breach of such agreements, like the remedy under FAA §§ 3 and 4, is specific performance, that is, a court order to arbitrate.[12] While the New York Convention requires enforcement of executory arbitration agreements, its provisions on that topic reflect less "drafting attention" than was given to its provisions on the topic of enforcing arbitration awards.[13] In other words, the gist of the New York Convention is less about getting parties to arbitration than it is about getting arbitrators' decisions enforced.

In contrast, the FAA's more important impact was on getting parties to arbitration because, prior to its enactment, courts around the United States generally refused to enforce executory arbitration agreements, but did enforce arbitration awards.[14] So the main arbitration law reform needed in the early 20th Century United States was holding parties to their promises to arbitrate rather than litigate, while the main arbitration law reform needed globally in the late 20th Century was holding States' to their promises to enforce arbitration awards against their own citizens.

(2) U.S. Ratification and Implementation of the New York and Panama Conventions

In 1970, the United States ratified the New York Convention and Congress enacted FAA §§ 201–208 to make the New York Convention enforceable in United States courts.[15] The ratification came with the reservation that it would be applied "on the basis of reciprocity, to the recognition and enforcement of only those awards

---

[11] New York Convention, supra note 3.

Each Contracting State shall recognize an agreement in writing under which the parties undertake to submit to arbitration all or any differences which have arisen or which may arise between them in respect of a defined legal relationship, whether contractual or not, concerning a subject matter capable of settlement by arbitration.

Id. art. II(1).

[12] Id. art. II(3).

The court of a Contracting State, when seized of an action in a matter in respect of which the parties have made an agreement within the meaning of this article, shall, at the request of one of the parties, refer the parties to arbitration, unless it finds that the said agreement is null and void, inoperative or incapable of being performed.

Id. See § 64(a).

[13] Gary B. Born, International Commercial Arbitration 710 (2009) ("Article II was added to the Convention in the closing days of negotiations. Little drafting attention was given to the Article.")

[14] Ian R. Macneil, Richard E. Speidel & Thomas J. Stipanowich, Federal Arbitration Law: Agreements, Awards, and Remedies under the Federal Arbitration Act ch.4 (1994). See also Ian R. Macneil, American Arbitration Law: Reformation, Nationalization, Internationalization 19 (1992).

[15] 9 U.S.C. § 201.

made in the territory of another Contracting State."[16] As a result, an arbitration award rendered in another Contracting State (or an agreement to arbitrate in another Contracting State) is generally enforceable in United States courts.[17] An arbitration award rendered elsewhere in the world may be enforceable in United States courts,[18] but the New York Convention does not make it so.[19] However, the United States and most States in the Western Hemisphere have ratified the Inter-American Convention on International Commercial Arbitration, also known as the Panama Convention.[20] The New York Convention does not govern "[i]f a majority of the parties to the arbitration agreement are citizens of a State or States" that have signed the Inter-American Convention,[21] which also enforces arbitration awards.[22] The Inter-American Convention "was obviously modeled"[23] on the New York Convention and the Second Circuit has stated that "Congress intended the Inter-American Convention to reach the same results as those reached under the New York

---

[16]   See http://www.uncitral.org/uncitral/en/uncitral_texts/arbitration/NYConvention_status.html (listing ratifying states and their reservations). See also New York Convention, art. I(3) ("When signing, ratifying or acceding to this Convention, or notifying extension under article X hereof, any State may on the basis of reciprocity declare that it will apply the Convention to the recognition and enforcement of awards made only in the territory of another Contracting State.")

[17]   Whether the New York Convention applies turns on where the arbitration award is made (or is to be made), not the citizenship of the parties. See, e.g., E.A.S.T., Inc. v. M/V Alaia, 876 F.2d 1168 (5th Cir.1989); Ministry of Defense of the Islamic Republic of Iran v. Gould, Inc., 887 F.2d 1357 (9th Cir.1989); Continental Transfert Technique Ltd. v. Federal Government of Nigeria, 697 F.Supp.2d 46, 56 (D.D.C.2010) ("the critical element is the place of the award: if that place is in the territory of a party to the Convention, all other Convention states are required to recognize and enforce the award, regardless of the citizenship or domicile of the parties to the arbitration") (quoting TermoRio S.A. E.S.P. v. Electranta S.P., 487 F.3d 928, 934 (D.C.Cir.2007)).

However, the New York Convention does not govern arbitration "entirely between citizens of the United States" unless their "relationship involves property located abroad, envisages performance or enforcement abroad, or has some other reasonable relation with one or more foreign states." 9 U.S.C. § 202.

[18]   Macneil, Speidel & Stipanowich, supra note 14, § 44.9.1.8, at 44:61–44:63.

[19]   There is doubt about whether the United States' reciprocity reservation applies to executory agreements as well as to completed arbitration awards. See Gary B. Born, International Commercial Arbitration: Commentary and Materials 141 (2d ed.2001).

[20]   9 U.S.C. § 305(1). See Inter-American Convention on International Commercial Arbitration, Jan. 30, 1975, 1975 O.A.S.T.S. No.42, 14 I.L.M. 336, available at http://www.oas.org/DIL/CIDIPI_convention_arbitration.htm (last visited Aug.1, 2011). See generally John P. Bowman, The Panama Convention and Its Implementation under the Federal Arbitration Act (2002).

[21]   9 U.S.C. § 305(1). For a list of signatories, see Department of International Law, http://www.oas.org/juridico/english/sigs/b-35.html (last visited Mar.11, 2017).

[22]   http://www.oas.org/en/sla/dil/inter_american_treaties_B-35_international_commercial_arbitration.asp.

[23]   Rau, Sherman & Peppet, supra note 5, at 968–69.

Convention."[24] However, while Article 1 of the Inter-American Convention provides that arbitration agreements are "valid," one of the Convention's "major deficiencies" is that it lacks a provision obligating courts to enforce arbitration agreements by ordering parties to arbitration.[25] Nevertheless, some U.S. courts have ordered parties to arbitration in reliance on FAA § 307, which provides that FAA "Chapter 1 [9 U.S.C. §§ 1–16] applies to actions and proceedings brought under this chapter to the extent chapter 1 is not in conflict with this chapter or the Inter-American Convention as ratified by the United States."[26] In this indirect fashion, courts have applied FAA § 2 and § 4 to order arbitration in Inter-American Convention cases.[27]

(3)   U.S. Exceptions from New York Convention

The general enforceability in United States courts of foreign arbitration agreements and awards is subject to two important exceptions found in FAA § 202.

First, the New York Convention does not govern an arbitration agreement or award "entirely between citizens of the United States" unless their "relationship involves property located abroad, envisages performance or enforcement abroad, or has some other reasonable relation with one or more foreign states."[28] Courts have held that agreeing to arbitrate in another State is not, without more, enough of a relation with a foreign state to bring the arbitration within the coverage of the Convention.[29]

Second, the United States ratified the New York Convention with the reservation that it does not govern an arbitration agreement or award not "considered as commercial."[30] However, FAA § 202's

---

[24]   Productos Mercantiles E Industriales, S.A. v. Faberge USA, Inc., 23 F.3d 41, 45 (2d Cir.1994). The Organization of American States promulgated the Inter-American Convention at a time when only three Latin American states had ratified the New York Convention. See Jonathan C. Hamilton, Three Decades of Latin American Commercial Arbitration, 30 U. Pa. J. Int'l L. 1099, 1100 (2009).

[25]   Claus von Wobeser, The Influence of the New York Convention in Latin America and on the Inter-American Convention on International Commercial Arbitration, 2 No. 1 Disp. Resol. Int'l 43, 51 (May, 2008).

[26]   9 U.S.C. § 307.

[27]   Paramedics Electromedicia Comercial Ltda. v. Medical Sys. Info. Techs., Inc., 2003 WL 23641529 (S.D.N.Y. June 4, 2003) (FAA§ 4); Siderurgica del Orinoco (SIDOR), CA v. Linea Naviera de Cabotaje, C.A., 1999 WL 632870 (S.D.N.Y. Aug. 19, 1999) (FAA § 2).

[28]   9 U.S.C. § 202.

[29]   Jones v. Sea Tow Services Freeport NY Inc., 30 F.3d 360 (2d Cir.1994); Reinholtz v. Retriever Marine Towing & Salvage, 1993 WL 414719 (S.D.Fla.1993); Brier v. Northstar Marine, Inc., 1992 WL 350292 (D.N.J. 1992). For critiques of these cases, see Rau, Sherman & Peppet, supra note 5, at 1008–09; Macneil, Speidel & Stipanowich, supra note 14, § 44.9.4.3.

[30]   9 U.S.C. § 202 ("An arbitration agreement or arbitral award arising out of a legal relationship, whether contractual or not, *which is considered as commercial,*

definition of "commercial" incorporates FAA § 2's "involving commerce," which has been broadly interpreted by the Supreme Court. As a result, the definition of "commercial" in United States law may be "the broadest of any signatory to the Convention."[31] For example, employment relationships are generally considered "commercial" by United States courts,[32] but courts of other States might disagree. What sorts of disputes might not be "considered as commercial"? Perhaps examples would include "family law disputes, state boundary disputes, and disputes presenting political issues."[33]

(4) Awards Made in the U.S. but "Not Considered as Domestic"

In addition to generally making enforceable in United States courts arbitration awards rendered in another Contracting State, the New York Convention also applies to awards made in the United States if those awards are "not considered as domestic."[34] As an oft-cited Second Circuit case, *Bergesen v. Joseph Muller Corp.*,[35] put it,

> awards "not considered as domestic" denotes awards which are subject to the Convention not because made abroad, but because made within the legal framework of another country, e.g., pronounced in accordance with foreign law or involving parties domiciled or having their principal place of business outside the enforcing jurisdiction.[36]

---

including a transaction, contract, or agreement described in section 2 of this title, falls under the Convention.") (emphasis added); New York Convention, Art. I(3) ("When signing, ratifying or acceding to this Convention, or notifying extension under article X hereof, any State * * * may also declare that it will apply the Convention only to differences arising out of legal relationships, whether contractual or not, *which are considered as commercial* under the national law of the State making such declaration.") (emphasis added).

[31] Macneil, Speidel & Stipanowich, supra note 14, § 44.9.3.3.

[32] Rogers v. Royal Caribbean Cruise Line, 547 F.3d 1148, 1155 (9th Cir.2008) ("The employment contracts of seafarers 'aris[e] out of legal relationship[s] . . . which [are] considered as commercial,' and therefore those contracts 'fall[ ] under the [C]onvention.' "); Bautista v. Star Cruises, 396 F.3d 1289, 1297–1300 (11th Cir.2005).

[33] Christopher R. Drahozal, Commercial Arbitration: Cases and Problems 306 (2d ed.2006). See also Island Territory of Curacao v. Solitron Devices, Inc., 356 F.Supp. 1, 13 (S.D.N.Y.1973) ("Research has developed nothing to show what the purpose of the "commercial" limitation was. We may logically speculate that it was to exclude matrimonial and other domestic relations awards, political awards, and the like.") See also Born, supra note 13, at 264–65.

[34] New York Convention, art. I(1) ("This Convention * * * shall also apply to arbitral awards not considered as domestic awards in the State where their recognition and enforcement are sought.")

[35] 710 F.2d 928, 932 (2d Cir.1983).

[36] Id. at 932. See also Ledee v. Ceramiche Ragno, 684 F.2d 184, 187 (1st Cir.1982) (relevant question is "Is a party to the agreement not an American citizen, or does the commercial relationship have some reasonable relation with one or more foreign states?"); Kaliroy Produce Co., Inc. v. Pacific Tomato Growers, Inc., 730 F.Supp.2d 1036, 1039 (D.Ariz.2010) (award rendered in Arizona "is non-domestic and within the scope of the Convention" because the case "involves one foreign party (ALP) and two

An award rendered in the United States may be "not considered as domestic" (and thus governed by the New York Convention) even if the arbitration was between United States citizens, so long as it involved performance abroad.[37]

(b) National Law

(1) Implementing Legislation

In addition to the New York Convention and other treaties, international arbitration is also governed by national arbitration law. "In virtually all Contracting States, the New York Convention has been implemented through national legislation."[38] While many States have implemented the New York Convention by adopting the United Nations Commission for International Trade Law (UNCITRAL) Model Law on International Arbitration,[39] the United States has not.[40] Instead, the United States legislation implementing the New York Convention is Chapter 2 of the FAA.[41] The United States legislation implementing the Panama Convention is Chapter 3 of the FAA.[42] These chapters of the FAA are the core of the United States' national law on international commercial arbitration. In addition, U.S. law on international commercial arbitration includes

---

domestic parties (PTG and Kaliroy), and principally involved conduct and contract performance in the United States and Mexico. Moreover, the Tribunal applied Arizona law in issuing the Award."); Matter of Arbitration Between Trans Chemical Ltd. and China Nat. Machinery Import and China National Machinery Import and Export Corp., 978 F.Supp. 266, 297 (S.D.Tex.1997) ("adopt[ing] the Bergesen definition of 'nondomestic' as encompassing actions to confirm arbitration awards rendered in the United States between two foreign parties.")

[37]   See Lander Co., Inc. v. MMP Investments, Inc., 107 F.3d 476, 482 (7th Cir.1997). In Lander Co., the Seventh Circuit held that such cases are governed by both the Convention and the FAA. Id. at 481. Accord Freudensprung v. Offshore Technical Services, Inc., 379 F.3d 327, 341 (5th Cir.2004); Bergesen v. Joseph Muller Corp., 710 F.2d 928, 934 (2d Cir.1983) ("no reason to assume that Congress did not intend to provide overlapping coverage between the Convention and the Federal Arbitration Act."). For reasons why it might matter that the Convention, not just the FAA applies, see Rau, Sherman & Peppet, supra note 5, at 1003–05.

[38]   Born, supra note 13, at 99–100.

[39]   See http://www.uncitral.org/uncitral/en/uncitral_texts/arbitration/1985Model _arbitration_status.html

[40]   However, California, Texas and a few other U.S. states have enacted the UNCITRAL Model Law. Id.

[41]   9 U.S.C. §§ 201–08. And one might say Chapter 1 of the FAA also implements the New York Convention because FAA § 208 provides that "Chapter 1 applies to actions and proceedings brought under this chapter to the extent that chapter is not in conflict with this chapter or the Convention as ratified by the United States."

[42]   9 U.S.C. §§ 301–07. And one might say Chapter 1 of the FAA also implements the Panama Convention because FAA § 307 provides that "Chapter 1 applies to actions and proceedings brought under this chapter to the extent chapter 1 is not in conflict with this chapter or the Inter-American Convention as ratified by the United States."

case law and the American Law Institute is producing a restatement on The United States Law of International Commercial Arbitration.[43]

If an arbitration agreement or award is covered by (within the scope of) the New York Convention or other treaty then the treaty might be expected to supersede any conflicting national law. But national courts have not always readily subordinated their national laws to the treaties.[44] For instance, in the United States "acts of Congress remain on a par with treaties,"[45] "the Constitution trumps treaties,"[46] and at least one court has refused to enforce an international commercial arbitration award on constitutional grounds.[47] In sum, "the practical effect" of the New York Convention depends on national law—including case law interpreting the Convention and statutes implementing it—and therefore varies from State to State.[48]

With national law on arbitration continuing to vary from State to State, cases can still turn on the question of which State's arbitration law governs. This question is generally determined by the seat of arbitration.

(2) The Choice of National Arbitration Law: The "Seat" of Arbitration

The place (or "seat") in which an international commercial arbitration occurs is significant because, under widely recognized choice-of-law principles, it is the seat State's *arbitration* law that governs the dispute, even if some other State's *substantive* law governs that dispute.[49] For instance, a contract might contain a New

---

[43]   See   http://www.ali.org/index.cfm?fuseaction=projects.proj_ip&projectid=20. See George A. Bermann, Jack J. Coe, Jr., Christopher R. Drahozal & Catherine A. Rogers, Restating the U.S. Law of International Commercial Arbitration, 113 Penn St. L. Rev. 1333 (2009).

[44]   Margaret L. Moses, The Principles and Practice of International Commercial Arbitration 17 (2008) (the New York Convention "should supercede domestic law regarding the proper form of an arbitration agreement. However, State courts have not always viewed the Convention as superceding their domestic law.") For example, the United States Supreme Court has held "that an Act of Congress * * * is on a full parity with a treaty, and that when a statute which is subsequent in time is inconsistent with a treaty, the statute to the extent of conflict renders the treaty null." Breard v. Greene, 523 U.S. 371, 376 (1998) (quotations omitted).

[45]   William W. Park, Treaty Obligations and National Law: Emerging Conflicts in International Arbitration, 58 Hastings L.J. 251, 252 (2006).

[46]   Id.

[47]   Base Metal Trading, Ltd. v. OJSC "Novokuznetsky Aluminium Factory," 283 F.3d 208 (4th Cir. 2002) (due process requirements for personal jurisdiction). For contrary authority on that personal jurisdiction issue, see Christopher R. Drahozal, Commercial Arbitration: Cases and Problems 620–22 (3d ed.2013).

[48]   Born, supra note 13, at 99–100.

[49]   "Typically, when the parties have chosen a law, the arbitrators will apply that law * * * . [A]lthough parties typically do not specifically choose a procedural law, they

York choice-of-law clause but provide for arbitration in Mexico. While the arbitrators would likely apply New York substantive law to the merits of the underlying dispute, any judicial involvement in the arbitration would likely be by a Mexican court applying Mexican arbitration law.[50] Possible topics for such judicial involvement (all likely governed by the seat's arbitration law) include arbitrator selection, the arbitration process, and the enforcement (confirmation) or setting aside (vacatur) of the arbitration award.[51]

With the seat's arbitration law governing all this, a lot can turn on the choice of seat. Thus, that choice may be a topic of negotiation at the time a contract is formed. "Parties frequently choose a seat of arbitration in a country where neither party's business interests are located. In addition, the seat may be chosen simply because it is convenient to both parties."[52] The seat can, many authorities suggest, be different from where the arbitration hearing actually occurs.[53] If, for example, the parties want English arbitration law to apply, they

---

do usually choose the seat of the arbitration, and almost inevitably, the procedural law of the arbitration will be considered the arbitration law of the seat." Moses, supra note 44, at 64. Note that what Moses calls "the procedural law of the arbitration" is the relevant State's arbitration law, rather than the procedural rules of an arbitration organization, such as the International Chamber of Commerce, which the parties often choose as their arbitration's equivalent to the rules of civil procedure. See § 57.

[50]   See International Standard Elec. Corp. v. Bridas Sociedad Anonima Petrolera, Indus. Y Comercial, 745 F.Supp. 172 (S.D.N.Y.1990). In *Bridas*, the arbitration occurred in Mexico City under a contract with a New York choice of law clause. The federal court in New York held that it lacked jurisdiction to set aside award because New York Convention art. V's reference to the country "under the laws of which [the] award was made" refers

> exclusively to procedural and not substantive law, and more precisely, to the regimen or scheme of arbitral procedural law under which the arbitration was conducted, and not the substantive law of contract which was applied in the case.

> In this case, the parties subjected themselves to the procedural law of Mexico. Hence, since the situs, or forum of the arbitration is Mexico, and the governing procedural law is that of Mexico, only the courts of Mexico have jurisdiction under the Convention to vacate the award. ISEC's petition to vacate the award is therefore dismissed.

Id. at 178.

[51]   Rau, Sherman & Peppet, supra note 5, at 962. See also Born, supra note 13, at 1307–08.

[52]   Moses, supra note 44, 56.

[53]   Macneil, Speidel & Stipanowich, supra note 14, § 44.40.1.3, at 44:275("American parties engaged in a joint venture in Thailand might very well choose the FAA to govern but at the same time wish to conduct any arbitration in Thailand, where records, witnesses, local counsel familiar with the facts, and the like are readily available."); Rau, Sherman & Peppet, supra note 5, at 994–1000; Moses, supra note 44, at 58; English Arbitration Act of 1996 § 100(2) ("an award shall be treated as made at the seat of the arbitration, regardless of where it was signed, despatched or delivered to any of the parties.")

can contractually designate England as the seat of arbitration and then hold the arbitration hearings in some other country.[54]

The parties' contract can select the seat of arbitration directly by naming it or indirectly by delegating the choice to the arbitration organization selected to administer the arbitration, such as the International Chamber of Commerce. Another such organization is the American Arbitration Association. When the AAA decides the seat (or "locale") of arbitration, it will consider:

1.   Location of parties and attorneys.

2.   Location of witnesses and documents.

3.   Location of records.

4.   Where the evidence is located (i.e. location of a construction site).

5.   Consideration of the relative difficulty in traveling and cost to parties.

6.   Place of performance of the contract.

7.   Place of previous court actions.

8.   Location of most appropriate panel.

9.   Any other reasonable arguments that might affect the locale determination.[55]

What happens if the parties neither select the seat of arbitration directly nor by delegating seat-choice to an arbitration organization? If such parties cannot resolve their dispute about where to seat the arbitration they may litigate the question in national courts. However, most States' arbitration laws deny courts the power to select an arbitral seat. Instead, most States' arbitration laws give arbitrators and arbitration organizations the power to select an arbitral seat but these laws only apply to arbitrations already seated within that State.[56] Accordingly, some States' arbitration laws hold that arbitration clauses that do not specify an arbitral seat or a

---

[54]   "England is one of the leading jurisdictions in the world for international commercial arbitration (the other two top contenders are France and Switzerland)." S.I. Strong, Border Skirmishes: The Intersection Between Litigation and International Commercial Arbitration, 2012 J. Disp. Resol. 1, 5 (2012).

[55]   AMERICAN ARBITRATION ASSOCIATION, *Locale Determinations: ICDR*, available at https://www.adr.org/cs/idcplg?IdcService=GET_FILE&dDocName=ADRSTG_013009&RevisionSelectionMethod=LatestReleased.

[56]   Born, supra note 13, at 1703 ("[T]he absence of agreement on the arbitral seat arguably prevents application of [national arbitration law] statutory mechanisms that empower the arbitrators to select an arbitral seat."). So a court may refuse to select a seat and refuse to grant anyone else the power to select a seat. In sum, circularity or bootstrapping problem arises.

means of selecting the arbitral seat are invalid.[57] And when national courts do decide the arbitral seat, there is a risk that different States' courts will select different arbitral seats for the same case.[58]

Parties sometimes agree pre-dispute to an arbitral seat that post-dispute turns out to be unattractive to one party. If that party asks a court to invalidate the parties' agreement to the seat, that party will generally find little supportive authority, including under the doctrine of *forum non conveniens*, which permits courts to dismiss litigation where the plaintiff's chosen form is inconvenient.[59]

(c) Contracting for the Procedural Rules and Substantive Law to Be Applied to a Particular Case

As noted above, international commercial arbitration typically involves major disputes between large and sophisticated parties. While such arbitration is typically slower and more costly than domestic arbitration,[60] that is not much of a criticism of international commercial arbitration. The alternative to international arbitration for parties engaged in international activities is not domestic arbitration but international litigation. Parties often fear litigation in foreign courts for a variety of reasons, including fear of a local bias in the process of foreign litigation and fear of foreign substantive law.[61]

International arbitration avoids the procedures and possible bias of foreign courts by substituting the procedures and arbitrators agreed to by the parties.[62] International commercial arbitration

---

[57]   *Id.*

[58]   See Tonicstar Ltd v. Am. Home Assur. Co. [2004] EWHC 1234 (Q.B.). This case involved parallel judicial proceedings in New York and England, and later requests for arbitration in both England and New York. The English courts issued an antisuit injunction to prevent the respondents from getting a U.S. court to compel arbitration in New York. The English court reasoned that the dispute was more closely connected to England, and that English courts should therefore decide the arbitral seat. Although there was no conflicting US court decision, such a scenario is conceivable.

[59]   Born, supra note 13, at 1723–25. See also Y. Derains & E. Schwartz, A Guide to the ICC Rules of Arbitration 218 (2d ed.2005) ("Thus far, to the authors' knowledge, no ICC Arbitral Tribunal has found the parties' choice of a place of arbitration should be considered to be nullified by changed circumstances").

[60]   Rau, Sherman & Peppet, supra note 5, at 631 ("It is inevitable that international arbitration will often turn out to be considerably more protracted and expensive than its domestic counterpart.")

[61]   Edward Brunet, Charles B. Craver & Ellen E. Deason, Alternative Dispute Resolution: The Advocate's Perspective 442–44 (4th ed.2011). "Parties choose international arbitration primarily because they fear being subject to the potentially biased decisions of the national courts of their business-partner-turned-adversary." Bermann, Coe, Drahozal & Rogers, supra note 43, at 1342.

[62]   International commercial arbitration offers a "time-tested blend of common law and civil law procedures (as opposed to international litigation, which typically gives one party a home-court advantage in terms of procedure)." S.I. Strong,

agreements often incorporate the procedural rules of an arbitration organization such as the International Chamber of Commerce (ICC[63]) or the London Court of International Arbitration (LCIA).[64] These organizations provide procedural rules and administer arbitrations according to them. In contrast, another organization—the United Nations Commission for International Trade Law (UNCITRAL)— promulgates a popular set of procedural rules but does not administer arbitration.[65]

Parties in international arbitration can avoid application of foreign law through *amiable composition*, the arbitrator's power to ignore any State's law and apply instead the customs of international commerce,[66] but parties rarely choose this sort of arbitration.[67] More often, they include a choice of law clause agreeing that a particular State's substantive law will govern any dispute they have.

2.   FORMATION OF ENFORCEABLE INTERNATIONAL COMMERCIAL ARBITRATION AGREEMENTS
Table of Sections

Navigating the Borders Between International Commercial Arbitration and U.S. Federal Courts: A Jurisprudential GPS, 2012 J. Disp. Resol. 119, 124.

[63]   Rau, Sherman & Peppet, supra note 5, at 628 ("A large number of other organizations besides the AAA compete in the administration of international commercial arbitrations; by far the most important of these is the International Chamber of Commerce (ICC) in Paris.") See generally International Chamber of Commerce, International Court of Arbitration, http://www.iccwbo.org/court/ arbitration/id4424/index.html (last visited Aug.1, 2011).

[64]   See London Court of International Arbitration (LCIA), available at http:// www.lcia.org/.

[65]   See   http://www.uncitral.org/uncitral/en/uncitral_texts/arbitration/2010 Arbitration_rules.html. UNCITRAL rules may be used in arbitrations administered by other arbitration organizations and in ad hoc (un-administered) arbitrations. Moses, supra note 44, at 9.

[66]   See generally Lex Mercatoria and Arbitration (Thomas Carbonneau ed., Rev.ed.1998); Brunet, Craver & Deason, supra note 61, at 443.

[67]   Christopher R. Drahozal, Contracting Out of National Law: An Empirical Look at the New Law Merchant, 80 Notre Dame L. Rev. 523 (2005).

§ 64   Formation

(a)   Enforcement of Executory Arbitration Agreements

The New York Convention makes executory arbitration agreements enforceable. Article II(1) says:

> Each Contracting State shall recognize an agreement in writing under which the parties undertake to submit to arbitration all or any differences which have arisen or which may arise between them in respect of a defined legal relationship, whether contractual or not, concerning a subject matter capable of settlement by arbitration.[68]

Just as the remedy for breach of a domestic executory arbitration agreement is specific performance, rather than money damages,[69] the New York Convention also does not direct courts to award money damages for breach of international executory arbitration agreements. Rather it directs courts to "refer the parties to arbitration," that is, specifically enforce the agreement to arbitrate:

> The court of a Contracting State, when seized of an action in a matter in respect of which the parties have made an agreement within the meaning of this article, shall, at the request of one of the parties, refer the parties to arbitration, unless it finds that the said agreement is null and void, inoperative or incapable of being performed.[70]

For example, if Buyer sues Seller despite an international commercial arbitration agreement between them, Seller can get a court to stay[71] or dismiss[72] Buyer's lawsuit.

---

[68]   New York Convention, art. II(1).

[69]   See § 4(c).

[70]   New York Convention, art. II(3). See also Domenico Di Pietro & Martin Platte, Enforcement of International Arbitration Awards 66 (2001) ("refer the parties to arbitration" "means that the Court becomes incompetent to entertain the case and must stay proceedings"); 9 U.S.C. § 206 ("A court having jurisdiction under this chapter may direct that arbitration be held in accordance with the agreement at any place therein provided for, whether that place is within or without the United States. Such court may also appoint arbitrators in accordance with the provisions of the agreement."). FAA § 208 provides that "Chapter 1 applies to actions and proceedings brought under this chapter to the extent that chapter is not in conflict with this chapter or the Convention as ratified by the United States." As Chapter 1 includes FAA § 3 staying litigation, this provision presumably applies to actions under FAA Chapter 2. See Macneil, Speidel & Stipanowich, supra note 14, § 44.8.3, at 44:41.

[71]   Rhone Mediterranee Compagnia Francese Di Assicurazioni E Riassicurazioni v. Lauro, 555 F.Supp. 481, D.V.I. (1982), aff'd, 712 F.2d 50 (3d Cir.1983).

[72]   Filanto, S.p.A. v. Chilewich Intern. Corp., 789 F.Supp. 1229 (S.D.N.Y.1992). For conflicting authority on dismissal, see supra § 4(c) n.33.

(b) National Law Governs Formation

Suppose though, that Buyer denies that its contract with Seller contains an arbitration clause. That is, suppose Buyer denies that "the parties have made an agreement within the meaning of" Article II of the New York Convention. These facts arose in *Matter of Ferrara S.p.A.*,[73] in which the arbitration clause apparently appeared, not right above the signature line, but rather on the back of the page containing signatures of the parties' agents.[74] This location of the arbitration clause made it unenforceable under Italian law, according to the buyer.[75] The buyer argued that Italian law governed the question whether the parties formed an arbitration agreement.[76] In contrast, according to the court, the arbitration clause *would* be enforceable under United States law. So the *Ferrara* court confronted a choice-of-law question, that is, whether Italian or United States law governed the question whether the parties formed an arbitration agreement.

The *Ferrara* court chose to apply United States law. Other United States cases similarly apply U.S. law to determine whether the parties have formed an international arbitration agreement.[77] This is understandable, as Article II of the New York Convention provides courts with little guidance about how to determine whether the parties have formed an arbitration agreement. The little Article II does provide is its requirement that the agreement be "in writing."[78] But Article II provides no legal rules on mutual assent, offer and acceptance, consideration, or any other topics that might play a role in determining whether the parties have formed an arbitration agreement. Nor does Article II tell courts where to look to find such legal rules. In other words, Article II lacks a choice-of-law rule.[79] It does not say, for example, to apply the law of the State in which the agreement was allegedly formed. Or to apply the law of the

---

[73] 441 F.Supp. 778 (S.D.N.Y. 1977), aff'd mem., 580 F.2d 1044 (2d Cir. 1978).

[74] Id. at 779.

[75] Id. at 780.

[76] Id.

[77] Born, supra note 13, at 461, nn. 252–53.

[78] See § 64(c).

[79] As Gary Born explains:

Article II's terms reflect the fact that the New York Convention was, until late in its drafting process, directly solely at the recognition of arbitral awards, and not arbitration agreements. When Article II of the Convention was expanded, to require recognition of arbitration agreements, relatively little thought was directed towards choice-of-law or other issues relating to the new provisions.

Born, supra note 13, at 462.

State in which the alleged agreement would be performed (the "seat" of arbitration).

With all this lacking from Article II, it is understandable that United States courts apply their own national law to determine whether the parties have formed an international arbitration agreement. Nevertheless, commentators have criticized this practice and tried to develop an alternative approach.[80] This alternative approach, building on the fact that the New York Convention does have a choice-of-law rule on the enforcement of arbitration *awards,* would apply this choice-of-law rule also to issues about arbitration agreement formation.[81] United States courts have, however, rejected this alternative approach.[82] So United States courts are likely to apply United States law (summarized in sections 2.19–2.28 of this chapter) to issues of whether an international arbitration agreement has been formed, except when those issues relate to the one formation topic addressed in the New York Convention, the requirement of a writing.

(c) The Requirement of a Writing

Under domestic United States law, an oral arbitration agreement is likely unenforceable[83] and many other States' national laws also enforce only written arbitration agreements.[84] Similarly, the New York Convention suggests that only written arbitration agreements are enforceable, as it provides that "Each Contracting State shall recognize an *agreement in writing* under which the parties undertake to submit to arbitration."[85] It then defines "agreement in writing" to "include an arbitral clause in a contract or

---

[80]   Id. at 460–66.

[81]   See Id. at nn. 263–64. Article V(1)(a) of the Convention provides that enforcement of an award may be refused if the arbitration "agreement is not valid under the law to which the parties have subjected it or, failing any indication thereon, under the law of the country where the award was made." In other words, under Article V(1)(a)'s choice-of-law rule, the relevant State's law is the law the parties have chosen in a choice-of-law clause ("the law to which the parties have subjected it") or, if there is no party choice of law, then the relevant State's law is the law of the country where the award was made, that is, the "seat" of arbitration.

[82]   Rhone Mediterranee Compagnia Francese Di Assicuraziono E Riassicurazoni v. Achille Lauro, 712 F.2d 50, 53 (3d Cir. 1983) (Article V's choice-of-law rule is not incorporated into Article II(1) because Article II(3)'s ambiguity was "deliberate"); Meadows Indem. Co. v. Baccala & Shoop Ins. Sers., Inc., 760 F.Supp. 1036, 1042 (E.D.N.Y. 1991) (Article II(3) does not incorporate Article V's choice-of-law rule).

[83]   See § 4(d) n.18.

[84]   See, e.g., UNCITRAL Model Law, art. 7 (Option I, as amended); Swis PILA, art. 178(I); English Arbitration Act, § 5; French Code of Civil Procedure, art. 1443.

[85]   New York Convention, art. II(1).

an arbitration agreement, signed by the parties or contained in an exchange of letters or telegrams."[86]

The reference to "letters or telegrams" evokes the technology of the era in which the Convention was written, over half a century ago. In contrast, international commercial arbitration agreements formed through more-modern electronic communication, such as email, may be enforceable but few reported cases have addressed the question.[87]

Even if the communications technology used by the parties fits within the Convention's definition of "agreement in writing," the arbitration agreement may not be enforceable due to the signature requirement. As noted above, Article II(2) defines "agreement in writing" to "include an arbitral clause in a contract or an arbitration agreement, *signed by the parties* or contained in an exchange of letters or telegrams."[88] To what does this signature requirement apply? Most United States courts hold that the signature requirement does not apply to "an exchange of letters or telegrams,"[89] but does apply to both "an arbitral clause in a contract or an arbitration agreement."[90] In other words, most courts hold that the

---

[86] New York Convention, art. II(2). Whether an "agreement in writing" in fact occurred can be a fact-intensive inquiry. See, e.g., Filanto, S.p.A. v. Chilewich Intern. Corp., 789 F.Supp. 1229, 1236–37 (S.D.N.Y.1992).

[87] See § 4(d) n.18. There is a United Nations Convention on the Use of Electronic Communications in International Contracts (ECC). G.A. Res. 60/21, U.N. Doc. A/Res/60/21, U.N. Sales No E.07.V.2 (Dec. 9, 2005), available at http://www.uncitral .org/pdf/english/texts/electcom/06-57452_Ebook.pdf. It provides that "[w]here the law requires that a communication or a contract should be in writing, or provides consequences for the absence of a writing, that requirement is met by an electronic communication if the information contained therein is accessible so as to be usable for subsequent reference." Id. art.9(2). The ECC applies to the New York Convention. Id. art. 20(1). See also Chloe Z Fishing Co., Inc. v. Odyssey Re (London) Ltd., 109 F.Supp.2d 1236, 1250 (S.D.Cal.2000) ("Under plaintiffs' unduly restrictive definition, only a written message sent in an envelope with a signature or a message transmitted by telegraph would satisfy the letter and telegram requirements respectively. However, the Court finds that Article II section 2 of the Convention could not have intended to exclude all other forms of written communications regularly utilized to conduct commerce in the various signatory nations by failing to provide an exhaustive list of 'letters' or 'telegrams.' ") But see Decision of the Hologaland Court of Appeal, 16 August 1999, Yearbook on Commercial Arbitration XXVII, at 519 (2002) (exchange of emails did not satisfy writing requirement).

[88] New York Convention, art. II(2) (emphasis added).

[89] See Standard Bent Glass Corp. v. Glassrobots Oy, 333 F.3d 440, 449–50 (3d Cir.2003).

[90] See id.; Kahn Lucas Lancaster, Inc. v. Lark International Ltd., 186 F.3d 210, 217 (2d Cir.1999) ("Grammatically, the comma immediately following 'an arbitration agreement' serves to separate the series ('an arbitral clause in a contract or an arbitration agreement') from the modifying phrase ('signed by the parties or contained in an exchange of letters or telegrams'), and suggests that the modifying phrase is meant to apply to both elements in the series. Indeed, this comma can serve no other grammatical purpose.") But see Sphere Drake Insurance PLC v. Marine Towing, Inc., 16 F.3d 666, 667–69 (5th Cir.1994) (signature not required to enforce "arbitral clause in a contract").

signature requirement applies to both the typical pre-dispute arbitration agreement (the "arbitral clause in a contract") and a standalone "arbitration agreement," which is more often formed post-dispute and called a "submission agreement," but does not apply to an arbitration agreement formed by "an exchange of letters or telegrams."

§ 65　Separability

In the domestic United States context, the Supreme Court has repeatedly held that "a challenge to the validity of the contract as a whole, and not specifically to the arbitration clause, must go to the arbitrator."[91] This "separability doctrine"[92] is even more firmly established in the international commercial context, as many States' national laws adopt it.[93] While the New York Convention does not expressly adopt the separability doctrine,[94] at least one leading commentator argues that the Convention "rests on the premise that parties may, and ordinarily do, intend their arbitration agreements to be separable."[95]

In addition, many international commercial agreements incorporate arbitration-organization rules that provide for separability. For example, the International Chamber of Commerce Arbitration Rules provide "if any party * * * raises one or more pleas concerning the existence, validity or scope of the arbitration agreement, * * * the arbitration shall proceed and any question of jurisdiction * * * shall be decided directly by the arbitral tribunal."[96]

§ 66　Contract Law Defenses

A contract containing an international arbitration clause is subject to the same general defenses as other contracts.[97] These may

---

[91]　Buckeye Check Cashing, Inc. v. Cardegna, 546 U.S. 440, 449 (2006). See §§ 19–21.

[92]　Which the Supreme Court has taken to calling the "severability doctrine." 546 U.S. 445–47.

[93]　Born, supra note 13, at 311 ("An international arbitration agreement is almost invariably treated as presumptively 'separable' or 'autonomous' from the underlying contract within which it is found.") See, e.g., UNCITRAL Model Law, art. 16; English Arbitration Act § 30; UNCITRAL rules, art. 21(I); LCIA Rules, art. 23(I).

[94]　Born, supra note 13, at 317, 319.

[95]　Id. at 319.

[96]　ICC Rules, art. 6(3). The arbitral tribunal may be overruled by the Court of Arbitration of the International Chamber of Commerce, but that "court" is more like an appellate arbitrator than a "court" in the ordinary sense of governmental adjudication.

[97]　Born, supra note 13, at 705 ("The categories of substantive invalidity of international arbitration agreements contained in the Convention and most developed national arbitration legislation are limited to cases where such agreements are invalid

include: fraud (misrepresentation), duress, undue influence, mistake, impracticability, frustration of purpose, the statute of limitations, the statute of frauds, and illegality. These defenses to enforcement of contracts containing international arbitration clauses are, however, subject to the separability doctrine.[98] The separability doctrine holds that arbitrators, not courts, hear challenges to the enforceability of contracts containing arbitration clauses unless those challenges are "directed to the arbitration clause itself" rather than to the whole contract containing that clause (the "container contract").[99] Under the separability doctrine, arbitrators rather than courts will address the aforementioned defenses in nearly all cases because those defenses are rarely "directed to the arbitration clause itself."[100] A party alleging that its container contract is unenforceable due to one of the grounds listed above will likely be sent to arbitration to make that argument.

In contrast, parties in some cases have contract law defenses directed to the arbitration clause itself, rather than to the broader contract containing that clause. How are those defenses handled in international agreements? The New York Convention requires courts to enforce arbitration agreements unless a court finds that a particular agreement "is null and void, inoperative or incapable of being performed."[101] This phrase may sound foreign to United States lawyers but most of the standard United States contract law defenses seem to fall into one of the Convention's three categories: "null and void," "inoperative," or "incapable of being performed."[102] According to Gary Born:

- "null and void" refers to "cases in which an arbitration agreement was defective or invalid from the outset," such as "fraud * * *, unconscionability, illegality and mistake."[103]

- "inoperative" "refers to agreements that were at one time valid, but which thereafter ceased to have effect

---

on generally-applicable contract law grounds (e.g., mistake, fraud, unconscionability, impossibility, waiver.)")

[98] See §§ 19–21.

[99] See Prima Paint Corp. v. Flood & Conklin Manufacturing Co., 388 U.S. 395, 402 (1967).

[100] See § 21. See also Macneil, Speidel & Stipanowich, supra note 14, § 19.2.1.

[101] New York Convention, art. II(3).

[102] Lindo v. NCL (Bahamas), Ltd., 652 F.3d 1257, 1272 (11th Cir.2011) (reiterating court's earlier holding "that Article II's 'null and void' clause was confined to standard breach-of-contract defenses and that the limited scope of the Convention's null and void clause must be interpreted to encompass only those situations—such as fraud, mistake, duress, and waiver—that can be applied neutrally on an international scale.") (internal quotes omitted).

[103] Born, supra note 13, at 711.

(or to be 'operative'), * * * includ[ing] cases of waiver, revocation, repudiation, or termination of the arbitration agreement, or failure to comply with jurisdictional time limits prescribed by the arbitration agreement."[104]

- " 'incapable of being performed' includes cases where the parties have agreed upon a procedure that is physically or legally impossible to follow."[105]

What law determines whether an agreement "is null and void, inoperative or incapable of being performed"? An oft-cited Third Circuit case said:

None of the limited secondary literature sheds so clear a light as to suggest a certain answer. However, we conclude that the meaning of Article II section 3 which is most consistent with the overall purposes of the Convention is that an agreement to arbitrate is "null and void" only (1) when it is subject to an internationally recognized defense such as duress, mistake, fraud, or waiver, or (2) when it contravenes fundamental policies of the forum state. The "null and void" language must be read narrowly, for the signatory nations have jointly declared a general policy of enforceability of agreements to arbitrate.[106]

In other words, the New York Convention, like FAA § 2, allows courts to decline to enforce arbitration agreements only on such grounds as exist at law or in equity for the revocation of any contract. As with domestic arbitration agreements, parties who deny the enforceability of an international commercial arbitration agreement generally must find their arguments in contract law, not in some other body of law.[107]

---

[104] Id. at 711–12.

[105] Id. at 712.

[106] Rhone Mediterranee Compagnia Francese Di Assicurazioni E Riassicurazoni v. Lauro, 712 F.2d 50, 53 (3d Cir.1983) (citations omitted). See also Ledee v. Ceramiche Ragno, 684 F.2d 184, 187 (1st Cir.1982) ("must be interpreted to encompass only those situations—such as fraud, mistake, duress, and waiver—that can be applied neutrally on an international scale."); DiMercurio v. Sphere Drake Ins., PLC, 202 F.3d 71, 80 (1st Cir.2000); Chloe Z Fishing Co., Inc. v. Odyssey Re (London) Ltd., 109 F.Supp.2d 1236, 1259 (S.D.Cal.2000); Prograph Intern. Inc. v. Barhydt, 928 F.Supp. 983, 989 (N.D.Cal.1996).

[107] See, e.g., *Ledee*, 684 F.2d at 187 (rejecting provision in Puerto Rico Dealers Act that invalidated, on public policy grounds, arbitration clauses in dealers' contracts, and stating, "[A]n expansive interpretation of the [null and void] clause would be antithetical to the goals of the Convention.")

§ 67   Non-Contract Law Defenses: Inarbitrable (Non-Arbitrable) Claims

The New York Convention only requires enforcement of agreements to arbitrate disputes "concerning a subject matter capable of settlement by arbitration."[108] Article II(1) provides:

> Each Contracting State shall recognize an agreement in writing under which the parties undertake to submit to arbitration all or any differences which have arisen or which may arise between them in respect of a defined legal relationship, whether contractual or not, concerning a subject matter capable of settlement by arbitration.[109]

In other words, the Convention does not require enforcement of agreements to arbitrate inarbitrable (or "non-arbitrable"[110]) claims.

This topic of "inarbitrability" in the domestic United States context is discussed in sections 2.27–2.28, which summarize the United States Supreme Court's 1980's arbitration law revolution. Prior to the 1980's, nearly all domestic arbitration occurred in two contexts: (1) labor disputes, and (2) disputes among businesses. With arbitration limited to these contexts, domestic arbitration seemed largely confined to contract claims and little attention was given to the arbitration of non-contract claims. Beginning in the 1980's, (and spurred by an international arbitration case from 1975,[111]) the Supreme Court enforced agreements to arbitrate other claims such as antitrust, securities, and employment discrimination.[112] Domestically, only a few claims are now inarbitrable.[113]

---

[108]   New York Convention, art. II(1). See also id., art. V(2).

   2.   Recognition and enforcement of an arbitral award may also be refused if the competent authority in the country where recognition and enforcement is sought finds that:

   (a) The subject matter of the difference is *not capable of settlement by arbitration* under the law of that country; or

   (b) The recognition or enforcement of the award would be contrary to the public policy of that country.

Id. (emphasis added).

[109]   New York Convention, art. II(1).

[110]   Born, supra note 13, at 766–67.

[111]   Scherk v. Alberto-Culver Co., 417 U.S. 506, 515–520 (1974) (enforcing international agreement to arbitrate a claim arising under the Securities Exchange Act of 1934 notwithstanding Court's assumption, arguendo, that its precedents would bar such enforcement in a domestic context.)

[112]   See § 27.

[113]   See § 28. One type of claim that may be inarbitrable in domestic United States arbitration—insurance—may nevertheless be arbitrable in international arbitration. See ESAB Group, Inc. v. Zurich Ins. PLC, 685 F.3d 376 (4th Cir.2012).

Similarly, in the international commercial context, most claims are arbitrable. But in many States, including the U.S., "criminal matters, child custody, family matters, and bankruptcy are not arbitrable. It would be against the law or the public policy of the local jurisdiction to try to arbitrate disputes in these areas."[114] Also, the validity of a patent is generally not arbitrable.[115] Suppose a particular claim is arbitrable under the national law of one party but inarbitrable under the national law of the other party? Most courts, including United States courts, have applied the inarbitrability rules of the forum where litigation over the arbitration agreement is pending.[116]

3.   TERMS OF INTERNATIONAL COMMERCIAL
     ARBITRATION AGREEMENTS
     Table of Sections

---

[114]   Moses, *supra* note 44, at 31. See also Born, *supra* note 13, at 768; Jean-Francois Poudret & Sebastien Besson, Comparative Law of International Arbitration 295–314 (2007) (under the law of some States, inarbitrable claims may include those relating to property rights and laws that regulate markets or protect consumers and employees).

[115]   Moses, *supra* note 44, at 31. William Grantham, The Arbitrability of International Intellectual Property Disputes, 14 Berkeley J. Int'l L. 173 (1996); Deming Liu, Think Twice Before Arbitrating a Patent Dispute?, 23 Am. Rev. Int'l Arb. 313 (2012).

[116]   Born, *supra* note 13, at 521 & n.520.

§ 68   Contractual Arbitrability (Scope of Arbitration Agreement)

In domestic arbitration under the FAA, if a party seeks to litigate, rather than arbitrate, a particular claim, the court will send that claim to arbitration only if the parties agreed to arbitrate that claim.[117] That the parties agreed to arbitrate *some* claim is not enough. They must have agreed to arbitrate *that* claim. Whether or not they did so, the question of "contractual arbitrability," is a question of interpreting the scope of the arbitration agreement.

The threshold issue regarding contractual arbitrability is who, court or arbitrator, decides whether a claim is arbitrable. The FAA presumptively sends contractual arbitrability (scope) disputes to courts, rather than to arbitrators.[118] However, parties can contract around this rule by using an arbitration agreement that says contractual arbitrability disputes shall be resolved by the arbitrator, rather than the court.[119]

In the international commercial context, parties do this frequently, such as by agreeing to arbitrate under the International Chamber of Commerce's Rules of Arbitration.

> Article 6(2) of the ICC Rules provides that "any decision as to the jurisdiction of the Arbitral Tribunal shall be taken by the Arbitral Tribunal itself," while making clear that the jurisdictional issues identified for arbitral decision include "pleas concerning the . . . scope of the arbitration agreement." Virtually all other leading institutional arbitration rules are to the same effect.[120]

The New York Convention arguably "require[s] Contracting States to 'recognize' such agreements (like other agreements to arbitrate) and to 'refer' the parties to such agreements to arbitration."[121]

Suppose, however, that the parties have not agreed to arbitrate disputes about the scope of the arbitration agreement. Consider, for example, a contract between Buyer and Seller obligating each party to arbitrate any "controversy or claim arising out of or relating to this contract, or the breach thereof." Suppose that Buyer sues Seller, alleging antitrust violations, and Seller moves to stay the litigation

---

[117]   See § 30.

[118]   Id.

[119]   Id.

[120]   Born, supra note 13, at 932–33.

[121]   Id. at 860.

and to compel arbitration. Buyer may argue that, while the parties agreed to arbitrate breach-of-contract claims, they did not agree to arbitrate antitrust claims. Therefore, Seller's motion to compel arbitration should be denied. In other words, Buyer may argue contractual arbitrability.

If Buyer's case is brought outside the United States then the court may grant Seller's motion. Some States' laws give arbitrators, not courts, the initial power to rule on questions of contractual arbitrability.[122] Under such laws, Buyer must go to arbitration to persuade the arbitrator that the parties did not agree to arbitrate antitrust claims. In other words, Buyer must go to arbitration to persuade the arbitrator that the arbitration clause should be interpreted not to cover Buyer's claim. Only after getting a ruling from the arbitrator to that effect, or successfully challenging in court a contrary ruling,[123] can Buyer proceed to litigate the antitrust claim.

Arguably, this reasoning is required by New York Convention Article II(3) which provides

> The court of a Contracting State, when seized of an action in a matter in respect of which the parties have made an agreement within the meaning of this article, shall, at the request of one of the parties, refer the parties to arbitration, unless it finds that the said agreement is null and void, inoperative or incapable of being performed.[124]

---

[122]   See id. at 902 ("the general rule in France is that parties may not obtain judicial resolution of jurisdictional disputes until *after* an arbitral tribunal has ruled on the issue.") However, "a French court is permitted to question arbitral jurisdiction [when] no arbitral tribunal has yet been constituted and the agreement to arbitrate is, for one reason or another, manifestly ineffective or unenforceable." George A. Bermann, The "Gateway" Problem in International Commercial Arbitration, 37 Yale J. Int'l L. 1, 17 (2012). See generally Thomas E. Carbonneau, Beyond Trilogies: A New Bill of Rights and Law Practice Through the Contract of Arbitration, 6 Am.Rev.Int'l Arb. 1, 17 (1995) (most nations' laws "contain the *kompetenz-kompetenz* doctrine, under which arbitral tribunals are given the authority to rule initially at least upon questions of contractual inarbitrability. These determinations are subject to judicial review * * * at the stage of enforcement when a final award can be challenged on the basis of an invalid or non-existent arbitration agreement or for excess of arbitral authority.").

[123]   See id. See also William W. Park, Determining an Arbitrator's Jurisdiction: Timing and Finality American Law, 8 Nev. L.J. 135, 139 (2007) (same).

[124]   New York Convention, art. II(3). See also Pietro & Platte, supra note 70, at 66 ("refer the parties to arbitration" "means that the Court becomes incompetent to entertain the case and must stay proceedings"); 9 U.S.C. § 206 ("A court having jurisdiction under this chapter may direct that arbitration be held in accordance with the agreement at any place therein provided for, whether that place is within or without the United States. Such court may also appoint arbitrators in accordance with the provisions of the agreement."). FAA § 208 provides that "Chapter 1 applies to actions and proceedings brought under this chapter to the extent that chapter is not in conflict with this chapter or the Convention as ratified by the United States." As Chapter 1 includes FAA § 3 staying litigation, this provision presumably applies to

According to Gary Born, "[t]his language is most naturally read as establishing an exception to the general obligation to refer parties to arbitration only in cases where the parties' arbitration agreement is null and void, inoperative or incapable of being performed—and *not* in cases where the scope of the arbitration agreement allegedly does not encompass the parties' dispute."[125] This reading of the Convention would, in the above example, require a court to refer Buyer's claim to arbitration because Buyer concedes that it formed an enforceable arbitration agreement with Seller and is merely arguing about the best interpretation of that agreement. While this reading of the Convention is plausible, many courts do not follow it. "Most national courts have routinely considered disputes concerning the scope of the arbitration agreement in interlocutory judicial proceedings."[126] That is, most national courts have not required Buyer go to arbitration to persuade the arbitrator that the arbitration clause should be interpreted not to cover Buyer's claim.

§ 69 Multi-Party Disputes

(a) Claims by or Against Those Not Party to the Arbitration Agreement

The previous section discusses contractual arbitrability, the question of whether a particular arbitration agreement covers a particular claim.[127] A specific application of that question is whether a particular arbitration agreement covers claims by or against a particular person who is not a party to the arbitration agreement.[128] This "non-party" issue arises with some frequency in international commercial arbitration.[129]

As in domestic arbitration, the non-party issue can arise in various procedural contexts. Three examples include:

(1) a party to the arbitration agreement seeks to litigate its claims against a non-party to the agreement but that non-party seeks to compel arbitration of those claims;

---

actions under FAA Chapter 2. See Macneil, Speidel & Stipanowich, supra note 14, § 44.8.3, at 44:41.

[125] Born, supra note 13, at 861.

[126] Born, supra note 13, at 861, n.40.

[127] See § 68.

[128] Those not party to the arbitration agreement are often called "non-signatories" but this usage should be avoided if it misleads some into believing that the only way to be a party to an arbitration agreement is to sign it. Other methods of manifesting assent sometimes make one a party to an international commercial arbitration agreement. See § 64.

[129] See generally W. Laurence Craig, Introduction, in Multiple Party Actions and International Arbitration (The Permanent Court of Arbitration, eds. 2009).

(2) a party to the arbitration agreement seeks to arbitrate its claims against a non-party to the agreement and that non-party refuses to participate in arbitration of those claims (denying that the arbitrator has jurisdiction over those claims); and

(3) a non-party to the agreement seeks to arbitrate its claims against a party to the agreement and that party refuses to participate in arbitration of those claims (denying that the arbitrator has jurisdiction over those claims).

Depending on the procedural context, the relevant legal doctrines may include those noted in this book's discussion of them in the domestic context[130]—third-party beneficiaries, estoppel, agency, assumption of contractual duties, corporate veil piercing.[131] With respect to all of these doctrines, the relevant law is national,[132] or international principles found outside the New York Convention,[133] as the Convention itself has no provisions on point.

(b) Consolidation of, and Stays Pending, Related Proceedings

As explained in Section 33, rules of civil procedure encourage courts to consolidate related cases and to join multiple parties in a single action if their disputes arise out of the same transaction or occurrence.[134] This consolidation and joinder avoids multiple litigation over the same facts, thus saving time and money and helping to avoid inconsistent results. These same goals also argue for arbitrators to consolidate cases and to join parties. The obstacle to doing so, however, is the contractual nature of arbitration. Parties who have not agreed to arbitrate have a right to litigate rather than arbitrate. And parties who have agreed to arbitrate have a right to arbitrate rather than litigate.

> Equally important, parties agree to arbitrate with particular other parties, according to specified procedures— not to arbitrate with anybody, in any set of proceedings. Accordingly, most national legislatures, courts and arbitral tribunals have resolved questions of consolidation, joinder and intervention by reference to the parties' arbitration agreement(s), providing for consolidation, joinder and/or

---

[130]   See § 32.

[131]   Born, supra note 13, at 1142–1205.

[132]   Id. at 1214–17.

[133]   Id. at 1212–14.

[134]   Born, supra note 13, at 2069. See, e.g., Fed.R.Civ.P. 14 (third-party practice), 19 (joinder of persons needed for just adjudication), 20 (permissive joinder of parties), 22 (interpleader), 23 (class actions), and 24 (intervention).

intervention where contemplated—and only where contemplated—by the parties' agreement.[135]

This result is consistent with the New York Convention, which has no provisions specifically addressing the consolidation of multiple arbitrations. The Convention's general provisions requiring Contracting States to enforce executory arbitration agreements support national law deferring to party autonomy.[136]

§ 70   Arbitration Procedure

(a) Overview

Section 2.35, on domestic arbitration procedure, explained that

> The presentation of evidence and argument in litigation is governed by rules of procedure and evidence enacted by government. In contrast, the rules of procedure and evidence in arbitration are, with few exceptions, whatever the parties' arbitration agreement says they are. The procedures of arbitration are largely determined by contract.

This point also applies to international commercial arbitration, as the New York Convention does not regulate the procedures of arbitration. In their international commercial arbitration agreement, the parties can select rules of procedure and evidence, along with the arbitration's location, language, governing law, and other matters. "In essence, the parties create their own private system of justice."[137]

Of course, few parties start from scratch in their agreement in creating their own, completely customized, system of justice. Just as many domestic arbitration agreements incorporate the rules of an arbitration organization, such as the American Arbitration Association's Commercial Rules, many international commercial arbitration agreements incorporate the rules of an arbitration organization, such as the International Chamber of Commerce or the London Court of International Arbitration.[138]

---

[135]   Born, supra note 13, at 2072.

[136]   Id. at 2074.

> Put concretely, if a party has a contractual right to arbitrate particular claims in a consolidated arbitration, or with the presence of a particular party, then Articles II(1) and II(3) of the Convention require recognition of these rights * * * . Conversely, if a party has a contract right to arbitrate in a non-consolidated proceeding, or without the presence of additional parties, Articles II(1) and II(3) again safeguard these rights.

Id.

[137]   Moses, supra note 44, at 17. See also Born, supra note 13, at 1748–50.

[138]   Born, supra note 13, at 1753–55.

International commercial arbitration procedures often consist of compromises between procedures familiar in legal systems (like the United States system) based on the English common law and procedures used in the civil law systems prevalent in continental Europe, South America, and East Asia. One major difference between the common law and civil law traditions is "that what common lawyers think of as a trial in civil proceedings does not exist in the civil law world."[139]

While a trial in the United States brings together the parties, lawyers, judge, and jury in a single, concentrated event, civil law systems use "an entirely different approach" with "no such thing as a trial in our [common law] sense; there is no single, concentrated event. The typical civil proceeding in a civil law country is actually a series of isolated meetings of and written communications between counsel and the judge, in which evidence is introduced, testimony is given, procedural motions and rulings are made, and so on."[140]

Why this major difference between common law and civil law systems? "The reason is that the right to a jury in civil actions, traditional in the common law world, has never taken hold in the civil law world."[141] Following the civil law approach of a series of isolated meetings at which some, but not all, evidence is introduced would not be practical with a jury because the "lay jury cannot easily be convened, adjourned, and reconvened several times in the course of a single action without causing a great deal of inconvenience."[142] So in common law systems a trial must be a single, concentrated event. In contrast, civil law systems can spread out the case over several appearances with each involving the examination of only one witness or the introduction of "only one or two pieces of material evidence."[143]

International commercial arbitration procedures generally look somewhat "civilian" to a lawyer trained in the United States, which is not only a common law jurisdiction, but the common law jurisdiction with the strongest and most broadly applicable civil jury right.

---

[139]   John Henry Merryman & Rogelio Perez-Perdomo, The Civil Law Tradition 113 (3d ed. 2007).

[140]   Id.

[141]   Id.

[142]   Id.

[143]   Id. at 114.

(b) Pre-Hearing

(1) Selection of Arbitrators

Section 2.36 explained that nearly all arbitrations have either one or three arbitrators. While international commercial arbitration sometimes has one arbitrator, three is especially common. For this reason, discussions of international commercial arbitration often refer, not to "the arbitrator," but to "the tribunal." "[W]hen there are substantial amounts of money at stake, most parties feel more comfortable with three arbitrators. * * * In addition when the parties are from different cultural or legal backgrounds, a party may want at least one arbitrator to have some knowledge and understanding of its own culture and legal system."[144] For these reasons, many international commercial arbitration agreements provide for *tripartite* arbitration, in which each party picks one arbitrator and those two agree on the third. This method of arbitrator selection is also the usual method under the rules of important international arbitration organizations, such as the International Chamber of Commerce and London Court of International Arbitration. Many international commercial arbitration agreements provide that arbitration will be conducted according to the rules of these organizations.

(2) Pleadings

An expert on international commercial arbitration says parties seek "fair and neutral procedures that are flexible, efficient and capable of being tailored to the needs of their particular dispute, without reference to the formalities and technicalities of procedural rules applicable in national courts."[145] While litigation generally begins with a complaint filed and served by the plaintiff, and domestic arbitration typically begins with a *demand* for arbitration filed and served by the *claimant*, the corresponding document in international arbitration is often called (more politely) a *request* for arbitration or *notice* of arbitration.[146] This document typically states the basic substantive claims, the relief sought, and the jurisdiction of the arbitrators conferred by the agreement to arbitrate. The request for arbitration may also include the claimant's views about the appropriate number or manner of selecting arbitrators and, if that is tripartite arbitration, the request for arbitration may also include claimant's nomination of an arbitrator. One challenge in drafting this—or any—pleading in international arbitration is making it

---

[144] Moses, supra note 44, at 42.

[145] Born, supra note 13, at 1741.

[146] Id. at 1795.

"understandable and persuasive to readers from other legal and linguistic backgrounds."[147]

After a request for arbitration is served, the respondent may reply in any number of ways. It might answer the claimant's allegations and/or assert counterclaims. It might nominate an arbitrator or it might object to the arbitrators' jurisdiction to hear the dispute, perhaps arguing that there is no enforceable arbitration agreement or that any such agreement does not cover this dispute.

(3) Discovery

Like other aspects of international commercial arbitration procedure, discovery is governed primarily by the arbitration agreement, so the parties have great freedom to choose the amount and types of discovery that will be required in their arbitration.[148] Often parties exercise this freedom by agreeing to arbitrate under the rules of an arbitration organization so the parties indirectly choose the amount and types of discovery provided by those rules. And the rules, in turn, generally give arbitrators broad discretion over the amount and types of discovery they will require.[149]

While domestic arbitration tends to have less discovery than litigation in the United States,[150] this is even more true of international commercial arbitration—where discovery "is usually materially less extensive and intrusive than in common law litigation."[151] Comfort with extensive and intrusive discovery may be widespread among arbitrators from the United States, and perhaps arbitrators from other systems based on the English common law, but that sort of discovery is generally foreign to arbitrators from the civil law systems prevalent in continental Europe, South America, and East Asia. In most civil law jurisdictions, "[e]vidence-taking is largely controlled by the court and the parties have no (or virtually

---

[147] Born, supra note 13, at 1798.

[148] "[A]rbitration legislation is most developed jurisdictions recognizes the parties' autonomy to agree upon the existence, scope and timing of disclosure within the arbitration (as an aspect of the parties' more general procedural autonomy)." Born, supra note 13, at 1879. Gary Born suggests that this is required by the New York Convention. Id. at 1880 ("A Contracting State's refusal to give effect to the parties' agreement granting (or denying) the arbitrators disclosure powers would amount to a failure to recognize a material term of the agreement to arbitrate, contrary to Articles II(1) and II(3)."

[149] "The prevailing view is, and is increasingly firmly-held, * * * that, even absent express authorization, the power to order discovery or disclosure is inherent in an international arbitral tribunal's mandate. This does not obligate a tribunal, in a particular case, to permit or order discovery, but instead (absent contrary agreement) leaves the decision whether or not to order discovery to the tribunal's discretion." Id. at 1891.

[150] See § 36(d).

[151] Born, supra note 13, at 1821.

no) right to demand relevant materials from one another or from witnesses."[152] In much of the world, "United States-style" discovery is as alien and suspect as that other anomalous feature of United States litigation, the civil jury.[153] International commercial arbitration procedures often consist of compromises between the common law and civil law traditions, and this is reflected in international commercial arbitration typically having less discovery than litigation in the United States and in that lesser discovery consisting primarily in the disclosure of documents, rather than interrogatories or depositions.[154] For these reasons, the word "discovery" might even be ill-suited to international commercial arbitration,[155] but this book uses the word because it is familiar to lawyers in the United States.

What happens if a party disobeys an arbitrator's discovery order? International commercial arbitrators are "likely to draw adverse inferences from a party's refusal to produce requested documents or witnesses."[156] In addition, it is "possible, but unusual," for arbitrators to seek court enforcement of their discovery orders.[157] Similarly, parties denied discovery may seek to involve courts, who are authorized by some national laws to help parties in arbitration obtain discovery from recalcitrant opponents and non-parties. For instance, a United States statute gives federal courts the power to order discovery from specified persons "for use in a proceeding in a foreign or international tribunal,"[158] and some courts have held that this covers an international commercial arbitration tribunal.[159]

---

[152] Id. at 1893–94.

[153] On the connections between the civil jury and broad discovery, see Merryman & Perez-Perdomo, supra note 139, at 114; Stephen J. Ware, Consumer and Employment Arbitration Law in Comparative Perspective: The Importance of the Civil Jury, 56 U.Miami L.Rev. 865, 868–69 (2002) (quoting John H. Langbein, The German Advantage in Civil Procedure, 52 U.Chi.L.Rev. 823, 831 (1985), and Paul D. Carrington, The Seventh Amendment: Some Bicentennial Reflections, 1990 U.Chi.Legal F. 33, 40 (1990)).

[154] Born, supra note 13, at 1896 ("The most common and significant mode of disclosure in international arbitration is the production of documents."); id. at 1902 ("interrogatories are infrequently used outside of common law settings."); id. at 1903 ("Depositions are not infrequently used in domestic United States arbitrations, but are much less common in international arbitration."); Carolyn B. Lamm, et al., International Arbitration in a Globalized World, Disp.Resol.Mag., Winter 2014, at 4, 6 (trend "toward broader document disclosure" but "depositions and interrogatories[ ] are not commonly used in international arbitration").

[155] Peter Ashford, Document Production in International Arbitration: A Critique from 'Across the Pond', 10 Loy. U. Chi. Int'l L. Rev. 1, 1–2 (2012).

[156] Born, supra note 13, at 1919.

[157] Id. at 1918.

[158] 28 U.S.C. § 1782.

[159] Born, supra note 13, at 1935. Roger P. Alford, Ancillary Discovery to Prove Denial of Justice, 53 Va. J. Int'l L. 127, 133–42 (2012).

(c) Hearing

(1) General Comparison with Trial

International commercial arbitration hearings resemble arbitration hearings and trials in the United States, insofar as all three types of proceedings involve adversaries trying to persuade a neutral adjudicator by presenting evidence and making arguments. All three typically proceed with opening statements, presentation of witnesses by the claimant for examination and cross-examination, followed by similar presentation of the respondent's witnesses and ending with closing statements.

However, international commercial arbitration hearings often differ from United States trials and domestic arbitration hearings in ways that seem to follow from international commercial arbitration's frequent blending of the common law and civil law traditions.[160] While trials and hearings in the United States and other legal systems based on the English common law generally allow parties (through their lawyers) great latitude in presenting their cases— including the direct and cross-examination of witnesses— "arbitrators with civil law backgrounds (principally in Continental Europe, Japan, Korea and China) can often be expected to adopt somewhat more 'inquisitorial' procedures, with the tribunal being primarily responsible for identifying issues, seeking evidence and probing the record."[161] Also, civil law systems "favor proof through documents, rather than witness testimony,"[162] and where witnesses are heard, it is generally the judge who examines them.[163] Cross-examination "continues to play virtually no role" in civil law litigation,[164] and in some civil law jurisdictions the parties, their relatives, and other interested persons are disqualified from appearing as witnesses.[165]

With international commercial arbitration generally blending the common and civil law traditions, it is no surprise that international commercial arbitration "tends to rely more heavily on documentary evidence and written witness statements than oral testimony."[166] Unlike most litigation in the United States, even

---

[160] See § 70(b)(3).

[161] Born, supra note 13, at 1787.

[162] Id. at 1788.

[163] In the civil law, "even the questions asked a witness during civil proceedings are often asked by the judge on the basis of questions submitted in writing by counsel for the parties." Merryman & Perez-Perdomo, supra note 139, at 115.

[164] Born, supra note 13, at 1842. Accord Merryman & Perez-Perdomo, supra note 139, at 116.

[165] Merryman & Perez-Perdomo, supra note 139, at 116.

[166] Born, supra note 13, at 1826.

domestic U.S. arbitrations often permit evidence to be introduced by affidavit or declaration.[167] And international commercial arbitration generally leans still further in the direction of written, rather than oral, evidence.

(2) Rules of Evidence

The New York Convention does not create rules of evidence for arbitration. The same is true of the FAA; so in United States law arbitration's evidentiary rules (like other aspects of arbitration) are primarily determined by the arbitration agreement.[168] In a slight contrast, other national arbitration laws, particularly those based on the UNCITRAL Model Law, provide that "[t]he power conferred upon the arbitral tribunal includes the power to determine the admissibility, relevance, materiality and weight of any evidence."[169] This contrast is slight because allowing parties to determine evidentiary rules in their arbitration agreement reaches the same result as a statute giving arbitrators the power to decide evidentiary issues if, as is often true, parties agree to arbitrate pursuant to the rules of an arbitration organization that gives arbitrators the power to decide evidentiary issues. However, parties may not wish to give arbitrators complete discretion over evidentiary issues, so some arbitration clauses include an agreement that the arbitration be conducted according to the International Bar Association (IBA) Rules on the Taking of Evidence in International Commercial Arbitration.[170] "These rules provide a good harmonization of civil and common law approaches to taking evidence, and provide parties with a fair amount of certainty about the tribunal will deal with documents, witnesses, and experts."[171]

As in domestic United States arbitration, "technical rules of evidence are usually not observed" in international commercial arbitration and arbitrators tend to "err substantially on the side of permitting presentation of the facts that a party desires."[172] Rather than holding defective evidence inadmissible, arbitrators can just give it little or no weight. However, the IBA Rules noted in the previous paragraph give arbitrators the power to exclude evidence on

---

[167]   Instead of requiring an oral presentation in "open court," that is, the hearing itself.

[168]   See § 37(d).

[169]   Uncitral Model Law, Art. 19(2).

[170]   http://www.ibanet.org/Publications/publications_IBA_guides_and_free_materials.aspx

[171]   Moses, supra note 44, at 44–45.

[172]   Born, supra note 13, at 1853.

several grounds including irrelevance, privilege, and unreasonable burden.[173]

(3) No Hearing; Dispositive Motions

While much litigation in the United States ends on a grant of a motion to dismiss or for summary judgment, such motions are generally less likely to succeed in arbitration,[174] including international commercial arbitration. However, that does not mean a live hearing is required for an international commercial arbitration award to be enforceable in court. Just as domestic arbitration may result in a default award against a party who does not participate in arbitration, the same is true internationally.[175] A more difficult situation arises when arbitrators decide to forgo live testimony and decide the case on the documentary evidence submitted, despite a party's request for a live hearing. While there is some domestic United States authority in favor of confirming such awards,[176] a leading scholar of international commercial arbitration writes that "[o]ral hearings are mandatory in virtually all international arbitrations (save where the parties agree otherwise)."[177] "Failure to hear oral evidence, when requested by a party to do so, would invite a challenge to the resulting award for failure to afford the protesting party the opportunity to present its case."[178]

(4) Written Awards; Reasoned Opinions

While in some types of domestic arbitration the arbitrators' awards tend to be very brief and conclusory, international commercial awards tend to resemble the opinions issued by many courts—lengthy, "careful discussions of the parties' positions and the tribunal's factual and legal analysis."[179]

(d) Remedies

This book's discussion of remedies in domestic arbitration begins "Remedies, like other aspects of arbitration, are primarily determined by the arbitration agreement."[180] The same is true in

---

[173] IBA Rules on the Taking of Evidence, Art. 9(2).

[174] See § 37(e).

[175] Born, supra note 13, at 1865–68.

[176] See § 37(e).

[177] Born, supra note 13, at 1831. See id. at 2747 ("In some context, 'documents only' arbitrations are customary (conducted without oral hearings or testimony). Most national courts have rejected arguments that such procedures are necessarily procedurally improper or inadequate.")

[178] Id. at 1832.

[179] Id. at 1871.

[180] See § 38(a)(1).

international commercial arbitration.[181] While most international commercial arbitration awards are of money damages, courts in both common law and civil law jurisdictions "have routinely upheld [arbitrators'] grants of injunctive relief, including specific performance of contractual obligations."[182] In addition, "international arbitration tribunals generally possess (and exercise) the authority to award the prevailing party in an arbitration the costs of arbitration, including its legal costs."[183] In contrast, awards of punitive damages "are arguably contrary to public policy in some civil law jurisdictions."[184]

The above section on remedies in domestic arbitration noted that "arbitration is generally less suited than litigation as a forum for an emergency remedy, such as a temporary restraining order. This is because arbitration cannot award any remedy until an arbitrator has been appointed. The party against whom a restraining order is sought likely can delay that appointment until it does whatever the other party sought to restrain."[185] This problem applies as well in international commercial arbitration[186] so "parties to international arbitration agreements who require urgent provisional relief at the outset of a dispute must often seek the assistance of national courts."[187] Some (but probably a minority) of courts in the United States have been reluctant to provide such assistance on the ground that the purpose of the New York Convention is best carried out by restricting pre-arbitration judicial action to enforcement of executory arbitration agreements, that is, sending parties to arbitration.[188]

4. ENFORCEMENT AND VACATUR OF INTERNATIONAL COMMERCIAL ARBITRATION AWARDS
Table of Sections

---

[181]   Born, supra note 13, at 2478 ("The remedial powers of an international arbitral tribunal are defined in the first instance by the parties arbitration agreement. * * * Under most developed national arbitration regimes, arbitrators have broad discretion in fashioning relief.")

[182]   Id. at 2481.

[183]   Id. at 2488.

[184]   Id. at 2487.

[185]   See § 38(b). For attempts to remedy this problem, see Erin Collins, Pre-Tribunal Emergency Relief in International Commercial Arbitration, 10 Loy. U. Chi. Int'l L. Rev. 105 (2012).

[186]   Born, supra note 13, at 1970–71.

[187]   Id. at 2028–29.

[188]   Id. at 2030–37.

§ 71   Enforcement of International Arbitration Awards

The primary purpose of the New York Convention is to make arbitration awards rendered in one State enforceable in the courts of other States.[189] Accordingly, the Convention begins "[t]his Convention shall apply to the recognition and enforcement of arbitral awards made in the territory of a State other than the State where the recognition and enforcement of such awards are sought."[190] The Convention states that "[e]ach Contracting State shall recognize arbitral awards as binding and enforce them,"[191] and the Convention permits only a narrow list of grounds upon which "[r]ecognition and enforcement of the award may be refused."[192]

To recognize and enforce an award, the Convention prescribes a fairly quick and easy process:

    1.   To obtain the recognition and enforcement mentioned in the preceding article, the party applying for recognition and enforcement shall, at the time of the application, supply:

    (a)   The duly authenticated original award or a duly certified copy thereof;

    (b)   The original agreement referred to in article II or a duly certified copy thereof.

    2.   If the said award or agreement is not made in an official language of the country in which the award is relied upon, the party applying for recognition and enforcement of

---

[189]   Rau, Sherman & Peppet, supra note 5, at 960.
[190]   New York Convention, supra note 3, art. I(1).
[191]   Id. art. III.
[192]   Id. art. V. See § 72(b).

the award shall produce a translation of these documents into such language. The translation shall be certified by an official or sworn translator or by a diplomatic or consular agent.[193]

The speed and ease of this process is facilitated by national courts' "taking a practical and relatively flexible approach" to it,[194] for example by excusing non-compliance with the translation requirement where the award could nonetheless be comprehended by the court.[195]

The Convention's distinction between award recognition and enforcement generally relates to which party—claimant or respondent—prevailed in arbitration. Prevailing claimants typically seek award enforcement to collect the money or other remedy awarded in arbitration, while prevailing respondents typically seek award recognition to increase the award's finality and preclude further arbitration or litigation of the claim respondent defeated in arbitration.[196]

In implementing the New York Convention, Chapter 2 of the FAA provides:

> Within three years after an arbitral award falling under the Convention is made, any party to the arbitration may apply to any court having jurisdiction under this chapter for an order confirming the award as against any other party to the arbitration. The court shall confirm the award unless it finds one of the grounds for refusal or deferral of recognition or enforcement of the award specified in the said Convention.[197]

This provision enables federal[198] courts to confirm awards "falling under" the Convention.[199] For example, if an arbitration tribunal seated outside the United States awards the claimant money damages from the respondent and the respondent has assets in the United States then the claimant does not need to involve a

---

[193]　Id. art. IV.

[194]　Born, supra note 13, at 2703.

[195]　Born, supra note 13, at 2704.

[196]　Park, supra note 45, at 260.

[197]　9 U.S.C. § 207.

[198]　An action to confirm an award falling under the Convention triggers the original, but not exclusive, jurisdiction of the federal courts. 9 U.S.C. § 203. Such an action may be brought in state court but the defendant may then remove it to federal court. 9 U.S.C. § 205. See also Christopher R. Drahozal, The New York Convention and the American Federal System, 2012 J. Disp. Resol. 101, 109–111 (discussing application of FAA Chapter 2 in state court).

[199]　For a summary of the scope of the Convention, see § 63(a)(1).

court at the seat of the arbitration. The claimant can get a federal court to confirm the award, which converts the award into a judgment of the court.[200] A confirmed award is enforced in the same manner as other court judgments: through orders to turn over property, judicial liens, etc.

Conversely, if an arbitration tribunal seated in the United States awards the claimant money damages from the respondent and the respondent has assets abroad, say in England, then the claimant does not need to involve a U.S. court before seeking enforcement of the award by an English court.[201]

§ 72   Vacatur and Non-Enforcement of International Arbitration Awards

(a) Introduction: National Law of Vacatur

While the primary purpose of the New York Convention is to make arbitration awards rendered in one State enforceable in the courts of other States, Article V says that "[r]ecognition and enforcement of the award may be refused [if the award] has been set aside or suspended by a competent authority of the country in which, or under the law of which, that award was made."[202] As a result, a party displeased with an international arbitration award can get a national court (of the State that is the seat of the arbitration) to vacate ("set aside" or annul) the award and then use that vacatur as a defense to enforcement of the award in other States.[203] Crucially, the standards for vacatur are found, not in the New York Convention, but in the national law of the arbitration's seat.[204] For example,

---

[200]   See § 39.

[201]   Oriental Commercial & Shipping Co. v. Rosseel, N.V., 769 F. Supp. 514, 516 (S.D.N.Y. 1991) ("Under the Convention, it is no longer necessary to seek leave to enforce in the rendering jurisdiction: the party seeking to enforce an award may proceed directly to the jurisdiction in which it wishes to enforce the award and may apply directly to that jurisdiction's court for an order of enforcement.")

[202]   New York Convention, supra note 3, art. V(1)(e).

[203]   Born, supra note 13, at 2404 ("the Convention limits actions to annul to (a) the place where the arbitral award was made; and (b) if different, and only exceptionally, the state 'under the law of which' the award was made.")

[204]   "The choice of the seat of arbitration is effectively a choice of law with respect to judicial review of the award." William Laurence Craig, Uses and Abuses of Appeal from Awards, 4 Arb. Int'l 174, 178 (1988). Karaha Bodas Co., L.L.C. v. Perusahaan Pertambangan Minyak Dan Gas Bumi, 364 F.3d 274, 287–88 (5th Cir.2004) ("the courts of the country of the arbitral situs * * * may apply their own domestic law in evaluating a request to annul or set aside an arbitral award"). Compare Born, supra note 13, at 2554 (citing Yusuf Ahmed Alghanim & Sons v. Toys "R" Us, Inc., 126 F.3d 15, 22–23 (2d Cir.1997) ("Most national courts and commentators have * * * concluded that the New York Convention imposes no limits on the grounds with may be relied upon to annul an award in the arbitral seat."), with id. at 2556–60 (contending that "while this position is very widely repeated, it produces anomalous results which are very difficult to justify in light of the Conventions's overall structure and purposes.")

vacatur of an arbitration award rendered in Mexico City is governed by Mexican law and should only be done by a Mexican court.[205] Vacatur of an arbitration award rendered in New York is governed by FAA § 10 and should only be done by a United States court.[206]

While vacatur of an award by a court of the State that is the seat of arbitration nearly always prevents the award from being enforced by the courts of other States,[207] a rare and well-known exception involved an arbitration award in favor of a United States company against the Government of Egypt. The award was vacated by an Egyptian court but nevertheless enforced by a United States court in *Chromalloy Aeroservices v. Arab Republic of Egypt.*[208] The United States court said that, while Article V of the New York Convention says the United States court "*may*, at its discretion, decline to enforce the award," Article VII:

> *requires* that, "The provisions of the present Convention *shall not* . . . deprive any interested party of any right he may have to avail himself of an arbitral award in the manner and to the extent allowed by the law . . . of the count[r]y where such award is sought to be relied upon." 9 U.S.C. § 201 note (emphasis added). In other words, under the Convention, CAS [the United States company] maintains all rights to the enforcement of this Arbitral Award that it would have in the absence of the Convention. Accordingly, the Court finds that, if the Convention did not exist, the Federal Arbitration Act ("FAA") would provide CAS with a legitimate claim to enforcement of this arbitral award.[209]

Here, the *Chromalloy* court reasoned that the quoted language from Article VII of the Convention makes arbitration awards enforceable to the extent permitted by the domestic arbitration law of the State in which enforcement is sought even if the award has been set aside by a court at the seat of arbitration.[210] Perhaps it was

---

[205]   International Standard Elec. Corp. v. Bridas Sociedad Anonima Petrolera, Indus. Y Comercial, 745 F.Supp. 172 (S.D.N.Y.1990).

[206]   Yusuf Ahmed Alghanim & Sons v. Toys "R" Us, Inc., 126 F.3d 15, 21 (2d Cir.1997) ("We read Article V(1)(e) of the Convention to allow a court in the country under whose law the arbitration was conducted to apply domestic arbitral law, in this case the FAA, to a motion to set aside or vacate that arbitral award.")

[207]   "An arbitration award does not exist to be enforced in other Contracting States if it has been lawfully 'set aside' by a competent authority in the State in which the award was made." TermoRio S.A., E.S.P v. Electranta S.P, 487 F.3d 928, 936 (D.C. Cir. 2007).

[208]   939 F.Supp. 907 (D.D.C.1996).

[209]   Id. at 909–10.

[210]   For arguments against *Chromalloy*, see Rau, Sherman & Peppet, supra note 5, at 988.

relevant that, at least according to its lawyer, CAS "was able to show that Egyptian courts had a disturbing propensity to nullify awards in favor of foreign parties against Egyptians or its government for seemingly arbitrary reasons."[211] *Chromalloy* is not unique,[212] but courts generally decline to enforce under their own domestic arbitration law awards that have been vacated by a court of the State that is the seat of arbitration.[213]

In contrast, purported vacatur of an award by a court of a State *not* the seat of arbitration should *not* prevent enforcement of the award by the courts of any State.[214] In fact, the Convention does not even authorize a court to vacate or modify an award made in another State.[215] "The reason for this is evident from the limited purpose of the Convention[ ]: to effectuate the enforceability of awards in foreign nations outside the nation primarily legally responsible for the awards."[216]

To summarize, a party displeased with an international arbitration award has two ways to prevent or limit enforcement of the award. First, that party can try to persuade a court at the seat of arbitration to "set aside" (vacate), rather than confirm, the award. Vacatur by a court at the seat nearly always prevents enforcement of the award by the courts of any State. Second, even if the court at the

---

[211] Gary H. Sampliner, Enforcement of Foreign Arbitral Awards After Annulment in Their Country of Origin, 11 (9) Mealey's Int'l Arb.Rep., Sept.1996, at 22, 28.

[212] W. Laurence Craig, Some Trends and Developments in the Laws and Practice of International Commercial Arbitration, 30 Tex.Int'l L.J. 1, 32 (1995) ("the French statute does not permit nonenforcement on the ground that the award has been set aside by the courts of the country where the arbitration took place. Instead of automatic nonenforcement, the French court will independently examine any reasons for nonrecognition, including the reasons which led to its annulment abroad, in the exercise of its control function.")

[213] See, e.g., Baker Marine (Nig.) Ltd. v. Chevron (Nig.) Ltd., 191 F.3d 194 (2d Cir.1999) (distinguishing *Chromalloy* and affirming district court holding that "it would not be proper to enforce a foreign arbitral award [rendered in Nigeria] under the Convention when such an award has been set aside by the Nigerian courts."); Spier v. Calzaturificio Tecnica, S.p.A., 77 F.Supp.2d 405 (S.D.N.Y.1999).

[214] See Karaha Bodas Co., L.L.C. v. Perusahaan Pertambangan Minyak Dan Gas Bumi Negara, 364 F.3d 274 (5th Cir.2004) (Swiss court refused to set aside arbitration award made in Switzerland but then Indonesian court purported to set it aside; Fifth Circuit held that Indonesian court's ruling could not a be a defense to enforcement under the New York Convention: "there is only one national court system that has jurisdiction to consider an application for annulment of an award."). Accord W. Michael Reisman, Systems of Control in International Adjudication and Arbitration: Breakdown and Repair 114 (1992).

[215] Macneil, Speidel & Stipanowich, supra note 14, § 44.40.1.3, at 44:272; Tesoro Petroleum Corp. v. Asamera (South Sumatra) Ltd., 798 F.Supp. 400, 405 (W.D.Tex.1992) (the Convention "not appear to this Court to authorize a suit to be initiated for the purpose of vacating an arbitral award, but instead sets forth the specific, limited circumstances in which, in a suit to enforce an award, a court may decline to do so.")

[216] Macneil, Speidel & Stipanowich, supra note 14, § 44.40.1.3, at 44:273.

seat of arbitration confirms the award, that confirmation only makes the award enforceable in that State so the party displeased with the award can seek to prevent other States' courts from recognizing and enforcing it.[217] This second topic of enforcement (but not the first topic of vacatur) is governed by the New York Convention, which provides:

1. Recognition and enforcement of the award may be refused, at the request of the party against whom it is invoked, only if that party furnishes to the competent authority where the recognition and enforcement is sought, proof that:

(a) The parties to the agreement referred to in article II were, under the law applicable to them, under some incapacity, or the said agreement is not valid under the law to which the parties have subjected it or, failing any indication thereon, under the law of the country where the award was made; or

(b) The party against whom the award is invoked was not given proper notice of the appointment of the arbitrator or of the arbitration proceedings or was otherwise unable to present his case; or

(c) The award deals with a difference not contemplated by or not falling within the terms of the submission to arbitration, or it contains decisions on matters beyond the scope of the submission to arbitration, provided that, if the decisions on matters submitted to arbitration can be separated from those not so submitted, that part of the award which contains decisions on matters submitted to arbitration may be recognized and enforced; or

(d) The composition of the arbitral authority or the arbitral procedure was not in accordance with the agreement of the parties, or, failing such agreement, was not in accordance with the law of the country where the arbitration took place; or

(e) The award has not yet become binding on the parties, or has been set aside or suspended by a competent authority of the country in which, or under the law of which, that award was made.

2. Recognition and enforcement of an arbitral award may also be refused if the competent authority in the

---

[217] As noted above, confirmation by the seat is not required before a court outside the seat can enforce an award. See § 71.

country where recognition and enforcement is sought finds that:

(a) The subject matter of the difference is not capable of settlement by arbitration under the law of that country; or

(b) The recognition or enforcement of the award would be contrary to the public policy of that country.

These grounds for denying recognition and enforcement to awards are permissive. The Convention does not require States to invoke the grounds in Article V, but merely permits States to.[218] Occasionally, "national courts have recognized awards where the Convention imposed no obligation to do so."[219]

The Convention's grounds for denying recognition and enforcement are discussed in the following subsections.

(b) The Convention's Grounds for Non-Enforcement of Award

(1) Arbitration Agreement Invalid

Article V(1)(a) of the New York Convention says recognition and enforcement of an arbitration award may be refused if "The parties to the agreement referred to in article II were, under the law applicable to them, under some incapacity, or the said agreement is not valid under the law to which the parties have subjected it or, failing any indication thereon, under the law of the country where the award was made."[220] This provision refers to and relates to Article II, which generally requires enforcement of executory arbitration agreements. While Article V(1)(a) has a choice-of-law rule not found in Article II,[221] generally, "the same substantive analysis that applies in the context of the enforcement of [executory] arbitration agreements is equally applicable in resolving an application to recognize [or deny enforcement to] an arbitral

---

[218] Born, supra note 13, at 2722–23 ("The English language text of Article V is unmistakably permissive, providing that Contracting States *"may"* refuse recognition of an award").

[219] Id. at 2725.

[220] New York Convention, supra note 3, art. V(1)(a).

[221] Article V(1)(a) provides that enforcement of an award may be refused if the arbitration "agreement is not valid under the law to which the parties have subjected it or, failing any indication thereon, under the law of the country where the award was made." Under this choice-of-law rule, the relevant State's law is the law the parties have chosen in a choice-of-law clause ("the law to which the parties have subjected it") or, if there is no party choice of law, then the relevant State's law is the law of the country where the award was made, that is, the "seat" of arbitration.

award."[222] That analysis is summarized above in the context of the enforcement of executory arbitration agreements.[223] An example at the award-enforcement stage is *Sarhank Group v. Oracle Corp.*,[224] in which the Second Circuit held that a district court could find that a parent corporation was not bound by its subsidiary's agreement to arbitrate.[225] Another case denied recognition and enforcement of an arbitration award on the ground that there was no "exchange of letters" or other agreement to arbitrate as required by Article II of the New York Convention.[226]

(2) Inadequate Opportunity to Present Case

Article V(1)(b) of the New York Convention says recognition and enforcement of an arbitration award may be refused if "[t]he party against whom the award is invoked was not given proper notice of the appointment of the arbitrator or of the arbitration proceedings or was otherwise unable to present his case."[227] Some courts have read this provision to "essentially sanction[ ] the application of the forum state's standards of due process."[228] In contrast, a leading commentator says this provision "is best viewed as providing the basis for uniform international standards of procedural fairness" and "[m]ost authorities have held that Article V(1)(b) must be applied in light of the Convention's general pro-enforcement objectives."[229]

Nevertheless, some cases rely on Article V(1)(b) in denying enforcement to an arbitration award. These cases include facts like: lack of an oral hearing,[230] inadequate notice of the hearing,[231] and denial of an opportunity to present evidence. In an example of the latter, the Second Circuit held that arbitrators (the Iran-United

---

[222] Born, supra note 13, at 2780. But see China Minmetals Materials Import and Export Co., Ltd. v. Chi Mei Corp., 334 F.3d 274 (3d Cir.2003) ("there is indeed some distinction between Article II and Article V. The former explicitly requires an 'agreement in writing' while the latter requires only that the parties have reached an agreement as to arbitrability under ordinary contract principles.")

[223] See §§ 63–65.

[224] 404 F.3d 657 (2d Cir.2005).

[225] Id. at 662–63 (remand[ing] to the district court to find as a fact whether Oracle agreed to arbitrate, by its actions or inaction, or by reason of any action of Systems [Oracle's subsidiary] as to which Oracle clothed Systems with apparent or actual authority to consent on its behalf to arbitration, or on any other basis recognized by American contract law or the law of agency").

[226] Dynamo v. Ovechkin, 412 F.Supp.2d 24 (D.D.C.2006).

[227] New York Convention, supra note 3, art. V(1)(b).

[228] Parsons & Whittemore Overseas Co., Inc. v. Societe Generale De L'Industrie du Papier (RAKTA), 508 F.2d 969, 975 (2d Cir.1974). Accord Karaha Bodas Co., L.L.C. v. Perusahaan Pertambangan Minyak Dan Gas Bumi, 364 F.3d 274, 298 (5th Cir.2004).

[229] Born, supra note 13, at 2738.

[230] See § 70(c)(3).

[231] Born, supra note 13, at 2750.

States Claims Tribunal[232]) denied a party (Avco) the opportunity to present its claim by first "approving the method of proof proposed by Avco, namely the submission of Avco's audited accounts receivable ledgers," and then ruling against Avco because it did not submit actual invoices.[233] Apart from such cases, showing that a party lacked an opportunity to present its case may require a fact-intensive inquiry about the extent to which arbitrators can reasonably be expected to accommodate the schedule of a party or its witnesses, and courts generally defer to arbitrators' judgment about the timing and conduct of the arbitration proceedings.[234]

(3) Arbitrators Exceeded Their Jurisdiction

Article V(1)(c) of the New York Convention says recognition and enforcement of an arbitration award may be refused if

> The award deals with a difference not contemplated by or not falling within the terms of the submission to arbitration, or it contains decisions on matters beyond the scope of the submission to arbitration, provided that, if the decisions on matters submitted to arbitration can be separated from those not so submitted, that part of the award which contains decisions on matters submitted to arbitration may be recognized and enforced.[235]

This ground for non-enforcement resembles FAA § 10(a)(4), which permits courts to vacate an arbitration award where, among other things, "the arbitrators exceeded their powers."[236] Courts and commentators generally speak interchangeably of arbitrators exceeding their powers, exceeding their authority, or exceeding their jurisdiction. Importantly, however, whether one calls it the arbitrators' "power," or "authority," or "jurisdiction," it comes from the parties.[237] It is jurisdiction conferred by contract, not by statute or other law, so arbitrators exceed this jurisdiction when they decide

---

[232]   The Iran-United States Claims Tribunal is discussed further in § 76.

[233]   Iran Aircraft Industries v. Avco Corp., 980 F.2d 141 (2d Cir.1992) ("Having thus led Avco to believe it had used a proper method to substantiate its claim, the Tribunal then rejected Avco's claim for lack of proof. * * *We believe that by so misleading Avco, however unwittingly, the Tribunal denied Avco the opportunity to present its claim in a meaningful manner.")

[234]   Parsons & Whittemore Overseas Co., Inc. v. Societe Generale De L'Industrie du Papier (RAKTA), 508 F.2d 969, 973–74 (2d Cir.1974) (rejecting Article V(1)(b) argument).

[235]   New York Convention, supra note 3, art. V(1)(c).

[236]   9 U.S.C. § 10(a)(4). Parsons, 508 F.2d at 976 (Article V(1)(c) "tracks in more detailed form" FAA § 10(a)(4). "Both provisions basically allow a party to attack an award predicated upon arbitration of a subject matter not within the agreement to submit to arbitration.")

[237]   See §§ 43(d), 44.

matters beyond the scope of the arbitration agreement. This is clear in Article V(1)(c) of the New York Convention which refers to "matters beyond the scope of the submission to arbitration."

Courts will enforce an arbitration award on a claim only if the parties agreed to arbitrate that claim. That the parties agreed to arbitrate *some* claim is not enough. They must have agreed to arbitrate *that* claim.[238] However, courts generally presume that the arbitrators acted within their powers,[239] and rarely decline to enforce awards as beyond the submission to arbitration.[240] Parties often take this issue away from courts by giving it to arbitrators. That is, parties often agree to arbitrate pursuant to an arbitration organization's rules giving the arbitrators power to decide whether particular claims are within the scope of the arbitration agreement.[241] Where parties have done this, the arbitrators' "jurisdictional decision should generally not be subject to subsequent judicial review."[242]

(4) Improper Arbitral Procedure or Composition of Arbitral Authority

Article V(1)(d) of the New York Convention says recognition and enforcement of an arbitration award may be refused if "[t]he composition of the arbitral authority or the arbitral procedure was not in accordance with the agreement of the parties, or, failing such agreement, was not in accordance with the law of the country where the arbitration took place."[243] The gist of this provision is that arbitration procedure is a matter of contract; it is governed by the parties' agreement and if that agreement has gaps the law of the seat of arbitration fills those gaps. Cases relying on Article V(1)(d) in

---

[238]   Like that ground of the FAA, this ground of the Convention relates to the "contractual arbitrability (scope of arbitration agreement)" topic discussed in a previous chapter. See §§ 30–31.

[239]   Management & Technical Consultants S.A. v. Parsons-Jurden Intern. Corp., 820 F.2d 1531, 1534 (9th Cir.1987) (stating, in a case to enforce a foreign arbitral award, "Federal arbitration law has established a presumption that an arbitral body has acted within its powers"); *Parsons*, 508 F.2d at 976 (referring to the "powerful presumption that the arbitral body acted within its powers."); Whirlpool Corp. v. Philips Electronics, N.V., 848 F.Supp. 474, 480 (S.D.N.Y.1994) (arbitrator's "decision as to the scope of its arbitral authority is entitled to deference").

[240]   Albert Jan van den Berg, New York Convention of 1958: Refusals of Enforcement, 18(2) ICC Int'l Ct. Arb. Bull. 15, 24 (2007) (finding only two reported cases, neither of which was from the United States).

[241]   "As a practical matter, parties in many international commercial arbitration will be found to have submitted disputes over the scope of their arbitration clause to the arbitrators for resolution. That is in large part because the terms of most institutional arbitration rules expressly provide that jurisdictional questions are for arbitral resolution." Born, supra note 13, at 932. See, e.g., International Chamber of Commerce Rules of Arbitration, Art. 6, https://iccwbo.org/dispute-resolution-services/arbitration/rules-of-arbitration/#article_6.

[242]   Born, supra note 13, at 2802.

[243]   New York Convention, supra note 3, art. V(1)(d).

denying enforcement to an arbitration award include facts such as the arbitrators' failure to:

- render an award or conduct the proceedings within prescribed time limits,

- conduct the arbitration in the agreed arbitral seat,

- make a reasoned award,

- apply agreed rules of procedure, or

- apply provisions regarding consolidation of arbitrations.[244]

That said, courts are generally reluctant (even in cases with facts like those just listed) to overturn awards for arbitrators' minor violations of agreed procedures.

A leading commentator states that "the most difficult issues that arise under Article V(1)(d) involve cases where the parties' agreed arbitral procedures violate the mandatory laws of the arbitral seat,"[245] and "the weight of authority is that for purposes of Article V(1)(d), the parties' agreed arbitral procedures must be given effect, regardless of the law of the arbitral seat."[246] "Under Article V(1)(d), the procedural law of the arbitral seat may only serve to supplement gaps in the parties' agreement, not to override or nullify that agreement."[247] However, whether a particular agreement contains a gap on a particular topic can be a matter of dispute. Like other aspects of contract interpretation, reasonable people can disagree in close cases.

(5) Set Aside by Court at Seat of Arbitration

Article V(1)(e) of the New York Convention says recognition and enforcement of an arbitration award may be refused if "The award has not yet become binding on the parties, or has been set aside or suspended by a competent authority of the country in which, or under the law of which, that award was made."[248] Whether a particular award has "become binding on the parties" can be in some cases be debated, but confirmation of an award by a court in the arbitral seat is not necessary to make an award binding.[249] Courts generally hold

---

[244] Born, supra note 13, at 2765–66.
[245] Id. at 2768.
[246] Id.
[247] Id.
[248] New York Convention, supra note 3, art. V(1)(e).
[249] Born, supra note 13, at 2818–19.

awards to be binding even when a party displeased with the award might seek to have it set aside by a court in the arbitral seat.[250]

The setting aside of an arbitration award by a court at the seat of arbitration is discussed above.[251] A related provision is Article VI of the Convention which provides:

> If an application for the setting aside or suspension of the award has been made to a competent authority referred to in article V(1)(e), the authority before which the award is sought to be relied upon may, if it considers it proper, adjourn the decision on the enforcement of the award and may also, on the application of the party claiming enforcement of the award, order the other party to give suitable security.[252]

At least one United States court has adjourned its enforcement pending a decision by a court at the seat of arbitration, India, on whether to set aside the award.[253]

(6) Inarbitrability (Non-Arbitrability)

Article V(2)(a) of the New York Convention says recognition and enforcement of an arbitration award may be refused if "the competent authority in the country where recognition and enforcement is sought finds that: The subject matter of the difference is not capable of settlement by arbitration under the law of that country."[254] This provision relates to Article II(1), discussed above, which requires enforcement of agreements to arbitrate only disputes "concerning a subject matter capable of settlement by arbitration."[255] Generally, "if arbitration of a claim cannot be compelled under Article II(1), because it is non-arbitrable, then an arbitral award dealing with that claim is unenforceable under Article V(2)(a), subject only to possible

---

[250] Id. at 2819.

[251] See § 72(a).

[252] New York Convention, supra note 3, art. VI.

[253] Fertilizer Corp. of India v. IDI Management, Inc., 517 F.Supp. 948, 956–59 (S.D.Ohio 1981) ("The award is presently before the Indian courts for a ruling."); id. at 962 ("this Court has determined to adjourn its decision on enforcement of the Nitrophosphate Award until the Indian courts decide with finality whether the award is correct under Indian law. FCI, of course, may apply to this Court for suitable security, as provided by Article VI.") See also Europcar Italia, S.p.A. v. Maiellano Tours, Inc., 156 F.3d 310, 317–18 (2d Cir. 1998) (listing factors courts should consider when deciding whether to adjourn enforcement proceedings to await the outcome of parallel foreign proceedings).

[254] New York Convention, supra note 3, art. V(2)(a).

[255] See § 67.

waiver arguments."[256] Inarbitrability has not often been relied on by courts in declining enforcement of awards.[257]

(7) Public Policy

Article V(2)(b) of the New York Convention says recognition and enforcement of an arbitration award may be refused if "the competent authority in the country where recognition and enforcement is sought finds that * * * [t]he recognition or enforcement of the award would be contrary to the public policy of that country."[258] This provision has been interpreted narrowly by United States courts. As the Second Circuit recognized long ago,

> [a]n expansive construction of this defense would vitiate the Convention's basic effort to remove preexisting obstacles to enforcement. Additionally, considerations of reciprocity—considerations given express recognition in the Convention itself—counsel courts to invoke the public policy defense with caution lest foreign courts frequently accept it as a defense to enforcement of arbitral awards rendered in the United States.[259]

Therefore, the court held "enforcement of foreign arbitral awards may be denied on this basis only where enforcement would violate the forum state's most basic notions of morality and justice."[260] Similarly, one commentator observes that courts, especially in developed countries, exercise "a substantial degree of restraint and moderation in the application of public policies under Article V(2)(b)."[261] In contrast, "some less-developed states have taken relatively expansive views of public policy, relying on the doctrine's 'unruly' character to refuse recognition to foreign arbitral awards on a variety of grounds."[262]

---

[256] Born, supra note 13, at 2863. However, if non-enforcement of an award (Art. V) is sought in a different State than non-enforcement of an executory agreement (Art. II) than different standards may apply.

[257] Jan van den Berg, supra note 240, at 1.

[258] New York Convention, supra note 3, Art. V(2)(b).

[259] Parsons & Whittemore Overseas Co., Inc. v. Societe Generale De L'Industrie du Papier (RAKTA), 508 F.2d 969, 973–74 (2d Cir.1974). Accord Fertilizer Corp. of India v. IDI Management, Inc., 517 F.Supp. 948 (S.D.Ohio 1981).

[260] *Parsons*, 508 F2d. at 974. For an example, see Karen Mar. Ltd. v. Omar Int'l, Inc., 322 F. Supp. 2d 224, 229 (E.D.N.Y. 2004) (contract undertaking to boycott Israel violated U.S. anti-boycott law; "if [e]nforcement of the award * * * legitimized or perpetuated the Arab boycott of Israel, [enforcement] would violate basic American notions of morality and justice.")

[261] Born, supra note 13, at 2833.

[262] Id. at 2859.

§ 73   Overview of International Public Law Arbitration

International arbitration is commonly divided into commercial arbitration and public law arbitration. Of the two, international commercial arbitration is more similar to the domestic arbitration discussed earlier in this book.[263] Most basically, this book began by defining arbitration as private (non-government) adjudication.[264] It said "the essence of arbitration is that it is a private-sector alternative to government courts." This basic point applies just as broadly to international commercial arbitration as it does to domestic arbitration.[265] In the international commercial context, "[w]hen parties agree to arbitrate their disputes, they give up the right to have those disputes decided by a national court. Instead, they agree that their disputes will be resolved privately, outside any court system."[266]

By contrast, in the international public law context the word "arbitration" is not typically used to describe a private-sector alternative to government courts. International public law disputes often involve claims by and against States. These are generally claims for which there is no national court with jurisdiction to enter judgment against the defending State because the doctrine of sovereign immunity prevents such jurisdiction.[267] So when States

---

[263]   Macneil, Speidel & Stipanowich, supra note 14, § 44.1.1, at 44:18.

[264]   See supra § 1, n.1.

[265]   Born, supra note 13, at 221 ("The non-governmental identity of the decision-maker is a fundamental, distinguishing feature of 'arbitration' agreements.")

[266]   Moses, supra note 44, at 17.

[267]   See, e.g., Andreas F. Lowenfeld, International Litigation and Arbitration ch.7 (3d ed.2006). Sovereign immunity is less of a force in commercial arbitration than in public law arbitration because sovereign immunity often does not protect a State insofar as it is engaged in "commercial," rather than governmental, activity. See, e.g., 28 U.S.C. § 1605.

A foreign state shall not be immune from the jurisdiction of courts of the United States or of the States in any case—

"arbitrate" their *public law* disputes with each other, they are not giving up the right to have those disputes decided by a national court because they never had any such right. International public law arbitration is not an alternative to international litigation, but rather an alternative to the other ways States interact, such as diplomacy and war. The same is also generally true of public international law arbitration involving claims against States by private parties who are citizens of different States; for example, investment arbitration generally involves claims that would otherwise be barred by sovereign immunity.

Because the claims in public international law arbitration are generally against States, enforcement of an award arising out of such arbitration may face an obstacle not likely present in international commercial arbitration, let alone domestic arbitration: how does a party enforce an arbitration award against a State whose national courts are part of the State and thus share the State's opposition to enforcement of the award?

* * *

(1) in which the foreign state has waived its immunity either explicitly or by implication, notwithstanding any withdrawal of the waiver which the foreign state may purport to effect except in accordance with the terms of the waiver;

(2) in which the action is based upon a *commercial activity* carried on in the United States by the foreign state; or upon an act performed in the United States in connection with a commercial activity of the foreign state elsewhere; or upon an act outside the territory of the United States in connection with a *commercial activity* of the foreign state elsewhere and that act causes a direct effect in the United States;

* * *

(6) in which the action is brought, either to enforce an agreement made by the foreign state with or for the benefit of a private party to submit to arbitration all or any differences which have arisen or which may arise between the parties with respect to a defined legal relationship, whether contractual or not, concerning a subject matter capable of settlement by arbitration under the laws of the United States, or to confirm an award made pursuant to such an agreement to arbitrate, if (A) the arbitration takes place or is intended to take place in the United States, (B) the agreement or award is or may be governed by a treaty or other international agreement in force for the United States calling for the recognition and enforcement of arbitral awards, (C) the underlying claim, save for the agreement to arbitrate, could have been brought in a United States court under this section or section 1607, or (D) paragraph (1) of this subsection is otherwise applicable.

Id. § 1605(a) (emphasis added). See also Cargill Intern. S.A. v. M/T Pavel Dybenko, 991 F.2d 1012, 1018 (2d Cir.1993) ("the [New York] Convention is exactly the sort of treaty Congress intended to include in the arbitration exception" of 28 U.S.C.§ 1605(a)(6).); 9 U.S.C. § 15 ("Enforcement of arbitral agreements, confirmation of arbitral awards, and execution upon judgments based on orders confirming such awards shall not be refused on the basis of the Act of State doctrine.")

Public international arbitration agreements can be divided into three types.[268] The first consists of an arbitration clause that is included in a treaty with the purpose of resolving disputes regarding the application of that treaty. A prominent example of this first type is investment arbitration. The second type of public international arbitration agreement "consists of treaties whose sole function is to establish a method for the resolution and arbitration of whatever disputes might arise between the parties in the future."[269] And the third type consists of post-dispute arbitration agreements, such as the one establishing the Iran-U.S. Claims Tribunal.[270] These three types of public international law arbitration are discussed in the following three sections.

§ 74 Investment Arbitration

The parties to major transnational business transactions often consist entirely of private-sector businesses based in the most economically-developed parts of the world. The contracts facilitating such transactions often have a clause providing for international *commercial* arbitration of any disputes. In contrast, other transnational business transactions involve a country's government (a State) as a party. This is especially likely when the transaction will exploit natural resources or require a large investment (e.g., mining) in a less-developed country.[271] With at least one State as a party, arbitration arising out of such transactions is international *public law* arbitration, and commonly falls under the heading of "investment arbitration."[272]

---

[268] Thomas Buergenthal & Sean D. Murphy, Public International Law in a Nutshell 71–72 (4th ed.2007).

[269] Id. at 71.

[270] Id. at 72.

[271] Rau, Sherman & Peppet, supra note 5, at 628–29 ("In many countries the government assumes a far more active role in economic transactions—particularly those involving capital investment and the exploitation and development of national resources—than it does in the United States."); Julian D. Lew, Loukas A. Mistelis & Stefan M. Kroll, Comparative International Commercial Arbitration 764 (2003) ("The investment may be considerable which may need years for the investor to recover. In developing countries foreign investment often relates to core components of the national economy. These factors make foreign investment particularly vulnerable to possible interference by the host state.").

[272] Strong, supra note 62, at 124 ("international commercial arbitration is a private dispute resolution mechanism that relies heavily on the agreement of the parties, both as a means of demonstrating consent to arbitration and as a way of describing the shape of the proceedings. * * * International investment arbitration, on the other hand, is a treaty-based procedure that is rooted in public international law."); Irene M. Ten Cate, International Arbitration and the Ends of Appellate Review 44 N.Y.U. J. Int'l L. & Pol. 1109, 1113 (2012) ("The paradigmatic commercial arbitration case involves contract claims arising out of business transactions between private parties. Investment disputes, on the other hand, always involve claims against state party respondents concerning their interference with investments made by foreign

While international *commercial* arbitration arises out of an ordinary contract between the parties, (either a pre-dispute arbitration agreement or a post-dispute submission agreement,) the "contract" underlying investment arbitration is typically quite different. Generally, the State in which the investment occurred (the "host" State) previously consented to arbitration by acceding (agreeing) to a treaty providing for the arbitration of investment disputes or by enacting similar legislation. Such a treaty or legislation "constitute[s] a unilateral standing offer" to arbitrate disputes with any investor fulfilling the requirements of the treaty or legislation.[273]

> In what amounts to a sophisticated choice of forum clause, some treaties require investors to choose between litigating their treaty claims in national courts and arbitrating their investment claims before an arbitral panel * * * . Other treaties require investors to arbitrate their claims, but let the investors choose the arbitral body that will administer the dispute.

> Investors have overwhelmingly accepted Sovereigns' standing offers to arbitrate.[274]

States typically agree to investment arbitration to attract foreign investment.[275] Historically, investors had been vulnerable to host State seizure of assets (expropriation) or regulation tantamount to expropriation.[276] The doctrine of sovereign immunity might prevent investors from bringing a claim against the host State in the investor's home courts[277] or the courts of the host State.[278] The only remedy available to the investor would be diplomatic or military support from its home State against the host State. With investors' home states generally reluctant to do this,[279] investors continued to fear expropriation and similar actions by host states. Reducing these fears is a goal of international investment treaties and their arbitration provisions. Relatedly, collecting on an international

---

investors (often, but not always, in state-sponsored projects). The private-public distinction also holds true for the sources that govern the disputes.")

[273] Lew, Mistelis & Kroll, supra note 271, at 764.

[274] Susan D. Franck, The Nature and Enforcement of Investor Rights Under Investment Treaties: Do Investment Treaties Have a Bright Future, 12 U.C.Davis J.Int'l L. & Pol'y 47, 54–55 (2005). "The offer is accepted by the investor when it initiates arbitration proceedings against the state." Lew, Mistelis & Kroll, supra note 271, at 764.

[275] Christopher F. Dugan et al., Investor-State Arbitration 6 (2008).

[276] Jeswald W. Salacuse, The Law of Investment Treaties 285 (2010).

[277] Dugan et al., supra note 275, at 20–21.

[278] Id. at 14.

[279] See id. at 29.

investment arbitration award against a State "may be difficult, but political repercussions of treaty-based arbitration claims have compelled countries to honor awards—obviating the investor's need to pursue collection through the courts."[280]

The terms of international investment treaties vary. In most, host states do not forego a right of expropriation altogether.[281] Rather, host states limit the circumstances where expropriation can take place and provide for compensating the foreign investor.[282] Host states agree to provide foreign investors with the better of treatment provided to investments of nationals of the host State or of investments of nationals of any other country.[283] Investment treaties usually prohibit the host country from requiring the investment project to export a percentage of its production, use local content, or hire local workers.[284] Investment treaties ensure that the investor can transfer money freely between the host State and the investor's home State.[285]

The number of parties to international investment treaties varies. Some involve only two countries, that is, they are bilateral investment treaties (BITs). A typical BIT obligates the host State to provide foreign investors protection against various forms of expropriation and discrimination by the State.[286] For example, in the Supreme Court's 2014 case of *BG Grp., PLC v. Republic of Argentina*, a British investor in Argentina argued "that Argentina's new laws and regulatory practices violated provisions in the [BIT] forbidding the 'expropriation' of investments and requiring that each nation give 'fair and equitable treatment' to investors from the other."[287]

---

[280]   Michael S. Greco & Ian Meredith, Getting to Yes Abroad: Arbitration as a Tool in Effective Commercial and Political Risk Management, Bus.L.Today, March/April 2007, at 23, 25. For a different view, see Joseph M. Cardosi, Precluding the Treasure Hunt: How the World Bank Group Can Help Investors Circumnavigate Sovereign Immunity Obstacles to Icsid Award Execution, 41 Pepp. L. Rev. 125, 126–27 (2013) (although a State agreeing to arbitration "acts as a waiver of sovereign immunity as to jurisdiction, prevailing investors may encounter the obstacle of sovereign immunity following the arbitration when attempting to execute an award against a noncompliant state. If a state refuses to comply with an award, investors must set off on a worldwide search for assets held by that state; if and when investors find state assets, they must overcome the obstacle of sovereign immunity laws governing access to those assets.")

[281]   Salacuse, supra note 276, at 288.

[282]   Id.

[283]   Id. at 245.

[284]   Id. at 329.

[285]   Id. at 256–57.

[286]   Greco & Meredith, supra note 280, at 26. "To facilitate the flow of capital to lesser-developed countries, the United States and other Western nations have entered into more than 2,800 BITs with capital-importing countries. A critical feature of these treaties is that they protect the foreign investor against expropriation or other conduct." Peter B. Rutledge, Arbitration and the Constitution 51–52 (2013).

[287]   BG Grp., PLC v. Republic of Argentina, 134 S.Ct. 1198, 1204 (2014).

Some BITs commit the host State to arbitrate a broad array of claims by foreign investors, while others are more narrow. Some treaties allow investors to choose[288] whether the arbitration will be unadministered (ad hoc) arbitration under the UNCITRAL rules or administered by an organization such as the International Chamber of Commerce (ICC)[289] or the International Centre for Settlement of Investment Disputes (ICSID). ICSID was created by the World Bank to resolve investment disputes,[290] and (unlike arbitration awards under the New York Convention,) "ICSID awards are directly enforceable in signatory states, without any method of review in national courts."[291] Instead, when a party challenges an ICSID award, the Chairman of the Administrative Council of ICSID can appoint an ad hoc committee to review, and possibly annul (vacate), awards.[292]

Investment arbitration arises not only from BITs but also from broader treaties on international trade, such as the North American Free Trade Agreement (NAFTA) involving the United States, Canada and Mexico. Chapter 11 of NAFTA gives investors of one contracting State the right to initiate binding arbitration against another contracting State under the ICSID Convention, the ICSID Additional Facility Rules, or as an ad hoc arbitration under UNCITRAL Rules.[293] NAFTA arbitration awards are enforceable in domestic courts.[294]

§ 75 Treaties Focused on Arbitration of Future Public Law Disputes

The Permanent Court of Arbitration (PCA) was established by the 1899 Hague Convention on the Pacific Settlement of International Disputes.[295] "It is not really a court since it is not composed of a fixed body of judges."[296] Rather, it is a panel of persons nominated by the (hundred or so) contracting States. "Where contracting states wish to go to arbitration, they are entitled to choose the members of the tribunal from the panel. Thus, [the PCA]

---

[288] Franck, supra note 274, at 54–55.

[289] See supra note 63 and accompanying text.

[290] Born, supra note 13, at 105.

[291] Id. at 106.

[292] Id.

[293] North American Free Trade Agreement, art. 1120, Jan. 1, 1994, available at http://www.sice.oas.org/Trade/NAFTA/NAFTATCE.ASP.

[294] See, e.g., International Thunderbird Gaming Corp. v. United Mexican States, 473 F.Supp.2d 80 (D.D.C.2007), aff'd, 255 Fed.Appx. 531 (D.C.Cir.2007).

[295] For the text of the Convention of July 29, 1989, see Treaties and Other International Agreements of the United States of America 1776–1949, Vol. I, 230–46 (Charles I. Bevans ed., 1968).

[296] Malcom N. Shaw, International Law 953 (5th ed.2003).

is in essence machinery facilitating the establishment of arbitral tribunals."[297] The PCA says its caseload includes "territorial, treaty, and human rights disputes between states, as well as commercial and investment disputes."[298] The PCA's website contains a partial list of its cases; that list shows no cases between 1935 and 1998, but dozens of cases more recently.[299]

The International Court of Justice (ICJ), also known as World Court, was created as part of the United Nations in 1945. Judges are elected to it when they receive a majority vote in each of the U.N. Security Council and General Assembly.[300] Only States may be parties to contentious (as opposed to advisory) cases before the ICJ[301] and "the most common, and uncontroversial, way for the Court to receive a case" is through the parties' agreement to submit their existing dispute to the ICJ.[302] This post-dispute arbitration agreement is often used for matters, such as boundary disputes, in which "[b]oth sides are prepared to lose [the dispute], in effect, so submitting it to the adjudication of the Court provides a valuable, 'face-saving' device for an embattled government."[303] An increasing number of pre-dispute agreements to resolve disputes before the ICJ are found in various treaties.[304] Examples include the 1948 Genocide Convention, the 1965 Convention on Investment Disputes, the 1965 Convention on the Elimination of All Forms of Racial Discrimination, and the 1970 Hague Convention on Hijacking.[305]

Compliance with ICJ decisions has been characterized in a variety of ways. While some see "the record of compliance" as "only marginally satisfactory,"[306] others say that States have generally, but not always, complied with ICJ decisions.[307] Perhaps all can agree that ICJ decisions have an impact "on a political level," and thus

---

[297]   Id.

[298]   http://www.pca-cpa.org/showpage.asp?pag_id=1027.

[299]   http://www.pca-cpa.org/showpage.asp?pag_id=1029.

[300]   "The ICJ adjudicates two types of cases: contentious and advisory. In contentious cases, only states may be parties. Statute of the International Court of Justice, Stat 1055, 33 UN Treaty Ser 993, Art 34 (June 26, 1945) (ICJ Statute). In contrast, an advisory opinion may be given in response to 'any legal question at the request of whatever body may be authorized by or in accordance with the Charter of the United Nations to make such a request.' Id at Art 65." Michael P. Scharf & Margaux Day, The International Court of Justice's Treatment of Circumstantial Evidence and Adverse Inferences, 13 Chi. J. Int'l L. 123 (2012).

[301]   Shaw, supra note 296, at 972.

[302]   Id. at 254.

[303]   Id.

[304]   Id.

[305]   Shaw, supra note 296, at 977.

[306]   Shaw, supra note 296, at 996.

[307]   Buergenthal & Murphy, supra note 268, at 91.

"should not necessarily be exclusively evaluated on the legal plane" of enforcement.[308] Failure to comply violates the U.N. Charter and would ultimately be enforceable by the Security Council but each of its five permanent members (China, France, Russia, the United Kingdom, and the United States) maintains a veto power.[309]

The two institutions discussed in this section—the Permanent Court of Arbitration and the International Court of Justice (or World Court)—both have the word "court" in their names. This may suggest a higher level of "governmental-ness," than is found in international investment arbitration or the Iran-United States Claims Tribunal discussed in the next section. Relatedly, some scholars distinguish international "adjudication" before the PCA or ICJ from international "arbitration" before other bodies[310]—perhaps because "arbitration" tends to connote "non-governmental-ness."

§ 76   Public International Arbitration Tribunals Arising out of Post-Dispute Arbitration Agreements

The leading example of a public international arbitration tribunal established by post-dispute agreement is the Iran-United States Claims Tribunal. It was established in 1981 through the Algiers Declarations as part of the resolution of the Iran Hostage Crisis.[311] The Tribunal hears two categories of claims: private claims, which are claims brought by a national of one State against the other State, and inter-governmental claims, which are claims brought by one State against the other, alleging either a violation of the Algiers Declarations or breach of contract.[312] The Tribunal has decided nearly 4,000 cases and awarded more than $2.5 billion approximately $1 billion to Iran and Iranian nationals and a substantially higher amount to the United States and United States nationals.[313] "While successful U.S. nationals were paid out of a security account in the Netherlands, in cases where Iran prevailed but the U.S. national

---

[308]   Shaw, supra note 296, at 997.

[309]   Id.

[310]   See e.g., Stephen E. Gent, The Politics of International Arbitration and Adjudication, 2 Penn St. J. L. & Int'l Aff. 66, 67 (2013) ("The two methods primarily differ with respect to the identity of the third party. In arbitration, an individual, state, NGO, or panel of states hands down a decision. On the other hand, adjudication is conducted by an international court, such as the International Court of Justice.")

[311]   Declaration of the Government of the Democratic and Popular Republic of Algeria, Jan. 19, 1981, 1 Iran-U.S.C.T.R. 3; Declaration of the Government of the Democratic and Popular Republic of Algeria Concerning the Settlement of Claims by the Government of the United States of America and the Government of the Islamic Republic of Iran, Jan. 19, 1981, 1 Iran-U.S.C.T.R. 9.

[312]   Yulia Andreeva, et al., International Courts, 43 Int'l Law. 425, 439 (2009).

[313]   Id.

refused to pay, Iran successfully enforced its awards in U.S. Courts through resort to the New York Convention."[314] The Iran-United States Claims Tribunal still exists.[315]

---

[314]   Buergenthal & Murphy, supra note 268, at 76–77 (citing Iran v. Gould, 887 F.2d 1357 (9th Cir.1989)).

[315]   http://www.iusct.net/Pages/Public/A–About.aspx.

Chapter 9

PROCESSES SIMILAR
TO ARBITRATION

Table of Sections

§ 77   Private Judging and Business Courts

(a) Private Judging ("Rent-a-Judge")

Litigation is *adjudication*[1] in a court or other government forum. Arbitration is adjudication in a private (non-government) forum. Private judging is somewhere in between. It is adjudication in a quasi-government forum.

Arbitration is a creature of contract. Not only does the parties' contract determine *whether* a dispute goes to arbitration, the contract also largely determines *what occurs* during arbitration.[2] Parties to arbitration agreements generally have the freedom of contract to determine the identity of the arbitrator(s), the rules of procedure and evidence, and the secrecy of the proceedings.[3] Judicial enforcement of arbitration awards is contractual in its rationale. The parties agreed to comply with the arbitrator's decision and if the losing party

---

[1]   See supra § 1, n.1.
[2]   See §§ 35–38.
[3]   See §§ 35–37.

refuses to do so then that party is in breach of contract—even if the arbitrator's decision is wrong.[4]

In contrast, private judging is a less contractual, less privatized, process. Party agreement, usually formed post-dispute, does send a case to private judging, and parties generally can determine the time and place of trial, as well as the identity of the judge. However, unlike arbitration, privately judged trials may (depending on state law[5]) be:

(1)   required to use the same rules of procedure and evidence used in ordinary litigation;[6]

(2)   exposed to public view;[7]

(3)   adjudicated only by a former judge;[8] and

(4)   subject to appeal in the same manner as other trial verdicts.[9]

In sum, private judging is essentially an ordinary bench trial except that the parties select and pay for the judge.

Private judging "has been used primarily in technical and complex business litigation involving substantial amounts of money."[10] It has also been used in family law matters.[11] It allows parties to such disputes to "jump the line" waiting for a trial and get an early trial at the cost of paying (often at a very high hourly rate) for the judge or "referee." Private judging has been labeled "Rent-A-Judge" and criticized as, "an unconstitutional, elitist institution that unfairly grants privileges to the wealthy."[12]

---

[4]   See §§ 42–44.

[5]   Unlike the Federal Arbitration Act, which makes arbitration law nearly uniform around the country, the law on private judging varies from state to state. California is the leader in private judging. See Cal.Const.art. VI, § 21; Cal.Civ.Proc.Code §§ 638–645. Compare, e.g., N.H.Rev.Stat.Ann. § 519:9; N.Y.Civ.Proc.L. & R. 4301–21; Tex.Civ.Prac. & Rem.Code §§ 151.001–151.013; Wash.Rev.Code.Ann § 4.48.010—.130.

[6]   Tex.Civ.Prac. & Rem.Code § 151.005.

[7]   Cal.Ct.R. 2.833.

[8]   Tex.Civ.Prac. & Rem.Code § 151.003 (West 2015).

[9]   Id. § 151.013.

[10]   Barlow F. Christensen, Private Justice: California's General Reference Procedure, 1982 Am.Bar Found.Research J. 79, 82.

[11]   Jacqueline St. Joan, Privatizing Family Law Adjudications: Issues and Procedures, 34 Colo.Law. 95 (2005); Ned I. Price, Binding Arbitration, Voluntary Trial Resolution, and Med-Arb Proceedings in Family Law, Fla.B.J., Nov. 2012, at 48, 50 (explaining that parties in family law disputes in Florida may agree to private judging called "voluntary trial resolution" in which the parties choose a member of the Florida Bar who is in good standing for more than 5 years to act as a private trial resolution judge).

[12]   Anne S. Kim, Note, Rent-A-Judges and the Cost of Selling Justice, 44 Duke L.J. 166, 199 (1994). See also Note, The California Rent-A-Judge Experiment:

(b) Business Courts

The previous subsection invoked the distinction between government and the private sector to describe private judging as somewhere in between litigation (adjudication in a government forum) and arbitration (adjudication in a non-government forum). Similarly, several states have business courts that, although technically parts of (government) trial courts, often have some features commonly associated with arbitration, such as specialized, expert adjudicators, and expedited case management procedures emphasizing ADR.[13] However, business courts differ from arbitration and private judging in giving parties less choice of adjudicator, as parties generally must take whichever judge the business court assigns to their case; some business courts automatically receive business cases, while others receive cases on party request or a judge's recommendation.[14] Also, business courts tend to:

- have lower filing fees than arbitration, as government subsidizes the cost of business courts;

- generally lack the confidentiality of arbitration; and

- generally have full rights to appeal, as opposed to the narrower grounds for vacating an arbitration award.[15]

In contrast however, a Delaware statute tried to create a business court similar to arbitration on all three of these factors, and even described this court's process as "arbitration" in granting its Court of Chancery "the power to arbitrate business disputes."[16] This forum had high filing fees ($12,000), appeal only under the deferential standards of FAA § 10, and confidential proceedings barring public access.[17] This confidentiality—"[a]ttendance at the proceeding is limited to 'parties and their representatives,' and all 'materials and communications' produced during the arbitration are

---

Constitutional and Policy Considerations of Pay-As-You-Go Courts, 94 Harv.L.Rev. 1592 (1981).

[13]   Christopher R. Drahozal, Business Courts and the Future of Arbitration, 10 Cardozo J. Conflict Resol. 491, 492 (2009); Ralph Peeples & Hanne Nyheim, Beyond the Border: An International Perspective on Business Courts, Bus. L. Today, Mar.-Apr. 2008.

[14]   Drahozal, supra note 13, at 498; Anne Tucker Nees, Making a Case for Business Courts: A Survey of and Proposed Framework to Evaluate Business Courts, 24 Ga.St.L.Rev. 477, 515 (2007).

[15]   Drahozal, supra note 13, at 498–500.

[16]   H.B. 49, 145th Gen. Assemb. (Del. 2009), cited in Delaware Coal. for Open Gov't, Inc. v. Strine, 733 F.3d 510, 512 (3d Cir.2013), cert. denied, 134 S.Ct. 1551 (2014).

[17]   733 F.3d at 512–13. Arbitration petitions are "considered confidential" and are not included "as part of the public docketing system." Tit. 10, § 349(b); Del. Ch. R. 97(4). Del. Ch. R. 98(b).

protected from disclosure in judicial or administrative proceedings"—led the Third Circuit to hold that Delaware's business court violated the First Amendment's right of public access to trials.[18]

The Third Circuit pointed out that arbitration's "[c]onfidentiality is a natural outgrowth of the status of arbitrations as private alternatives to government-sponsored proceedings."[19] By contrast, "Delaware's government-sponsored arbitrations * * * differ fundamentally from other arbitrations because they are conducted before active judges in a courthouse."[20] In sum, while arbitration can be highly confidential because it is non-governmental adjudication,[21] a government court—even if it calls itself "arbitration"—is subject to a constitutional right of public access.

§ 78   Non-Contractual, yet Binding, Arbitration

(a) Introduction

There are two types of arbitration, contractual and non-contractual.[22] The duty to arbitrate a dispute can be created by contract or by other law. If the duty to arbitrate is created by contract, then enforcement of that duty is unlikely to violate the constitutional right to a jury trial. Courts typically hold that, by forming a contract to arbitrate, a party waives its right to a trial by jury.[23] In contrast, the parties to non-contractual arbitration have rarely waived the right to a jury trial. Therefore, non-contractual arbitration generally must be non-binding to avoid violating this right.[24] Non-binding arbitration has less in common with arbitration

---

[18]   Delaware Coal. for Open Gov't, Inc. v. Strine, 733 F.3d 510, 521 (3d Cir.2013),

[19]   Id. at 518.

[20]   Id.

[21]   See § 37(b), which explains that arbitration hearings are generally closed to non-participants and a few state statutes even protect arbitration materials from discovery or admissibility in litigation.

[22]   Many examples of "non-contractual" arbitration do involve a contract, such as an employment contract or a contract for the sale of an automobile. So in these contexts the duty to arbitrate is, in a sense, assumed by contract. The difference between "contractual" and "non-contractual" arbitration is whether it is possible to form a contract of the relevant sort without assuming the duty to arbitrate. For example, in transportation industries governed by the Railway Labor Act, it is not possible to form an employment contract without assuming the duty to arbitrate. See § 78(b)(4). In contrast, it is possible to form such an employment contract elsewhere in the private sector. See § 47. Accordingly, transportation employment arbitration is "non-contractual," while other labor and employment arbitration is "contractual."

[23]   See § 2.

[24]   Kimbrough v. Holiday Inn, 478 F.Supp. 566, 570–71 (E.D.Pa.1979)(non-binding arbitration did not violate jury trial right); Hamm v. Arrowcreek Homeowners' Ass'n, 183 P.3d 895, 903 (Nev.2008) (same); Lisanti v. Alamo Title Ins. of Tex., 55 P.3d 962 (N.M.2002)(state statute requiring arbitration of all title disputes under one million dollars violated state constitutional right to jury trial); Cooper v. Poston, 483 S.E.2d 750, 751 (S.C.1997)(state statute allowing one party unilaterally to divert an

than it does with mediation and other processes in aid of negotiation. Accordingly, non-binding arbitration is discussed, not in this book, but in a companion book.[25] The difference between binding and non-binding can be a matter of degree relating to the degree of deference courts show the arbitrators' awards.[26]

Non-contractual, yet binding, arbitration is discussed in this book. There are several examples of non-contractual, yet binding, arbitration. Some avoid violating the right to jury trial; others may violate it.

The United States Constitution's Seventh Amendment, preserving the right to jury trial, and most state constitutional provisions recognizing this right,[27] were enacted prior to the merger of law and equity. Courts generally interpret these constitutional provisions to confer a jury trial right only in cases arising at law, as opposed to cases in equity.[28] That basically means there is a right to a jury trial of claims for money damages, but not for equitable remedies like injunctions and specific performance.

Legislatures and administrative agencies have created new claims that did not exist at the time the constitutional provisions regarding the right to a jury trial were enacted. Whether there is a right to a jury trial of these claims is determined by the language of the statute creating the claim and by whether these claims bear more resemblance to legal or to equitable claims.[29] For example, the

---

action for monetary damages arising out a motor vehicle accident to binding arbitration would "abrogate another party's constitutional right to a jury trial"); Grace v. Howlett, 283 N.E.2d 474 (Ill.1972)(state statute requiring arbitration of certain automobile injury cases violated right to jury trial under Illinois Constitution); Jersey Cent. Power & Light Co. v. Melcar Utility Co., 59 A.3d 561, 575 (N.J.2013)(statute requiring binding arbitration for disputes involving low-dollar damages to underground facilities violated the constitutionally guaranteed right to a trial by jury for a common-law cause of action in negligence).

[25]   See Stephen J. Ware, Principles of Alternative Dispute Resolution § 4.32 (3d ed.2016).

[26]   See § 78(b)(6) (no-fault insurance).

[27]   While the Seventh Amendment is one of the few amendments in the Bill of Rights that constrains only federal, not state, government, see Curtis v. Loether, 415 U.S. 189, 192 n.6 (1974), nearly all state constitutions contain a provision that similarly protects the right to trial by jury. See Martin H. Redish, Legislative Response to Medical Malpractice Insurance Crisis: Constitutional Implications, 55 Tex.L.Rev. 759, 797 (1977); Eric J. Hamilton, Federalism and the State Civil Jury Rights, 65 Stan. L. Rev. 851, 855 (2013)("Today, forty-seven state constitutions provide for the right to a jury trial in civil cases, and most do so in the "Declaration of Rights" article, the state constitution counterpart to the U.S. Constitution's Bill of Rights.")

[28]   See, e.g., Feltner v. Columbia Pictures Television, Inc., 523 U.S. 340, 347–48 (1998); Pichler v. UNITE, 542 F.3d 380, 388 (3rd Cir.2008); Marseilles Hydro Power, LLC v. Marseilles Land & Water Co., 299 F.3d 643 (7th Cir.2002); State v. O'Malley, 95 S.W.3d 82 (Mo.2003); Motor Vehicle Mfrs.Ass'n v. State, 551 N.Y.S.2d 470 (N.Y.1990).

[29]   The Seventh Amendment's jury trial right

Supreme Court of New Jersey held that a statute requiring binding arbitration for disputes involving low-dollar damages to underground facilities violated the constitutionally guaranteed right to a trial by jury for a common-law cause of action in negligence.[30]

(b) Examples

(1) Federal Programs

Federal law requires arbitration of certain disputes under particular federal programs.[31] These disputes may involve claims by private parties against the federal government or claims between private parties relating to the rights and duties specified by the particular federal program. Examples of such federal laws include the Comprehensive Environmental Response, Compensation and Liability Act,[32] the Federal Insecticide, Fungicide, and Rodenticide Act,[33] and the Multiemployer Pension Plan Amendments Act.[34] In all these examples, the duty to arbitrate is created by statute in the absence of any contract providing for arbitration. This form of non-contractual arbitration does not, however, violate the constitutional right to a jury trial because that right does not attach to claims under these programs.[35]

(2) Government Employees—Federal

The Civil Service Reform Act ("CSRA") authorizes employees of the federal government to form labor unions and requires employers (the various federal government agencies) to bargain in good faith with these unions.[36] The CSRA states that the collective bargaining agreement "shall provide procedures for the settlement of

---

applies not only to common-law causes of action, but also to actions brought to enforce statutory rights that are analogous to common-law causes of action ordinarily decided in English law courts in the late 18th century, as opposed to those customarily heard by courts of equity or admiralty. To determine whether a statutory action is more analogous to cases tried in courts of law than to suits tried in courts of equity or admiralty, we examine both the nature of the statutory action and the remedy sought.

Feltner, 523 U.S. at 348 (internal citations omitted). See, e.g., Braunstein v. McCabe, 571 F.3d 108, 123 (1st Cir.2009)("Courts have held that [bankruptcy code] § 549 actions are equitable rather than legal and do not include a jury trial right.")

[30]   Jersey Cent. Power & Light Co. v. Melcar Util. Co., 59 A.3d at 561 (2013).

[31]   See Ian R. Macneil, Richard E. Speidel & Thomas J. Stipanowich, Federal Arbitration Law ch.12 (1994).

[32]   42 U.S.C. §§ 9601–9675.

[33]   7 U.S.C. §§ 136—136y.

[34]   29 U.S.C. §§ 1381–1461.

[35]   See, e.g., Thomas v. Union Carbide Agricultural Products Co., 473 U.S. 568 (1985); Connors v. Ryan's Coal Co., 923 F.2d 1461 (11th Cir.1991).

[36]   Civil Service Reform Act of 1978, Pub. L. 95–454, 92 Stat. 111 (codified as amended in scattered sections of 5 U.S.C.).

grievances."[37] "[A]ny grievance not satisfactorily settled under the negotiated grievance procedure shall be subject to binding arbitration."[38] Herein lies the non-contractual source of the duty to arbitrate. A statute, rather than a contract, imposes the duty to arbitrate.

Either party to a federal employment arbitration may appeal to the Federal Labor Relations Authority and may further appeal that Authority's decision to a federal court.[39] For further discussion of federal labor arbitration see Section 61.

(3) Government Employees—State and Local

Some state and local government employees are covered by grievance arbitration systems similar to those found in the private sector.[40] What stands out about arbitration in the context of state and local employees, however, is the prevalence of interest arbitration.[41] Interest arbitration is often used to determine the terms of employment for public school teachers, police, firefighters, etc. Such government employees:

> are usually forbidden to engage in strikes; economic pressure, and the usual tests of economic strength used in the private sector to determine contract terms after a bargaining impasse, are therefore limited in the public interest. "Interest" arbitration to determine the terms of a new contract when bargaining fails provides a common alternative mechanism. In many cases, in fact, state statutes impose this as a *mandatory* means of settlement. * * * Such legislation in effect gives to public employee unions the "right" to resort to the arbitration mechanism to determine the future terms of employment.[42]

Such arbitration is not so much the application of law to resolve a dispute as it is quasi-legislative policymaking, requiring consideration of government spending and taxation priorities.[43] For

---

[37]   Id. § 7121(a)(1).

[38]   Id. § 7121(b)(1)(C)(iii).

[39]   Id. § 7122(a), 7123(a). See generally Dennis Nolan, Labor and Employment Arbitration in a Nutshell 83–87, 199–201 (2d ed.2007).

[40]   Nolan, supra note 39, at 87–89.

[41]   See § 60; Ronald Hoh, Interest Arbitration, 32 Mont.Law. 8 (2007) ("By 1990, 35 states and the District of Columbia had adopted some form of interest arbitration as a means of resolving disputes over new contract terms for some or all of their public employees.")

[42]   Alan Scott Rau, Edward F. Sherman & Scott R. Peppet, Processes of Dispute Resolution: The Role of Lawyers 615 (4th ed.2006). See, e.g., R.I.Gen.Laws §§ 28–9.1–1 to.2–1

[43]   Clyde W. Summers, Public Sector Bargaining: Problems of Governmental Decisionmaking, 44 U.Cin.L.Rev. 669, 672 (1975).

additional discussion of interest arbitration and public sector labor arbitration see Sections 60 and 61.

(4) Railway Labor Act

Employers and employees in certain transportation industries, such as railroads and airlines, are governed by the Railway Labor Act ("RLA").[44] The RLA creates a National Railroad Adjustment Board consisting of representatives selected by the employers and representatives selected by the employees' labor unions.[45] The RLA requires employers and unions to submit certain disputes to the Adjustment Board for decision.[46] Thus, the RLA requires arbitration, rather than litigation, of these disputes. Appeals of Adjustment Board decisions may be taken to federal court. Judicial review of these Boards' determinations has been characterized as "among the narrowest known to the law."[47] For additional discussion of the RLA, see Section 56.

(5) State "Lemon" Laws

Many states have enacted "lemon" laws with the goal of ensuring that auto manufacturers satisfy their warranty obligations to consumers. New York State requires manufacturers to arbitrate lemon law disputes with their customers if the customer chooses arbitration over litigation.[48] New York's highest court rejected the manufacturers' contention that this mandatory, binding arbitration violates their constitutional right to a jury trial.[49] However, because Lemon Law arbitration is "imposed on" manufacturers, judicial review of its arbitration awards is fairly rigorous.[50]

---

[44]   45 U.S.C. §§ 151–188.

[45]   Id. § 153(a).

[46]   Id. § 153(i).

[47]   Union Pacific R. Co. v. Sheehan, 439 U.S. 89, 91 (1978) (citation omitted); Martino v. Metro North Commuter R. Co., 582 Fed. Appx. 27, 29 (2d Cir.2014)("the scope of judicial review of a labor board's arbitral decision is "the narrowest known to law" ").

[48]   N.Y.Gen.Bus.L. § 198–a(k), (m); Lyeth v. Chrysler Corp., 929 F.2d 891 (2d Cir.1991); Star Boxing, Inc. v. Daimlerchrysler Motors Corp., 840 N.Y.S.2d 357, 357–58 (App.Div.2007)("Once the petitioner selected alternative arbitration, the appellant manufacturer was required to 'submit to such alternative arbitration'" (General Business Law § 198–a[k])).

[49]   Motor Vehicle Mfrs.Ass'n v. State, 551 N.Y.S.2d 470 (N.Y.1990).

[50]   Star Boxing, Inc. v. Daimlerchrysler Motors Corp., 840 N.Y.S.2d 357, 357–58 (App.Div.2007) ("Once the petitioner selected alternative arbitration, the appellant manufacturer was required to 'submit to such alternative arbitration'" (General Business Law § 198–a[k]). Since arbitration was imposed upon the appellant, the appellant is entitled to the 'expanded judicial review available in compulsory arbitration'. In order to be upheld, an arbitration award must have evidentiary support and cannot be arbitrary and capricious.")

(6)   State Auto Insurance Laws

Many states have enacted "no-fault" auto insurance. For example, New York State requires every vehicle owner to provide herself and certain others with compensation for economic loss resulting from injuries occasioned by the use or operation of that vehicle, regardless of fault.[51] The insurer is statutorily-required to arbitrate disputes over benefits if the claimant chooses arbitration over litigation.[52] When insurers challenged this requirement on a number of federal and state constitutional grounds, a federal court abstained from ruling on whether the requirement conflicts with the state constitutional right to a jury trial.[53] While New York's no-fault-insurance arbitration is binding, the statute "permits an insurer or a claimant to institute a court action to adjudicate the dispute de novo where the master arbitrator's award is $5,000 or greater."[54]

In another example of non-contractual, yet binding, arbitration in the auto insurance context, some states require arbitration of uninsured motorist claims.[55] The Illinois Supreme Court held that such a requirement did not violate the state constitutional jury trial right.[56] Illinois' uninsured motorist arbitration awards are largely binding, but not completely so because the Illinois statute provides: "Any decision made by the arbitrators shall be binding for the amount of damages not exceeding $75,000 for bodily injury to or death of any one person, $150,000 for bodily injury to or death of 2 or more persons in any one motor vehicle accident, or the corresponding policy limits for bodily injury or death, whichever is less."[57]

---

[51]   N.Y.Ins.L. § 5103 (McKinney 2011).

[52]   Id. § 5106(b).

[53]   Country-Wide Ins. Co. v. Harnett, 426 F.Supp. 1030, 1033–34 (S.D.N.Y.1977)("Since this is a novel and important issue as to which the state law is evolving, it would appear that this Court should exercise its discretion to refuse to decide this pendent issue of state law.") Other constitutional challenges to New York's "no fault" regime have also been rejected. Green v. Liberty Mutual Insurance Co., 791 N.Y.S.2d 630 (App.Div.2005); 563 Grand Med. P.C. v. New York State Insurance Dept., 787 N.Y.S.2d 613 (Sup.Ct.2004).

[54]   Ave. C Med., P.C. v. Encompass Ins. of MA, 130 A.D.3d 764, 764, 12 N.Y.S.3d 578, 579 (N.Y.App.Div.2015).

[55]   215 Ill.Comp.Stat.Ann. § 5/143a (West 2015); Cal.Ins.Code § 11580.2(f); and Mass.Gen.Laws ch. 175, § 111D.

[56]   Reed v. Farmers Ins.Group, 720 N.E.2d 1052, 1060 (Ill.1999).

[57]   215 Ill. Comp. Stat. Ann. 5/143a. See Phoenix Ins. Co. v. Rosen, 242 Ill. 2d 48, 58–59, 949 N.E.2d 639, 646–47 (2011) (upholding this provision against challenge that it "unfairly favors the insurer over the insured.")

(7) Attorney Fee Disputes

Some states require lawyers to arbitrate fee disputes with their clients if the client chooses arbitration over litigation.[58] Courts have rejected the contention that this mandatory, yet binding, arbitration violates the lawyer's constitutional right to a jury trial.[59] The courts hold that by accepting a license to practice law the lawyer waived his or her jury trial right for these sorts of disputes.

---

[58] Anderson v. Elliott, 555 A.2d 1042 (Me.1989); BiotechPharma, LLC v. Ludwig & Robinson, PLLC 98 A.3d 986, 992 (D.C.2014) (D.C. Bar rules "give clients the power to require arbitration of fee disputes"); In re LiVolsi, 428 A.2d 1268 (N.J.1981).

[59] BiotechPharma, LLC v. Ludwig & Robinson, PLLC, 98 A.3d 986, 995–96 (D.C. 2014) ("Although other jurisdictions impose rules similar to D.C. Bar Rule XIII, no such rule has ever been struck down for denying an attorney's right to a jury trial. Rather, it has been held that attorneys give up that right by practicing law in a jurisdiction subject to the challenged rule"); Guralnick v. Supreme Court of New Jersey, 747 F.Supp. 1109, 1116 (1990); Kelley Drye & Warren v. Murray Indus., 623 F.Supp. 522, 525, 527 (D.N.J.1985); Shimko v. Lobe, 790 N.E.2d 335 (Ohio App.2003); Anderson v. Elliott, 555 A.2d 1042 (Me.1989); In re LiVolsi, 428 A.2d 1268 (N.J.1981).

Appendix A

FEDERAL ARBITRATION ACT

9 U.S.C. §§ 1–307

CHAPTER 1. GENERAL PROVISIONS

§ 1. "Maritime Transactions," and "Commerce" Defined; Exceptions to Operation of Title

"Maritime transactions", as herein defined, means charter parties, bills of lading of water carriers, agreements relating to wharfage, supplies furnished vessels or repairs to vessels, collisions, or any other matters in foreign commerce which, if the subject of controversy, would be embraced within admiralty jurisdiction; "commerce", as herein defined, means commerce among the several States or with foreign nations, or in any Territory of the United States or in the District of Columbia, or between any such Territory and another, or between any such Territory and any State or foreign nation, or between the District of Columbia and any State or Territory or foreign nation, but nothing herein contained shall apply to contracts of employment of seamen, railroad employees, or any other class of workers engaged in foreign or interstate commerce.

§ 2. Validity, Irrevocability and Enforcement of Agreements to Arbitrate

A written provision in any maritime transaction or a contract evidencing a transaction involving commerce to settle by arbitration a controversy thereafter arising out of such contract or transaction, or the refusal to perform the whole or any part thereof, or an agreement in writing to submit to arbitration an existing controversy arising out of such a contract, transaction, or refusal, shall be valid, irrevocable, and enforceable, save upon such grounds as exist at law or in equity for the revocation of any contract.

§ 3. Stay of Proceedings Where Issue Therein Referable to Arbitration

If any suit or proceeding be brought in any of the courts of the United States upon any issue referable to arbitration under an agreement in writing for such arbitration, the court in which such suit is pending, upon being satisfied that the issue involved in such suit or proceeding is referable to arbitration under such an agreement, shall on application of one of the parties stay the trial of the action until such arbitration has been had in accordance with the terms of the agreement, providing the applicant for the stay is not in default in proceeding with such arbitration.

§ 4. Failure to Arbitrate Under Agreement; Petition to United States Court Having Jurisdiction for Order to Compel Arbitration; Notice and Service Thereof; Hearing and Determination

A party aggrieved by the alleged failure, neglect, or refusal of another to arbitrate under a written agreement for arbitration may petition any United States district court which, save for such agreement, would have jurisdiction under Title 28, in a civil action or in admiralty of the subject matter of a suit arising out of the controversy between the parties, for an order directing that such arbitration proceed in the manner provided for in such agreement. Five days' notice in writing of such application shall be served upon the party in default. Service thereof shall be made in the manner provided by the Federal Rules of Civil Procedure. The court shall hear the parties, and upon being satisfied that the making of the agreement for arbitration or the failure to comply therewith is not in issue, the court shall make an order directing the parties to proceed to arbitration in accordance with the terms of the agreement. The hearing and proceedings, under such agreement, shall be within the district in which the petition for an order directing such arbitration is filed. If the making of the arbitration agreement or the failure, neglect, or refusal to perform the same be in issue, the court shall proceed summarily to the trial thereof. If no jury trial be demanded by the party alleged to be in default, or if the matter in dispute is within admiralty jurisdiction, the court shall hear and determine such issue. Where such an issue is raised, the party alleged to be in default may, except in cases of admiralty, on or before the return day of the notice of application, demand a jury trial of such issue, and upon such demand the court shall make an order referring the issue or issues to a jury in the manner provided by the Federal Rules of Civil Procedure, or may specially call a jury for that purpose. If the jury find that no agreement in writing for arbitration was made or that there is no default in proceeding thereunder, the proceeding shall be dismissed. If the jury find that an agreement for arbitration was made in writing and that there is a default in proceeding thereunder, the court shall make an order summarily directing the parties to proceed with the arbitration in accordance with the terms thereof.

§ 5. Appointment of Arbitrators or Umpire

If in the agreement provision be made for a method of naming or appointing an arbitrator or arbitrators or an umpire, such method shall be followed; but if no method be provided therein, or if a method be provided and any party thereto shall fail to avail himself of such method, or if for any other reason there shall be a lapse in the naming of an arbitrator or arbitrators or umpire, or in filling a vacancy, then upon the application of either party to the controversy the court shall designate and appoint an arbitrator or arbitrators or umpire, as the case may require, who shall act under the said agreement with the same force and effect as if he or they had been specifically named therein; and unless otherwise provided in the agreement the arbitration shall be by a single arbitrator.

§ 6. Application Heard as Motion

Any application to the court hereunder shall be made and heard in the manner provided by law for the making and hearing of motions, except as otherwise herein expressly provided.

§ 7. Witnesses   Before   Arbitrators;   Fees;   Compelling Attendance

The arbitrators selected either as prescribed in this title or otherwise, or a majority of them, may summon in writing any person to attend before them or any of them as a witness and in a proper case to bring with him or them any book, record, document, or paper which may be deemed material as evidence in the case. The fees for such attendance shall be the same as the fees of witnesses before masters of the United States courts. Said summons shall issue in the name of the arbitrator or arbitrators, or a majority of them, and shall be signed by the arbitrators, or a majority of them, and shall be directed to the said person and shall be served in the same manner as subpoenas to appear and testify before the court; if any person or persons so summoned to testify shall refuse or neglect to obey said summons, upon petition the United States district court for the district in which such arbitrators, or a majority of them, are sitting may compel the attendance of such person or persons before said arbitrator or arbitrators, or punish said person or persons for contempt in the same manner provided by law for securing the attendance of witnesses or their punishment for neglect or refusal to attend in the courts of the United States.

§ 8. Proceedings Begun by Libel in Admiralty and Seizure of Vessel or Property

If the basis of jurisdiction be a cause of action otherwise justiciable in admiralty, then, notwithstanding anything herein to the contrary, the party claiming to be aggrieved may begin his proceeding hereunder by libel and seizure of the vessel or other property of the other party according to the usual course of admiralty proceedings, and the court shall then have jurisdiction to direct the parties to proceed with the arbitration and shall retain jurisdiction to enter its decree upon the award.

§ 9. Award of Arbitrators; Confirmation; Jurisdiction; Procedure

If the parties in their agreement have agreed that a judgment of the court shall be entered upon the award made pursuant to the arbitration, and shall specify the court, then at any time within one year after the award is made any party to the arbitration may apply to the court so specified for an order confirming the award, and thereupon the court must grant such an order unless the award is vacated, modified, or corrected as prescribed in sections 10 and 11 of this title. If no court is specified in the agreement of the parties, then such application may be made to the United States court in and for the district within which such award was made. Notice of the application shall be served upon the adverse party, and thereupon the court shall have jurisdiction of such party as though he had appeared generally in the proceeding. If the adverse party is a resident of the district within which the award was made, such service shall be made upon the adverse party or his attorney as prescribed by law for service of notice of motion in an action in the same court. If the adverse party shall be a nonresident, then the notice of the application shall be served by the marshal of any district within which the adverse party may be found in like manner as other process of the court.

§ 10.　　Same; Vacation; Grounds; Rehearing

(a)　In any of the following cases the United States court in and for the district wherein the award was made may make an order vacating the award upon the application of any party to the arbitration—

(1)　Where the award was procured by corruption, fraud, or undue means.

(2)　Where there was evident partiality or corruption in the arbitrators, or either of them.

(3)　Where the arbitrators were guilty of misconduct in refusing to postpone the hearing, upon sufficient cause shown, or in refusing to hear evidence pertinent and material to the controversy; or of any other misbehavior by which the rights of any party have been prejudiced.

(4) Where the arbitrators exceeded their powers, or so imperfectly executed them that a mutual, final, and definite award upon the subject matter submitted was not made.

(b) Where an award is vacated and the time within which the agreement required the award to be made has not expired the court may, in its discretion, direct a rehearing by the arbitrators.

(c) The United States district court for the district wherein an award was made that was issued pursuant to section 580 of title 5 may make an order vacating the award upon the application of a person, other than a party to the arbitration, who is adversely affected or aggrieved by the award, if the use of arbitration or the award is clearly inconsistent with the factors set forth in section 572 of title 5.

§ 11.   Same; Modification or Correction; Grounds; Order

In either of the following cases the United States court in and for the district wherein the award was made may make an order modifying or correcting the award upon the application of any party to the arbitration—

(a) Where there was an evident material miscalculation of figures or an evident material mistake in the description of any person, thing, or property referred to in the award.

(b) Where the arbitrators have awarded upon a matter not submitted to them, unless it is a matter not affecting the merits of the decision upon the matter submitted.

(c) Where the award is imperfect in matter of form not affecting the merits of the controversy.

The order may modify and correct the award, so as to effect the intent thereof and promote justice between the parties.

§ 12.   Notice of Motions to Vacate or Modify; Service; Stay of Proceedings

Notice of a motion to vacate, modify, or correct an award must be served upon the adverse party or his attorney within three months after the award is filed or delivered. If the adverse party is a resident of the district within which the award was made, such service shall be made upon the adverse party or his attorney as prescribed by law for service of notice of motion in an action in the same court. If the adverse party shall be a nonresident then the notice of the application shall be served by the marshal of any district within which the adverse party may be found in like manner as other process of the court. For the purposes of the motion any judge who might make an order to stay the proceedings in an action brought in the same court may make an order, to be served with the notice of motion, staying the proceedings of the adverse party to enforce the award.

§ 13. Papers Filed with Order on Motions; Judgment; Docketing; Force and Effect; Enforcement

The party moving for an order confirming, modifying, or correcting an award shall, at the time such order is filed with the clerk for the entry of judgment thereon, also file the following papers with the clerk:

(a) The agreement; the selection or appointment, if any, of an additional arbitrator or umpire; and each written extension of the time, if any, within which to make the award.

(b) The award.

(c) Each notice, affidavit, or other paper used upon an application to confirm, modify, or correct the award, and a copy of each order of the court upon such an application.

The judgment shall be docketed as if it was rendered in an action.

The judgment so entered shall have the same force and effect, in all respects, as, and be subject to all the provisions of law relating to, a judgment in an action; and it may be enforced as if it had been rendered in an action in the court in which it is entered.

§ 14. Contracts Not Affected

This title shall not apply to contracts made prior to January 1, 1926.

§ 15. Inapplicability of the Act of State Doctrine

Enforcement of arbitral agreements, confirmation of arbitral awards, and execution upon judgments based on orders confirming such awards shall not be refused on the basis of the Act of State doctrine.

§ 16. Appeals

(a) An appeal may be taken from—

(1) an order—

(A) refusing a stay of any action under section 3 of this title,

(B) denying a petition under section 4 of this title to order arbitration to proceed,

(C) denying an application under section 206 of this title to compel arbitration,

(D)   confirming or denying confirmation of an award or partial award, or

(E)   modifying, correcting, or vacating an award;

(2)   an interlocutory order granting, continuing, or modifying an injunction against an arbitration that is subject to this title; or

(3)   a final decision with respect to an arbitration that is subject to this title.

(b)   Except as otherwise provided in section 1292(b) of title 28, an appeal may not be taken from an interlocutory order—

(1)   granting a stay of any action under section 3 of this title;

(2)   directing arbitration to proceed under section 4 of this title;

(3)   compelling arbitration under section 206 of this title; or

(4)   refusing to enjoin an arbitration that is subject to this title.

CHAPTER 2. CONVENTION ON THE RECOGNITION AND ENFORCEMENT OF FOREIGN ARBITRAL AWARDS

Sec. 201.   Enforcement of Convention

The Convention on the Recognition and Enforcement of Foreign Arbitral Awards of June 10, 1958, shall be enforced in United States courts in accordance with this chapter.

Sec. 202.   Agreement   or   award   falling   under   the Convention

An arbitration agreement or arbitral award arising out of a legal relationship, whether contractual or not, which is considered as commercial, including a transaction, contract, or agreement described in section 2 of this title, falls under the Convention. An agreement or award arising out of such a relationship which is entirely between citizens of the United States shall be deemed not to fall under the Convention unless that relationship involves property located abroad, envisages performance or enforcement abroad, or has some other reasonable relation with one or more foreign states. For the purpose of this section a corporation is a citizen of the United States if it is incorporated or has its principal place of business in the United States.

Sec. 203.   Jurisdiction; amount in controversy

An action or proceeding falling under the Convention shall be deemed to arise under the laws and treaties of the United States. The district courts of the United States (including the courts enumerated in section 460 of title 28) shall have original jurisdiction over such an action or proceeding, regardless of the amount in controversy.

Sec. 204.   Venue

An action or proceeding over which the district courts have jurisdiction pursuant to section 203 of this title may be brought in any such court in which save for the arbitration agreement an action or proceeding with respect to the controversy between the parties could be brought, or in such court for the district and division which embraces the place designated in the agreement as the place of arbitration if such place is within the United States.

Sec. 205.   Removal of cases from State courts

Where the subject matter of an action or proceeding pending in a State court relates to an arbitration agreement or award falling under the Convention, the defendant or the defendants may, at any time before the trial thereof, remove such action or proceeding to the district court of the United States for the district and division embracing the place where the action or proceeding is pending. The procedure for removal of causes otherwise provided by law shall apply, except that the ground for removal provided in this section need not appear on the face of the complaint but may be shown in the petition for removal. For the purposes of Chapter 1 of this title any action or proceeding removed under this section shall be deemed to have been brought in the district court to which it is removed.

Sec. 206.   Order to compel arbitration; appointment of arbitrators

A court having jurisdiction under this chapter may direct that arbitration be held in accordance with the agreement at any place therein provided for, whether that place is within or without the United States. Such court may also appoint arbitrators in accordance with the provisions of the agreement.

Sec. 207.   Award of arbitrators; confirmation; jurisdiction; proceeding

Within three years after an arbitral award falling under the Convention is made, any party to the arbitration may apply to any court having jurisdiction under this chapter for an order confirming the award as against any other party to the arbitration. The court shall confirm the award unless it finds one of the grounds for refusal or deferral of recognition or enforcement of the award specified in the said Convention.

Sec. 208.   Chapter 1; residual application

Chapter 1 applies to actions and proceedings brought under this chapter to the extent that chapter is not in conflict with this chapter or the Convention as ratified by the United States.

Sec. 301.   Enforcement of Convention

The Inter-American Convention on International Commercial Arbitration of January 30, 1975, shall be enforced in United States courts in accordance with this chapter.

Sec. 302.   Incorporation by reference

Sections 202, 203, 204, 205, and 207 of this title shall apply to this chapter as if specifically set forth herein, except that for the purposes of this chapter "the Convention" shall mean the Inter-American Convention.

Sec. 303.   Order to compel arbitration; appointment of arbitrators; locale

(a)   A court having jurisdiction under this chapter may direct that arbitration be held in accordance with the agreement at any place therein provided for, whether that place is within or without the United States. The court may also appoint arbitrators in accordance with the provisions of the agreement.

(b)   In the event the agreement does not make provision for the place of arbitration or the appointment of arbitrators, the court shall direct that the arbitration shall be held and the arbitrators be appointed in accordance with Article 3 of the Inter-American Convention.

Sec. 304.   Recognition and enforcement of foreign arbitral decisions and awards; reciprocity

Arbitral decisions or awards made in the territory of a foreign State shall, on the basis of reciprocity, be recognized and enforced under this chapter only if that State has ratified or acceded to the Inter-American Convention.

Sec. 305.   Relationship between the Inter-American Convention and the Convention on the Recognition and Enforcement of Foreign Arbitral Awards of June 10, 1958

When the requirements for application of both the Inter-American Convention and the Convention on the Recognition and Enforcement of Foreign Arbitral Awards of June 10, 1958, are met, determination as to which Convention applies shall, unless otherwise expressly agreed, be made as follows:

(1) If a majority of the parties to the arbitration agreement are citizens of a State or States that have ratified or acceded to the Inter-American Convention and are member States of the Organization of American States, the Inter-American Convention shall apply.

(2) In all other cases the Convention on the Recognition and Enforcement of Foreign Arbitral Awards of June 10, 1958, shall apply.

Sec. 306. Applicable rules of Inter-American Commercial Arbitration Commission

(a) For the purposes of this chapter the rules of procedure of the Inter-American Commercial Arbitration Commission referred to in Article 3 of the Inter-American Convention shall, subject to subsection (b) of this section, be those rules as promulgated by the Commission on July 1, 1988.

(b) In the event the rules of procedure of the Inter-American Commercial Arbitration Commission are modified or amended in accordance with the procedures for amendment of the rules of that Commission, the Secretary of State, by regulation in accordance with section 553 of title 5, consistent with the aims and purposes of this Convention, may prescribe that such modifications or amendments shall be effective for purposes of this chapter.

Sec. 307. Chapter 1; residual application

Chapter 1 applies to actions and proceedings brought under this chapter to the extent chapter 1 is not in conflict with this chapter or the Inter-American Convention as ratified by the United States.

Appendix B

NEW YORK CONVENTION

Convention on the Recognition and Enforcement of Foreign Arbitral Awards Done at New York, 10 June 1958; entered into force, 7 June 1959 United Nations, Treaty Series, vol. 330, p. 38, No. 4739 (1959).

Article I

1.   This Convention shall apply to the recognition and enforcement of arbitral awards made in the territory of a State other than the State where the recognition and enforcement of such awards are sought, and arising out of differences between persons, whether physical or legal. It shall also apply to arbitral awards not considered as domestic awards in the State where their recognition and enforcement are sought.

2.   The term "arbitral awards" shall include not only awards made by arbitrators appointed for each case but also those made by permanent arbitral bodies to which the parties have submitted.

3.   When signing, ratifying or acceding to this Convention, or notifying extension under article X hereof, any State may on the basis of reciprocity declare that it will apply the Convention to the recognition and enforcement of awards made only in the territory of another Contracting State. It may also declare that it will apply the Convention only to differences arising out of legal relationships, whether contractual or not, which are considered as commercial under the national law of the State making such declaration.

Article II

1.   Each Contracting State shall recognize an agreement in writing under which the parties undertake to submit to arbitration all or any differences which have arisen or which may arise between them in respect of a defined legal relationship, whether contractual or not, concerning a subject matter capable of settlement by arbitration.

2.   The term "agreement in writing" shall include an arbitral clause in a contract or an arbitration agreement, signed by the parties or contained in an exchange of letters or telegrams.

3.   The court of a Contracting State, when seized of an action in a matter in respect of which the parties have made an agreement

317

within the meaning of this article, shall, at the request of one of the parties, refer the parties to arbitration, unless it finds that the said agreement is null and void, inoperative or incapable of being performed.

Article III

Each Contracting State shall recognize arbitral awards as binding and enforce them in accordance with the rules of procedure of the territory where the award is relied upon, under the conditions laid down in the following articles. There shall not be imposed substantially more onerous conditions or higher fees or charges on the recognition or enforcement of arbitral awards to which this Convention applies than are imposed on the recognition or enforcement of domestic arbitral awards.

Article IV

1.　To obtain the recognition and enforcement mentioned in the preceding article, the party applying for recognition and enforcement shall, at the time of the application, supply:

(a)　The duly authenticated original award or a duly certified copy thereof;

(b)　The original agreement referred to in article II or a duly certified copy thereof.

2.　If the said award or agreement is not made in an official language of the country in which the award is relied upon, the party applying for recognition and enforcement of the award shall produce a translation of these documents into such language. The translation shall be certified by an official or sworn translator or by a diplomatic or consular agent.

Article V

1.　Recognition and enforcement of the award may be refused, at the request of the party against whom it is invoked, only if that party furnishes to the competent authority where the recognition and enforcement is sought, proof that:

(a)　The parties to the agreement referred to in article II were, under the law applicable to them, under some incapacity, or the said agreement is not valid under the law to which the parties have subjected it or, failing any indication thereon, under the law of the country where the award was made; or

(b)　The party against whom the award is invoked was not given proper notice of the appointment of the arbitrator or of the arbitration proceedings or was otherwise unable to present his case; or

(c)   The award deals with a difference not contemplated by or not falling within the terms of the submission to arbitration, or it contains decisions on matters beyond the scope of the submission to arbitration, provided that, if the decisions on matters submitted to arbitration can be separated from those not so submitted, that part of the award which contains decisions on matters submitted to arbitration may be recognized and enforced; or

(d)   The composition of the arbitral authority or the arbitral procedure was not in accordance with the agreement of the parties, or, failing such agreement, was not in accordance with the law of the country where the arbitration took place; or

(e)   The award has not yet become binding on the parties, or has been set aside or suspended by a competent authority of the country in which, or under the law of which, that award was made.

2.   Recognition and enforcement of an arbitral award may also be refused if the competent authority in the country where recognition and enforcement is sought finds that:

(a)   The subject matter of the difference is not capable of settlement by arbitration under the law of that country; or

(b)   The recognition or enforcement of the award would be contrary to the public policy of that country.

Article VI

If an application for the setting aside or suspension of the award has been made to a competent authority referred to in article V(1)(e), the authority before which the award is sought to be relied upon may, if it considers it proper, adjourn the decision on the enforcement of the award and may also, on the application of the party claiming enforcement of the award, order the other party to give suitable security.

Article VII

1.   The provisions of the present Convention shall not affect the validity of multilateral or bilateral agreements concerning the recognition and enforcement of arbitral awards entered into by the Contracting States nor deprive any interested party of any right he may have to avail himself of an arbitral award in the manner and to the extent allowed by the law or the treaties of the country where such award is sought to be relied upon.

2.   The Geneva Protocol on Arbitration Clauses of 1923 and the Geneva Convention on the Execution of Foreign Arbitral Awards of 1927 shall cease to have effect between Contracting States on their

becoming bound and to the extent that they become bound, by this Convention.

Article VIII

1.   This Convention shall be open until 31 December 1958 for signature on behalf of any Member of the United Nations and also on behalf of any other State which is or hereafter becomes a member of any specialized agency of the United Nations, or which is or hereafter becomes a party to the Statute of the International Court of Justice, or any other State to which an invitation has been addressed by the General Assembly of the United Nations.

2.   This Convention shall be ratified and the instruments of ratification shall be deposited with the Secretary-General of the United Nations.

Article IX

1.   This Convention shall be open for accession to all States referred to in article VIII.

2.   Accession shall be effected by the deposit of an instrument of accession with the Secretary-General of the United Nations.

Article X

1.   Any State may, at the time of signature, ratification or accession, declare that this Convention shall extend to all or any of the territories for the international relations of which it is responsible. Such a declaration shall take effect when the Convention enters into force for the State concerned

2.   At any time thereafter any such extension shall be made by notification addressed to the Secretary-General of the United Nations and shall take effect as from the ninetieth day after the day of receipt by the Secretary-General of the United Nations of this notification, or as from the date of entry into force of the Convention for the State concerned, whichever is the later

3.   With respect to those territories to which this Convention is not extended at the time of signature, ratification or accession, each State concerned shall consider the possibility of taking the necessary steps in order to extend the application of this Convention to such territories, subject, where necessary for constitutional reasons, to the consent of the Governments of such territories.

Article XI

In the case of a federal or non-unitary State, the following provisions shall apply:

(a) With respect to those articles of this Convention that come within the legislative jurisdiction of the federal authority, the obligations of the federal Government shall to this extent be the same as those of Contracting States which are not federal States;

(b) With respect to those articles of this Convention that come within the legislative jurisdiction of constituent states or provinces which are not, under the constitutional system of the federation, bound to take legislative action, the federal Government shall bring such articles with a favourable recommendation to the notice of the appropriate authorities of constituent states or provinces at the earliest possible moment;

(c) A federal State Party to this Convention shall, at the request of any other Contracting State transmitted through the Secretary-General of the United Nations, supply a statement of the law and practice of the federation and its constituent units in regard to any particular provision of this Convention, showing the extent to which effect has been given to that provision by legislative or other action

Article XII

1. This Convention shall come into force on the ninetieth day following the date of deposit of the third instrument of ratification or accession.

2. For each State ratifying or acceding to this Convention after the deposit of the third instrument of ratification or accession, this Convention shall enter into force on the ninetieth day after deposit by such State of its instrument of ratification or accession.

Article XIII

1. Any Contracting State may denounce this Convention by a written notification to the Secretary-General of the United Nations. Denunciation shall take effect one year after the date of receipt of the notification by the Secretary-General.

2. Any State which has made a declaration or notification under article X may, at any time thereafter, by notification to the Secretary-General of the United Nations, declare that this Convention shall cease to extend to the territory concerned one year after the date of the receipt of the notification by the Secretary-General.

3. This Convention shall continue to be applicable to arbitral awards in respect of which recognition or enforcement proceedings have been instituted before the denunciation takes effect.

Article XIV

A Contracting State shall not be entitled to avail itself of the present Convention against other Contracting States except to the extent that it is itself bound to apply the Convention.

Article XV

The Secretary-General of the United Nations shall notify the States contemplated in article VIII of the following:

(a) Signatures and ratifications in accordance with article VIII;

(b) Accessions in accordance with article IX;

(c) Declarations and notifications under articles I, X and XI;

(d) The date upon which this Convention enters into force in accordance with article XII;

(e) Denunciations and notifications in accordance with article XIII.

Article XVI

1. This Convention, of which the Chinese, English, French, Russian and Spanish texts shall be equally authentic, shall be deposited in the archives of the United Nations

2. The Secretary-General of the United Nations shall transmit a certified copy of this Convention to the States contemplated in article VIII.

Appendix C

EXCERPTS FROM LABOR MANAGEMENT RELATIONS ACT

29 U.S.C. §§ 173, 185

Section 203 (29 U.S.C. § 173)

* * *

(d) Final adjustment by a method agreed upon by the parties is hereby declared to be the desirable method for settlement of grievance disputes arising over the application or interpretation of an existing collective-bargaining agreement. The [Federal Mediation and Conciliation] Service is directed to make its conciliation and mediation services available in the settlement of such grievance disputes only as a last resort and in exceptional cases.

Section 301 (29 U.S.C. § 185)

(a) Suits for violation of contracts between an employer and a labor organization representing employees in an industry affecting commerce as defined in this Act, or between any such labor organizations, may be brought in any district court of the United States having jurisdiction of the parties, without regard to the citizenship of the parties.

(b) Any labor organization which represents employees in an industry affecting commerce as defined in this Act and any employer whose activities affect commerce as defined in this Act shall be bound by the acts of its agents. Any such labor organization may sue or be sued as an entity and in behalf of the employees whom it represents in the courts of the United States. Any money judgment against a labor organization in a district court of the United States shall be enforceable only against the organization as an entity and against its assets, and shall not be enforceable against any individual member or his assets.

* * *

Table of Cases

Index

References are to Section Number